Personal Computer
Applications
in the Social Services

Personal Computer Applications in the Social Services

David A. Patterson
The University of Tennessee, Knoxville

Allyn and Bacon

Boston • London • Toronto • Sydney • Tokyo • Singapore

Senior Series Editor, Social Work and Family Therapy: Judy Fifer
Vice-President, Social Sciences: Karen Hanson
Series Editorial Assistant: Julie Cancio
Marketing Manager: Jackie Aaron
Production Editor: Christopher H. Rawlings
Editorial-Production Service: Omegatype Typography, Inc.
Composition and Prepress Buyer: Linda Cox
Manufacturing Buyer: Julie McNeill
Cover Administrator: Jenny Hart
Electronic Composition: Omegatype Typography, Inc.

Between the time Website information is gathered and then published, it is not unusual for some sites to have closed. Also, the transcription of URLs can result in unintended typographical errors. The publisher would appreciate notification where these occur so that they may be corrected in subsequent editions. Thank you.

Library of Congress Cataloging-in-Publication Data

Patterson, David A.
    Personal computer applications in the social services / David A. Patterson.
        p. cm.
    Includes bibliographical references and index.
    ISBN 0-205-28537-6 (alk. paper)
    1. Social service—Data processing.   2. Human services—Data processing.   3. Microcomputers.   I. Title.
HV29.2.P37   2000
361'.00285'416—dc21   99-31864
                                          CIP

Printed in the United States of America

10 9 8 7 6 5 4 3 2 1   04 03 02 01 00 99

Contents

Chapter 3   Software: Basic Tools   49

Chapter 4   Spreadsheets: Multipurpose Tools   71

**Chapter 5   Databases: Information When
and How You Want It   122**

**Chapter 6   Graphics: Visual Representation
of Practice Information   161**

Chapter 7   Beyond Word Processing   192

Chapter 10   Ethical Applications of Information Technology in Social Service Practice   298

Preface

At this point in history, the act of learning about information technology is a bit like trying to comprehend a river by examining the contents of a cup recently dipped into the river. One can carefully observe the temperature, clarity, purity, acidity, salinity, and taste of the water in the cup. However, by the time one has come to know the qualities of the river in the cup, the river at one's feet is no longer the same water.

In this book I have attempted to construct a craft to allow social service students and professionals to move with the flow of emerging information technology. Adaptive application by social service providers of information technology tools requires a fine balance between knowledge of how to use certain tools and an appreciation of principles that apply across both tools and tasks. Often, texts on information technology focus excessively on the "how to" of a particular piece of software or hardware. This type of information is extremely useful with the particular software or hardware, but does not always generalize to other software and hardware. Yet some users of information technology find it extremely helpful, especially in the early phases of learning a new skill, to have clear descriptions of the steps involved in accomplishing specific tasks with a software program or with a piece of hardware. Specific steps to completing a task can both allay anxiety and build confidence to learn new skills.

"Coming on board" with information technology requires not only application- or hardware-specific knowledge, but also necessitates knowledge of guiding principles and key concepts to structure one's interaction with current and emerging technologies. In this book, I have tried to steer a course between providing, where necessary, step-by-step descriptions of specific uses of personal computers in social service tasks and delineating principles, concepts, and skills that transcend particular software, hardware, or tasks. For instance, it may be important to know the process of creating a graph from rows and columns of data in a particular spreadsheet program. Conversely, it is equally important to appreciate how the resultant graph can be used in a range of word processing, e-mail, and Web applications to communicate to one's intended audience. The intention of this book is for the reader not to be bound to a particular type of hardware, software, or a rigid following of prescribed steps to accomplish a task. Instead, the goal here is for the reader to come away from this text with the knowledge, skills, and confidence sufficient to fluidly adapt existing and emergent information technology to the service of clients.

Audience

I wrote this book with two audiences in mind. It is meant for undergraduate and graduate students in the social service professions, including social work, counseling, psychology, and other human services programs. For these students, this text may serve as a primary textbook in information technology courses and as a secondary text in courses teaching research, program evaluation, or administration. This book is intended to help students become agents of change in social service agencies, advancing the use of information technology to serve clients.

This book is also directed toward social service professionals wishing to update their skills in the use of personal computers and information technology. Many social service professionals now find themselves confronted with a dizzying array of new types of information technology for which they were not prepared in their undergraduate or graduate education. For this audience, the purpose of this book is to provide a means for these readers to augment their professional skills with new knowledge and skills in using personal computers and information technology as tools of social service practice.

Acknowledgments

This book is the result of the remarkable generosity and grace of friends, colleagues, and family. In particular I wish to thank my friends and colleagues John Orme, Terri Combs-Orme, Bill Nugent, Jim Post, Mary Roggie, Roger Nooe, Paul Campbell, Mark Perry, Kris Nelson, Jay Wysocki, and Judith Fiene. Each of these individuals made a unique, though perhaps unknown to them, valuable contribution to this book. Thanks also to my dean, Karen Sowers, for promoting an atmosphere of growth and potential at the University of Tennessee's College of Social Work. Thanks also to my advisor during my doctoral studies, Mark Fraser, who continues to model the rare combination of scholarly excellence and extraordinary humanity. I also wish to thank the book's reviewers: Jerry Finn, University of New Hampshire; Stephen M. Marson, University of North Carolina at Pembroke; Thomas E. Smith, Florida State University; and Leon F. Williams, Boston College.

My sincere thanks are offered to my parents, Georgell and Douglas Patterson, whose unsparing generosity, love, and support were instrumental in the completion of this book. Their editing of the first drafts of this text was above and beyond the call of parental duty.

I offer my deep appreciation to my daughters Kaitlyn and Hannah, who shared their radiant light and liberating bliss throughout the writing of this book. This effort might never have begun and would certainly never have been completed without the unflagging love, encouragement, and profound support of my wife, Melanie McGhee. No words of thanks are sufficient to express my gratitude for her presence in my life.

This book is dedicated to the great beings who founded and sustain the PRASAD Project. The PRASAD (Philanthropic Relief, Altruistic Service and Development) Project is an international, voluntary, not-for-profit organization. PRASAD's mission is to improve the quality of life for people living in conditions of poverty and offers opportunities for self-reliance. PRASAD provides service in rural family health care, eye and dental care, nutrition, clean water, community assistance and education in India, rural New York State, and Mexico.

D.A.P.

chapter **1**

Comes a Revolution

This chapter provides an introduction and rationale for the use of information technology in social service practice. It describes some of the reasons for the limited use of information technology (IT) in social service practice to date. It introduces the concept of the personal computer as a tool of practice and illustrates it with a tale of a day in the life of a laptop. The capacity of personal computers to facilitate communication, collaboration, and cooperation is discussed. The chapter describes how information accessed through information technology can serve practitioners. It advocates for the utility of openness to learning and experimentation in advancing one's skills in the use of IT. To conclude, some of the essential limitations of information technology in social service practice are articulated.

In this transmillenium period, much of how human civilization works and communicates is being transformed by information technology. The term *IT* refers to computer hardware and software, the networks that link computers, and the mechanisms that change information and images into digital formats, for example, digital cameras and scanners. The combined impact of the rapid and continuing increases in the computational power of computers, the dramatic increase in their ease of use, and the development of global networks linking computers is creating a revolution in human culture. We are in the midst of a revolution that is transforming how we relate to and understand one another, how we access and use information, and how we understand our world.

This revolution is impacting virtually every level of social system. Individuals find a sense of community and support through Internet-based discussion groups. Family members and friends around the world readily stay in touch with one another via e-mail. Nonprofit agencies disseminate information about their charitable work and solicit contributions over the World Wide Web. The federal government publishes information on governmental policy and congressional actions on a host of Web servers. International investors track the fluctuations of financial markets and the actions of global corporations through steady streams of fiscal data that flow across continents around the clock. Images from the video eye of a small robot on the surface of Mars travel across space and appear on the screens of computers in science classes around the globe. Ground controllers on earth point the Hubble Space Telescope to the heavens and pictures of the vastness of space course over the Internet, transforming desktop computers into windows on the universe through which we fly.

Revolutions are often thought of as dramatic political upheavals in which power changes hands from one group to another. One of the revolutionary aspects of the advancement of information technology is the multiple forms of empowerment it brings to individuals and groups. The fruits of the IT revolution include a number of powerful tools. Word processing has changed the written expression of ideas from hard copy typing with its intrinsic time penalty for error correction to the flow of easily correctable letters across an electronic display. As a result, people worldwide have been freed to express their ideas and readily distribute them via the Internet or in printed materials. Electronic databases have made it possible for groups and organizations to readily compile, access, and utilize addresses and phone numbers of supporters and contributors in the service of their cause. Vast quantities of medical information on a wide range of diseases are now available on the Web. Consequently, patients and family members who take the time to look for the material can become conversant in the course of a disease, the range of treatment protocols being utilized, and current research trials testing new treatment procedures. Access and utilization of this medical information alters the power differential between medical personnel and the patients and families they serve. In each instance cited here, the tools of information technology have increased the power and efficacy of those who employ them. The IT revolution is manifest not by blood in the streets, but by the use of the tools of information technology to acquire, use, transform, and disseminate information.

To date, professionals in the social services have been slow to take up the tools of the IT revolution (Phillips & Berman, 1995). The power and efficacy of computers and the other tools of information technology are insufficiently employed in the aid of individuals and groups seeking social services (Rafferty, Steyaert, & Colombi, 1995). The sources of this reticence to embrace IT are manifold. Social service workers fear the loss of their professional roles as information providers and networking facilitators (Howard, 1995; Plant, 1991). Inadequate training and limited access to agency computers have been shown to be detrimental to computer use in human service organizations (Mutschler & Hoefer, 1990). Gerstman (1996) found that the attitudes that directors of agencies have about computer use and their involvement in computerization can affect computer use in agencies. Murphy and Pardeck (1986, 1988, 1992) have repeatedly warned that the social work profession is endangered by information technology because, in their view, it threatens the essential role of the interpersonal relationship between social worker and client.

This is not to say that IT has not been engaged in the provision of social services. The journals *Computer in Human Services* and *New Technology in the Human Services* regularly publish articles on a range of specific software and hardware applications employed in social service agencies. Academics, researchers, practitioners, and social service administrators regularly convene at HUSITA (Human Service Information Technology Applications) conferences to discuss advances in the use of IT in their respective areas. In the introduction to a collection of selected papers from the 1997 HUSITA 4 conference, the editor, Bryan Glastonbury, declared that "Whatever criticism may be leveled, it is a reality that IT is now indispensable to the health and social services, and carries out a wide range of tasks to almost uniform satisfaction" (1997, p. 3). While Glastonbury's assertion that IT is "indispensable" may offer some reassurance of its recognized importance, it does not imply that the potential utility of IT in social services is widely recognized or valued.

It can be argued that the major thrust of IT in social service agencies has been toward the collection of administrative and management information (Pardeck, Umfress, & Murphy, 1990). IT systems in agencies have been focused on capturing data on fiscal transactions, client demographics, service utilization, and to a lesser extent, broad services outcome information (Phillips & Berman, 1995). Historically, these IT systems have used database software for collection, storage, retrieval, and reporting purposes. Social service workers have input data on either desktop terminals or personal computers linked to either a mainframe computer or file server. Actual access to information in the database that is of use to frontline social service workers has either been extremely limited or unavailable (Steyaert, Colombi, & Rafferty, 1996). This constrained access to practice-relevant information has often been due to the fact that programmers and administrators design systems for administrative and fiscal information needs, with limited consideration of information needs of actual service providers. There has been extremely limited conceptualization, training, or application of personal computers for the direct provision of services and support of individuals and groups. There has been even less effort expended to explicate how a personal computer, with a moderate range of commonly available software applications and a modem, can become a powerful tool to assist in the provision of a wide array of social services. Such an effort is the central focus of this book.

The Personal Computer as a Tool of Practice

The conceptualization of a personal computer as a tool of practice is critical to developing a sense of personal efficacy in regard to IT and to cultivating a willingness to explore a wide range of applications for the personal computer in the social services. Much of the resistance to IT in social services stems from a sense that IT impinges on professional autonomy (Williams & Foster, 1988), the absence of models showing how to integrate computers into practice, and the historical difficulty in learning how to use a computer (Lamb, 1990). Concern over the complexity involved in learning computer skills was especially valid in the days before graphic user interfaces when one had to give written commands in operating systems and remember the functions of various keys. Software on personal computers now almost universally employs icons and menu bars that represent available functions. Users express their command wishes by pointing and clicking on icons or functions available in the menu bars. For social service professionals, the personal computer has been transformed of late from an object with questionable utility and indiscernible operation into a tool that advances professional autonomy rather than impinges on it.

In beginning to think of the personal computer as a tool of practice in the social services, it is essential to first reflect on the nature of tools in professions. Surgeons spend years learning how to use a scalpel, how to suture a wound, how to read an X-ray. Musicians devote their lives to mastering their instruments. Photographers spend thousands of hours with their cameras learning the subtleties of the interactions between light, lens, and time. These three examples illustrate both the dedication that is requisite for professionals to become proficient in using tools of their trade and the necessary time commitment. Moreover, development and mastery of distinct tools of practice is the means by which a profession distinguishes itself from other professions and vocations.

It can readily be argued that the primary tool, although intangible, of the social services is the capacity to form a relationship with the clients, be they individuals, groups, or organizations, and to utilize that relationship in the service of the clients' goals. It is within the context of that relationship that social service professionals convey information, another tool of the profession. The information conveyed is specific to the domain of practice in which the professional works. Family therapists provide information to families about how family systems work. Welfare benefit workers give information on application procedures and available resources. Mental health workers may inform a client of how self-defeating thoughts contribute to depressive episodes. In each instance, the information cited is only a small part of the information the worker will utilize and disseminate to the client and to systems associated with the client, for instance, managed care organizations. The proper use of information as a tool of practice is dependent on a number of necessary attributes of the information. The information must be relevant to the client's problem, accurate, up to date, comprehensible, and delivered in a manner in which the client can use it.

Given the important role of information in the provision of social services, the personal computer employed for information acquisition, production, transformation, and communication represents an extremely flexible and robust tool of practice. Use of a personal computer can allow the social service professional to gain access to a vast amount of information relevant to the field of practice or germane to a particular client's specific problem. Once found, that information can be assessed for its accuracy and timeliness relative to other available information. Imagine, for instance, a medical social worker using the World Wide Web to find information on a rare type of tumor that has recently been diagnosed in a client. The worker collects information from various Web sites, selects the information regarding treatment, prognosis, and support groups that seems most appropriate and comprehensible to the client and the family, prints it out, and provides the information to the family in an information packet. The worker then saves the locations of the Web sites and electronically stores the information packet so that it can be updated and made available to future clients.

As with any tool, learning to use a personal computer as a tool of practice requires a commitment of time to master its range of uses. The actual amount of time any user requires is of course dependent on their experience in using personal computers, the range and complexity of tasks to be learned, and the user's motivation. The notion of mastering the personal computer is perhaps erroneous or at least unhelpful. The development of skills in applying a personal computer as a tool of social service practice is best thought of as an ongoing process that unfolds in the interplay of each individual's creativity, curiosity, employment tasks, motivation, and openness to learning.

Given this fact, one of the best ways to make use of the contents of this book is to first cultivate within oneself an awareness and appreciation of the fact that personal computers represent powerful tools that can be harnessed in service of those whom we serve. For too long, workers in the social services have viewed themselves as being harnessed to IT by the fiscal and managerial data demands of agency administration. Alternatively, we can view the personal computer as a tool for enhancing the capacity to perform the duties of our positions. If we see the personal computer as a tool for personal and creative expression, as an opportunity to develop skills of value in an age of information, we are thereby empowered by embracing the utility of the personal computer. Moreover, and perhaps more importantly, we are enabled in the performance of our duties to those whom we serve.

A Day in the Life of a Laptop

To further illustrate the potential of the personal computer to enhance social service practice, consider this story of "A Day in the Life of a Laptop."

Joan is a clinical social worker at Maximum Mental Health, a community mental health center that has recently made a commitment to the use of IT to enhance worker efficacy, promote communication, and meet the information demands of managed care agencies. As a result, Joan was provided a range of computer training, access to computer support personnel, and a laptop computer that links to the agency's computer network from work and home. On this Tuesday morning before leaving for work, Joan dials into the agency's network to check her e-mail and schedule for the day. She has an e-mail message from a social work student that she is supervising. The student's e-mail poses a brief clinical question regarding one of the student's clients. In checking her schedule Joan noted that she had a cancellation of her first appointment so she composes a response to the student's question and sends it off via e-mail. With the extra time she has available this morning, she completes her case notes on a client she saw the previous evening at the clinic. She e-mails the case notes to the medical records specialist at the clinic who will take the message and paste it into the client's electronic medical record.

Upon arriving at the clinic, Joan plugs her laptop into the network and again checks her e-mail and schedule. She has a group scheduled for the morning. She has been collecting information in the group on how the group is meeting the needs of its participants. At the end of each session, she asks the group members to complete a brief questionnaire that measures a number of dimensions of the group's functioning. Joan enters this information into a spreadsheet and plots it on a chart. From the chart she can see that there has been a gradual decline over the last three weeks in the level of trust in the group. As this seems like an important issue for the group to address at this point in its development, she prints a copy of the chart and will hand it out in group and use as it as a means to facilitate discussion of trust in the group session. Following group, Joan writes her group notes and sends them via e-mail to medical records.

After lunch, Joan makes a number of phone calls to people in the community regarding clients she is case managing. To do this, she opens the address book database and selects the number of the person she wishes to call. The computer dials the selected number and Joan picks up the receiver of her phone when the party on the other end answers. At the end of each conversation, she makes a brief note for the case record and sends it off to medical records.

In the late afternoon, Joan is scheduled to do a presentation to the local mental health association. As part of her final preparation for the talk, she checks a number of sites on the World Wide Web that focus on mental health issues. At one site she finds information on a recent change in government policy relevant to the topic she is speaking on later today. She saves the information to her laptop. She then opens her word processing program and edits the information she found on the Web into several talking points for her presentation. She then opens the presentation software in which she has developed her talk, takes the edited information from the word processor and pastes it into the appropriate location in her presentation.

She arrives at the mental health association meeting half an hour later with her laptop in hand. The laptop is connected to a screen projector and she is ready to deliver her talk from the presentation software. The talk contains text-based information, diagrams, graphics, and a brief animated video film clip she found on the Web of the theorized action in the brain of a new medication being used in the clinic.

Later at home and after dinner she checks her e-mail one last time for the day. There is a brief note from her social work student thanking her for the case supervision earlier that day. The note also contains a follow-up question. Instead of answering it now, she decides it can wait till tomorrow. She has other things to do.

Communication, Collaboration, and Cooperation

Essential to the notion of the personal computer as a tool of professional practice in the social services is the requirement that using the computer brings added value or benefit to the practitioner in return for the time invested in learning how to use it. Stated more succinctly, what is gained by the practitioner in taking up the personal computer as a tool of social service practice? Readily identifiable are several areas in which specific advantages in communications, collaboration, and cooperation are derived from the use of a personal computer over standard practice methods. These advantages include (1) communication that is not time and place dependent, (2) a range of tools for ready assessment and visual representation of practice outcomes, (3) enhanced capacity to communicate to clients, peers, and constituents, and (4) greater freedom as to when and where work is conducted.

A distinct advantage to using a personal computer in communications via e-mail is that it frees the parties involved from having to be either simultaneously in the same place, as in face to face discussions, or from their communication exchange having to occur at the same time, as in a phone conversation. E-mail makes possible asynchronous communication, in that individuals can read and respond to messages as their schedules allow, thereby reducing the number of intrusive phones calls and the length of time consumed by excessively verbose callers. Unlike phone or face to face communications, e-mail exchanges can be kept very focused on the intent of the communication, the subject. Additionally, e-mail allows for the instantaneous dissemination of information within an agency or to peers and colleagues around the globe. As will be discussed below, the use of e-mail cannot and probably should not be a complete substitute for face to face and/or voice communication. The subtleties of human communication are far too rich to be captured in text alone. However, e-mail is a valuable tool for a wide range of messages.

Another advantage that the personal computer as a tool of social service practice makes available is a wide range of options for assessing and graphically representing practice outcomes. *Practice outcomes* refers to a broad spectrum of indicators of the impact of social services at the clinical, administrative, policy, or community level. Assessment of practice outcome represents a collaborative effort between the service provider and the service recipient in which there is an exchange of information. Examples of practice outcome indicators might be the numbers of individuals attending community organization meetings, monthly cost savings secondary to changes in administrative procedures, or weekly changes in measured level of depression in a psychotherapy client. Software tools for practice evaluation range from programs specifically developed for clinical application, such as Walter Hudson's CASS program (1996), to employing spreadsheets as a means of collecting and graphically depicting financial change over time. The value of using personal computers instead of paper-based methods in practice evaluation includes, but is not limited to, (1) time savings from the automatic calculations of scores on clinical instruments, (2) the ability to readily update graphs and reports as new data become available, (3) greater ease in the use of statistical procedures to calculate change magnitude, and (4) greater fluidity in the sharing of practice outcomes with interested parties.

An example of this last point is a community organization raising funds to build a new homeless shelter tracking weekly contributions on a spreadsheet. The spreadsheet is configured to produce a bar graph to represent the goal of the campaign and the current level of pledged support. The graph is posted on the organization's World Wide Web page and distributed as a file attached to e-mail sent out weekly to update the employees, donors to the agency, and board of directors. This e-mail distribution includes the agency's e-mail address to which recipients can respond with questions and suggestions.

The fund-raising example represents how the power of personal computers can enhance a social service practitioner's capacity to communicate with clients, peers, and constituents. Personal computers make possible the transmission of information in multiple forms, as text, sound, digital images, animation, graphs, and video. The aptness with which personal computers receive, produce, modify, display, publish, and distribute multimedia information has increased dramatically in recent years. The World Wide Web is perhaps the best manifestation of how the increased multimedia functionality of personal computers is harnessed to disseminate information. Browsing the Web, one encounters digitized video clips, music excerpts, pages with multiple fonts in multiple colors, animated images that dance across the screen, and digital images and other art forms produced and enhanced by graphics software. Granted, the message is often lost in the medium. Nonetheless, it is clear that the personal computer is rapidly becoming a fundamental tool of communication and expression in this transmillenium period.

The question now facing social service providers is how do we employ the personal computer to inform and collaborate with our clients, peers, and constituents? It is clearly impossible to produce a complete list of the possible applications of the personal computer for communications. The quantity and resultant manifestations of global, collective human imagination now directed toward employing IT to convey information is incalculable and perhaps inexpressible. There are, however, methods or channels of communications available through the personal computer that can be listed. These channels include e-mail, news groups, printed materials, Web pages, Usenet, CD-ROMS, and electronic presentations. Each of these channels represents potentially powerful and effective media through which to communicate with our clients, peers, and constituents. Each of the channels of communications is described and explained in subsequent chapters.

The capacity of personal computers to expand the range of channels of communications in social services also results in greater freedom as to when and where work is conducted. At first blush, an increased ability for practitioners to work when and where they want to may seem like a trivial issue meaning nothing more than that the worker can write case notes at home while wearing pajamas. One of the recent changes in social service delivery is the move away from centralization of service delivery to an increasingly decentralized model in which services are delivered in the homes of clients and in their communities. Home health care agencies provide a range of medical and mental health services in the client's residence. Family preservation programs provide counseling, parenting education, and case management services to families in their homes. The revitalization of communities and housing rehabilitation is advanced by the presence of social service workers on-site (Cohen & Phillips, 1997; Morrison, et al., 1997).

Each of these examples offers an opportunity to glimpse the potential of personal computers to alter when and how service could be provided. Upon visiting an elderly client and noting concerns over the client's health status, a home health care social worker might use a laptop to leave an e-mail message requesting an immediate visit from the nurse involved in the case. A family preservation worker working with a family in which there is considerable conflict between the parents and their two teenage sons might each week have the family members complete on a laptop the Hudson's Index of Family Relations in order to measure change in the family relations. Entering the summed scores of the four family members into a spreadsheet and graphing the results over time, the worker can readily communicate with the graph the progress, or lack thereof, the family is making toward their goal of decreasing family conflict. A social service worker employed in a housing rehabilitation project could assist residents in searching for employment by linking to the Internet with a laptop and showing job seekers how to find jobs listed on the local employment commission's Web page. At the core of each of these examples is the personal computer being used as a tool of communication, collaboration, and cooperation in the service of improved social service practice. More fundamentally, information is being communicated and forms the basis of the cited collaboration and cooperation. The fact that information is the essential element the personal computer brings to social service practice suggests the value of practitioners enhancing their capacity to use personal computers as tools of information retrieval and application.

Information Serving the Practitioner

Rivard, Madrigal, and Millan (1997) report that social service practice is developing extremely diverse areas of professional activity. This branching out into new sectors of practice, such as home health care, corrections, employee assistance, and substance abuse treatment, requires access to new domains of information if workers are to deliver effective services. In addition, it is increasingly clear that undergraduate and graduate education cannot provide students seeking careers in the social service professions all the necessary information to sustain a career that may encompass several areas of practice over three or more decades. Consequently, it is necessary for students and professionals to recognize the importance of lifelong learning and to develop competence with tools that make sustained learning possible.

A personal computer with a connection to the Internet makes available to a social service worker a staggering range of information. The use of the Internet as a source for practice information will be elaborated on in Chapter 9. As we develop our understanding and appreciation of the personal computer as a tool of practice, it is essential to realize that the Internet provides the practitioner with near instantaneous access to state of the art information on a wide array of topics. Of course, along with learning to access and retrieve information from the Internet, it is equally important to develop discrimination in regard to the source and quality of the available information.

Imagine, for instance, that the director of a children's services agency is asked to speak to a parents group on child discipline. In particular, members of the parents group have heard news reports of research on the detrimental effects of spanking children and they ask the agency director to specifically address the topic in her talk. The director first searches the Web for sites with information on child discipline and spanking. She visits those sites and copies relevant information into a file on her office personal computer. She next visits the Web sites of several national newspapers and searches their online archives for recent stories on the topic. As she finds relevant information and quotes, she saves them to a file on her computer. The director then visits a Web site that provides full text copies of research journal articles for a fee. This director, as the person responsible for ensuring that the practitioners who work for her have access to up-to-date research, has previously set up an account with this Web-based information service provider. She then searches the available database and comes up with three articles that appeared in the last two years, one of which was published a month ago, reporting the problems spanking creates for parents and children. Later, the director will compile the information she collected on the Web into an "electronic presentation" she will present at the parents group meeting.

Concomitant with the need to access practice information that is both relevant and timely, practitioners across all levels of organizational hierarchies increasingly are being required to produce information on service outcomes and activity. Expectations for service outcome and activity reporting now come from funding agencies, service contractors, and managed care organizations. Although service outcome evaluation and activity reporting may not generally be construed as information serving the practitioner, upon further consideration their utility to the practitioner becomes apparent. *Service outcome evaluation* refers to a wide range of indicators of the effectiveness of social services that have been provided to an individual or population. *Activity reporting* represents an accounting of what services have been delivered, to whom, for what duration, and with what frequency. The generation and analysis of information regarding service outcomes provides social service workers at all organizational levels with information on how well their clients or constituents are responding to the services rendered. Clear information on service outcomes allows practitioners and organizations to adjust their practices in response to outcome information so as to better serve their clients or constituents. Moreover, outcome information and activity information can be used to justify continuing or increased funding, utilized in contract negotiations, and used as justification for increases or changes in staffing.

As a tool of practice, the personal computer offers a distinct advantage of information fluidity in providing information in the service of practitioners. Negroponte (1995) points out that one of the fundamental changes of our time is that we are increasingly moving from atom-based information to information represented as electronic bits. This book is an example of information in the form of atoms. It has substance, it can be held in one's hand. On the other hand, computers represent information as electronic bits. A *bit* is the presence or absence of an electronic pulse or magnetized spot on a disk. *Information fluidity* refers to the fact that information in the form of bits can readily be moved between computer software applications or across the globe. For instance, imagine the following scenario. In an interfaith counseling center, each week prior to the beginning of an assertiveness training group clients rate their overall level of assertiveness for the week. To do this, they stop at a table where the group leaders have placed a laptop computer. On the computer screen, there is a form that has been created in a database program. The clients enter the last four digits of their social security numbers and then rate their overall assertiveness for the week. The database is linked to a spreadsheet. Changes in clients' levels of assertiveness over the course of the group can readily be transformed from numbers to a chart representing changes over time. This information allows the group leaders to adapt the group content and materials in response to the information provided in the client self-reports. This chart can then be pasted into a word processing program where it forms the core of a report on the groups' treatment outcome. This report is then distributed as an e-mail attachment to clinicians and administrators within the agency that sponsored the group.

There are two important elements in this scenario. First, at no point in this example did the information move from bits to atoms. The informational fluidity evidenced here was made possible by initially capturing the assertiveness data in electronic form and by having it remain as bits. Information that is collected on paper has the distinct disadvantage of requiring additional time and effort to transfer it into electronic format before it can be analyzed and readily disseminated. Social service agencies around the globe have untold volumes of potentially useful paper-based information sitting in files which will likely not be used due to the labor required to extract information. The second noteworthy element in the group scenario is that the outcome information gathered can serve the practitioner in multiple ways. The charts of individual clients' progress over time can be a vital motivator for clients to continue to make changes in their thoughts, feelings, and behaviors. The group's combined change in assertiveness over time provides the practitioner with valuable information on the efficacy and utility of the intervention methods used. Moreover, this information can be used by agency administrators in support of funding decisions and in demonstrating agency effectiveness to current and potential funding sources.

Daring to Imagine and Experiment

In recent years social service practitioners increasingly sought to apply personal computers and information technology to a wide range of practice problems (Rondero, 1998). Taking up the personal computer as a tool of practice and using information technology in social services requires a willingness to imagine and experiment. The idea that computer use is best approached through experimentation and imagination may seem odd. The operation of computers is often viewed as a clearly delineated series of steps that one performs in order to have the computer complete the function that the operator intends. In one sense this perspective is entirely correct. If one wishes to save a word processing file, one selects File from the available items in a menu bar, then selects Save, names the file to be saved, and selects the directory in which the file is to be saved: a straightforward, clearly specified set of steps that, if followed to the letter, will result in saving the file.

The problem with approaching personal computers in particular and information technology generally as a series of steps to be remembered and carried out in a set order is that it constrains our thinking and therefore our capacity to fully make use of these tools. Returning again to the simple example of saving a word processing file, for most word processors there are in fact several ways to save a file. One can use the procedure described in the preceding paragraph. Additionally, files can be saved by clicking an icon from the menu bar or by using a simple keyboard command such as Control S. Moreover, one may wish to save a file in a different format so it can be shared with someone who is using a different word processor. This requires using a different command, Save As, and then selecting the type of file format to use. The point is that many functions and tasks that personal computers can perform can be accomplished by more than one method or set of procedures. Openness to learning alternative ways of accomplishing tasks on a personal computer increases flexibility and resiliency in dealing with a wide range of IT challenges.

Awareness of the fact that there are often different procedures to accomplish the same end can initially seem overwhelming or frustrating. "Just tell me how to do it" is not an uncommon response, and it is certainly understandable. We often learn computer skills on a "need to know" basis. It can certainly be argued that if we learn to use computers through this need to know process, at some point we will know what we need to know. The problem with this approach is that it constrains our imagination and creativity, and it can limit our experimentation with the use of a personal computer. Experimentation and the application of creative solutions are essential to fully adapting information technology to the particular needs of each practice setting. To achieve the goal of finding the optimal application of the personal computer and other IT tools to serve one's clients, work setting, and personal professional information needs requires experimentation. This experimentation is necessary in order to discern which tools and applications augment practice and which ones are excessively time consuming, overly complex, and/or superfluous.

Drawing upon imagination and creativity in finding new ways to adapt the tools of information technology to social service practice is needed because to date there has been limited conceptualization and application of these tools to the wide range of settings in which social services are delivered. As a profession, and despite the fact that information technology has been developing for over forty years, we are in the early stages of learning how to utilize personal computers and more broadly IT in social service practice (Caputo, 1988). This book provides a foundation in the use of a broad array of software tools that can be creatively adapted to the task and information demands of each practitioner's particular work setting and client populations. The profession will be enhanced by each reader's willingness to imagine and experiment with these tools in their own practice settings, in the task and problems they face with the rich array of clients the profession serves.

Cultivating an Attitude of Openness

The willingness to engage in creativity and experimentation in learning how to optimally apply IT tools to particular social service settings is predicated on a basic understanding of the working principles of IT hardware and software and an attitude of openness to technology. The working principles of IT hardware and software will be covered in subsequent chapters. Let us consider for a moment what is meant by an attitude of openness to information technology. This idea should not be construed as an embracing of all technology without regard to its function or potential deleterious effects. For our purposes, *an attitude of openness* will be defined as a cognitive and emotional state in which one strives to perceive the world, or in this case information technology, with clarity unimpaired by presuppositions and emotional bias. The goal is to interact with IT while holding a perspective unclouded by either our historically held attitudes or beliefs. Henry Miller (1970) said, "Everything we shut our eyes to, everything we run away from, everything we deny, denigrate or despise, serves to defeat us in the end. What seems nasty, painful, evil can become a source of beauty, joy and strength, if faced with an open mind. Every moment is a golden one for him who has the vision to recognize it as such" (p. 101).

An attitude of openness can change the way one learns new computer skills and the way one solves problems related to information technology. If one approaches computers and other tools of IT with dread, fear, and loathing, then one's experience with them is likely to be most unpleasant. The attitudinal state that one holds upon sitting down in front of a computer colors one's reaction to everything that happens in the interaction. For instance, John has the attitude, "I hate computers." He often repeats this most unhelpful mantra to himself and his coworkers. Naturally, each time his computer experiences a problem reading a disk, connecting to the Internet, or carrying out some function in a software application, John again repeats his mantra, "I hate computers." Holding tenaciously to this attitude and strengthening his grip on it with each repetition of his mantra, John cognitively and emotionally limits his ability to see or find solutions to his computer problems as they present themselves.

The truth is that in recent years computers have become more reliable, user-friendly, and generally easier to use, but complications with hardware and software are not uncommon. Viruses can infect machines. Hard drives can and do fail. Complications with software can and do arise. However, if one cultivates an attitude of openness in response to the occasional travails of computer use, then one is far better prepared to both seek and find solutions to the problems. An attitude of openness allows one to more readily and clearly move through a process to solve a problem. Attempts to figure out what is wrong, if clouded by anger, fear, anxiety, or helplessness, may miss important elements of the problem which may hold the key to solving it. While attempting to identify resources that can offer assistance with the obstacle one is facing, an attitude of openness allows full consideration of all the possible sources of assistance, such as Help files with software applications, telephone hardware and software support lines, friends or colleagues, and Web-based assistance.

Often, once a source of assistance is identified it is tempting to seize upon the first possible solution offered. If, however, one remains open, solicits a range of options, and carefully considers the options, one increases the chances of selecting a workable solution. Finding workable solutions to information technology problems often requires experimentation, the testing of solutions until a robust one is found. Again, holding an attitude of openness, practicing patience, and letting go of one's attachment to an immediate solution can often result in the problem getting fixed faster than will seizing on the first possible solution and holding doggedly to it despite evidence suggesting it's not working.

There are several practices that can facilitate the cultivation of an attitude of openness in computing. Contemplation of attitudes and beliefs about information technology can be a helpful first step in developing an attitude of openness. One way of contemplating this is to sit in a quiet place, perhaps with paper and pen nearby or a computer with a word processing program open. Allow yourself to breath slowly and deeply and after a few moments close your eyes. Contemplate the questions, "How do I feel about computers?" "What do I think about my ability to use computers?" "What do I believe about their usefulness in my work?" Just allow these questions to be held in your mind as you continue breathing in a slow, regular manner. It is not necessary to try to answer these questions during this time, but instead allow yourself to contemplate them. After a while, open your eyes, type or jot down the questions, and then write out the answers that came to you. When you are through, consider what you have written. Are there attitudes and beliefs that you hold that represent obstacles to holding an attitude of openness to information technology? Awareness of these possible limiting attitudes and beliefs is the first step in considering whether you wish to hold on to them or consider changing them or letting them go.

Another practice that can foster an attitude of openness in dealing with personal computers is simply pausing and breathing. While this sounds deceptively simple, it is in fact a potent means to disrupt the rushed thinking and distracting emotions that often go along with either learning a new computer skill or trying to solve some complex IT problem. There are three steps in this practice. First, take your hands away from the keyboard and mouse and let them rest in your lap. Second, change your breathing. One way to do this is to take a deep breath and hold it for a moment. Then release it, breathing out completely. Again, take a deep breath and this time pause for a moment and let yourself rest in that moment between the in breath and the out breath. As you breathe out deeply, again pause in the moment between the end of the exhalation and the inhalation. Allow your attention to focus on this pattern of breathing. If your attention shifts back to the computer, gently return it to your breathing. The third step is optional. You may want to close your eyes while you practice this breathing exercise. Closing your eyes allows you to move away from the computer for a moment; it allows you to take a brief break from the task at hand. It allows you to rest your eyes from the strain of staring at the screen. This can have a soothing effect on both your thoughts and emotions. If you choose not to close your eyes, find something else to rest your gaze on for a while as you breathe. It may be that you can look at a picture on your desk, gaze out a window, or simply look at your hands folded in your lap while you focus on your breathing. This practice of pausing and breathing can be refreshing and allow one to bring greater openness and energy to problem solving and skill acquisition. M. McGhee suggests reminding yourself of this practice by putting a small sign on your computer, perhaps on your monitor, that reads "BREATHE" (personal communication, July 15, 1997). It's a very useful reminder to cultivate this practice of pausing and breathing.

The third practice in developing an attitude of openness is sitting and contemplating the task to be learned or the problem to be resolved. Pirsig published (1970) an account of the application of Zen Buddhist practice in everyday life. In this book, he described how often the first step of repairing his motorcycle engine was the act of sitting before the engine and contemplating its parts, their functions, and their relations to each other. Instead of rushing into a poorly understood problem and attempting to fix it with an incomplete or ill-considered solution, one often arrives at a better solution if one first sits with the task and contemplates it. To try this practice, spend some time looking at Figure 1.1. Allow yourself to pause and notice each bit of information, each icon, each menu label, each arrow in the figure. Take your time. Just sit and look at Figure 1.1. After a while, consider how much richer your knowledge of the figure is now than when you first glanced at it. What do you see now that you did not see at first? What question arose for you as you looked at the icons and considered what functions they represented?

Sitting and contemplating a task or a problem is similar to what happens when one sits or stands before a work of art in a museum. The subtleties of the artist's effort can begin to emerge from the work. The use of color, the arrangement of shadow and light, the brush strokes in the paint, and emotional tones conveyed in the work come to one's

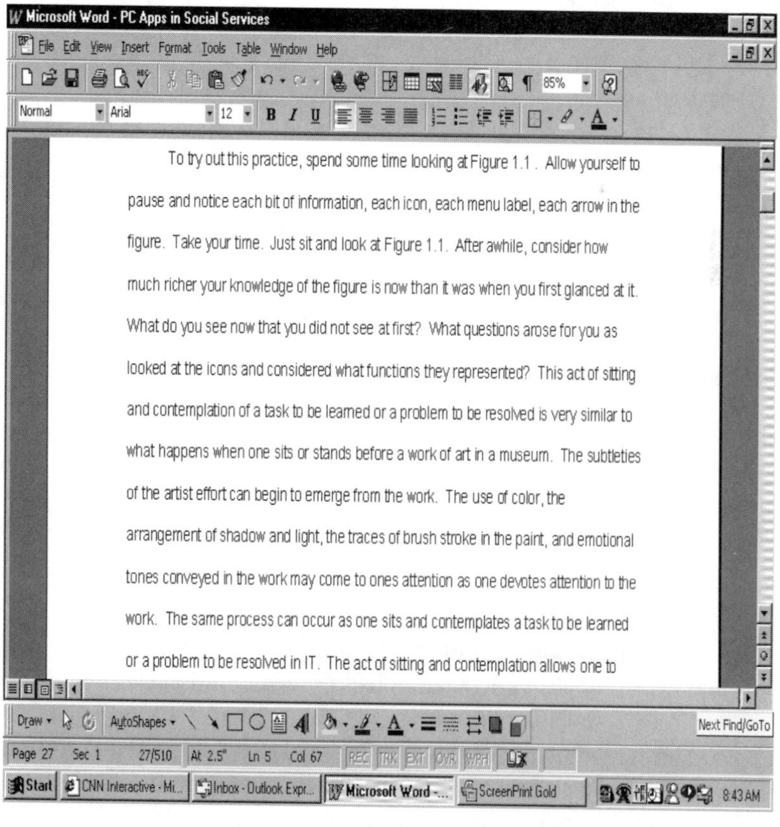

FIGURE 1.1   Computer Screen for Contemplation

attention as one devotes attention to the work. The same process occurs as one sits and contemplates a task in IT. Contemplation allows one to see the problem more completely, to remember what is already known, to notice what has previously escaped attention, to intellectually grasp the task or problem more completely, to open up to possible solutions. Of course, breathing during this time of sitting and contemplating probably would not hurt.

The fourth practice to employ in developing an attitude of openness to IT is letting go. There are times when one can spend a considerable amount of time attempting to learn some new computer skill, complete some task, or solve some problem. However, despite your best efforts and the application of the practices described above, you simply get stuck, you cannot figure out the problem. The solution does not come to you. This type of impasse is often best solved by letting go of the problem for a while. This act of detachment can be manifested in a variety of ways. You may simply want to get up from your desk and take a walk around the office, the house, or the block. Another option is to put the problem or task away and go on to something else. A third option is to let go of the desire to solve the problem on your own and to seek assistance. Each of these options allows you to disengage from the task or problem for a time.

A highly skilled information technology manager/social worker, J. A. Post, reports that he often uses all three of these options (personal communication, September 29, 1997). He reports that walking away from the problem for a time allows him to develop fresh ideas and renewed energy. When he puts the task or problem away for a while and moves on to something else, it allows him to remain productive and avoid wasting time on efforts that are going nowhere fast. The time away from the task or problem allows him to devote additional time in contemplating the issue and to seek advice from others. Finally, despite his considerable expertise in a wide range of hardware and software applications, he does not hesitate to call on others for their advice and expertise. This openness only serves to enhance his skills. The point here is that everyone runs into obstacles in dealing with IT that may seem at times insurmountable. Taking excessive pride in being able to solve IT problems, working unrelentingly, and never giving up may in fact be a deterrent to finding a solution, learning a new skill, or completing a task. An attitude of openness allows one to let go of the problem for a while and open up to new information from other sources.

Essential Limitations

Barring any presently unforeseen retreat of postmodern society away from information technology or apocalyptic alterations in the current course of world events, it appears that the range, functionality, power, and utility of IT will continue to expand in the near term. This growth in the capacity of personal computers to capture, hold, process, transform, and represent information is both exhilarating and challenging. The major thrust of this chapter so far is that the personal computer and information technology represent robust and powerful tools that can dramatically enhance the capacity of social service practitioners to deliver a range of effective and creative social services. It is further suggested that alteration in the attitudes and beliefs about information technology held by the practitioner can enhance the ability to learn and develop proficiencies in the use of IT with the resultant creative and novel applications of information technology in social services. Given the great and expanding potential for creative and useful application of IT in the service of clients, it is possible to overlook the essential limitations of IT in the provision of social services. However, consideration of limits of technology in social service practice can help to more clearly identify and define promising applications of the personal computer and IT. Our appreciation of the light is made possible by our perception of shadow.

What then are the essential limitations in the application of personal computers and IT in social service practice? Perhaps the foremost limitation is that as a tool of interactive communication the personal computer is an inadequate substitute for face to face interaction. Personal computer–mediated dialog between two or more people is made possible via e-mail; real time, text-based exchanges; or two-way audio/video linkage over the Internet. Clearly, personal computer–mediated interaction is being used for therapeutic purposes. Finn (1996) describes computer-based self-help/mutual aid (CSHMA) groups in which addiction recovery is facilitated in the exchanges between recovering individuals via e-mail. Levenson (1997) describes a range of applications of online counseling including question and answer e-mail exchanges, real time "chat" discussions, and the utility of these methods with homebound clients. Despite the possible clinical utility of these methods, the experiential poverty of the interaction is difficult to dispute.

Computer-mediated communications represent a useful alternative to in-person interactions for a wide range of tasks and situations. However, it should be acknowledged that as a species, human beings have an extremely long evolutionary history over which our brains adapted to recognize and respond to the subtleties of in-person social exchange. We attend to the interpersonal cues communicated in multiple nonverbal forms such as dress, gestures, facial expressions, personal space, hygiene, eye contact, odors, and speed of speech. Certainly, there are cultural differences in the meaning of some of these nonverbal expressions of interpersonal information, but regardless of this cultural variability, nonverbal interpersonal information is to varying degrees missing in computer-mediated communication. A portion of the richness of the interaction is lost when we utilize computer-mediated communication. Given this fact, there are certainly a wide range of social service activities for which the essential limits of computer-mediated communication are reached. Examples include psychosocial assessment of emotionally disturbed individuals, child protection evaluations, most forms of psychotherapy, and in-home assessments, to name a few.

A second essential limitation of personal computers and information technology is that sometimes, for some tasks, older, low-tech solutions simply work better and faster and are more versatile. Imagine, for instance, that you are leaving your office, heading out for a home visit. Your supervisor stops you and asks to schedule an appointment for supervision later in the week. In your briefcase you have a laptop computer and an appointment calendar. To schedule the appointment on the laptop, you have to pull the laptop from your briefcase, hope you have remembered to charge the battery or look for a nearby electrical outlet, turn the computer on, wait for it to boot up, and then open your scheduling software and enter the time and date of the meeting. Once it is entered, you then have to exit the scheduling software and wait for the computer to cycle through its shut-down routine. It's far easier and faster to schedule the meeting by noting it in an appointment calendar. This paper-based information tool is immediately available, provides a durable permanent record of activities, does not require batteries, and does not necessitate making awkward small talk with your boss while your laptop cycles through a start-up and shut-down cycle.

For many tasks of information retrieval, storage, and presentation, paper-based methods are presently faster and more versatile. To find a local phone number it is simply easier to look it up in a phone book than to log on to the Web and look for it in phone number directories via search engines. Taking notes when talking to clients, especially in informal situations such as homes and hospital rooms, is for most people more readily and comfortably accomplished with a notepad than with a laptop. In health or psychoeducational settings, it is far more likely that clients will read educational materials if they are provided as paper handouts than if the clients are told to look up the information on your Web page. In each of the situations cited here, the task can be accomplished with IT, but there is no readily apparent added benefit in its use.

With broad sectors of society rushing to embrace and apply computer and information technology to a wide range of tasks and problems, this discussion of the essential limitations of computers and information technology may appear to be rather neo-Luddite in its tone. The Luddites were English laborers who in the early nineteenth century destroyed textile machinery in riots protesting the occupational and social impact of that new technology. However, unlike the Luddites who were clearly threatened by technology, this text seeks to find the optimal application of technology in the provision of social services, balanced by the awareness of the essential limitations of its applications. Ironically, some of the clients we now serve are individuals and families whose lives, like the Luddites, have been disrupted by the technological changes in their workplaces. The essential balance we seek is to enhance our provision of services through personal computers and IT while through the alchemy of human interaction conveying the profession's fundamental compassion and concern.

Summary

This chapter has provided an introduction to the concept that the personal computer has great, and so far largely untapped, potential as a tool for social work practice. The chapter described some of the historical and psychological impediments faced by practitioners in the application of information technology in social services. Described here is the role of the personal computer in communication, collaboration, and cooperation. The chapter discussed ways to cultivate openness to learning information technology skills and concluded with a discussion of some of the fundamental limitations of information technology in the provision of social services.

Exercises

1. Describe in writing how personal computers and other information technology are currently used in your practice setting. What impediments to the use of IT do you see within the practice setting? How is the use of personal computers and IT prompted in the practice setting?

2. Discuss with a group of peers your own experiences in acquiring personal computer and IT skills. What are the common themes in terms of attitudes and behaviors that have supported and deterred the acquisition of skills?

3. Discuss with a group of peers your perceptions of the limitations of information technology in social service practice. Then consider and discuss the unmet potentials for applying IT in social service practice.

chapter 2

Hardware
The Basics and Beyond

This chapter presents an introduction to information technology hardware. It reviews the basic forms and functions of personal computers. Described is hardware for inputting information, computer processing capabilities, information output devices, and a variety of information storage devices. This chapter provides a rationale for working with and retaining information in electronic form, as opposed to creating unnecessary hard copies. It also provides a discussion of the use of notebook computers as a tool of social service practice. Guidelines of how and where to buy personal computers are provided. The intent of this overview of information technology hardware is to provide social service practitioners with a foundation to make informed decisions regarding the purchase and deployment of IT.

Information technology is made possible by the marriage of hardware and software. *Hardware* refers to the physical devices utilized in IT. *Software,* on the other hand, denotes the sets of electronically based instructions and procedures that give hardware function and utility. More broadly, the term software also denotes any electronically encoded information such as a data file, word processing document, or digitized sound file. In this chapter, we will review a wide range of informational technology hardware used in interaction with the personal computer. The goal of this chapter is to provide a working understanding of the functions of the hardware described without overwhelming the reader with technological detail. Fundamental knowledge of IT hardware, including the basic components of a personal computer, makes it possible for social service workers to more readily employ the wide array of hardware devices available. A related goal of this chapter is to provide an examination of the relative merits of various configurations of personal computers as well as factors to consider in making hardware purchases.

In and Out of the "Black Box"

Readers to whom the fundamental architecture of personal computers is well known may wish to lightly review this section. However, for many social service professionals and students, the components of personal computers and their respective functions remain shrouded in mystery. To many, the personal computer is akin to the proverbial "black box" which mysteriously transforms input from the keyboard and mouse into output on the computer's screen and printer. For them, the contents of the "black box" and the magic that results from its unknown operations are often viewed as being of little consequence as long as the computer works. The question then arises, Why would any noncomputer professional want or need to know anything about the contents or workings of the "black box"?

The truth is that having a basic understanding of the architecture of a personal computer and knowing something of how it operates makes learning to use the machine optimally much easier. For instance, understanding that information in the form of documents can be stored on a 3½-inch floppy disk, the computer's hard drive, or perhaps a removable hard drive is important to know. It allows one to make decisions about if, when, and how information may be stored, shared, transported, and retrieved. Additionally, a working knowledge of the basic components of a personal computer and their functions is extremely important when attempting to understand and solve a problem in the computer's operations. Whether one is trying to solve the problem alone or seeking help from a technician in person or over the phone, the more complete one's understanding, the easier it is to track down a problem and communicate about its manifestations.

Many of the major computer manufacturers have telephone help lines. The technicians who take calls from customers have numerous stories of callers who had very limited understanding of their machines. From time to time these stories are circulated via e-mail and posted on Web sites. One customer sent in a Xerox copy of a diskette in response to the technician's request for a copy of the problematic diskette. Another man reported the fax software on his computer was not working because despite holding the intended fax in front of his monitor and hitting the send key, nothing happened. Then there was the customer who inserted a diskette encased in a plastic cover into her machine to prevent it from becoming infected with a computer virus. In order to avoid having our misunderstandings of personal computer architecture and functions distributed and archived on the Internet, we will now review the basics of computer form, function, and vocabulary.

Basic Personal Computer Forms and Functions

The shape and configuration of personal computers are varied and ever changing. There are basic forms and within those forms some fundamental configurations of components. Personal computers are manufactured as notebooks (or laptops), desktop machines, towers (mini and full), and all-in-one machines. Notebooks vary in size, weight, and array of components, but are distinguished by their portability and a screen integrated into a folding case that encloses the keyboard. Desktops are intended, as their name suggests, for placement on a desktop. Internally, their components are horizontally arranged as opposed to the vertical configuration of components in tower models. The vertical configuration of towers makes it possible for users to place these machines either under or to the side of a desk, thereby freeing desktop space. Alternatively, towers can be placed on a desktop with a monitor beside them. The tower configuration is also used to allow more space for the adding of multiple components such as CD-ROMs, data storage drives, and cards that add functionality to personal computers such as sound and video digitization cards. While it is certainly possible to add these enhancing components to desktop models, their horizontal configuration requires the building of machines that consume considerable desktop space. The space required for a machine on a desktop is generally referred to as its *footprint*. Desktop machines with the capacity to hold a large number of cards and devices often have the drawback of having a large footprint. A final configuration of the personal computer is the all-in-one machine which has the monitor included in the case housing the computer's other components. The Apple iMac is one example of such a computer. All-in-one machines are apparently preferred by users who desire either the aesthetic simplicity of their design or users who do not wish to make decisions in selecting both computer and monitor. The main drawback to this design is that if the monitor fails, one loses the use of the entire machine until the monitor is replaced or repaired. This same drawback applies to notebooks as well.

Despite the variability in personal computer form described here, all of these types of machines have the same basic components that make possible four basic functions (Schoech, 1990). These functions are input, information processing, output, and storage. *Input* refers to the range of ways in which information and instructions are entered into the computer. Commonly used input components include keyboards, mice, joysticks, digital scanners, digital cameras, modems, network cards, CD-ROMs (compact disk—read only memory), DVD (digital versatile/video disc), hard drives, floppy-disk drives, data storage devices, microphones, video cameras, and electronic drawing pads.

The *information processing* component of a personal computer generally means the central processing unit (CPU). The CPU is often referred to as the chip or the microprocessor. The CPU is the brain of the computer, the means by which inputs are transformed into outputs, keystrokes become letters on the screen, and columns of numbers become solved equations. Computer chip manufacturers like Intel who make the Pentium chip and Motorola who make the Power PC chip are constantly striving to make faster CPUs. The faster the CPU, the faster information is transformed. The faster the CPU, the more complex the series of tasks a computer can perform. Tasks such as voice recognition, which transforms words spoken into a microphone connected to a computer into text on the computer screen, require very sophisticated software. In order for the software to recognize as distinct words the vibrations of speech that have been transformed by the computer into digital patterns, large numbers of operations must be carried out at high rates of speed. The faster the CPU, the more calculations or operations a computer can perform in a given length of time. In recent years, the speed of CPUs has climbed dramatically from 8 MHz to 550 MHz and higher, thereby allowing personal computers to handle increasing complex tasks such as voice recognition and photographic image manipulation.

The products of the work of a CPU are *outputs.* Computers can produce multiple forms of output. Output can be displayed on computer screens as images, text, videos, animations, and graphics. Output can be printed, faxed, distributed as e-mail, and displayed as pages on the World Wide Web. Personal computers can produce and transform music, sound, and speech. Outputs are, in essence, why we use personal computers; they are the reason for the existence of information technology.

The fourth function of personal computers is information storage. Storage of information is the means by which the outputs are stored and without which the use of IT would be a rather ephemeral enterprise. If we were unable to capture and store the output from CPUs, the products of our endeavors would be much like the elaborate and beautiful mandalas made from colored sand by Buddhist monks and Hindu devotees, gone with the passing of a strong breeze, or in the case of IT, with the turning off of the machine. Fortunately, such is not the case. Outputs are stored on floppy disks, they reside on hard disk drives, are held on CD-ROMS, cached on removable drives, and preserved on tape back-up systems. The storage space available on these various storage media continues to grow in order to accommodate the growing quantities of information captured through scanners and digital cameras, from the Internet and other sources. Additionally, as software programs grow more complex, the space required to store them on hard drives grows proportionally. Only a few years ago, a 40-megabyte hard drive was considered more than adequate for most home computers. Now, 8-gigabyte hard drives, that is a 200-fold increase in size, are common.

Stored outputs are not simply stored and then retrieved for examination, but also used as inputs for further processing of the information. For instance, data on the progress several clients have made in individual cognitive behavioral therapy sessions can be retrieved and combined to assess the overall effectiveness of this intervention method in a clinic. In this example, data from multiple stored files are input into a single file, processed by calculating the combined average level of depression at each therapy session, and then graphically represented as an average depression level for the group over time. The output, the resultant graph, is then printed, saved in the combined data file, and also inserted into a report being written in a word processing document. The interaction of these four functions of the personal computer give it its utility in the collection, processing, management, and representation of information. This process is illustrated in Figure 2.1.

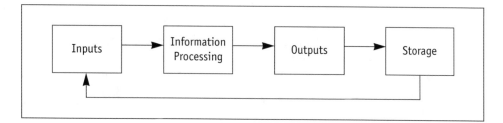

FIGURE 2.1   Four Functions of a Personal Computer

Information In: Keyboards to Captured Video

The means by which personal computers can receive information have dramatically expanded in recent years. Information and instructions were entered into early models of personal computers with keyboards. In 1984, Apple Computers introduced the Macintosh, which was the first personal computer to use a mouse as a means to give the computer instructions and enter information. As is widely known now, the mouse is a hand-held device with one or more buttons that works in tandem with software to enhance the ease of operation of personal computers. Software that works in interaction with a mouse generally has a graphic user interface (GUI). The GUI will be discussed in greater detail in the next chapter, but for now it is important to understand that GUI software uses menus and icons or pictures on the computer screen to represent instructions or functions of the software.

There are a number of distinct advantages in using a mouse in conjunction with GUI software as a mechanism to input instructions and information. The user does not have to remember keyboard commands in order to activate functions such as printing a document or saving a file. When exploring the Web, pointing and clicking on highlighted words or images with a mouse allows the user to navigate through the content of a single Web page or across myriad pages linked to each other on the Web. In graphics programs, a mouse makes it possible for a user to select an icon of a geometric shape, such as a circle, place the shape on a page, expand or contract its size, drag it to another location on the page, and graphically link it to other shapes or objects. In spreadsheet programs, charts can be reshaped, rotated, and reconfigured with instructions from a mouse, without ever touching a keyboard. Each of these graphic functions is considerably more complex, if not impossible, using only keyboard commands. As an input device, the mouse along with GUI software has played a major role in the information technology revolution in the last twenty years.

Another critical element in the information technology revolution has been the growing ease and capacity to digitize information. *Digitization* means the transformation of information, whether sound, graphics, images, or video, into a format that can be understood and processed by a computer. This is accomplished by converting information into *bits,* ones or zeros, the fundamental elements of language in computing (Green, 1997). Hardware input devices such as digital cameras, scanners, video capture cards, and microphones connected to sound cards all perform this function of digitization. Once an image, a sound, or a video (in essence a series of images) has been digitized, it can be altered and enhanced in the personal computer according to the needs and wishes of the user. Furthermore, once information is in digital form it can be compressed in size and transferred over a computer network to the office next door, the agency on the other side town, or made available to interested parties around the world over the Internet.

The capacity to input digital information from multiple media sources such as video, sound, and images has markedly expanded the functionality of the personal computer. The handling of text-based information, numbers and words, is still a key function of the personal computer. However, the ability to enhance documents with digitized images, add sound to Web pages, and capture, transform, store, and display video represent only a few examples of how digitized input has enhanced and enriched computer-based information. The potential applications of this capacity in social service practice will be explored in subsequent chapters.

There are several other means to input information and instructions into a computer including diskettes, CD-ROMS, DVD hard drives, data storage devices, network cards, and modems. The term *data storage devices* refers to a range of mechanisms such as tape back-up systems, optical drives, and removable hard disks, such as Zip disks. The diskette, CD-ROM, DVD, hard drive, and data storage devices are storage mechanisms that also serve as sources of data input that can be subsequently processed. For instance, a digitized image stored on a CD-ROM can be added to the computer's memory, altered or enhanced by graphics software, and then saved again in its revised or altered form to a data storage device such as a hard drive.

Unlike these storage devices, the input function of network cards and modems is derived from their ability to serve as conduits linking a personal computer to other computers and computer networks. For example, a school social worker preparing to lead a discussion with middle school students on the dangers of smoking might find on the Web several documents containing relevant information, which can be downloaded via modem to a personal computer. In addition, the social worker finds and downloads images of smoking-damaged lungs and a sound file on teenage smoking in the National Public Radio archives. Having input this information through the modem, these various documents can be combined into a single multimedia presentation used to facilitate the discussion group. The personal computer's capacity to handle these various sources of information is a function of its information processing ability.

Processing: Speed and Space

SPEED.   The capacity of a personal computer to process information is primarily a function of the speed of its central processing unit and the space it has available in its memory or RAM (random access memory) to hold information awaiting immediate processing. The speed of CPUs in personal computers has been increasing steadily since their introduction. In 1965, Gordon Moore, a founder of Intel Corporation, made a prediction that has since become known as Moore's Law (Green, 1997). Moore's Law "states that the power, speed, and capacity of microprocessors—'brains' of computers— would double every 18 months and the cost would be halved in the same period" (p. 9). Remarkably, Moore's Law has so far proved to be true, though there is debate about how long this trend can continue. The result of this rapid advancement of computer speed is the ability of computers to handle increasingly large and complex information files, easier-to-use and more intuitive operating systems, and a dramatic enhancement of the sophistication and utility of software.

The other reality of Moore's Law is that personal computers and the software to operate them become rapidly outmoded. For instance, in 1987 a personal computer with an Intel 286 processor, with approximately 100,000 transistors, ran at a speed of 7.5 megahertz (MHz). (A hertz denotes one cycle per second and *mega* equals one million; therefore, a 7.5 MHz processor would run at a speed of 7.5 million computing cycles per minute.) A personal computer with a 286 processor was a perfectly serviceable machine capable of word processing, running spreadsheet and database programs, as well as connecting to mainframe computers via a modem, albeit at glacial speed compared to today's modems. Since that time Intel has introduced the 386 processor, the 486 processor, the Pentium processor, and most recently the Pentium II chip. By way of comparison to the 286 processor, the fastest Pentium III chip has 9.5 million transistors on it and runs at 550 MHz (Intel Corportation, 1999). This continuing and extraordinary increase in processing speed of newly released computers often results in the perception that older and slower machines are antiquated. This process of machines becoming rapidly outdated is a function not only of perception, but is also the function of continual enhancement of software. As software applications and operating systems grow in complexity and functionality, they often will not run well or sometimes at all on machines with older processors that do not have the requisite speed or processing capacity.

Now that we have established the importance of the speed of a CPU in a personal computer, the question might still be asked, what exactly does the CPU do? The CPU was described above as the "brain" of the computer and as such it handles the logical and arithmetic functions required to change input to output, such as transforming keystrokes to words on a screen, or performing the calculations to solve an equation in a spreadsheet. It is in essence the computing part of the computer. Moreover, the CPU manages the interaction of all the parts of the computer. The CPU is located on what is called the motherboard. The *motherboard* is a piece of hardware inside the computer that links the various components together and allows them to communicate with each other via the CPU.

Take, for instance, the simple act of typing the word "simple" on a computer screen. The typing of each letter of the word sends from the keyboard a series of zeros and ones, representing each letter of the word, to the computer's CPU. Now the word "simple" arrives at the same time the computer is performing a number of other operations, such as running the software instructions that keep the word processing program in operation and continually displaying its image on the computer monitor. Depending on the speed of the CPU, the available RAM (random access memory), and the other programs that are also running, this input from the keyboard in the form of zeros and ones representing the word "simple" combines in the CPU with the operating word processing program and then is displayed on the computer screen nearly as soon as it is typed. If, however, the CPU is an older, slower processor, or the computer has a number of other programs running at the same time, there may be a delay between the striking of the key and the display of the letter on the screen. The delay can also be the result of insufficient memory to hold all the software activity being required at the moment, causing the CPU to have to swap bits of information out of the RAM and back to the hard drive for storage. The essential point here is that the information processing ability of a computer is a function of the interaction between the CPU and the RAM.

SPACE.   The available RAM on a computer is perhaps best thought of as the immediate space the machine has to hold information that is being processed by the CPU. The CPU uses the RAM to temporarily store information from the operating system or from other programs in use or running in the background waiting to be used. As such, computers are able to operate faster with more RAM. RAM is now typically measured in megabytes, also known as megs. To understand how large a megabyte is it is important to recall that a bit is a single unit of information in computer language, as in 1 or 0. Eight bits equal a byte. A byte can be thought of as a word in computer language, as computers are designed to process a byte as a single unit. A kilobyte is 1,028 bytes. In 1984, Apple Computers introduced the first Macintosh computer, which had 128 kilobytes of RAM. By way of comparison, a megabyte is composed of one million bytes of information. Today, most personal computers come with at least 16 megabytes of RAM, and it is not uncommon for machines to have 32, 64, or more megs of RAM.

RAM is manufactured as chips that are placed on small boards called SIMMs. The SIMMs are plugged into slots on the motherboard. Memory chips are also rated according to the speed with which they can exchange information with the CPU. The speed is measured in nanoseconds. A nanosecond is 1/1000 of a microsecond and a microsecond is one millionth of a second. In other words, a nanosecond is an extremely short period of time. Typical memory chips are rated at 60 and 70 nanoseconds. The lower the nanoseconds the faster the memory chip. Most computers are designed to allow ready increases in the RAM by swapping the existing SIMMs for SIMMs with more RAM.

To make the picture a little more complex, there exists between the CPU and the RAM a type of memory called *cache RAM*. Cache RAM allows the computer to temporarily store and access information without having to go to the main RAM, thereby speeding up the processing time. It is not uncommon for personal computers to use 512 kilobytes of cache RAM along with 16 to 32 megs of standard RAM. As an indicator of the progress of computing speed and capacity, a cache RAM of 512 kilobytes is four times the size of the standard RAM on the original Macintosh.

Taken together these advances in CPU speed and RAM space make available to today's personal computer users machines residing on desktops that have far greater speed and utility than machines that once occupied entire rooms. These new machines are capable of processing such complex tasks as translating spoken words to text, capturing sound and video as readily modifiable digital data, and converting scanned pages of words into editable text files. The output of this information processing capacity comes as either or both atoms (hard copy such as printed material) or as bits (electronic documents or files).

Information Out: Monitors and Screens

Unless one is working with audio files, computer monitors and screens provide the most immediate representation of the output from a computer's CPU. While the terms *monitors* and *screens* may initially seem redundant, the two words are used to designate the distinction between standalone computer monitors and the screens in notebook and other portable computers. However, both these types of display units perform the function of providing a primary means by which the user interacts with the computer to accomplish the task in which they are engaged. For simplicity's sake in this discussion, the term *screen* will be used to refer to the visual display on both personal computers and notebooks, unless otherwise indicated.

Imagine for a moment attempting to do anything on a computer without being able to see the results. It would make the operation of the computer extremely difficult and time consuming. Individuals who are blind or who have significant visual impairments face this challenge daily. Fortunately, software has recently become available that translates operating systems and software into audio cues that tell the visually impaired user where they are and what they are doing, thereby making navigation and work on the computer possible. Personal computers have always had some type of monitor for the display of input and output. However, early mainframe computers offered no such luxury. In the late fifties and early sixties, programming instructions and data were input on *punch cards* which were paper cards with holes punched into the cards to represent information. These cards were then read by the computer. Output from running the "punched in" data and operating instructions was printed out. More often than not, errors in the punch cards resulted in data or program errors, which had to be tracked down, corrected, and the cards then rerun. According to H. D. Patterson, the resultant time lag was known as the "balding period" due to the hair loss/hair pulling of those awaiting data with which to make decisions (personal communication, February 14, 1998). Needless to say, the absence of visual display of input and output made computing a tedious, complex, and time-consuming process.

The visual display of information on a screen is made possible by the interaction of the CPU, a video card on the computer's motherboard, and the monitor or screen. The video card is a device designed to handle the calculations and transmission of information about how the CPU wants the screen to appear at any moment (Kozierok, 1997). The video card has on it a type of memory called video memory that stores information about the screen's content. The video card continually sends information from the video memory to the screen on how the screen should look at that moment. As the CPU sends new information to the video card indicating changes in the screen, the necessary calculations for transforming the screen are performed by the video card. This updated screen information is stored in the video memory and sent from the memory to the screen. It is important to recognize that this process of continually updating or refreshing the screen occurs at high rates of speed. This process is referred to as the *refresh rate,* as it indicates the number of times per second that the display on the screen is redrawn or refreshed by the video card. Refresh rates generally range from 60 to 100 Hz. The slower the refresh rate, the more likely one is to notice the screen flicker. Most people do not notice screen flicker at 72 Hz or above (Kozierok, 1997). Again, it should be noted that the way the screen looks is an interaction between the speed and memory of the video card and the computer monitor or screen. The amount of video card memory affects the performance of the video card and ultimately the output displayed on the screen. Four megabytes of video RAM is not uncommon.

Video cards operate in interaction with the computer's monitor or the notebook's screen though the two types of displays produce video output in two different ways. When personal computers first became available, they all had monochrome displays. Color monitors were introduced in the mid-1980s. Monochrome displays are now seldom used, except in homes and offices that have delayed upgrading their equipment much too long.

Color computer monitors are in essence high-resolution television screens composed of blue, green, and red dots (Kozierok, 1997). The video card tells the monitor which dots, or pixels, to illumine and how bright, thereby producing the image that appears on the screen. The resolution of a monitor is determined by the number of pixels displayed on the screen. The resolution is indicated by two numbers, for instance 640 × 480. The higher the resolution, the more information that can be displayed on the screen at one time; however, high resolution on a small screen can make it very difficult to read characters on the screen. High resolution on a large screen can cause the video display performance to slow down if the video card and monitor are not configured to support extremely high resolution. See Kozierok (1997) for more detailed information on monitor performance and configuration. As a visual medium for the display of output, the quality and performance of a monitor is important as it has a direct impact on the comfort one experiences in using a personal computer. Eye strain from poor quality monitors can hamper the use of a computer. If one frequently experiences fatigue from time spent working on a computer, it is likely that one's perception of personal computers will be significantly affected. As a result, experienced computer users will often spend extra money for the purchase of a higher-quality monitor when purchasing a computer system.

Unlike desktop personal computers, notebooks come with screens integrated into the lid of the machine. The flat screen technology used in notebooks employs liquid crystal display (LCD) technology like that used in digital watches to create images on a flat screen. When notebooks were first introduced they had monochrome screens that produced images in shades of gray. Color displays on notebooks fall into two categories, passive matrix and active matrix. Passive matrix screens have historically been less expensive, but suffered from being difficult to read in bright light and having less vivid colors than active matrix. More recently, computer manufacturers have begun to use dual-scan passive matrix screens, which achieve colors that rival active matrix screens and require less power, thereby conserving battery life. Dual scan screens have two noteworthy limitations. They have a limited viewing area, which makes it difficult for people who are not directly in front of the screen to see it well. The second limitation is that they have slower screen refresh rates, which makes them less suitable for computer games and video display. Active matrix displays, which are also known as thin film transistor (TFT) displays, refresh the image on the screen at about twice the rate of passive matrix screens. As a result, active matrix screens are known for their vibrant colors and better usability in daylight. One drawback is that, because of their power demands, they deplete batteries at a faster rate than passive matrix screens. Active matrix screens are more costly to produce and are usually found on more expensive notebooks.

The advent in the flat screen technology used in both passive and active matrix screens is responsible for the recent revolution in portable computing. This technology enabled computers to no longer be tethered to large, heavy, and power hungry monitors, but instead opened the doors and made it possible for computers to "leave the building." Computing became mobile because of flat screen technology. As a result, information now flows into and output pours across screens and out of notebook computers around the far corners of the earth.

Bits to Atoms or Not

The products of a personal computer, whether a notebook or desktop, can take multiple forms. Take, for instance, writing a paper. To start, the irony of the term *paper* should not be missed. The term presupposes the resultant output. In other words, in this age of information technology, a document that once was called a paper does not have to be transformed from bits to atoms and end up as a paper-based manuscript. Once it is complete—once keystrokes have been transformed to arranged words on a screen, once the charts, graphs, and/or images have been imported from other software and inserted in their proper places, once the document is checked for spelling and grammatical errors by the word processing software—then its author is faced with the decision of what type of output to produce. Will the manuscript be changed from bits to atoms or not? In printing the document, ink or laser technology is applied to inscribe words and images on paper and in doing so the information contained in the document moves from electronic bits to atoms in the form of ink and paper.

Increasingly there are other choices about what to do with the results of information processing. The document described above could be saved as an electronic file and attached to an e-mail message that is sent to one or more people. Other choices for the distribution of the document include saving it in HTML (hypertext markup language) format and posting it on the World Wide Web. The document could be saved on a diskette, a CD-ROM, or a removable hard disk and mailed to its intended recipients. In each of these options, the document is retained in its electronic form, as bits. The decision to change it to atoms, to print it, is open to its readers in each of the electronic options described here.

Documents that remain in an electronic form retain their capacity to be enhanced, modified, or in some way further transformed. In an age in which teamwork on projects and collaboration among professionals have become increasingly important, the ability to share information products, such as the document described here, have become extremely important. Moreover, retaining documents as bits allows them to be readily and immediately shared with colleagues. As an example, a grant proposal for a collaborative project under development by several different social service agencies can be distributed as an attached file to e-mail. As each team member makes their respective contributions, they send the revised document to the rest of the team via e-mail. There is even software, such as Netscape Communicator and Lotus Notes, that allows collaborators to simultaneously examine, mark up, change, and enhance a document over the Internet. This is a far more efficient and fluid way to develop such documents as a team. The alternative is to distribute hard copies of the document through the postal service, let each member add their contributions and edits to the document, send them back, and then again redistribute the revised document in a slow, iterative process. Teamwork on paper-based documents is slow, cumbersome, and inefficient, not to mention the fact that it requires the consumption of considerable amounts of paper; a nontrivial consideration in an age of constrained agency budgets and diminishing global forest resources.

It is worth noting that retaining information in an electronic format provides additional advantages in storage, retrieval, and reuse. A primary advantage of documents in an electronic format, as bits, is one of space. Multiple documents can be stored as bits on a diskette, hard drive, or CD-ROM. Of course the actual number of documents on these storage medium is dependent on the size of the document and the space available on the storage medium. The essential point is that any of these storage options requires far less physical space than the printed versions of the electronic documents they might hold. By way of comparison, a single CD-ROM can hold up to 300,000 pages of text-based information, which as paper-based information would require a nontrivial amount of filing cabinet space (Internet.com, 1997).

A second advantage of storage of documents in bits instead of atoms is the ease with which information can be retrieved. Many types of software allow users to readily search storage devices for documents using a number of retrieval parameters such as a word in a title, file format type, text in the document, or date of storage to name a few. These search procedures will scan the storage device and quickly find all documents meeting the specified criteria. Locating paper-based documents is generally not so easy, even if one has been timely, mindful, and conscientious in filing documents. Moreover, paper-based documents are not readily modifiable.

This ability to modify and reuse electronic documents offers significant advantages over retaining only paper-based computer output. Electronic documents can evolve over time as new information becomes available. Several documents can be combined to produce a summary document. Template documents can be created for letters and reports that require frequent or regular production. For instance, a social worker may have to produce a monthly activity report. Each month she retrieves her activity report template from her hard drive. Her first act is to save the document under a new name so as to retain the original template in an unaltered form and to produce her report under the name of the new document. She adds to her activity report summary process notes from various clients' electronic charts, data she has collected in spreadsheets accounting for her time and travel, and research findings she has found on the Web related to the population she works with that she wants to draw to her supervisors attention. When her report is complete, she e-mails it to her supervisor, saves a copy on her personal computer's hard drive, and adds a copy of her report to the file she is creating to document her activities for the year. In this reporting activity she has employed an existing template, combined electronic information from several sources, electronically distributed her report, and added it to an evolving document.

From Screen to Hard Copy

In discussing information output so far, a case has been made for avoiding or at least minimizing paper-based output. There are many times when the production of a hard copy is unavoidable, necessary, and preferable. The two most commonly used tools for production of paper-based output are fax machines and printers.

A fax machine is a scanning and printing device capable of sending and receiving documents over phone lines. Fax machines are widely used for personal and business communications. They represent a relatively easy to use and inexpensive means to send documents. Most modems used by personal computers come with fax software that allows the user to fax documents directly from word processing and other software. This direct faxing from the personal computer over phone lines has the advantage of not having to print a copy of the document before taking it to a standalone fax machine to send. Additionally, personal computers with modems and the requisite fax software can receive faxes, assuming the computer is turned on and the phone line is open. One of the drawbacks of fax transmission of documents is that the image quality is generally not as high as that produced by printers. Moreover, once a fax is received, either by a fax machine or by a fax modem, it is extremely difficult to modify, append, or enhance. The printed fax produced by a fax machine can sometimes be scanned into a computer and, using a type of software known as optical character recognition (OCR) software, faxes can, depending on the image quality and the robustness of the OCR software, be translated into editable text files. A similar process can be applied to faxes received by a personal computer through a fax modem, though because the fax is already in the machine, it is not necessary to print it out and then scan it back into the computer. What should be apparent from this discussion is that while fax transmissions are convenient and widely used, if one wishes to receive an editable document, e-mail or Web-based distribution, or a document on a diskette sent through the postal service, are all far more reliable and accurate methods.

The other alternative for paper-based output is the printer. The two most commonly used types of printers are laser printers and ink jet printers. Laser printers are extensively used in offices and as low-cost laser printers have become available, they are increasingly employed in homes and home offices. Laser printers produce words and images on a page by creating characters on a drum that is electronically covered by a powder known as toner. As the drum rolls over the paper, the characters are transferred to the paper (Schoech, 1990). The output of most laser printers is monochrome, usually black. Color laser printers are available on the market, however, they are very expensive and generally used by people interested in very high quality image production.

The other type of printer popularly used is the ink jet printer. Ink jet printers create images and characters by spraying a stream of ink through a tiny jet or opening. This ink jet technology has been applied to the production of color printing by using colored inks. This has resulted in the wide availability of relatively low-cost, high image quality, color ink jet printers. Some of these printers can produce photograph quality images, though some require special paper and special ink cartridges (McCracken, 1996; Schorr, 1997).

The quality and capacity of printers is judged by the maximum resolution that they will print, their printing speed, and their standard and maximum RAM. Maximum resolution is measured in dots per inch (dpi) which indicates the clarity and crispness of the images and characters produced by the printer. The dpi of typical moderately priced monochrome printers can range from 600 by 600 to 2,400 by 600 (McCracken, 1996) whereas color printers range from 1,440 by 720 to 600 by 600 (Schorr, 1997). The printing speed of monochrome printers in this price range produce from 6 to 8 pages per minute (ppm). The speed of color printers ranges from 1.5 to 8 PPM. Standard RAM indicates the amount of random access memory on the printer and maximum RAM denotes the total amount of RAM the printer can accommodate. The available RAM on a printer affects how fast the printer can print and the size of documents the printer can handle without having to communicate with the computer from whence the document came. Standard RAM on printers ranges from 32k to 1 meg and maximum RAM ranges from 32k to 9 megs (McCracken, 1996).

These parameters of printer quality and capacity are continuing to improve. In deciding on a printer to purchase, recent printer product reviews in computer magazines should be examined to determine current standards. Additionally, consideration should be given to the type of documents that the printer will most frequently be called upon to produce. If the output will almost exclusively be monochromatic documents, the laser printer is often a good choice because of generally superior speed and character quality. If, on the other hand, color images, graphs, charts, and mixed colors of text are required, then color ink jet printers are the best moderately priced choice for most individuals and many agencies.

Storage and Retrieval

In the process of creating any document or file on a personal computer, whether it is a word processing document, a spreadsheet, an audio file, or some other output, it is generally necessary and certainly advisable to save the file. Now there are people who will write a letter, do a paper for school, or create a budget on a spreadsheet, then print the document out without ever bothering to save it. They will argue that it's just a short letter or paper and saving it takes too much time and they do not want to bother with finding a disk or creating a file on their hard drive. There are two major problems with this approach to computing. First, they deprive themselves of ever reusing the information product they have produced. Second, if they do not save their document as they work on it, they are gambling with losing the document should their machine crash, the power fail, or they inadvertently delete the document. It is difficult to find anyone who has used a computer for more than a year or two who does not have some woeful tale of data lost. For anyone who uses a computer, the consequential result of regularly saving files is that the user begins to accumulate large numbers of files they may wish to store over time. Two questions then arise. What are the choices for storage of electronic files? And, what are the relative merits of the various storage devices?

Diskettes

Perhaps the most widely used and commonly available storage device is the diskette. The diskette is a portable, magnetic disk that is inserted into the computer's disk drive in order to be used by the computer (Margolis, 1996). Diskettes are sometimes called floppy disks or floppies. Modern 3½-inch diskettes are neither flexible nor floppy. Their predecessors, the 5¼-inch diskettes, were, and the names floppy disks or floppies remain in use, despite the fact that the old disks are now seldom seen. The 3½-inch, high density diskettes, which are the most widely used, can store up to 1.44 megabytes of information when formatted for PCs and 1.2 megabytes when formatted for Apple Macintosh computers.

The term *PC* is used here to refer to personal computers that use either DOS or Windows operating systems and were originally developed by IBM. Diskettes used in PCs are formatted differently than those used in Apple Macintosh computers or *Macs* for short. As such, Macintosh diskettes cannot be used in PCs without special software that translates the files. This limited compatibility is due to the fact that the operating system of the Macintosh configures or formats information on diskettes in a different manner than PCs do. Most Macintoshes do have disk drives and the requisite software to allow them to read and save files on PC formatted diskettes. Some older PCs use double density diskettes, which have a storage capacity of 720 kilobytes (k) and some older Macs used only 400k or 800k disks. All three of these older types of disks now are rarely encountered in everyday use.

As a storage medium, the diskette has the great advantage of being compact and portable: ideal for transporting and saving small files. Given the diskette's maximum capacity of 1.4 megabytes, any file larger than that has to be compressed in order to be put on a diskette. The process of file compression will be covered in the next chapter, but for now it is sufficient to say that it is a process that doubles or triples the amount of information that may held on a storage medium. It is not uncommon for commercial software to come compressed on several diskettes.

There are several drawbacks to using diskettes. The first is the space limitation previously mentioned. Even with compression, many files are simply too large to be held on a diskette. This is especially true for audio, image, graphics, and video files. A second drawback in using diskettes is expense. This may initially seem to be an erroneous assertion given the low cost of diskettes. However, when compared on a cost per megabyte basis with other storage mediums such as hard drives, removable hard disks, and tape back-up systems, diskettes are the most expensive storage medium. A third disadvantage of the diskette is that because the disk drive's write/read head actually makes physical contact with the diskette, they have a greater propensity for data errors and loss (FamilyPC, 1998). A fourth problem is that diskettes are the slowest medium for data storage (Kozierok, 1997). Regardless of these drawbacks, diskettes' convenience, portability, and almost universal compatibility in personal computers virtually assures their continued use in the near term.

Hard Drives

The hard drive, like the diskette, is almost ubiquitously used in personal computers. The hard drive is a storage device that holds the computer's operating system and the software that gives the computer functionality. While RAM in a computer acts much like short-term memory in the brain, the hard drive performs the same function as the brain's long-term memory, that of storing information until it is needed (Kozierok, 1997). When software is installed on a computer, it is sent to the hard drive and saved there. The hard drive is housed within the case, cabinet, or box that contains the motherboard and as such is not readily removed or transported.

Like the diskette, the hard drive is a magnetic drive on which information is both saved and retrieved. The process by which information is saved and retrieved from a disk is called *read/write*. It refers to the device's ability to access (read) and store or save (write) information. This is an important point to note at this time as many of the devices reviewed in this section will vary considerably in their access speeds. As a matter of comparison, diskettes are much slower than hard drives in accessing information. Manufacturers will specify a hard drive's access speed as a basis of comparison. Access speed is also referred to as *seek time*. Both indicate how fast the drive can find a piece of information (Margolis, 1996).

The storage capacity of hard drives has increased dramatically in recent years. When hard drives first became available in the early 1980s they could hold 10 megabytes and cost about $100 per megabyte. Today hard drives commonly have several gigabytes of storage capacity. A gigabyte is 1,000 megabytes. The price of this enormously increased storage space is approximately ten cents per megabyte. Consequently, over about 15 years, the price of storage on hard drives declined 100,000 percent (Kozierok, 1997). The push to build ever larger hard drives is driven by the ever increasing size of software applications, operating systems, data files, and the immeasurable amount of information and software that is available for downloading from the Internet.

As a cautionary note, hard drives should not be thought of as permanent storage devices. The life span of a hard drive varies from 3 to 10 years or more depending on its care and maintenance. The unfortunate reality is that hard drives can and do fail. As a result, data and document files should be backed-up or stored on other storage media on a regular basis to prevent their loss in the event of a hard drive's failure. The term *back-up* refers to a process of saving all or part of the contents of the hard drive to another storage medium in order to prevent their loss. Floppy disks are certainly not the storage medium of choice for backing up a hard drive. To save the contents of a 1-gigabyte hard drive would require approximately $350 worth of diskettes (FamilyPC, 1998). More economical storage media for backing up hard drives and storing information are reviewed in the following sections.

Removable Hard Disks

A removable hard disk is a type of hard disk drive system that uses a removable magnetic disk (Howe, 1999; Margolis, 1996). The removable disk drive, into which removable hard disks are inserted, is either an external device or an internal device housed in the case of the personal computer. Their size can range from 60 megabytes to 2 gigabytes. Removable hard disks offer the portability of diskettes, but with far greater storage capacity. An additional advantage of removable disks is that their access speeds are comparable to hard drives. Removable hard disks can serve not only as a supplemental and portable hard drive, but also as a back-up medium for hard drives. As a back-up medium for hard drives, their price per gigabyte varies from $50 to $150 (FamilyPC, 1998). While removable hard disks are certainly a more economical means to back-up hard drives than diskettes, they are not as economical as tape drives.

Tape Drives

A tape drive is a device that operates much like a tape recorder as it reads and writes information to a magnetic tape (Margolis, 1996). The capacity of tape drives varies from 60 megabytes to 5 gigabytes. The speed at which they can transfer information (read/write) ranges up to 20 megabytes per minute. The chief advantage of using a tape drive for backing up a hard drive is that it is inexpensive. The price of storage on tape is $5 per gigabyte (FamilyPC, 1998). The primary disadvantage of a tape drive is that it requires linear or sequential access to information. To find any bit of information, the drive has to read all the tape that precedes the information one is seeking. The process is not unlike trying to find a particular piece of music on a cassette tape, fast forwarding until one finds the desired song. Diskettes, hard drives, and most other storage media make possible nonsequential or random access in information retrieval. The sequential-access process of the tape drive makes it a rather slow and inefficient means for general storage of files. However, the per gigabyte price of tape makes it an ideal medium for the partial and complete back-up of a hard drive.

CD-ROMs/DVDs

CD-ROMs (Compact Disk-Read Only Memory) are a storage medium unlike the media reviewed thus far. First, CD-ROMs come with information already on them. They have a storage capacity of 650 megabytes, which is equivalent to 700 diskettes (Internet.com, 1997). Because of the large amount of information they can hold, CD-ROMs are used to provide information content, games, and software to personal computer users. For instance, reference works such as encyclopedias, dictionaries, books of quotations, and thesauruses are commonly made available on CD-ROMs. Interactive computer games and multimedia works that combine music, photography, and video are distributed on CD-ROMs. They are increasingly used for installing large software applications from the CD-ROM to a hard drive. Information on the CD-ROM cannot be altered by the computer; instead, the information that was previously stored on it, such as the multimedia contents of an encyclopedia, are read from the CD-ROM. There are types of compact disks drives that can create or "master" CDs. They are discussed later.

The second significant point of differentiation between the CD-ROM and the diskette, hard drive, removable hard disk, and the tape drive (which store and save information as magnetic bits) is that the CD-ROM is an optical storage medium. Magnetic storage media are susceptible to loss or corruption of information if exposed to strong magnets. Additionally, as already noted, diskettes and hard drives can and do fail, which results in the loss or corruption of information. Magnets and wear and tear secondary to use are not a problem for CD-ROMs. Information is encoded on a CD-ROM by the creation of a series of microscopic pits on an aluminum disk that is then coated with plastic. A CD-ROM drive reads the information on the disk with an infrared laser that detects the pitted and unpitted areas on the disk and then translates this information into binary code that is sent to the computer. Since the infrared laser does not make physical contact with the optical disk, there is nothing to wear out (*Concise Columbia Encyclopedia,* 1991). However, dirt on the CD-ROM or on the CD-ROM drive's laser reading mechanism will cause data reading errors (Kozierok, 1997).

When CD-ROMs were introduced, the slowness of their access speed was a significant limitation for their use, especially with large video and graphics files. Most of the original CD-ROM drives had an access speed of 150 kilobytes per second. The speed of a CD-ROM is indicated by an "X" designation, as in 16X. A 16X CD-ROM drive reads information from CD-ROMs at 2,400 kilobytes per second (*PCWebopedia,* 1997), or 16 times as fast as the original CD-ROM drives. Speeds of CD-ROM drives have risen to 4,800 kilobytes per second, which allows for faster file transfers, quicker database searches, and dramatically improved multimedia display and interaction when compared to models with speeds under 24X (Sengstack, 1998).

There are three additional types of optical disks which have recently been developed and offer features not available with CD-ROMs. The first is the CD-R (Compact Disk-Recordable). As the name implies, this is a compact disk on which information can be recorded by someone other than a CD-ROM vendor. CD-R drives allow personal computer users to save information on CDs. As such, CD-R drives represent an ideal medium for the long-term storage of important data files or other documents that one wishes to preserve. Moreover, up to 74 minutes of music can be recorded on a blank CD-R disc. The chief disadvantage of the CD-R is that it can only be written to once. The disc cannot be erased and used again.

CD-RW (CD-Rewritable) drives can be erased and used again (Holsinger, 1997). Some manufacturers estimate CD-RWs can be erased up to 1,000 times. The CD-RW disks have two disadvantages. First, they are recorded using a format that cannot be read by all CD-ROM drives. Second, the CD-RW disc is currently about four times as expensive as a CD-R disk: $6 for the CD-R compared to $25 for the CD-RW. Both the CD-R disk and the CD-RW disk are thought not to be as durable as CD-ROMs manufactured by CD-ROM venders due to a slight difference in the type of disk used. This may change as competitors improve manufacturing processes and prices fall.

A fourth type of optical disk that recently became available is the DVD (digital versatile/video disk). As an emerging technology, the standards for and applications of DVD are still in development. DVD-ROM disks should be able to hold up to 17giga-bytes of information and/or multimedia content on a two-sided disk. DVD-ROM disks can provide theater quality audio and video playback (Andrews, 1998). DVD drives were initially unable to read CD-R and CD-RW disks, though this incompatibility problem is resolving. More importantly for information storage purposes will be the eventual development and standardization of DVD-RW (rewritable) disks with storage capacities in excess of 3 gigabytes. This will dramatically enhance the quantity and variety of information storable on a single disk.

File Servers

Increasingly, personal computers in agencies and other social services practice settings are linked together over a computer network. Networks are sometimes referred to as LANs (local area networks) and WANs (wide area networks). LANs are usually established within a building or between two or more buildings in close proximity to each other. WANs are computer networks that link computers across a wide geographic area. Both LANs and WANs generally have at least one or more file servers on the network. A *file server* is a computer and storage device on a computer network designated for the storage of files (Margolis, 1996). All the other storage media reviewed so far are either internal devices that are housed in the case of the computer or external devices which generally sit a short cable's length from the computer. A network file server may reside in the office next door, down the hall, or across the state. A user connects to the file server either from a computer linked to the network or by dialing from a computer with a modem to a modem that connects to the network. File servers are included in this listing of storage devices as they are increasingly used to store files that one may wish to share with others via the network or to utilize the storage capacity and security of the file server.

Files stored on file servers are sharable with other users on the network when the files are placed in what are referred to as publicly available directories. Files such as word processing documents in public directories are transferable to either a diskette or hard drive on one's personal computer, where they can be opened by the appropriate software application. As an example, the College of Social Work at The University of Tennessee created in 1995 a wide area network that linked the three locations of the college in Memphis, Nashville, and Knoxville via a statewide computer network. One of the purposes for creating the college's WAN was to support the use of distance education via interactive classrooms. In this distance education initiative, a professor at one branch of the college can deliver lectures and interact with students in all three locations over a closed circuit television network. Students in all locations can see and interact with both the professor and other students. The WAN makes it possible for professors to make available to students in all three locations files of lecture notes and syllabi by placing them in a public directory on a file server. Students can log on to the WAN and download to a diskette or hard drive course materials from the file server.

On many networks it is not always necessary to transfer or download a file server file to a diskette or hard drive in order to work with it. Depending on the speed of the network and configuration of the network's security, files can be opened, enhanced/ altered, and then saved across the network on the file server. The security consideration here is that one may not want files in a public directory altered. If, however, one was collaborating with a group of coworkers on a project, a file might be placed in a semipublic directory, to which access was limited to colleagues working on the project, each of whom had a password to access the directory.

In addition to sharing files, file servers can augment the storage capacity of a personal computer on a network. Network administrators, the individuals who run and maintain the operation of the network, can allocate to each user on the network a specified amount of storage space on the network's file server. This personal storage space on the file server is usually secure and can only be accessed by the user and the network administrator, who generally retain access privileges to all files on the network. A file server is often a good repository in which to archive important files that one wishes to save and does not need on a regular basis. There is an added advantage to archiving files on a file server if the network administrator regularly creates tape backups of the entire contents of the file server. Backing up the server every 24 hours is optimal. This security procedure ensures that archived files will be preserved should the file server fail.

This review of storage media is not exhaustive. Technologies for the storage of information are in continual development. The media reviewed here are either currently widely used or, like DVD, emerging technologies with broadly recognized potential. As the potential and ease of digitizing a wide range of information continues to expand, the capacity to store information for immediate use and long-term retrieval and use will become increasingly important. Selection of storage media devices should be made with consideration given to near-term versatility of the media and long-term capability with personal computers. Given this temporal perspective on data storage, it is generally advisable to select near-term storage media based on consideration of storage capacity, portability, cost, and type and size of application files that one is using on a regular basis. As for long-term storage, because of the broad adoption of CD-ROM drives and the developing compatibility between CD-ROMs and DVD drives, files that one wishes to retain long-term are likely best preserved on CD-ROM, until such time that DVD rewritable drives are generally available and affordable.

Notebooks: A Desktop Alternative

The four functions of a personal computer—input, information processing, output, and storage—are present in both desktop and notebook computers. For the purposes of this discussion, the term *desktop* is used to refer to nonportable personal computers, which are further differentiated as desktops, towers, and all-in-one machines. The intention here is to review the advantages and disadvantages of notebooks relative to desktops. Specific consideration is given to the use of notebooks in social service practice. The goal of this discussion is to assist social service workers in finding the best fit between the tasks, job setting, and information needs of their employment situation and the personal computer used. Granted, not all social service workers have personal computers, though hopefully the days of this condition are growing shorter. A secondary purpose of this discussion is to provide adequate information with which a social service worker can make an informed and reasoned argument for the purchase of a computer. The intent here is to create a good match between computer and task expectations, information requirements, and the range of locations where the computer will be used.

If the 1980s was the time when personal computers became commonplace and widely used, then the 1990s has seen the explosion of portable computing. When first introduced in the late 1980s, portable computers were slow, heavy machines with limited functionality. They were sometimes referred to as "luggables" due to their weight and size. Present-day notebook computers, available in a wide range of configurations, are both dramatically lighter and smaller than their predecessors. The term *notebook* refers to the fact that these machines are often the size of a notebook, albeit given the size and weight of some models the manufactures likely had in mind some very large notebooks. Despite the variability in size, notebook computers are commonly small enough to fit into a briefcase. The weight of notebooks ranges from as little as 1.8 pounds for a mininotebook to nearly 8 pounds for some fully equipped, multimedia machines. Notebook computers are also known as *laptops*, a reference to the fact that they are small enough to sit on one's lap (Margolis, 1996). Notebook computers are distinct from *hand-held* computers, which are very small computers with limited functionally and very constrained keyboards. Hand-held computers are generally used for electronic address books, appointment calendars, limited note taking, and e-mail/faxing (Lasky & McCracken, 1997). Due to their present limited functionality, hand-held computers are not further reviewed here. Readers considering the purchase of a hand-held computer should review recent issues of personal computer magazines as these devices are regularly reviewed.

The chief advantage of a notebook computer is its portability. The compact design and relatively light weight of a notebook computer allow a user to carry it between home and work, to agency meetings, to field locations like clients' homes, to public presentations, and on out-of-town travel. This portability makes it possible for a user to both collect and disseminate information in diverse locations without having to commit information to paper-based form and then transfer it to electronic files. Examples of this include making brief notes during interagency meetings, administering assessment of scales during home visits, sending and receiving e-mail, accessing the Web for referral and resource information, and collecting financial and service provision data for quality assurance assessment.

The portability of a notebook computer makes it possible to bring the computer to the information source instead of having to bring the information to the computer. This enables social service workers to collect information in a more timely and flexible manner with the additional benefit of reduction in information errors secondary to repeated recording of the information. Writing information down and then typing it into a computer doubles the likelihood of recording error when compared to simply entering the information directly into a computer. The portability of a notebook computer enables the user to not only collect information in diverse locations, but can also facilitate the ease of dissemination of information in an equally wide range of locations. Collected e-mail correspondence stored on a notebook can be found and referred to during a team meeting. Budget proposals residing on a notebook are retrievable and revisable during administrative meetings. Referral source information is readily available to a case worker who has set up a notebook computer on a family's kitchen table during a home visit. Each of the examples cited here illustrates how the portability of notebook computers can enhance the capacity of social service workers to deliver improved services beyond their offices.

The utility of notebook computers to perform a wide range of functions continues to improve. This enhanced usefulness is the result of advances in CPU speed, the size of RAM, integration of CD-ROM drives, enriched screen color and brightness, increased hard disk space, improved keyboard layouts, and faster modem speeds. Consequently, notebook computers now represent a viable alternative to desktop computers even if the reasons for selection of a computer do not include portability. Like desktop computers, notebook computers are easily connected to computer networks. Most notebook computers now come with PCMCIA slots, which accept PCMCIA network interface cards making possible the linkage of the notebook to the network. The PCMCIA (Personal Computer Memory Card International Association) card is about the size of a credit card and adds functionality to the notebook computer. There are PCMCIA memory cards for RAM and ROM, ethernet (network) connection, fax/modem capabilities, portable disk drives and, portable CD-ROM players.

Despite the portability, flexibility, and improved functionality of notebook computers, there are some noteworthy disadvantages. First, notebook computers are generally more expensive than desktop computers with comparable CPUs, hard drives, and RAM configurations. As components have to fit into the case of a notebook computer, significant redesign of the components is often required to reduce their size, weight, and power requirements, all of which increase cost. Second, as the speed of CPUs rise, there is always a lag time between when a faster CPU chip is available in desktop machines and when it is modified and available in notebook computers. Accordingly, tasks that require significant computational resources, such as broadcast-quality digital video capture and editing, high-quality image editing, and digital audio recording and editing, are mostly commonly done on desktop computers with the newest available CPUs. A third disadvantage is the complexity involved in upgrading components on a notebook computer. Whereas many upgrades of desktop computers are accomplished by opening the case and replacing, for instance, the hard drive or the CPU, such upgrades of notebook computers are complicated by the small size of their cases and the compact arrangement of parts within the machines. Upgrades of components that can often be accomplished with limited technical skill on a desktop computer generally require sending a notebook computer back to the manufacturer or a technician who specializes in notebook repair. A fourth disadvantage of notebook computers is that, due to their portability, they are subject to accidents that can render them inoperative. As such, it is generally a very good idea to purchase an extended warranty when buying a notebook computer. On balance, it should be said that notebook computers have dramatically improved in their durability and resiliency in recent years. A social psychologist friend who does international training in team building described how he had dropped his notebook computer off the back of a truck in Kenya. Once he got the driver to stop the truck, he walked back and picked up his computer, which lay in the dirt on the road. With great trepidation he turned it on. Remarkably, it started right up!

The fact that a notebook computer can operate in the middle of a road in rural Kenya is made possible by a battery as a power source, an option not found on desktop personal computers. Many of the components of notebook computers are distinct from those of personal computers and bear consideration if one is selecting a notebook. Noteworthy differences exist in keyboards, pointing devices, screens, batteries, floppy disk drives, component configurations, PC card slots, sound, and CD-ROM drives. Keyboards on notebook computers are often somewhat smaller than the full-size keyboards of desktop machines. The experience of typing on them can range from being barely different from desktop keyboards to seeming rather cramped and disorienting due to variations in the arrangement of nonalphabet keys. As such, it is advisable to test the feel and arrangement of the keyboard prior to purchasing a notebook. Many notebook models allow one to plug in a full-size keyboard, which can offer relief from a cramped keyboard when one is using the machine in one's primary work space. Notebook computers offer a range of pointing devices which substitute for an external mouse. This is done so that the notebook can be used in limited spaces, such as a laptop, from which it would be awkward to operate a mouse. Two types of pointing devices are most commonly used: the touch-pad and the stick pointer (Trivette, 1997). The touchpad is a "small, touch-sensitive pad used as a pointing device . . . which by moving a finger or object along the pad, you can move the pointer on the display screen" (Margolis, 1996, p. 486). A stick pointer is an integrated cursor pointing device found in the center of the keyboard that when touched, detects motion parallel to the keyboard (IBM, 1995). Both types of pointing devices employ left and right click buttons, which are generally located directly beneath the devices. The choice between the two types of devices is a matter of personal preference and is best made by experimenting with display models in computer stores. Again, most note-books have ports to plug in a standard mouse to use in lieu of the pointing device.

Like keyboards and pointing devices, there are several options available for display screens on notebook computers. The differences between the two most commonly used notebook displays, active and passive matrix screens, have already been reviewed. Most notebooks have a video-out port for connecting to a standard computer monitor. This makes possible two very important options. First, a user can attach a notebook to a monitor at home or work and thereby have a larger screen to work from. The second option is that the video-out port allows sending screen output to large screen display devices, LCD display panels, and through scan converters onto television monitors. These options are described in greater detail in Chapter 8. This is particularly useful for presentations.

In addition to variations in keyboards, pointing devices, and screens, notebook computers offer other configuration options. Notebook computers are powered either by a stand AC power plugged into an available socket or by battery. There are two primary types of batteries currently widely used in notebooks: nickel-metal hydride (NiMH) and lithium ion (Li Ion) (Trivette, 1997). The chief advantage of NiMH batteries is that they are less expensive than lithium ion batteries. They are widely used in notebooks, but they do not hold a charge as long as a lithium ion battery and they are generally heavier. Many users justify the additional expense of lithium ion batteries because of their lighter weight and 10 to 20 percent longer run time between charges.

The power demand of a notebook computer is impacted by a number of components. Floppy drives on notebook computers are either built-in/internal, removable, or external. Some notebooks with removable floppy disk drives offer the option of switching the floppy drive with an additional hard drive, a second battery, or a CD-ROM player. External floppy drives are generally available on lightweight notebooks, which achieve some weight savings by giving the user the option to carry along the external floppy drive. Likewise, CD-ROM drives may either be internal, external, or removable. External CD-ROM drives most often connect to the notebook through the PCMCIA card (PC card) slot.

There are three types of PC cards. Type I cards are 3.3 mm thick and are used as additional RAM or ROM for the notebook (Margolis, 1996). Type II are used as fax, modem, and network cards and can be up to 5.5 mm thick. Type III cards, 10.5 mm thick, are generally used as removable hard disk drives.

A final option available on notebook computers is sound. This is accomplished by the inclusion of a sound card in the notebook along with built-in speakers. This option is particularly useful if one frequently makes presentations that include multimedia displays such as video clips with sound tracks. It should be noted that when one is using the notebook's battery power, sound places an additional power demand on the battery, thereby decreasing the time available to use the notebook.

In summary, notebook computers offer a number of distinct advantages to social service workers. This is especially true for workers whose job requirements take them out of the office. Specifically, notebooks make possible in field settings access of Internet and network information resources, information/data collection, and information dissemination options ranging from simply providing a referral to a client from a social service resource database to presenting a multimedia presentation in a public lecture. A core advantage in using notebook computers in social service practice is their capacity to extend the information exchange between clients and worker beyond the doors of an agency and into the communities in which clients live their lives. Notebook computers can play a major role in the decentralization of social services. They make possible the extension of services to clients who are unable to come to an agency secondary to physical/emotional limitations, inadequate transportation, or rural isolation.

Purchasing a Personal Computer: Choices, Trade-Offs, and Sources

Purchase Considerations

Whether a social service worker is using a notebook or a desktop computer, unless they are donated, these machines have to be purchased from some source and at some price. The purchasing of a personal computer requires a number of decisions about source, configuration, price, and life span. Some agencies have management information or information technology departments which handle the purchasing of computers. Despite this fact, it is beneficial for managers and administrators who have supervisory responsibility over such departments to be independently informed of the array of options in purchasing decisions. For supervisors and social service workers who submit requests for the purchase of personal computers, knowledge of the purchasing options allows them to make better informed requests. Many independent practitioners, students, and social service workers, supervisors, managers, and administrators cannot channel purchase requests through a management information or information technology department. For them, an understanding of the purchase options and considerations may result in cost savings and a better match between the system purchased and the buyer's IT needs.

In order to make an informed and economical personal computer purchase, there are a number of questions to answer. A single answer to any of the following questions should not drive the eventual purchase. Instead, weighting and balancing the answers in relation to each other can produce an informed, thoughtful, and prudent personal computer purchase.

Perhaps the best starting point in considering buying a personal computer is: How much does one wish to spend on it? What is the budget for the purchase? The decision of a spending limit should not be made based on the maximum number of dollars available. Instead, a spending limit should be based on consideration of what tasks the machine will be used for, how long it will be used, and what peripheral devices will also need to be purchased to optimize the personal computer for the tasks it is to perform. One may well have $2,000 to spend on a computer, but word processing, Internet access, and e-mail represent 90 percent of the tasks the computer will be used for. These tasks may readily be accomplished on a $1,000 personal computer. The remaining $1,000 could either be saved or devoted to peripheral devices like a high-speed modem, a scanner, a tape drive back-up system, or software, all of which may improve the match between the purchased machine and its intended tasks. Therefore, decisions on budget allocations for the purchase of a personal computer should include analysis of the intended functions of the machine in conjunction with consideration of the requisite peripheral devices necessary to support the intended functions.

A long-standing axiom in some circles regarding the purchase of a personal computer is to "avoid the bleeding edge." The "bleeding edge" refers to the high cost of computers on the cutting edge. Bleeding edge computers are recently released models with the fastest CPUs, biggest hard drives, and the other latest and most innovative technologies. The truth in this axiom arises from two facts; the most recently released personal computer models are always going to be the most expensive and, given Moore's law, in 18 months the price will drop 50 percent. Two additional drawbacks of purchasing on the "bleeding edge" is that recently developed innovative technology is the most untested and industrywide standards for the technology are less likely to be agreed on. For instance, when the first DVD drives were introduced, they could not read CD-Rewritable and CD-Recordable disks (Andrews, 1998), a problem corrected in the second generation of DVD drives.

The alternative to buying on the "bleeding edge" is to shop for models introduced 6 to 18 months earlier. The advantage here is that the price of these models is often significantly discounted compared to their price when they were first introduced, yet they are generally compatible with present-day software and hardware standards. This purchasing strategy is particularly relevant if the tasks that the machine is intended to perform do not require blazing CPU speed, three-dimensional, high-speed graphics, or other state of the art computer functions. It should be noted that most of the computer tasks for social services presented in this book do not necessitate "bleeding edge" machines. In fact, this book is being written on an IBM Thinkpad 701 CS (a notebook computer) with a 75 MHz processor, 24 megs of RAM, and a 540 meg hard drive. With present-day CPU speeds exceeding 550 MHz, this humble Thinkpad may seem perfectly antiquated. However, it is perfectly serviceable. It runs sophisticated statistical software, links to a computer network, accesses the Web, and allows for the opening and running of several software applications at once. It was introduced three years ago and purchased 30 months later at less than one third of its introductory price. The point is that computer purchases should not be driven by pursuing the latest and fastest computers. In fact, the standard advice used to be to purchase the most powerful computer one could buy in order to protect against obsolescence (Halfhill, 1998), but it is now recognized that obsolescence is both unavoidable and manageable. The management strategy is to minimize costs by avoiding the "bleeding edge" and carefully matching the machine to its required tasks.

Where to Buy?

While the previous discussion addresses how to buy, the next question is, Where to buy? The purchase of any personal computer brings the buyer into a costly relationship with the purchasing source (Furger, 1997). There are four categories of sources from which to procure a personal computer: (1) retail outlets, (2) small, local PC assemblers, (3) the Internet, and (4) mail order. Each source offers a number of distinct advantages and varying degrees of disadvantage.

RETAIL OUTLETS.   The term *retail outlets* generally refers to venders who (a) exclusively sell personal computers and other information technology items, (b) sell a broad spectrum of electronic merchandise such as televisions, VCRs, and computers, or (c) office product stores that also sell computers. One advantage in purchasing a personal computer from retail outlets is that one can see and try out machines before deciding on which one to buy. This is often important to first-time buyers and for individuals who want to experience the "look and feel" of a machine before spending their money. An additional advantage is that one can most often take home the selected computer that day, thereby avoiding the wait that occurs when a machine has to be built and shipped.

There are several noted disadvantages of buying personal computers through retail outlets. Retail outlet employees are often not well trained or well informed about the specifics of the computers they are selling (Furger, 1997; McEvoy, Freeman, McCraken, Scisco, & Spanbauer, 1998). As a result, when purchasing through a retail outlet it is best to carefully research in advance the system one intends to purchase. Additionally, retail outlets generally do not carry the most recently released technologies, preferring instead to carry mainstream, commonly sought products. Moreover, customization of personal computer systems such as installing a different video card or hard drive is generally not possible. Buying cutting edge technologies and custom matching of a personal computer to a user's needs most often require shopping the three other sources of personal computers.

LOCAL PC ASSEMBLERS.   If one is seeking a customized system, state of the art technologies, and/or the ability to see and touch a system before buying it, then one viable option is to seek out small, local personal computer assemblers. These are usually small businesses devoted to custom building personal computers to buyers' specifications. These businesses survive in a highly competitive market by offering personal attention, customization, and knowledgeable service. The prices on personal computers available through local personal computer assemblers are competitive and price negotiation is possible (McEvoy et al., 1998). Because they are generally small operations with limited staff, they usually cannot offer the around-the-clock technical support available from large computer manufacturers. Additionally, before ordering a computer from a local assembler, it is important to ask about their policies and any charges for returning computers. They may be reticent to take back custom-built computers, or at least have in place policies that discourage the practice.

ONLINE VENDORS.   An alternative way to shop for a personal computer, whether a customized configuration or stock model, is online over the Web. Computer manufacturers and retail vendors have Web sites on which a wide range of information on their personal computer systems is available. Many such sites allow the potential buyer to compare features and prices of various models. Some manufacturers and online retailers will offer a range of options of components such as RAM, hard drives, monitors, CD-ROMs, and video cards. Often their Web sites are designed so that after selecting specific components, the exact price of the system, including shipping and taxes, is displayed. Most manufacturers and online retailers have configured their Web sites for secure online purchases of their personal computer systems. Buyers receive an order number and an estimated shipping date in exchange for their credit card number. One major drawback in online shopping for a personal computer is that it is often difficult to get questions answered. Although questions about particular systems, warranties, and other queries can be submitted by e-mail, at least one review of such systems found them slow and unreliable (McEvoy et al., 1998). An alternative to actually placing an order on the Web is to shop online for the system that best matches price, configuration, and task requirements and then place the order over the phone.

MAIL ORDER.   Mail order is the fourth commercial pathway to owning a personal computer. Through mail order, a new personal computer is only a phone call away, assuming one has a credit card, a phone, and some idea of the type of computer one wishes to purchase. Each month, personal computer magazines publish manufacturers' advertisements of their latest models. The prices and system configurations of various manufacturers and retailers are readily comparable, although often not at the same level of detail available on the Web. One significant advantage to mail order shopping, especially when directly from the manufacturer, is that the representatives often have a thorough understanding of the systems they are selling and are able to make knowledgeable recommendations about systems configurations and performance (Furger, 1997; McEvoy et al., 1998). Additionally, buyers can often find state of the art systems and prices lower than retail when mail order shopping directly from manufacturers. Drawbacks to mail order shopping include (a) the buyer is unable to try out the machine prior to purchasing it, (b) there is often a week or more delay between placing the order and delivery, and (c) computers and system components that need repair require shipping back to the manufacturer. Some manufacturers now offer on-site repairs for a limited time period at the discretion of the manufacturer.

Regardless of purchasing source, ultimately the selection and acquisition of a personal computer is only the first phase of a relationship between the owner/user and the computer. The goodness of fit or optimal match between the user, the computer, and its intended information tasks results from the interaction of these three elements. Consequently, purchase decisions must take into account the user's current level of information technology skills and anticipated/desired skills development. Consideration also should be given to the situations/locations in which the machine will be used and tasks to which it will be applied. The degree to which the selected machine or system matches the intended user and tasks will often profoundly shape both the attitudes the user holds about information technology and the extent to which they employ it in their work.

Summary

Information technology hardware represents a challenging and changing factor in applying IT to social service practice. This chapter described the basic forms and functions of present-day personal computers. Devices for inputting information into computers were described, including the keyboard, mouse, and digital capturing methods. Attention was devoted to the information processing power of personal computers, including the interaction of processor speed and available memory. Output is a critical function of computing. As such, a range of output methods were viewed, ranging from monitors to a host of printing options. Also discussed were the advantages and trade-offs of retaining information in digital form. The choices for storage of digital information were presented with an emphasis on selecting methods, or combinations thereof, that maximize data preservation. Notebook computers were described here as an alternative to desktop computers that may have particular utility for the diverse locations in which social service practice occurs and the diverse tasks required in practice. The last section of this chapter provided strategies for purchasing personal computers as well as the relative merits of a range of purchasing sources.

Exercises

1. Create a list of all the hardware you are currently using in your home or practice setting. Categorize this hardware by function. Then create a list of hardware, including upgrades of present equipment, that would enable you to better perform the social service tasks you do on a regular basis.
2. Discuss with a group of peers your experiences in purchasing hardware. Where have you made those purchases? How satisfied were you with the hardware and service provided? What would you do differently on your next hardware purchase?
3. Say your agency's director came to you and asked you to upgrade the agency's or your department's hardware. What choice would you make? Create a list of necessary hardware upgrades and a rationale for the purchase of each piece of equipment.

chapter **3**

Software
Basic Tools

This chapter describes the transformation of software with the advent of the graphical user interface (GUI). The six elements of GUI are (1) the use of a pointer to execute commands, (2) a pointing device that moves the pointer, commonly a mouse, (3) icons, (4) a desktop metaphor, (5) windows to display information, and (6) menus. Four basic functions of operating systems are described. They are (1) creating an interface between user and computer, (2) running applications, (3) controlling hardware, and (4) information management. The chapter describes the basic functions of commonly used applications including word processors, spreadsheets, databases, presentation software, personal information management software, application suites, Web browsers, and utilities.

The Changed Face of Software

The development of software with a graphical user interface was a critical factor that made possible the increasingly widespread adoption of information technology. The graphical user interface, generally referred to as GUI, was first developed by the Xerox Corporation in the 1970s and popularized with the introduction of the Apple Macintosh Computer in 1984 (Margolis, 1996). GUI software uses the computer's graphics capacity to represent visually the options available in an operating system or a software application. An operating system controls the activities of the computer, such as running applications, and the computer's interface with peripheral devices, such as a printer and a scanner. An *application* is a piece of software that performs a specific set of functions that make possible a specific set of tasks. Examples of applications include spreadsheets, word processors, and graphics programs.

Before the development of GUI software, anyone using a computer had to know or have at hand a reference manual of commands to type into the computer in order for the operating system to carry out any functions. IBM PCs and their subsequent clones used MS-DOS (Microsoft Disk Operating System) to run the basic task of the computer as well as to provide user access to software on the computer's hard drive. After turning on a PC, the user confronted a DOS prompt that looked like this: "C:/". It was incumbent upon the potential user to then type in a command after the DOS prompt in order to use the PC for any task. The term *potential user* denotes the significant obstacle to usability that the requirement of knowing and typing commands at a DOS prompt represented. Once a piece of DOS-based software was started, users moved the cursor about the screen, not by pointing and clicking, but by using directional arrows, the space bar, or the tab key. Many of the DOS-based programs used the function keys at the top of the keyboard to execute functions of the software. Again, one often had to have a guide of some form in order to know what functions were available. This was yet another dramatic deterrent to easy use of the PC. Given the level of difficulty one faced and the amount of a priori information one had to have in order to use a personal computer, it is not surprising that many people either eschewed their use or when use was unavoidable, learned only what they had to know in order to carry out the tasks they were required to perform. Figure 3.1 shows a DOS prompt as displayed in the Windows environment. Note, multiple mistakes in the written commands before successfully accessing the FTP (file transfer protocol) program. This exemplifies the difficulty of working in the DOS environment.

The introduction of the Apple Macintosh and the subsequent development of the Windows operating system for PCs made the GUI the standard means for users to operate personal computers. The graphical user interface removed the necessity to remember and type into the computer commands in order to use it. While the Macintosh and Windows operating systems differ in their appearance and how they implement their

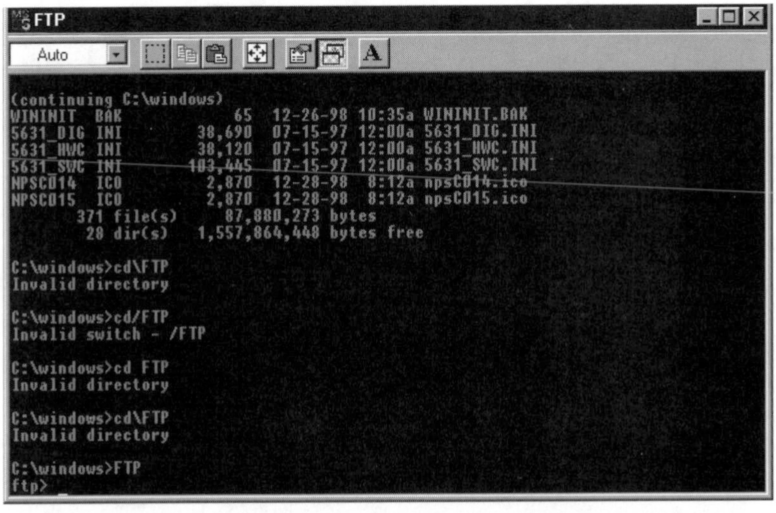

FIGURE 3.1   DOS Commands in the DOS Environment

GUIs, there are still six common elements (Margolis, 1996). First, both use on the display screen a pointer to execute commands and to highlight and select objects. The pointer may be a large or small arrow, or an I-beam pointer in the shape of a capital I. The shape of a pointer will often change depending on its location within a document. For instance, in a word processing document, the pointer will appear as an I-beam pointer when in the body of the text. It will change to an arrow when the pointer moves outside of the text and onto icons and menu bars.

The second element of a GUI is the pointing device that moves the pointer. The pointing device may be a mouse, a touch pad, a stick pointer, or some other device that directs the location of the pointer on the screen. In addition to moving the pointer, the pointing device allows the selection of commands and objects by clicking on them with a pointing device button.

The third element of a GUI is icons. Icons are small graphics or pictures that represent functions, files, windows, or software applications. Many programs use icons in conjunction with pop-up text fields that identify the function the icon represents. Placing the pointer on such an icon causes the pop-up text field identifying the function of the icon to appear. Clicking on the icon with the pointing device can activate a function such as Save, which saves the file to disk. Clicking on other icons can open a window, "an enclosed, rectangular area on a display screen" (Margolis, 1996, p. 516). The window can contain a range of additional functions or options, such as specification of the thickness of a line or the shape of a three-dimensional object that can be used in a graphic illustration. Icons can depict files and software applications that open when clicked on by the pointing device. Figure 3.2 shows the icons for a group of applications and folders in a directory.

The fourth element of a GUI is the desktop. The desktop is a metaphorical representation on the display screen of the files and tools (software applications) available in the computer, much as one would find on a real desktop without a computer on it. Users may arrange objects on the computer desktop, such as files and software, in accordance with their preferences. Like on a desktop, files are often stored in folders. The folder can contain multiple files and other folders. For instance, one may have a folder on a computer labeled My Documents. Within that folder, the user may create other folders to hold documents for various projects. The use of folders creates a way to visually organize information.

The fifth element of a GUI already mentioned briefly is windows. Microsoft's operating system of the same name should not be confused with the term *windows* in general. Windows in a GUI dramatically add to both the functionality and the information available on the desktop. The capacity to display within a window additional commands or functions for a software application increases its functionality. The ability to run multiple applications simultaneously in different windows further improves functionality. For instance, one might have Internet browser software open in one window, word processing in another, and a spreadsheet in a third. In such a scenario, information drawn from the Web and the spreadsheet could be readily incorporated into the

FIGURE 3.2   Icons of Applications and Folders

word processing document. The specifics of how to do this will be covered in subsequent chapters, but for now it is sufficient to understand that opening files and software in multiple windows facilitates the pooling of information in documents.

The sixth element of a GUI is menus. A menu is a list of available functions, commands, or files. The choices made available in software menus allow the user to see the available functions of the software. This eliminates the need to type commands into the computer or to refer to manuals to discern the possible functions of the software. Command menu choices appear in menu bars located on the top, bottom, or sides of the display screen. Pointing at a word in the menu bar and clicking activates menus. The list of options available under that item or word in the menu bar will appear in a window. The user can activate the desired function or option by pointing to the option and clicking. Some menu bars will have arrows beside some of the words in the list. Placing the cursor over these words with adjoining arrows causes additional command options to appear. These "cascading" menus add command options to a menu heading. Passing the cursor over any item in the menu list with an arrow beside it will cause the appearance of an additional window containing more choices. The cascading menu greatly expands the range of functions available through this element of the graphic user interface.

Operating Systems Basics

In the world of personal computing there is a wide range of operating systems available for use. This range of operating systems includes MS-DOS, Windows 3.1, Windows 95, Windows 98, Windows NT, IBM OS Warp, and the Apple Macintosh Operating System. At present, Windows 95 and 98 are the most commonly used operating systems throughout the world. This discussion of operating systems focuses on delineating the functions and features of contemporary operating systems. Instructions for the use of a particular operating system are beyond the scope and intent of this chapter and book. Readers should seek out specific reference texts for details on the intricacies of their particular operating system.

At their core, all operating systems have four basic functions (maranGraphics, 1996). First, the operating system is the most basic interface between the user and the computer. It is through the operating system's interface that the user starts applications and manages information in the computer, such as copying or deleting files. It is through the operating system interface that the user checks on system resources such as available RAM (random access memory) and hard disk space. The second function of the operating system is to run applications software. In order to accomplish this function, the software must be compatible with the operating system. For instance, while programs that were developed for the MS-DOS operating system will run under MS-DOS in Windows 95, software developed specifically for the Windows 95 operating systems, such as Microsoft Office 97, will not run on a computer using only MS-DOS. The capacity of an operating system to run software compatible with earlier operating systems is referred to as *backward compatibility*. The third function of an operating system is to control hardware. Intrinsic to this function is the capacity to receive input from input devices such as the keyboard and to send output to output devices such as the printer. As part of this controlling function, the operating system coordinates the interaction of all peripheral devices. Moreover, the operating system makes it possible to tailor the computer's interface to match the requirements of the user. For example, it is through the operating system that the resolution and color depth of the monitor are adjusted. The fourth function of the operating system is the management of information. The operating system accomplishes this by keeping track of files and the directories in which they are located. The operating system makes possible finding, viewing, sorting, copying, moving, and deleting files. For instance, in the Windows 95 Explorer a user can see icons representing the files on a disk. Figure 3.3 displays a Windows 95 Explorer application window. Files are copied by clicking on a file and dragging (copying) it from a floppy disk to a file folder on the hard drive. Files are copied from the hard drive to a floppy disk in the same way.

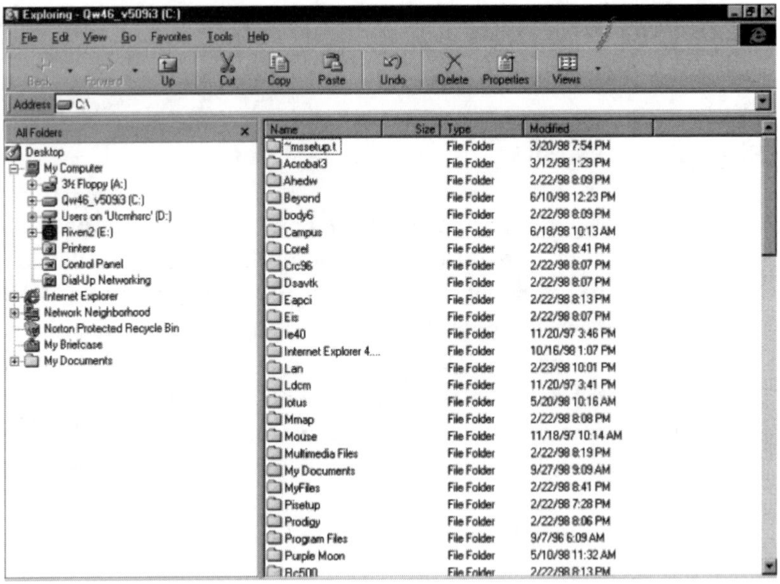

FIGURE 3.3 Windows 95 Explorer Window Displaying File Directories

Contemporary operating systems have a number of features that simplify their four basic functions. These systems employ GUI interfaces and visually represent files and folders on screen. A user clicks on a folder and a window appears displaying the files contained in the folder. Moving a file from one folder to another entails clicking on the file, holding down the mouse button, and dragging the file to the intended folder. This feature is called *drag and drop* (Margolis, 1996). Drag and drop makes it possible to move objects like graphics between applications. A drawing created in one program can be dragged into another, such as a word processing document. Files are deleted by dragging and dropping them into icons representing waste receptacles: a Recycling Bin in the Windows 95 OS and a Trash Can in the Macintosh OS.

Other GUI features of contemporary operating systems include scroll bars, title bars, menu bars, window sizing icons, and dialog boxes. Scroll bars, generally located at the right side and bottom of screens, allow a user to examine the contents of a window by scrolling through it. Title bars, which appear at the top of a window or open file, tell the user the name of the file or folder they have open. Menu bars, which generally appear below the title bar, offer a range of command choices to the user, such as cutting, pasting, opening, and saving. Window sizing icons allow a user to minimize or hide a window, maximize or fully open a window, or close a folder window or application. Dialog boxes are temporary windows that appear to either request information or provide information (Margolis, 1996). Each of these features expands the available information and functionality of the operating system by adding to the graphical user interface.

Plug and play and network connectivity are two additional features of contemporary operating systems that significantly expand the flexibility and functionality of personal computers. *Plug and play* refers to the ability of the operating system to automatically recognize and configure a device, such as a printer, or an expansion board, such as a sound card, to operate in conjunction with the computer. This feature appeared on Apple Macintosh computers in the mid-80s, but was not available for PCs until the introduction of Windows 95 (Margolis, 1996). Plug and play is an important innovation in an operating system as it dramatically improves the ease with which one can expand the range of devices used by the computer. Likewise, with the growth of computer networks and the Internet, contemporary operating systems have expanded their capacity to interface personal computers with networks. This network connectivity makes it possible to share files and applications with other computers, exchange e-mail, and share printers.

One recent advance in operating systems is their ability to run multiple software applications at the same time, a feature known as *multitasking*. Multitasking is important because it allows the user to share information easily between applications, thereby dramatically increasing work efficiency. Consider, for example, an agency manager who is preparing a budget report. With the use of multitasking, she can have running simultaneously on her computer a spreadsheet with the agency's budget, a word processing application in which the report is being written, and e-mail software from which she is drawing information from messages on budgetary matters sent to her from her department supervisors. Without multitasking and the capacity to cut and paste information from multiple applications, the manager would have to type in this disparate information from printed documents, a much more time consuming and inefficient method.

In summary, the operating system is the primary interface between the user and the personal computer. The operating system provides the software platform on which application software runs. It is through the operating system that peripheral devices interact with the computer. Management of information on the computer is made possible through the operating system. Contemporary operating systems visually represent command, file management, and viewing choices through icons, windows, and menu bars with graphic user interfaces. The inclusion of plug and play, network connectivity, and multitasking in operating systems have added functionality and flexibility to personal computers.

Applications: Tools for Tasks

An application is a software program that provides a specific set of functions making possible a defined set of tasks. Applications run on top of the operating system, which is to say that the operating system in the first level of software interfaces with the hardware. Applications interact with the computer's hardware through the operating system. Commonly used applications include word processors, spreadsheets, databases, presentation software, personal information management software, application suites, Web browsers, and utilities. The use of each of these types of software in social service practice is described in detail in subsequent chapters. The basic features of each of these applications are described in the following sections.

Word Processors

Word processing is the most common personal computer application (Internet.com 1997). Word processors are employed to create, edit, format, save, and print documents (Schoech, 1990). Word processing makes the creation and modification of documents far easier than it was in the technology that preceded it, the typewriter. Words, sentences, and paragraphs are easily moved within a document or from one document to another. Moreover, word processors make possible the ready creation of documents with images, diagrams, tables, and various fonts.

Most word processors include the following features.

1. Scrolling—As most documents are longer than can be displayed on a computer monitor, the ability to scroll up or down through a document is essential.

2. Editing—Cutting, copying, and pasting of information within and between documents facilitates editing.

3. Find and Replace—This is the capacity to search a document for a specified word or phrase. The Find command is particularly useful to locate specific information within a long document. For instance, the Find command might be employed to search a document for each instance where the term "hypermedia" is used. The Replace command searches for a word or phrase and replaces it with a designated word or phrase. This is useful in locating and changing, for instance, misspelled names.

4. Word wrap—As each line of text spans the width of a page, the cursor is automatically moved to the next line. Pressing the Enter key starts a new paragraph.

5. Print—The Print command allows for the creation of a hard copy of a document. The range, orientation, and number of copies of a document are specifiable.

6. View—Most word processors make available choices for viewing a document. These choices can include normal, outline, and page layout. Viewing options can include a range of editing and formatting toolbars. Toolbars can contain buttons and menus, which make available additional commands.

7. Mail merge—Merging information from a list of names, addresses, and other information into a document in which special symbols such as NAME and ADDRESS indicate where information is to be inserted to create form letters. This merging capacity is applicable to both letters and envelopes.

8. Font formatting—Fonts, which are sets of characters in different typefaces, may be selected and formatted, for instance, size, **bold**, *italics,* and underlined.

9. Spell checking, Thesaurus, and Grammar—Errors in spelling and grammar are detectable. The thesaurus in a word processor makes available synonyms.

10. Headers, Footers, and Page numbering—A header appears at the top of a page and a footer at the bottom of a page. Both options allow the writer to customize a document by including information such as report title or author's name. Page numbering automatically updates the page number for each page in a document.

11. WYSIWYG (what you see is what you get)—This feature in a word processor assures that the appearance of the document on the screen will be the same as its appearance on the printed page.

Taken together, these and other features of state of the art word processing programs make it possible to create complex and visually interesting documents that can rival professionally produced documents. Word processing software producers are in a continual battle to enhance the number of features and the ease of use of their products in order to gain market share. The end result is a continual escalation in the sophistication of word processing software. In turn, there has been a blurring of the line between word processors and desktop publishing systems, which historically have provided more choices in document layout and graphics (Margolis, 1996). The application of word processing software in social service practice is described in Chapter 7.

Spreadsheets

Like word processing software, spreadsheet software is widely used, though perhaps not commonly in social service practice. It is likely that social service workers have received limited training in the utility and versatility of spreadsheets. This is an unfortunate educational omission. Spreadsheets make it possible to collect, manage, and analyze both financial data and other types of information frequently collected in social service settings such as demographic and service utilization information.

A spreadsheet is essentially a table composed of rows, columns, and cells. A column is a vertical line of boxes with a letter identifying each column (maranGraphics, 1996). A row is a horizontal line of boxes with a number identifying each row. A cell is a single box in the spreadsheet, which is the intersection of a row and a column. The cell reference is the address of the cell, which is composed of the column letter and the row number. For instance, cell B4 is located in column B on row 4. Figure 3.4 shows a spreadsheet in which cell B4 is highlighted.

Three types of information may be entered into a cell: labels, values, and formulas. Labels are explanatory information such as the name of a variable that appears at the top of a column and identifies the information contained in the column. Values are the data, both numerical and text, that are collected in the spreadsheet. Formulas perform calculations, such as the average or sum of a column or row of values. Formulas are the means through which data in a spreadsheet are analyzed. Formulas make it possible to test a range of "what if" scenarios. For instance, in planning a budget, a manager might examine the impact of a 2%, 4%, or 5% salary increase for staff on her available annual resources. The formula would automatically recalculate her personnel budget as

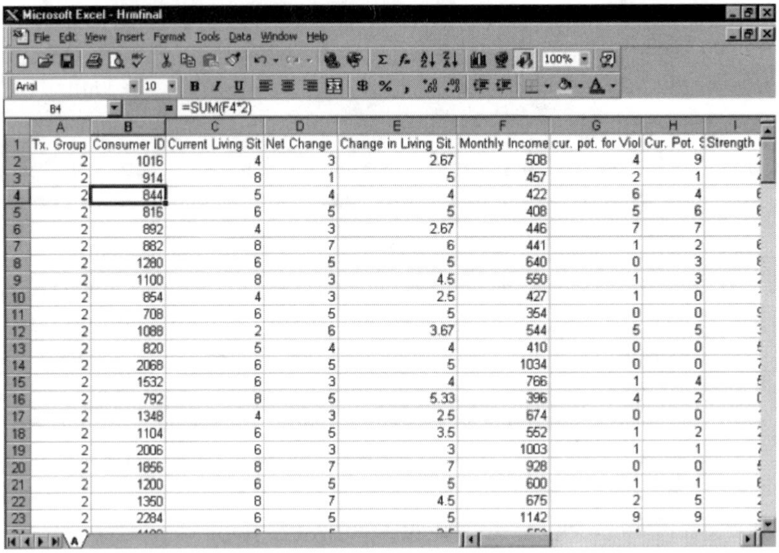

FIGURE 3.4   Spreadsheet of Client Data

she multiplied current salary cost by the possible 2%, 4%, or 5% salary increase. See Spreadsheet Exhibit 3.1 for an example. A caseworker also might help a client plan a household budget through exploring a range of "what if" scenarios around spending for the month. This capacity to test scenarios makes the spreadsheet a valuable tool in testing financial options in both administration and clinical practice settings.

The following features are commonly found in spreadsheets.

1. Graphing—Data in the spreadsheet can be visually represented in a range of graph and chart formats, such as bar charts and area graphs.

2. Formatting—Options in formatting of cell contents include bold, italics, underline, justification (right, left, center), number representation (percentage, scientific, decimal places, etc.), row and column height and width, and specification of cell border styles.

3. Data management—Information in spreadsheets can be sorted in a variety of ways, analyzed and summarized in tables, selected based on specified filters (e.g., all men over 50), and grouped in a variety of ways.

4. Drawing tools—A range of graphics tools are available to visually enhance spreadsheet documents. These tools may include lines, arrows, shapes, colors, and graphically augmented text tools, which add shape, color, and dimension to text.

5. Multidimensionality—Many spreadsheet programs create workbooks of spreadsheets (also known as worksheets) that allow the linkage of a series of spreadsheets by formulas. The result is that a change in one spreadsheet will affect all the other spreadsheets to which it is connected by a formula. For instance, an administrator could create a spreadsheet with the agency's budget on it. This spreadsheet would

SPREADSHEET EXHIBIT 3.1   Spreadsheet for Salary Increases

	A	B	C	D	E
1	Employee	Present Salary	2% Increase	4% Increase	5% Increase
2	J. P. Dole	32,000	32,640	33,280	33,600
3	Q. A. Smith	23,500	23,970	24,440	24,675
4	U. R. Wright	19,800	20,196	20,592	20,790
5	D. A. Day	18,000	18,360	18,720	18,900
6					
7	**Total**	93,300	95,166	97,032	97,965
8	Net Increase in Personnel Cost		1,866	3,732	4,665

be linked to three other spreadsheets in the same workbook, each spreadsheet representing a department's budget. The four spreadsheets might be linked by a formula that allocated a percentage of the agency's personnel budget to each of the three departments. Any change in the spreadsheet cell that contained the agency's budget would alter in turn the budget allocation for each department.

The utility of the spreadsheet in social service practice is not limited to financial applications, but extends to information management at the agency, program, group, or individual client level. Spreadsheets are highly flexible tools which can be readily adapted to a range of functions including monitoring and graphing client and/or group change, reporting of descriptive demographic information, compiling an inventory, or computing trends in client attendance. These and other applications of spreadsheets are presented in Chapter 4.

Databases

Database software can manage large quantities of information. Databases are used in a wide range of areas related to social service practice, including mailing lists, client records, referral resources, financial transactions, and donor contributions. Databases are a means to store information, like an electronic filing system (Margolis, 1996). Beyond the information storage, most databases provide options for summarizing data in reports, analyzing data, sorting data on specified parameters, and finding specific information. Data queries search for information meeting designated criteria, such as every case in a certain Zip code area between 18 and 50 years old.

Databases store information in one or more tables. Each table is composed of fields and records. A field is a single type of information, such as last name or city. Fields, like columns in spreadsheets, arrange information vertically in the table. A record is all the information about a single object or individual in the table. Records, like rows in a spreadsheet, display information horizontally across the table of a database. Figure 3.5 shows a data table in Microsoft Access.

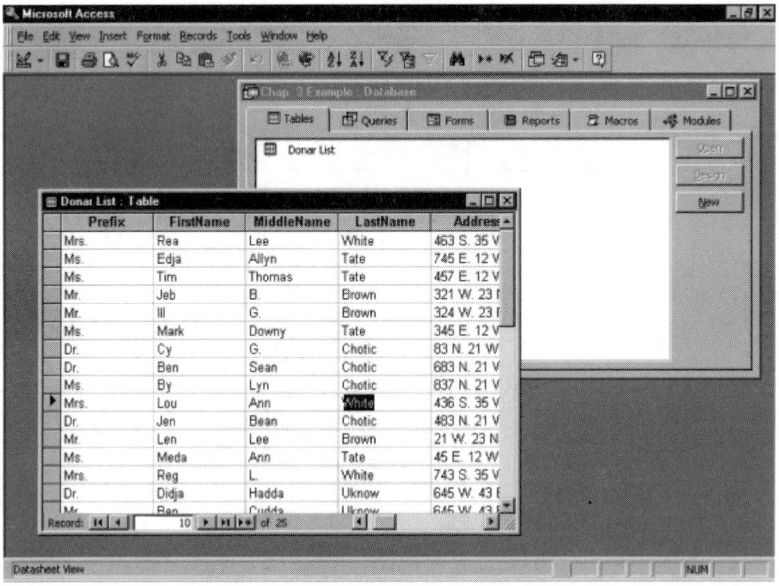

FIGURE 3.5   Database Table in Microsoft Access

There are two basic types of databases: flat file and relational. Flat file databases store information in one data sheet. The chief advantage of flat file databases is the ease of their set-up and use. Flat file databases are often developed for the storage and retrieval of information from simple lists, such as referral sources, mailing lists, or simple inventories. Relational databases, on the other hand, store information about one subject in a number of tables. The tables are linked or related by one type of information such as an employee number or item number. Each table having an identification field in common makes it possible to retrieve information from all the tables into a single report.

Information is entered into a database through a form. A form contains all the fields of the database. Each field is labeled and beside it is a box in which the field information is entered. The fields that appear on a form represent a record. For instance, a form for a mailing list database might contain fields for first name, last name, street address, city, state, and Zip code. The completed information in the database fields would comprise a single record in the database. This information can be viewed in combination with all other records in the database by examining the table that contains it. Each record can be examined sequentially in the form. Alternatively, a report can be designed and printed that presents selected information in a specified format.

The information in databases is examinable through a variety of means. The data in a table can be sorted on any field in ascending or descending (alphabetical or numerical) order. Many databases allow the user to apply filters to the data in order to find all the cases that meet the specified filtering criteria. A filter is a criterion or set of criteria that is applied to the data in order to select a subset of the data. For instance, a clinical social worker might want to review all of the cases from the caseload in the past four years that had a particular type of insurance. In the database table, simply clicking on the name of the particular insurer in the insurance provider field and then selecting the filter selection tool would generate a list of all cases with the specified insurer. Most databases will allow for additional filtering of the generated list. For instance, the user could then select all cases from the specified insurer who had a particular diagnosis. This type of incremental filtering of a database allows the user to examine carefully their database across a range of parameters. This can be extremely useful in examining large databases for very specific information.

Increasingly, database software is capable of storing not only text-based information but can also manage other forms of digital information, including images. One could create, for instance, a referral resource database of local social service agencies in which scanned photographs of the location and key staff members are included along with information on who to contact, address, phone number, and a map to the agency. The ability to show clients what the agency looks like and pictures of key staff members could enhance referral follow-through by clients as the agency and staff from whom they may seek assistance would no longer be faceless names.

In summary, databases are highly flexible tools for the collection, analysis, management, and reporting of information. For the information in a database to be useful, it is essential that the database be kept up to date through regular data entry. Moreover, in order to maximize the utility of a database, it should be designed to collect the information most relevant to the practice setting in which it is used. Database software, such as Lotus's Approach and Microsoft's Access, makes it possible to custom design a database for specific informational needs. They also provide templates to create commonly used databases. These template-created databases can be modified for distinct tasks and situations (McCracken, 1997; Robb, 1997). Both of these database applications have tools to turn reports generated from databases into Web publications by saving them in HTML (hypertext markup language). This feature makes it possible to publish information, such as progress to date on a fund-raising campaign, to wide audiences. The creation and use of databases are described in Chapter 5.

Presentation Software: Tools for Computer Slide Shows

Presentation software is used for the creation of computer-based slide shows. This type of software is sometimes called presentation graphics applications because of the integration in the presentation slides of text-based information and graphics such as digitized pictures, charts, diagrams, and even animations. Presentations are created and stored on a laptop or desktop computer. Depending on the size of the audience and the available equipment, the presentation is displayed on a laptop screen or desktop monitor, a large computer monitor, or an LCD (liquid crystal display) projector. The LCD projectors are expensive, with prices ranging from $2,000 to $5,000, and as such are generally available only in businesses, educational institutions, or hotels that cater to conferences. A lightweight, compact, and much less expensive alternative is a PC-to-TV converter. This type of device converts the video signal from the video port on a laptop or desktop computer to a format that can be displayed on a standard television screen. The price of these devices ranges from under $100 to around $300, depending on their output resolution. Their chief advantage is that televisions are commonly available in locations where social service workers are likely to make presentations, such as schools, churches, and agencies. A social service worker with a laptop, a PC-to-TV converter, and presentation software would be well equipped for a wide range of settings.

Presentation software makes possible the creation of informationally rich presentations that are both visually engaging and capable of holding the attention of an audience. Three widely used presentation software packages are Corel Presentations, Lotus Freelance Graphics, and Microsoft PowerPoint. Each of these presentation packages has features in common with the other two and unique features or options with which they hope to gain a competitive advantage. A review and comparison of these three presentation packages is presented in Chapter 8. The common features found in presentation software are described here.

The goal in developing presentations with presentation software is to create professional quality slide presentations that are both informative and engaging. There are a number of advantages to the development of slide presentations with presentation software over paper-based presentations using large paper tablets or posters or using overhead projector presentations with transparencies. First, presentation software can readily integrate content from other sources, including word processed documents; tables of numbers, charts, and graphs from spreadsheets; graphics; digitized images; and other content from the Web. Presentation software also can include animation and sound and video clips from a variety of sources. While one could argue that text, graphs, charts, and digitized images can be added to posters and transparencies, the addition of animations, sound, and video clips is not so readily accomplished. The second advantage of presentation software over posters and transparencies is the capacity to modify and adapt the presentation.

Once a presentation is developed, it is not fixed in stone, or as in the case of posters and transparencies, paper and plastic. Slide show presentations developed with presentation software can be easily revised. Figure 3.6 displays a slide created in Microsoft PowerPoint with content drawn from other sources. Text and graphics can be changed, removed, enhanced, and supplemented with additional material. Presentations can readily be adapted to meet the knowledge level and sophistication of audiences. A third advantage of presentation software over posters and transparencies is that they can readily be saved as Web pages (HTML files) for publication on the Web by placing the file on a Web server. A Web server is a computer that maintains a nearly continuous link to the Internet and runs Web server software that allows Internet users to view HTML files located on that server. One feature of this capacity to convert slide show presentations to Web pages is that once the presentation is over, it can be placed on the Web. Audiences then have access to the material and can review it again when they

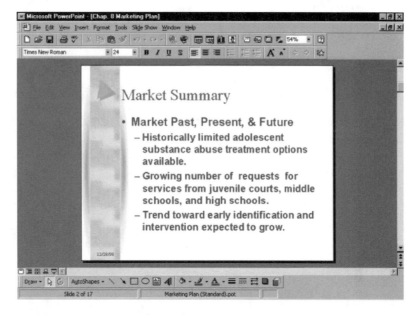

FIGURE 3.6   Presentation Software Slide Created in Microsoft PowerPoint

have a pressing need for the information. For example, an audience of middle school and high school parents may well appreciate being able to find and review on the Web information on recognizing possible signs of substance abuse in adolescents having once heard it in a presentation.

Presentations are created in presentation software either through choosing a template provided in the software package or using a blank presentation. Some presentation applications have guided, interactive presentation design tools known as wizards, which facilitate the creation of presentations. The wizard offers a series of choices about presentation design to the user and through this dialog the presentation is developed. Presentation templates define the appearance of the text and background of the presentation. Using a template has the advantage of making the appearance of each slide consistent and automates the formatting of every slide. Presentation templates are designed around types of presentations one might make, such as teaching a skill, presenting a financial report, strategy recommendations, or project planning. Blank presentations allow the user to start with a blank slate, focus first on the presentation content, and then add titles, bullets, graphics, and a background for the slide. The choice of type of presentation development tool to use depends on both the personal preferences of the user and the amount of experience the user has had with presentation software. Inexperienced users will likely find it easier to develop presentations either with an existing template or in interaction with a wizard. Whichever method is selected, presentation software applications have a great many tools which make it possible to develop very creative and engaging presentations. Readers are encouraged to express their creativity in their presentation development by experimenting with these tools which include graphics files, screen transitions, background choices, font size and color options, and sounds.

Personal Information Management Software: Organizing Your Life

Personal information management (PIM) software is a type of software designed to collect, organize, retrieve, and facilitate the use of a range of personal/professional information. PIM software packages vary in the types of components they offer, but generally include an address book, a scheduling calendar, a notebook/card file, a task or to-do list, and an e-mail interface. Each of these components serves to promote the organization and utilization of information germane to personal/professional tasks. Three commonly available PIM packages are Lotus Organizer, Corel Central, and Microsoft Outlook. Figure 3.7 displays the calendar page of Lotus Organizer. Note that some of the other features of the software are listed on tabs on the right side of the screen.

Some of the features of PIM software include:

1. Track contacts—Contacts are individuals with whom the software user has some form of interaction. Contacts could include individuals within an agency, clients, and employees of other agencies. PIM software allows the user to record a range of information about the contact. A wide array of address information may be collected, including business and home addresses, telephone and fax numbers, e-mail and Web

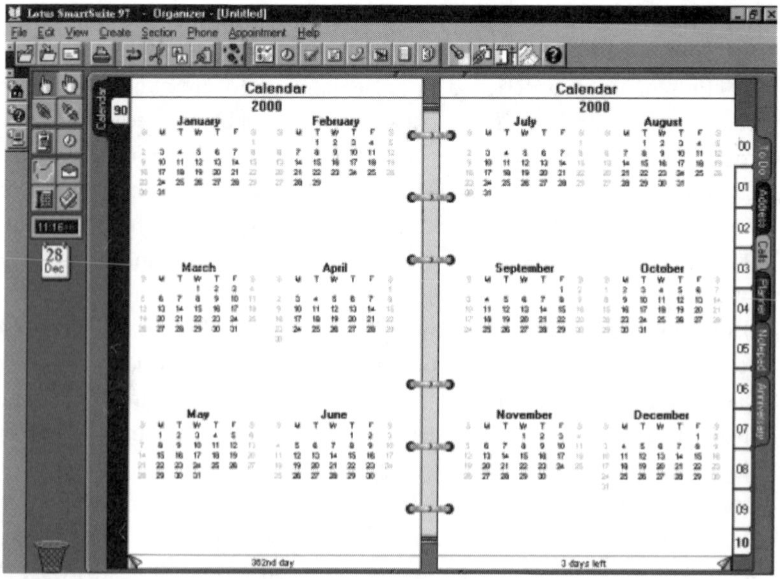

FIGURE 3.7 Lotus Organizer Personal Information Management Software

addresses, and job title. If a computer has a modem, contact telephone numbers can be dialed from the software. If a computer is connected to a network, e-mail message can be composed and sent by clicking on the e-mail address. In many PIM packages, one can make notes on meetings or telephone calls with clients and other contacts. The software will record the time, date, and duration of the contact. For caseworkers who have to produce activity reports or who have large, complex caseloads, a tool to record and manage contacts could be a great time saver. As an added feature, many PIM packages allow for the sharing of information with word processors, a feature that could facilitate report production. Moreover, address lists can be exported to word processor, database, and spreadsheet programs for the creation of mail merge letters.

2. Organize schedules—All PIM packages include a calendar for appointment scheduling. However, the sophistication of these calendars is far greater than a standard paper-based appointment calendar. For instance, many of them allow the user to change the calendar view from day, to week, to month with a simple click of an icon. Appointment entries in the calendar can specify single appointments or meetings, set reminder alarms for meeting times, and provide a space for reminder notes on the appointments. Some PIM packages make it possible to check the network-shared calendars of meeting participants in scheduling a meeting. Calendars can be printed in order to have a hard copy. Task lists may be integrated with calendars for the coordination of tasks and scheduling. Reoccurring appointments, events, and meetings can be automatically scheduled.

3. Task management—The specification and completion of tasks is an integral part of many jobs. Many PIM packages provide task or to-do lists which allow for the tracking of a range of information regarding each task, including a description of the task, status (e.g., not started, in progress, nearly complete), due date, and category of task (e.g., case management, supervision, outreach). Some PIM packages allow users to sort their task lists on these various categories of information. This can facilitate the grouping of similar tasks and may promote efficiency in task completion.

4. E-mail tool—A PIM package can help users organize their e-mail. PIM packages often have an e-mail component with which messages can be retrieved from the users' e-mail service/server. Retrieved messages are held in an inbox from which they may be read, deleted, forwarded to others, or replied to. Most PIM packages allow the user to save e-mail addresses from received e-mail in the PIM's address book. This feature makes it easy to both collect and retrieve e-mail addresses. E-mail can be composed either within the e-mail composing form or pasted into the form after being copied from a word processing document. E-mail can be sent to a single or multiple recipients with addresses entered from the address book or typed into the "To" or "CC" fields. This capacity facilitates communications with work groups. Attachments, which are compressed or uncompressed files, can be appended to e-mail messages. Clicking on an attachment icon opens a window from which the intended attachment file may be located, selected, and attached to an outgoing e-mail. The utility of attachments will be discussed in greater depth in Chapter 9. Finally, most PIM e-mail tools will track and, if desired, retain a copy of all e-mail correspondence.

The functions of PIM packages may be particularly useful to social workers who have to manage large caseloads, have extensive supervisory duties, or coordinate activities with other team members. Moreover, PIM packages often have group sharing features with which information may be shared with work groups whose computers are networked. In the case of client contact records, the password-protected sharing over the network of such information could facilitate case supervision and client case management in settings where teams of workers share cases.

Even for social service workers who do not have access to a computer network or need to share information with coworkers, the personal/professional information management tools in PIM packages represent valuable reasons for using a personal computer as a tool of social service practice. Users are not required or compelled to use all the tools available in a PIM package, but can pick and chose the tools that best fit their personal styles and information needs.

Application Suites: Tools That Work Together

One of the important advances in software applications in recent years is the development of integrated software suites. Software suites such as Microsoft Office, Corel Office, Microsoft Works, and Lotus Smart Suite integrate commonly used applications so they readily work in concert with each other. Each of these software suites has at minimum a word processor, spreadsheet, graphics tools, PIM tools, and presentation software. Graphics tools in software suites may not be standalone software applications but instead are often integrated in the word processing, spreadsheet, and presentation software. Some software suites include database software while others offer consumers a choice of versions that either include or exclude database software.

There are a number of advantages to purchasing software suites over individual software packages. One advantage is that software suites optimize the operation of each individual application to facilitate the sharing of information between applications in the suite. For instance, charts created in a spreadsheet are readily copied into the word processor or presentation software. Text from a word processor document may be pasted into presentation software or into a spreadsheet. The net effect of sharing content between applications is to dramatically increase the range and informational richness of the documents produced.

A second advantage of using software suites is cost. Generally, the cost of purchasing separately each of the applications in a software suite is greater than the cost of purchasing the software suite. Moreover, software companies will frequently make available updates of their software suites that are downloadable over the Web in order to maintain their customer base. This level of support represents an added level of value in a software suite.

A disadvantage of software suites is that the range of features in the applications contained in a software suite may not precisely match the needs of the user. For instance, a user may find that the word processor from one manufacturer may do a particular set of tasks that the user requires, while the database from another manufacturer has the data management features the user expects. In some instances, it may be less expensive to buy one software suite and use most of its applications, while purchasing separately a single, specifically required application from another manufacturer.

For social service workers, a software suite can be a very economical way to acquire a powerful set of software tools. The application tools available in most software suites are well suited for many of the procedures and tasks described in this book. There is also a distinct learning advantage in choosing one software suite and developing skills in its use over time. While all manufacturers now use a graphic user interface in their software suites and most applications have a similar look and feel, there are differences between how software manufacturers elect to have their software carry out some tasks. Switching between software suites from different manufacturers can be both comfortable and disconcerting. The comfort derives from the general similarity in the software interface between the same type of applications, for instance word processing, in different suites. The disconcerting aspect arises as one moves into doing tasks that are more complex. It then becomes apparent that there are notable differences between software suites in how to achieve the same end. As a result, if one wishes to advance skills and proficiency in using software applications to meet a range of employment task requirements, it seems far more time efficient to stay with one software suite over time, rather than switch software suites each time one is released with a new set of features.

Web Browsers

Despite the impressive range of features available in software suites, in order to examine information on the World Wide Web, one needs a Web browser. A Web browser is a specialized software application designed to allow a user to see and interact with information on Web pages. Through a Web browser one may see text, graphics, and animations present on the selected Web page. Some Web browsers allow a user to hear any music or sounds that are available on the Web page. Web browsers allow the user to bookmark or save the location of designated Web pages in order to return to the page in the future without having to either search for the page or reenter the Web address. Web browsers also retain a history of all the pages visited during a session on the Web. This feature allows the user to return to a page visited earlier in the session.

While the use of Web browsers has become increasingly commonplace, it is perhaps worth noting that the Web browsers are a recently developed type of software (Krol, 1992). The original work on development of the World Wide Web was done near Geneva, Switzerland, at the European Particle Physics Laboratory (CERN). Their intention was to develop a flexible tool for exploring the Internet. Their work exploited the ideas of hypertext and hypermedia. The term *hypertext* refers to the nonlinear linkage of information. Ted Nelson (1974) is generally credited with coining the phrase. He envisioned the nonsequential availability of information in large computer networks. The "hyper" portion of the term refers to multidimensional potential that users could encounter as they select idiosyncratic paths to move through the space of the information contained in the database. *Hypermedia* refers to the multimedia such as text, images, animations, video, and sound manifest in present-day Web pages. Not only can one click on a bit of text (hypertext) and be instantly linked to another page with associated information, but images are also hyperlinked. Web browsers provide the software interface to make possible this type of exploration of the informational space of the Web.

Historically, the concept of a hypertextlike system of informational management is credited to Vannevar Bush, President Franklin Roosevelt's Science Advisor (Tsai, 1988). In the 1940s, Bush predicted the information explosion that has occurred in the last half of this century. He proposed the creation of a machine called Memex that allowed for the linkage of documents stored on microfilm. Bush conceptualized that operation of the human mind was based on "omni-directional association" (Tsai, 1988, p. 4). Memex was to be designed to maximize the potential for user defined, associative information retrieval that mirrored Bush's conception of cognitive processes. Today's World Wide Web has expanded the idea of associative information retrieval to a global scale.

To facilitate exploration of the global information resources of the Internet, Web browsers have developed a number of common features. In many ways, Web browsers have moved beyond being just Web browsers to become Internet information management tools. Along with the capacity to explore Web sites, they now offer e-mail tools, news readers, HTML authoring tools, and the capacity to hold audio and text conferences. The utility of these features in social service practice will be discussed in Chapter 9. For now it is sufficient to emphasize that Web browsers not only allow a user to find, examine, and retrieve information from the Internet, but also they have become Internet communication tools. As such, they represent an extremely useful tool for social service practice.

Utilities

Utilities are programs designed to perform very specific functions (Margolis, 1996). Most operating systems have a number of utilities to aid in the management of computers. These utilities do things such as adding and removing files, finding files, adding and removing hardware, keeping track of time and date, and many more tasks. Utilities are differentiated from applications based on their size and functionality. Utilities are generally considerably smaller than applications. Utilities are limited in their functionality. They perform very specific tasks such as file compression, creating back-ups of files, folders, or drives, recovering lost and deleted files, and automating tasks that are routinely performed. A wide range of utilities is available for trial and purchase over the Web. The Yahoo web site (www.yahoo.com) has a wide range of utilities for downloading. Numerous other Web sites also offer downloadable utilities.

One type of utility, antivirus software, is especially important to the continued operation of a personal computer. Antivirus software is designed to seek out and destroy all viruses on a computer. A virus is a product of human intelligence and perhaps malevolence. It is a small program capable of reproducing itself. A virus can cause a computer to crash by filling up available memory. Even worse, some viruses can cause hard drives to fail, resulting in the loss of all documents and applications on the drive.

Computers become infected with viruses through sharing of floppy disks between computers, downloading files with viruses on them, or through e-mail with infected attached files (Miastkowski, 1997). Sharing of floppy disks between computers allows a virus-infected computer to infect the floppy disk and subsequently all the other computers in which the disk is inserted. Computer files on network servers and on the Internet can be infected with viruses. Downloading infected files to a computer can result in the release of the virus onto the computer's hard drive once the file is decompressed, run, or installed. Before 1995, it was not possible to receive a virus infection through e-mail. That year a type of virus called a macro virus emerged that was carried in Microsoft Word and Excel files attached to e-mail. Once the attached file was opened, the virus would infect the computer. Word 97, Excel 97, and later versions of these programs detect and eradicate common macro viruses.

To protect against virus infections and to eliminate viruses from personal computers, antivirus utilities must be used regularly. Some antivirus software has scheduling features that allow users to specify regular times for the software to scan the computer for viruses. In order to avoid infections from downloaded files, antivirus should be used each time a file is downloaded. In addition, because new viruses frequently appear, it is important to update antivirus software regularly. Most antivirus software manufacturers have Internet sites from which registered owners of their software can download software updates designed to detect newly released viruses. Utilities like antivirus software are now critical to the operation of a personal computer.

Summary

This chapter presented a broad review of the form and function of software presently in use in personal computers. The elements of a graphic user interface were described. The functions of operating systems were discussed with a focus on their current manifestations in popular operating systems. The operating system is perhaps best understood as the platform on which software applications run. This chapter provided an introduction to commonly used software applications, many of which are addressed in greater detail in subsequent chapters in this text. Software described here included word processors, spreadsheets, databases, presentation software, personal information management software, application suites, Web browsers, and utilities. A theme touched upon throughout this chapter is the ability to move information between software applications. The utility of this function is a theme that pervades this text.

Exercises

1. Create a list of software applications you commonly use and compare this list to the applications described in this chapter. What are the points of convergence between your list and the applications described here? Which applications described in this chapter do you feel most comfortable using? Which ones seem to have interesting uses you have not previously considered?

2. With a group of peers discuss how the applications described here might be used in your practice settings. What could be done with these software applications to improve client services that is not now being done? What prevents the use of these software applications in your practice settings? How could this situation be rectified?

3. What software applications would you like to see improved? How would you have the function or form of the software enhanced to improve its usefulness? How could this improved software be used in social service practice?

chapter 4

Spreadsheets
Multipurpose Tools

This chapter presents an overview and demonstrations of the use of spreadsheets in a range of common data collection, analysis, and graphing problems encountered by social service practitioners. Spreadsheets are a commonly available and relatively low-cost alternative to statistical software packages. This chapter illustrates the use of spreadsheets in data collection, random sampling, data cleaning, producing descriptive and some inferential statistics, single-system designs, and budgeting.

This chapter explores the use of spreadsheets for a variety of applications in social service practice. It examines the usefulness of spreadsheets as a tool in the collection of data[1] about clients, communities, and organizations. Once data is collected, the process of understanding it may be aided through a number of spreadsheet data analysis techniques presented here. Many data analysis tasks require descriptive and inferential statistics to fully understand the phenomena evident in the data and inherent in the relationships among variables. The capacity of spreadsheets in statistical analysis is demonstrated in this chapter. Graphical presentation of data can inform both the data analytic process and the audience for whom the analysis is intended. This chapter covers a number of methods for graphical representation in single-system practice evaluation designs.

The role of spreadsheets in social service practice extends beyond data collection, analysis, and reporting. Spreadsheets are also powerful tools for the collection, presentation, and analysis of fiscal data. The use of spreadsheets in the budget development process and in tracking fiscal data is demonstrated. Spreadsheets' applicability in decision support and "what if" analysis is explored.

The overarching purpose of the examination of this range of applications of spreadsheets in social service practice is the demonstration of spreadsheets' flexibility

---

[1]In the discussion of information technology thus far the term *information* has been used instead of the term *data*. The introduction of this term denotes the fact that, while text-based information may be used in spreadsheets, analytic methods generally require numerical information. Text-based information usually has to be numerically coded. As such, the term *data* is used throughout this chapter.

and analytic power as a tool of practice. Though spreadsheets are a commonly available software application, they have to date been underutilized in social service practice (Janzen & Lewis, 1990). The focus here is on demonstrating how recent advances in spreadsheet design have dramatically improved their ease of use, versatility, and usefulness as a tool of social service practice.

Capturing Data

A commonly used method for the collection of data on attitudes, beliefs, and preferences is survey research (Rubin & Babbie, 1997). Surveys of clients, customers, and workers are commonly conducted by social service agencies (Royse, 1992). Survey research is conducted through self-administered questionnaires, interview surveys conducted face to face, or telephone surveys. Self-administered questionnaires may be mailed, handed out to an assembled group, or hand delivered to a residence to be either mailed back or picked up at a later date. Each of these methods requires data management procedures that can be accomplished with the use of spreadsheets.

Mail Surveys

A prerequisite of conducting a mail survey is obtaining a list of individuals and their addresses. Mailing lists may be acquired from a variety of sources. Many agencies and organizations maintain databases containing name and address information. The methods for utilization of such electronic mailing lists are described later in this chapter and in Chapters 5 and 7.

If an electronic mailing list is unavailable, compilation of a list of survey recipients may require extracting names and addresses from case records or other sources. If such data must be hand entered to develop a mailing list, a data entry form can be constructed in a spreadsheet to facilitate the task. A data entry form uses the column names from the first row in a spreadsheet to create a form to simplify data entry (Rutledge, 1997). Figure 4.1 specifies the steps in this process in Microsoft Excel. Some spreadsheets do not make this type of data entry form available. In such a case, the variable names are typed in the first row of the spreadsheet. Data for each variable are entered in the rows below. In both methods, the Tab key moves the cursor or data insertion point between cells.

One drawback of the data entry in Excel is that the form is limited to 32 columns (variables). While most mailing lists contain only seven or eight variables, one may wish to use additional fields to collect other information or to enter survey results. If one is using a spreadsheet other than Excel or has more than 32 fields of data to enter, there are other options. The spreadsheet can be split horizontally so that the variable names at the top of the spreadsheet remain visible while data are entered in the rows below. This serves two purposes. First, a virtually unlimited number of variable (column) names can be entered in the first row. This is extremely helpful if one is developing a large

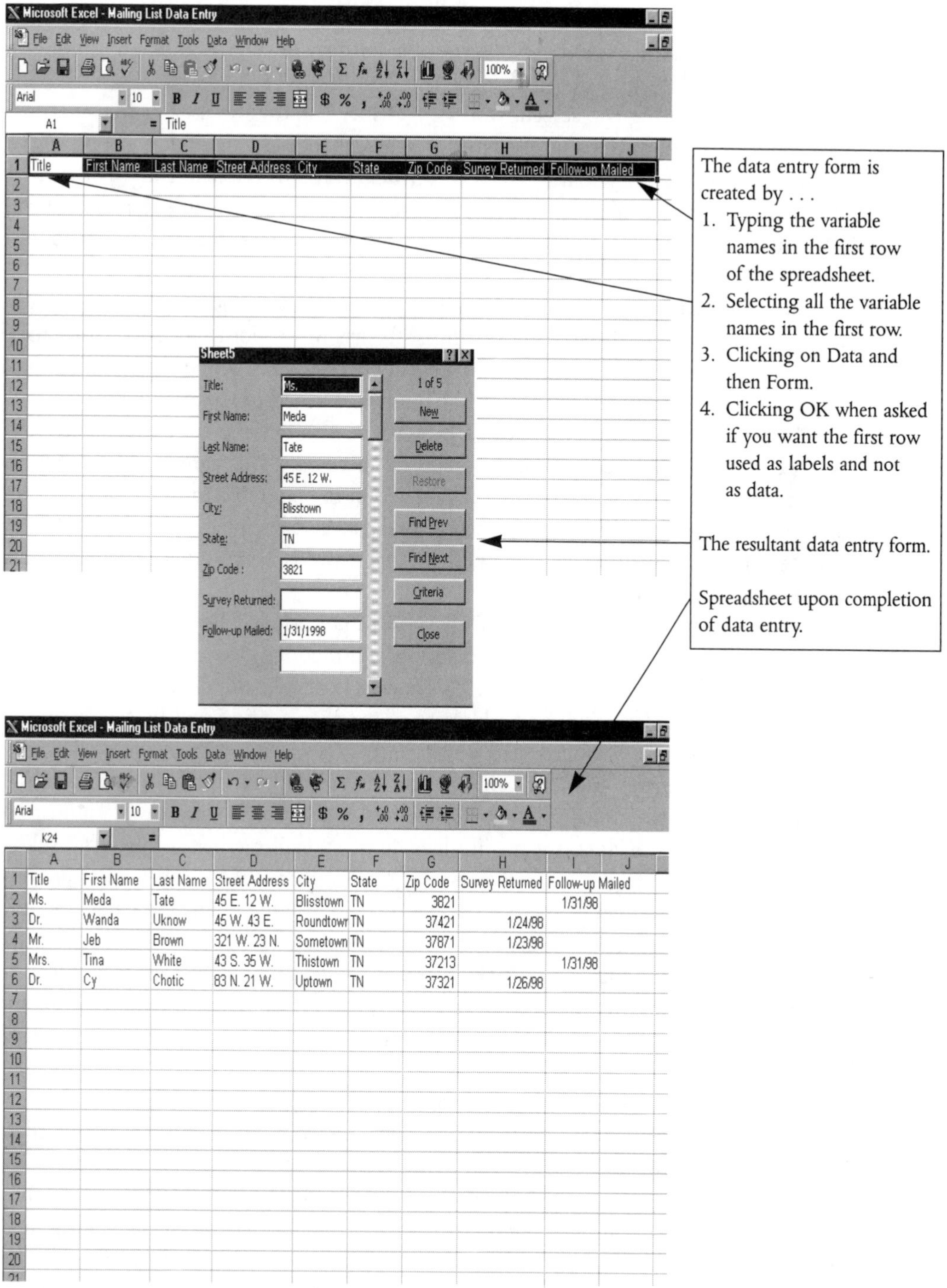

The data entry form is created by . . .

1. Typing the variable names in the first row of the spreadsheet.
2. Selecting all the variable names in the first row.
3. Clicking on Data and then Form.
4. Clicking OK when asked if you want the first row used as labels and not as data.

The resultant data entry form.

Spreadsheet upon completion of data entry.

FIGURE 4.1   Mailing List Data Entry

data set. Second, splitting the screen horizontally allows the variable names to remain visible as the data set expand beyond the initial number of rows that first appeared on the screen.

Instead of splitting the screen, some spreadsheets allow the user to freeze a portion of the screen so it does not scroll. If a spreadsheet has this option, the first row can be frozen while the remainder can be scrolled through for data entry. For further information on either of these options, click on Help in the Menu bar and click on Help Topics or Index, then type in "split" or "freeze" for more information on how to perform this function in the spreadsheet.

Once the mailing list is complete, it can be used to develop a mail merge document in conjunction with word processing software. Most word processors now have mail merge tools that facilitate the importing of spreadsheet mailing lists into the mail merge document. Mail merging is illustrated and described in Chapter 7.

The preceding discussion described how to create a mailing list by manually typing data into a spreadsheet. Though sometimes necessary, this can be a very tedious and time-consuming process. Whenever possible, it is preferable to obtain an existing electronic mailing list and import it into a spreadsheet or database (see Chapter 5) in order to produce a mail merge. The question that arises is how do we accomplish this feat of electronic magic?

Let us assume we work for the agency Maximum Mental Health. We have been asked to conduct a customer satisfaction survey of a random group of clients who have used the agency services in the past year. This request poses two important questions. First, how do we get a list of names and addresses of the clients who used the agency in the last year? The second question is how do we select a random sample of those clients?

Like many agencies, ours has address and service data in its client database. Unfortunately, as in many agencies that information is kept in some type of "industrial strength" database that does not readily lend itself to mail merges and random selection of clients. What to do? One option is to request from the person who maintains the database (the guardian of the database) a "flat file" that contains the name and address variables we will need to produce a mailing list. Moreover, we request that the file be limited to individuals who have received services within the last year. Now, it should be pointed out that requesting this type of information often requires a dialog with the person who is managing the databases. The purpose of this dialog is to maximize the clarity of the request, specify the format to create the flat file in, and decide on how the data will be delivered, over the network or on diskette. Most spreadsheets can read a variety of file formats including text files, dBase files, data exchange files, Excel files, Lotus files, and Quattro Pro files.

So, let us assume that the guardian of the database at Maximum Mental Health has extracted the information we requested, sent us a flat file over the agency's local area network along with an e-mail informing us that the file is saved in dbase format. We open the file in our spreadsheet with the File and Open commands in the menu bar and select dbase from the "Files of type" window. Once the file is open, we can save it in the file format used by our spreadsheet. For example, a Microsoft Excel file is saved with an .xls file extension.

Dragging the scroll bar to the bottom of the spreadsheet we see that there are the names and addresses of 1,000 clients in the spreadsheet. The question we now face is how large of a sample do we select? The complexities of specifying an appropriate sample size are beyond the scope of this discussion. For two different views on this matter see Rubin and Babbie (1997) and Williams, Unrau, and Grinnell (1998). Upon review of these two perspectives, we decide a sample of 200 is more than adequate for our purpose.

The next question we face is how to select a random sample. Spreadsheets make this a very simple process with the use of a formula or function. Different manufacturers use different terms, but essentially these are mathematical or logical procedures which are inserted in one or more cells and perform a calculation or logical operation. For our present purpose we are interested in generating a random number beside each case in the mailing list data set. With a random number beside each case, we will sort the entire list on the random number column. This produces a randomly sorted mailing list. This procedure is necessary to control for any possible selection bias in the order in which the database was selected. Once we have the randomly sorted mailing list, we select the top 200 cases for our survey. Since the list is now randomized, it does not matter where in the list we draw our 200 cases. For convenience sake, we select the top 200.

Simple Random Sampling Procedure

The steps in this randomization procedure are:

1. Click on A at the top of column A. This will select the entire column. Most spreadsheets have an Insert command in the Menu bar. Click on Insert and then click Column. This will insert a new column on the left side of the spreadsheet.

2. Click on the cell in the first column, second row. The cell reference is A2.

3. Again, click on the Insert command in the Menu bar. Then click on Function.

4. Most programs will show a list of function categories and a list of functions. Select Rand or Random and click Finish. This will insert the random number generator function in cell A2.

5. Copy cell A2 with the Copy command under Edit in the Menu bar.

6. Select the cells in Column A, Rows 3–1,001 and paste the copied function into them using the paste command under Edit in the Menu bar. Each case now has a random number beside it.

7. Select the entire data set.

8. In the Menu bar, under either Tools or Data (depending on the spreadsheet) select Sort. Make sure to sort on Column A. Sort in either Ascending or Descending order. This will sort the entire data set on the random number beside each case. Astute observers may note that once the data set is sorted, the random numbers

are not in sequential order. Once the sort is complete, the random number function generates new random numbers. Rest assured the data set is now randomized.

9. Select the top 200 cases. Copy them and then paste them into a new worksheet. Note that at the bottom of the spreadsheet page there are tabs. Clicking on any of these tabs opens a new page or worksheet in the spreadsheet. Paste the 200 cases into one of these worksheets.
10. The 200 randomly selected cases are now ready to use for the survey mail merge.

See Figure 4.2 for an illustration of a randomly sorted data set.

Systematic Sampling

Rubin and Babbie (1997) and Williams, Unrau, and Grinnell (1998) describe the process of creating a systematic sample in which every *k*th case is selected. For instance, we may decide to select every fifth case (1/5) from our 1,000 case data set. A systematic sample has no methodological advantage over the simple random sampling procedure described in the previous section. Nonetheless, some researchers prefer and are

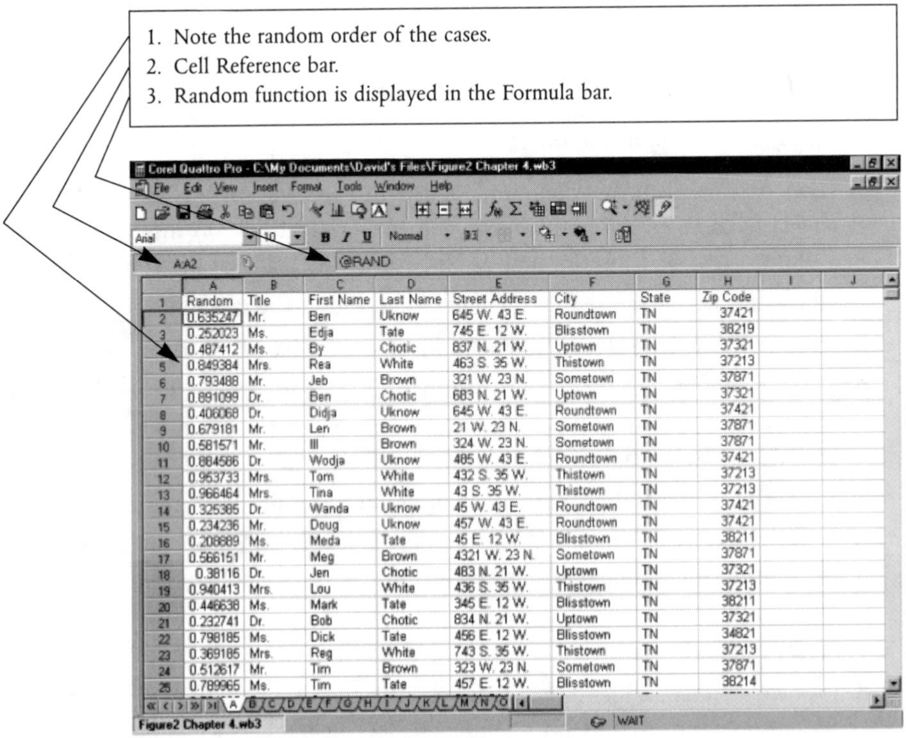

	A	B	C	D	E	F	G	H	I	J
1	Random	Title	First Name	Last Name	Street Address	City	State	Zip Code		
2	0.635247	Mr.	Ben	Uknow	645 W. 43 E.	Roundtown	TN	37421		
3	0.252023	Ms.	Edja	Tate	745 E. 12 W.	Blisstown	TN	38219		
4	0.487412	Ms.	By	Chotic	837 N. 21 W.	Uptown	TN	37321		
5	0.849384	Mrs.	Rea	White	463 S. 35 W.	Thistown	TN	37213		
6	0.793488	Mr.	Jeb	Brown	321 W. 23 N.	Sometown	TN	37871		
7	0.891099	Dr.	Ben	Chotic	683 N. 21 W.	Uptown	TN	37321		
8	0.406068	Dr.	Didja	Uknow	645 W. 43 E.	Roundtown	TN	37421		
9	0.679181	Mr.	Len	Brown	21 W. 23 N.	Sometown	TN	37871		
10	0.581571	Mr.	III	Brown	324 W. 23 N.	Sometown	TN	37871		
11	0.884586	Dr.	Wodja	Uknow	485 W. 43 E.	Roundtown	TN	37421		
12	0.953733	Mrs.	Tom	White	432 S. 35 W.	Thistown	TN	37213		
13	0.966464	Mrs.	Tina	White	43 S. 35 W.	Thistown	TN	37213		
14	0.325385	Dr.	Wanda	Uknow	45 W. 43 E.	Roundtown	TN	37421		
15	0.234236	Mr.	Doug	Uknow	457 W. 43 E.	Roundtown	TN	37421		
16	0.208889	Ms.	Meda	Tate	45 E. 12 W.	Blisstown	TN	38211		
17	0.566151	Mr.	Meg	Brown	4321 W. 23 N.	Sometown	TN	37871		
18	0.38116	Dr.	Jen	Chotic	483 N. 21 W.	Uptown	TN	37321		
19	0.940413	Mrs.	Lou	White	436 S. 35 W.	Thistown	TN	37213		
20	0.446638	Ms.	Mark	Tate	345 E. 12 W.	Blisstown	TN	38211		
21	0.232741	Dr.	Bob	Chotic	834 N. 21 W.	Uptown	TN	37321		
22	0.798185	Ms.	Dick	Tate	456 E. 12 W.	Blisstown	TN	34821		
23	0.369185	Mrs.	Reg	White	743 S. 35 W.	Thistown	TN	37213		
24	0.512617	Mr.	Tim	Brown	323 W. 23 N.	Sometown	TN	37871		
25	0.789965	Ms.	Tim	Tate	457 E. 12 W.	Blisstown	TN	38214		

FIGURE 4.2 Random Sampling Procedure

more familiar with systematic sampling. To produce a systematic sample we will again start with our 1,000 case mailing list.

1. Click on A at the top of column A. This will select the entire column. Most spreadsheets have an Insert command in the Menu bar. Click on Insert and then click Column. This will insert a new column on the left side of the spreadsheet.

2. Click on the cell in the first column, second row. The cell reference is A2.

3. To produce an every fifth case sample, type 1, 2, 3, 4, 5 down the next five rows of the column. To produce every tenth case sample, type 1–10 down the next ten rows of the column, cells A2 through A11. To produce a systematic sample for every fifth case using a random start (Rubin & Babbie, 1997), insert a random number, as described previously, into cell A1. Reading the random number from left to right, find the first number between 1 and 5. For instance, if the number is 0.751935, we start our sequence in the third row. In the row above we type 5, as it is the end of the sequence (remember the top row is the variable name). (See Spreadsheet Exhibit 4.1.)

4. Select and copy in Column A this 1–5 sequence.

5. Select all the remaining rows in the data set and click Paste. The 1–5 sequence will fill the column.

6. Select the entire data set.

7. In the Menu bar, under either Tools or Data (depending on the spreadsheet) select Sort. Make sure to sort on Column A. Sort in either Ascending or Descending order. This will sort the entire data set, grouping all the 1's, 2's, and so on.

8. Select, Copy and Paste one of the five groups into a new spreadsheet.

9. A systematically randomly selected sample of 200 cases is now ready to use in the survey mail merge.

SPREADSHEET EXHIBIT 4.1   Systematic Sample with a Random Start

	A	B	C	D	E	F	G	H
1	0.751935	Title	First Name	Last Name	Street Address	City	State	Zip Code
2	5	Mrs.	Rea	White	463 S. 35 W.	Thistown	TN	37213
3	1	Ms.	Edja	Tate	745 E. 12 W.	Blisstown	TN	38219
4	2	Ms.	Tim	Tate	457 E. 12 W.	Blisstown	TN	38214
5	3	Mr.	Jeb	Brown	321 W. 23 N.	Sometown	TN	37871
6	4	Mr.	Ill	Brown	324 W. 23 N.	Sometown	TN	37871
7	5	Ms.	Mark	Tate	345 E. 12 W.	Blisstown	TN	38211

Stratified Sampling

Before returning our discussion to survey data collection, one other sampling method that may be aided by spreadsheet methods requires review. Stratified sampling reduces the sampling error through random selection from subsets of the population (Rubin & Babbie, 1997). Drawing upon their example, let us assume that in our customer satisfaction survey for Maximum Mental Health, we wish to examine variation in customer satisfaction across ethnic groups. Toward that end, when we request our mailing list flat file from the guardian of the database, we ask for the inclusion of the field "Ethnic group." We may want to ask that the "Ethnic group" variable appear as either the first or last column in the flat file, as this makes the sorting more convenient.

Once we have the mailing list opened in our spreadsheet, we can sort the mailing list on the "Ethnic group" variable. We then copy the mailing list data for each ethnic group into a separate worksheet within the spreadsheet we are using. Next, we follow the procedures previously described for selection of either a simple random sample or a systematic random sample. Once we select a random sample for each ethnic group, we pool these samples into a spreadsheet by copying and pasting. We now have a stratified random sample for our mail survey. Of course, we will not use the field "Ethnic group" in the mail merge procedure.

Survey Data Collection

Each type of survey research—self-administered questionnaires, interview surveys conducted face to face, or telephone surveys—requires the recording of data. When mail surveys are returned, the answer to each question is entered into a computer in preparation for the data analysis. A spreadsheet is a versatile and easy to set up tool for data entry. Figure 4.1 illustrates the steps in a mailing list data entry.

The same process is applicable for survey data collection. Preparation of a spreadsheet for data entry requires both forethought and experimentation. One of the first issues to consider is whether a spreadsheet is the best tool for the data entry or whether a database application is more appropriate. This question is often a matter of experience with spreadsheets versus database applications. As we will see in Chapter 5, some spreadsheet and database software makes it possible to readily convert a spreadsheet into a database and to move a data sheet in a database into a spreadsheet application. The lines between the two types of applications are not always distinct.

One distinct advantage of a spreadsheet is the ease with which survey items are identified. Names or labels for each item (question) in the survey are simply typed into the first row of the spreadsheet. It is important to note that the column width is adjustable to the length of the survey item or question. To alter the width of a column, place the cursor at the top of the sheet on the line between two columns. A bidirectional arrow will appear. To expand the column, click it and hold, then drag it to the desired size. This means it is possible to type each entire question into the cells of the first row of each column, but this is generally not advisable. A single word or phrase summarizing each survey item is sufficient. This abbreviated labeling convention will minimize the time required to scroll through the spreadsheet. Additionally, in constructing the spreadsheet for survey data entry, be sure to maintain the sequential order in which questions (items) appear on the survey. This will reduce the possibility of data entry error due to the order of the items on the spreadsheet not matching the order on the survey.

Another consideration in setting up the spreadsheet for data entry is data format. The issue here is whether to enter information as text or in numerical code. Information entered as text will usually require recoding a numerical code if anything other than the most cursory analysis is to occur. It is generally preferable to precode a questionnaire (Rubin & Babbie, 1997). Precoding means each item in the questionnaire has a code for each possible response. For instance, the question "What is your gender?" would have (1) Female (2) Male beside it. The presence of the data numerical codes in the questionnaire decreases the possibility of data entry error.

An alternative procedure available in spreadsheets is the creation of comment windows. Comment windows are windows into which information pertaining to a cell in a spreadsheet is entered. Comment windows may either be set to be visible all the time or to pop up when the cursor is moved over the top of a cell containing a comment window. A cell with a comment window will have a small triangle in its upper left corner indicating the presence of a hidden comment window. A pop-up comment window is a useful tool by which to remember data codes when a questionnaire is not precoded. Comment windows are inserted by clicking Insert in the Menu bar and then clicking Comment. Figure 4.3 shows a spreadsheet with two comment windows activated.

These comment windows are not available in data entry forms. An alternative procedure is to enter the codes beside the field name. The codes will appear in the data entry form. See Figure 4.3 for an example of this method. In both methods, the availability of data codes on screen reduces the possibility of data entry error. Additionally, entering the data codes when the data are first entered saves time by avoiding recoding of text-based data (e.g., Married) into numerical data later.

The experimentation in spreadsheet data entry involves testing the ease with which data is transferred from the questionnaire to the spreadsheet. This involves entering data from several questionnaires to get a feel for the process. In a team project, everyone who will be entering data should try out the data entry spreadsheet to become familiar with the process. Evaluation of the data entry spreadsheet should include the following items: determination if all the necessary data codes are available; ensuring the column heading labels reflect the subject of the questionnaire items; checking that each item on the questionnaire has a column on the data entry spreadsheet; making sure everyone knows how and where to save data on the computer. This last item is particularly important. Saving the spreadsheet regularly, every five to ten minutes, and

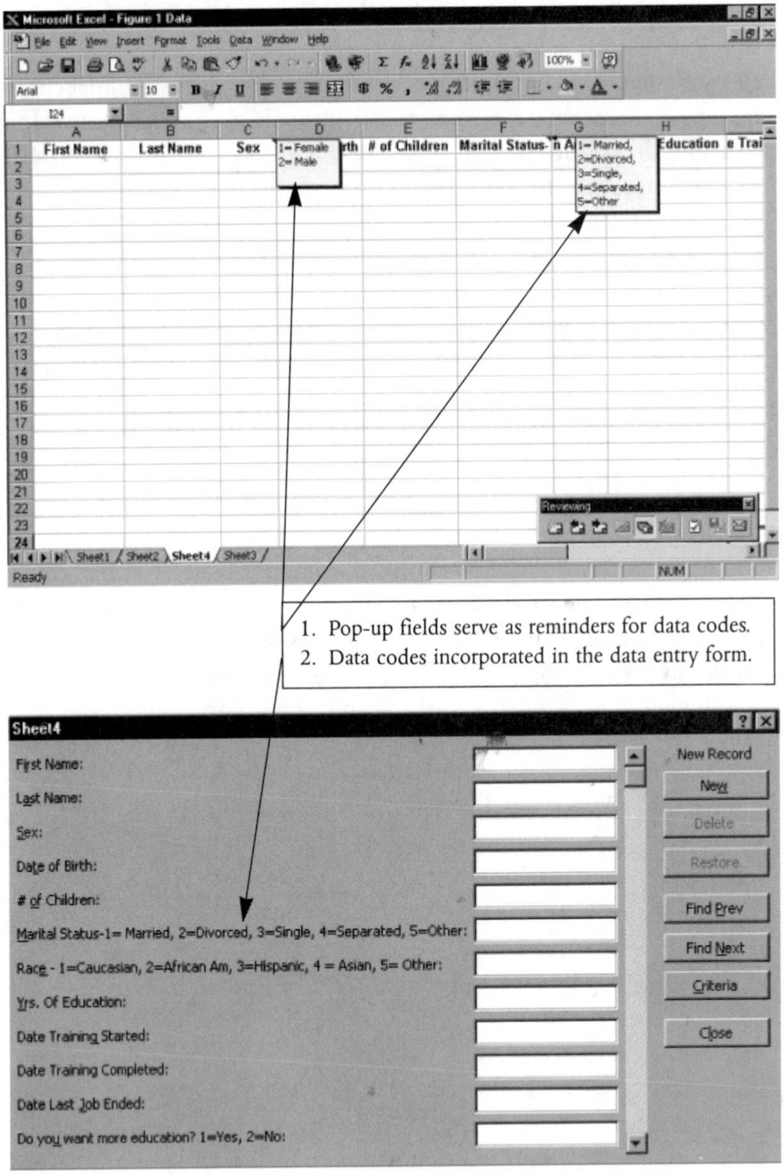

1. Pop-up fields serve as reminders for data codes.
2. Data codes incorporated in the data entry form.

FIGURE 4.3 Spreadsheet Data Entry Methods

to a directory where it may be easily located may prevent the considerable wailing and gnashing of teeth that inevitably follows the inadvertent loss of data.

Direct Data Entry

Interview surveys conducted face to face or telephone surveys require recording of participant responses. Often responses in face to face interviews or telephone surveys are recorded on paper and then rerecorded into a computer for data analysis. Direct data entry of survey responses into a database or spreadsheet saves time and effort. We have reviewed methods for creating a data entry form, expanding column width for short questions, and pop-up comment windows as reminders of numerical codes for variables.

In order to conduct face to face interviews or telephone surveys it is helpful to have the entire question, the possible responses, and their numerical codes visible. The following spreadsheet configuration makes this possible.

Configuring a spreadsheet for a direct entry survey requires the following steps.

1. Enlarge the height of the first row by moving the pointer on the line between rows 1 and 2 on the far left side of the spreadsheet, clicking and dragging the line down until the row reaches the desired height. The actual height and width of the cell will depend on the length of the question the cell will contain. The width of each column can be expanded by moving the pointer to the line between the column identification numbers, clicking, and dragging the column to the desired width.

2. Insert a text box into each of the cells of the first row for each of the items in the survey. Text boxes are usually available in the spreadsheet's Drawing Tools Toolbar. Check the spreadsheet's Help function if unsure of the location of the Text Box tool. Simply typing or pasting a question into the cell inserts the text as a single line, which necessitates creating very wide cells in order to see the entire question. A text box wraps the text to fit the size of the box.

3. In the order they appear on the survey, type or paste each question from the word processing file into the text boxes created in the first row.

4. Locate the split box at the top of the vertical scroll bar. The split box is a small, rectangular box. When the pointer is placed over the top of the split box, the cursor changes it to a bidirectional, up and down, arrow. After clicking on the box, drag it to the second row. This will keep the first row visible as data are entered into succeeding rows.

5. See Figure 4.4 for an example of a direct entry survey form created in a spreadsheet.

This method of configuring a spreadsheet for direct data entry is applicable for data collection purposes beyond interview surveys conducted face to face or telephone surveys. For instance, in social service agencies it is sometimes necessary to extract data from paper-based case records. Conducting this type of chart review by recording extracted information on a paper form and then entering it into a computer for analysis introduces unnecessary inefficiency to the process. Configuring a spreadsheet in the method described here, and then entering the requisite data from the charts directly into the computer eliminates the redundancy of recording data on paper and then rerecording it in the computer.

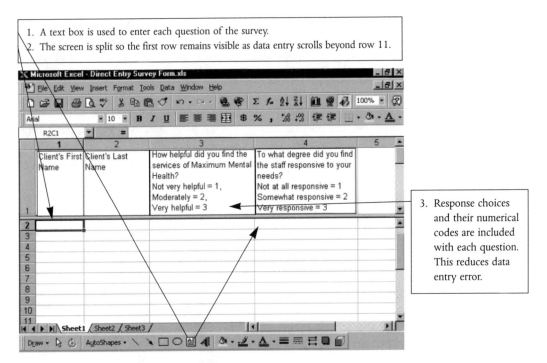

1. A text box is used to enter each question of the survey.
2. The screen is split so the first row remains visible as data entry scrolls beyond row 11.

3. Response choices and their numerical codes are included with each question. This reduces data entry error.

FIGURE 4.4   **Direct Entry Survey Form**

Data Analysis: Making Sense of It All

Whatever the purpose for which spreadsheets are employed in the collection of social service data, once the data are compiled in the spreadsheet, data analysis can begin. The process of data analysis involves data cleaning, production of descriptive statistics, graphs, and tables, and sometimes the use of inferential statistics (Royse, 1995; Rubin & Babbie, 1997; Weinbach & Grinnell, 1991; Williams, Unrau, & Grinnell, 1998). In recent years, with the increasingly wide availability of personal computers, social services workers in undergraduate and graduate education were taught to conduct data analysis with a range of statistical software packages. These statistical analysis programs include SPSS, Systat, SAS, StatView, and Jump. Unfortunately, social service workers often find themselves employed in practice settings in which they do not have access to statistical software packages. Spreadsheets are a widely available and relatively inexpensive alternative tool for a wide range of data analysis tasks including production of tables, graphics, and statistical analysis. In this section, we will examine how to conduct an array of data analysis procedures with spreadsheets.

Data Cleaning

Data cleaning is technically not a data analysis function, but instead a precursor of data analysis to ensure there were no errors made in the data entry (Rubin & Babbie,

1997). One issue is to ensure that each variable contains only values (numerical codes) specified for the attributes of the variable. For instance, Patterson and Lee (1998) in a study evaluating the use of intensive case management to prevent rehospitalization of severely and persistently mentally ill outpatients coded the variable rehospitalization as 1 = rehospitalization and 0 = no rehospitalization. Therefore, only the values 1 and 0 should appear in columns containing this variable. One simple way to check for data entry errors is to "eyeball" the data. This simply means to scroll down the column looking for values other than 1 or 0. For small data sets or when a variable has a very constricted range of values, this is often the quickest and most straightforward way to check for errors.

Another way to check for values in a variable outside the specified range is to sort the variable. Values outside the specified range will appear either at the top or bottom of the variable, depending on whether the variable is sorted in ascending or descending order. This method should be used with some caution. If only one variable in a data set is sorted, then the values in the variable will no longer be in the same row as the other variables for that case. This will render bivariate analysis meaningless. The alternative is to select the entire data set and then sort by one variable at a time, examining each variable for values outside of the expected range. To do this, once the entire data set is selected, click on Data (Microsoft Excel) or Tools (Quattro Pro), then click Sort. Select the column to sort and order to sort in, ascending or descending.

Still another way to examine variables for data errors is to create separate worksheets for each variable. Worksheets are created within the spreadsheet by clicking on the Insert command in the Menu bar and selecting Worksheet or Sheet, depending on spreadsheet manufacturer. Copy each variable into its own worksheet while leaving the original data set intact and unchanged. The advantage of doing this in checking for data errors is that it can facilitate the univariate analysis procedures described later. Once a variable is in its own worksheet, select the entire column by clicking on the letter at the top of the column. Sort the column by clicking on the Sort command under the Data or Tools command in the Menu bar. Then examine the column for values outside of the expected range.

The next method of data cleaning, construction of a frequency distribution, provides results that are useful also in univariate data analysis. A frequency distribution counts the number of times each value in a variable appears (Weinbach & Grinnell, 1991). To illustrate the construction of a frequency distribution, we return to some data from Patterson and Lee's (1998) study. Data were collected on how compliant each client was in taking medication prescribed for psychiatric symptomology. Case managers rated each client on a scale of 0 to 9, with 0 representing noncompliance and 9 indicating full compliance. We construct a frequency distribution to determine the number of cases at each level on the scale. We then sum the total number of cases counted by the frequency distribution procedure. If the sum is less than the total number of cases in the study, in this study $N = 196$, then we know the variable contains values outside the range of values in the variable. Again, if the total number of cases in the frequency distribution is less than the study's N, then a data error exists. The steps to construct a frequency distribution are outlined in Figure 4.5.

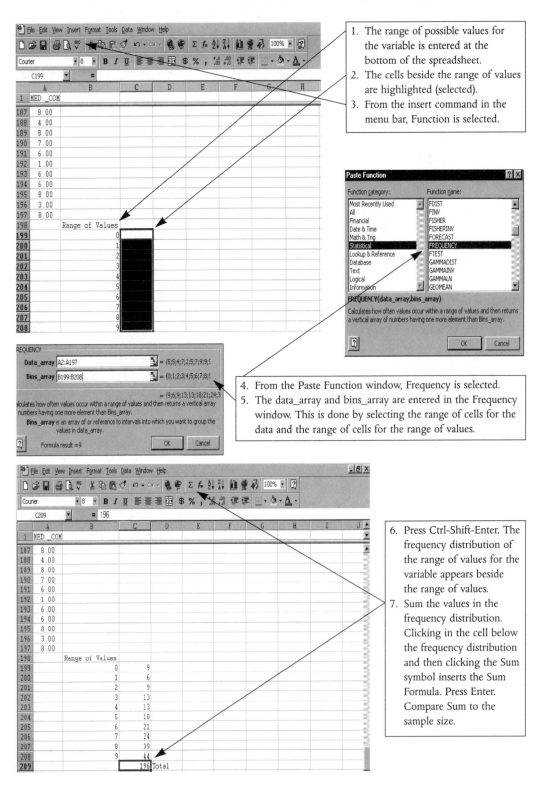

FIGURE 4.5 Frequency Distribution Creation

Simple Statistics (Not an Oxymoron!)

Descriptive Statistics

Descriptive statistics provide a description and summary of the variables in a data set (Rubin & Babbie, 1997; Weinbach & Grinnell, 1991; Williams, Unrau, & Grinnell, 1998). Descriptive statistics reduce the quantity and detail of information in a data set to a form in which it becomes manageable and understandable. Reporting the specifics of how each of 200 people surveyed responded to each item of a 40-question survey would be beyond the comprehension, much less the attention span of most people. Descriptive statistics are a means of reducing complexity and enumeration to a cognitively graspable format. We will examine three categories of descriptive statistics, univariate, bivariate, and multivariate.

Univariate Statistics: Frequency Distribution

Described in Figure 4.5 is the process for creating a frequency distribution with a spreadsheet. At times it is important to know not only the frequency count (absolute frequency) of each attribute or value in a variable, but also the cumulative frequency, the absolute percentage, and the cumulative percentage (Weinbach & Grinnell, 1991). These three descriptive statistics are readily computable with simple formulas in spreadsheet.

Formulas define the calculations the spreadsheet is to perform (Parsons, Oja, Auer, 1995). A formula is initiated by clicking on the cell in which the results of the calculation are to appear. Every formula has an operation symbol indicating to the spreadsheet the presence of a formula. In Microsoft Excel, the operation symbol that appears at the beginning of any formula is the equal sign (=), whereas Lotus 1-2-3 and Corel Quattro Pro use the "at" symbol (@). For instance, this formula in an Excel spreadsheet tells the application to add the numbers contained in the formula =45+56+75. In Lotus 1-2-3 and Quattro Pro the formula would be @SUM(45+56+75). Once the values are entered into the formula, pressing the Enter key returns the numerical result of the formula's calculations. Likewise, formulas can use values in other cells by entering their cell references into the formula. For example, in Spreadsheet Exhibit 4.2 the formula summing the three numbers could be expressed as =sum(B1+B2+B3) or as =sum(B1:B3). Column C contains a set of values that will be added with the formula in cell C4. Note that in both formulas the term sum follows the equal sign (=). Sum is a function. "A function is a special prewritten formula that provides a shortcut for commonly used calculations" (Parsons, Oja, Auer, 1995, p. 32). Examples of functions include Average, Standard Deviation, Random, and Median. Note also the use of a colon between B1 and B3 in the second formula. The colon tells the spreadsheet to include all the cells between B1 and B3. A colon in a formula is particularly useful when calculating a long series of values.

SPREADSHEET EXHIBIT 4.2
Simple Formula Example

	A	B	C
1		45	53
2		56	76
3		75	15
4	Sum	176	=sum(C1:C3)

To calculate the cumulative frequency, start by typing the first value of Absolute Frequency column into the Cumulative Frequency column. In this example the value is 9. Click the cell (C3) below the first value in the Cumulative Frequency column and start the formula, =sum(. Click the cell of the first value in the Cumulative Frequency column (9), type the plus sign (+), then click the second cell of the Absolute Frequency column (6), close the formula with a close parenthesis symbol), and hit Enter. The formula appearing in the formula bar is =sum(C2+B3) and the sum appearing in the cell (C3) is 15. Now copy the cell by clicking the cell and then selecting Edit, Copy from the menu bar. Copying the cell actually copies the formula. Select the remaining cells in the Cumulative Frequency column that have an Absolute Frequency value beside them. Pressing Enter will paste the formula into the selected cells and calculate the cumulative frequency for each cell. See Spreadsheet Exhibit 4.3 for the results.

To calculate an absolute percentage and a cumulative percentage frequency distribution with the data in Spreadsheet Exhibit 4.3 we will use two different formulas. To compute the absolute percentage, type the following formula into the first cell of the Absolute % column (E2), =sum(B2/196)*100, then hit the Enter key. Note that in this algebraic equation, we enclose B2/196 in parentheses, indicating to the spreadsheet that this calculation is performed first. The result of B2/192 then is multiplied by 100, producing a percentage. Remember, B2 refers to the value in the cell B2. The next step is to copy the formula in E2 and paste it into cells E3 through E11.

To calculate the cumulative percentage frequency distribution, we use the same process we used to calculate the cumulative frequency. Copy the value from cell E2 into cell F2. In cell F3 enter the formula =sum(F2+E3) and hit Enter. Now copy cell F3

SPREADSHEET EXHIBIT 4.3		Simple Formula Example	
	A	B	C	D
1	Range of Values	Absolute Freq.	Cumulative Freq.	
2	0	9	9	
3	1	6	15	
4	2	9	24	
5	3	13	37	
6	4	13	50	
7	5	18	68	
8	6	21	89	
9	7	24	113	
10	8	39	152	
11	9	44	196	

and paste it into cells F4 through F11. Upon hitting Enter, the cumulative frequency distribution appears in the spreadsheet. The results of the formulas for absolute and cumulative frequency distributions are in Spreadsheet Exhibit 4.4.

Univariate Statistics: Central Tendency and Dispersion

Measures of central tendency are commonly used to report information on the average, the most common, or the typical in the variable of interest (Rubin & Babbie, 1997; Weinbach & Grinnell, 1991; Williams, Unrau, & Grinnell, 1998). The three measures of central tendency are the mode, the median, and the mean. The mode is the most frequently occurring value of a variable. The median is the midpoint of the distribution of values in a variable. The mean, which is commonly referred to as the average, is the arithmetic average. Spreadsheet functions will calculate each of these measures of central tendency.

Dispersion refers to the degree to which values are distributed around some measure of central tendency. Dispersion is sometimes referred to as variability. Common measures of dispersion include the range, variance, and standard deviation. The range is composed of the maximum and minimum values in a variable (Rubin & Babbie, 1997). The variance is the sum of the squared deviations from the mean divided by the total number of cases minus 1 (Weinbach & Grinnell, 1991). The variance is not commonly reported in the social service research or practice literature. Perhaps the most widely used measure of dispersion is the standard deviation. The standard deviation of any variable is the square root of the variance. What is more important to understand

SPREADSHEET EXHIBIT 4.4   Absolute and Cumulative Percentage Frequency Distribution

	A	B	C	D	E	F
1	Range of Values	Absolute Freq.	Cumulative Freq.	Absolute %	Cumulative %	
2	0	9	9	4.59	4.59	
3	1	6	15	3.06	7.65	
4	2	9	24	4.59	12.24	
5	3	13	37	6.63	18.88	
6	4	13	50	6.63	25.51	
7	5	18	68	9.18	34.69	
8	6	21	89	10.71	45.41	
9	7	24	113	12.24	57.65	
10	8	39	152	19.90	77.55	
11	9	44	196	22.45	100.00	

is that when the values in a variable are normally distributed (in the shape of a normal curve), 68.6 percent of the values occur plus or minus one standard deviation from the mean. In this same normally distributed variable, 95.44 percent of the values are found within plus or minus two standard deviations from the mean (Rubin & Babbie, 1997). The standard deviation is a ready indicator of the degree to which values in a variable are clustered around the mean.

Values in a variable are not always normally distributed. Skewed distributions are commonly seen in social service data. The skewness of data indicates the degree of asymmetry of a distribution of values around the mean of the variable. A variable that is positively skewed to the right side of the distribution will form a tail extending further from the modal value than the left side. In negatively skewed distributions the tail will extend to the left. Remember, in a normal distribution the mode, mean, and median are the same value. In a positively skewed distribution the value of the mode is the lowest of the three, with the median higher and the mean the highest value of the three. The opposite is true for negatively skewed distributions. The Skew function in a spreadsheet indicates the degree and direction of the skewness of a distribution. Taken together, measures of central tendency, dispersion, and skew provide valuable information about the distribution of values in a variable. As a note of caution, remember that these measures are most appropriately used with continuous variables such as age, income, or years of education (Rubin & Babbie, 1997). The use of measures of central tendency, dispersion, and skew with discrete (nominal level) variables such as gender, diagnosis, or treatment group is inappropriate. Frequency distributions are more appropriate for discrete or categorical variables. Ordinal variables that measure rank order, such as degree of medication compliance, technically are appropriate only for mode as a descriptive statistic (Weinbach & Grinnell, 1991). Rubin and Babbie (1997) point out that this convention is commonly violated by the use of a mean to describe the "average" case. In Figure 4.6, all the measures of central tendency, dispersion, and skew are applied to the ordinal variable, Medication Compliance. This is a technical violation of the conventions of the mean, median, standard deviation, variance, and skew. Their use in Figure 4.6 illustrates their informative utility. The negative skew of values and their broad distribution in this variable are apparent by examining the full range of computed statistics in the figure.

Figure 4.6 also illustrates the steps in finding the modal value for the variable (Age) in the second column. These steps are applicable to each of the statistics labeled in the first column. Once the functions for each of the descriptive statistics is inserted into the cells adjoining the labels in the first column, calculating these statistics for the two other variables is a matter of copying and pasting. Copy cells B199 through B206. Then paste them into cells C199 through C206 and D199 through D206. The formulas automatically adjust their calculations to each of the new columns. This is illustrated in Spreadsheet Exhibit 4.5 which contains the formulas for the measures of central tendency and dispersion computed by the spreadsheet in Figure 4.6.

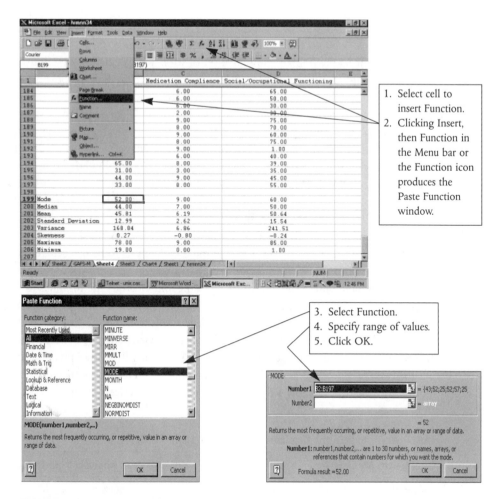

FIGURE 4.6   Measures of Central Tendency and Dispersion

SPREADSHEET EXHIBIT 4.5   Formulas for Measures of Central Tendency and Dispersion

	A	B	C	D
1	Mode	=MOD(B2:B197)	=MOD(C2:C197)	=MOD(D2:D197)
2	Median	=MEDIAN(B2:B197)	=MEDIAN(C2:C197)	=MEDIAN(D2:D197)
3	Mean	=AVERAGE(B2:B197)	=AVERAGE(C2:C197)	=AVERAGE(D2:D197)
4	Standard Deviation	=STDEV(B2:B197)	=STDEV(C2:C197)	=STDEV(D2:D197)
5	Variance	=VAR(B2:B197)	=VAR(C2:C197)	=VAR(D2:D197)
6	Skewness	=SKEW(B2:B197)	=SKEW(C2:C197)	=SKEW(D2:D197)
7	Maximum	=MAX(B2:B197)	=MAX(C2:C197)	=MAX(D2:D197)
8	Minimum	=MIN(B2:B197)	=MIN(C2:C197)	=MIN(D2:D197)

Data Analysis Tools

Most spreadsheets provide an alternative set of tools for calculating descriptive statistics and a wide range of other statistical procedures. These data analysis tools have much of the functionality of a standalone statistical software package. Table 4.1 contains a list of data analysis tools available in two popular spreadsheets. The collection of statistical procedures available in both spreadsheets contains tools for univariate, bivariate, and multivariate analysis. In Corel Quattro Pro, this set of data analysis tools is referred to as the Analysis Experts. It is accessed in the Menu bar under Tools, Numeric Tools, Analysis. In Microsoft Excel, the collection of data analysis tools is labeled Data Analysis. However, in Excel the data analysis tools are not initially configured in the available menu options. To add data analysis to the Excel menu, click on Tools in the Menu bar, then click on Add-Ins and select Analysis ToolPak. Excel then adds Data Analysis to the Tools menu. Clicking on Data Analysis makes available the data analysis tools listed in Table 4.1.

Note that both spreadsheet packages have a Descriptive Statistics option. Using this option to compute descriptive statistics saves time and effort as the formulas for each descriptive statistic (mean, median, mode, etc.) does not have to be entered into the spreadsheet. Figure 4.7 shows the windows that appear in Quattro Pro and Excel when their data analysis tools are accessed. In Figure 4.7, the steps to generate descriptive statistics for both programs are specified. Spreadsheet Exhibit 4.6 contains the Descriptive Statistics output for two variables, age and GAFS-M (a measure of social and occupational functioning). In Spreadsheet Exhibit 4.6 it is evident that the Descriptive Statistics tool provides

TABLE 4.1   Excel and Quattro Pro Data Analysis Tools

Excel's Data Analysis Tools	Quattro Pro's Analysis Experts Tool
Anova: Single Factor	Advanced Regression
Anova: Two-Factor With Replication	Amortization Schedule
Anova: Two-Factor Without Replication	ANOVA: One-Way
Correlation	ANOVA: Two-Way with Replication
Covariance	ANOVA: Two-Way without Replication
Descriptive Statistics	Correlation
Exponential Smoothing	Covariance
F-Test Two-Sample for Variances	Descriptive Statistics
Fourier Analysis	Exponential Smoothing
Histogram	Fourier
Moving Average	*F*-Test
Random Number Generation	Histogram
Rank and Percentile	Mortgage Refinancing
Regression	Moving Average
Sampling	Random Number
t-Test: Paired Two Sample for Means	Rank and Percentile
t-Test: Two-Sample Assuming Equal Variances	Sampling
t-Test: Two-Sample Assuming Unequal Variances	*t*-Tests
z-Test: Two Sample for Means	*z*-Test

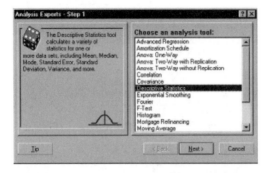 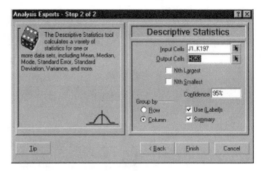

GAFS-M		MED._COM	
Mean	50.64	Mean	6.18
Standard Error	1.11	Standard Error	0.19
Median	50	Median	7
Mode	60	Mode	9
Standard Deviation	15.54	Standard Deviation	2.62
Variance	241.51	Variance	6.87
Kurtosis	-0.18	Kurtosis	-0.39
Skewness	-0.24	Skewness	-0.79
Range	84	Range	9
Minimum	1	Minimum	0
Maximum	85	Maximum	9
Sum	9925	Sum	1212
Count	196	Count	196
Confidence Level(0.950000)	2.18	Confidence Level(0.950000)	0.37

Corel's Quattro Pro Analysis Experts Tool for Statistical Analysis.

1. Open the tool by selecting Tools in the Menu bar, then select Numeric Tools, and then select Analysis.
2. In the window Analysis Experts – Step 1, select Descriptive Statistics.
3. In Step 2, specify Input Cells (range) and Output Cells.
4. The table to the left contains the results.

Data Analysis

Analysis Tools

- Anova: Single Factor
- Anova: Two-Factor With Replication
- Anova: Two-Factor Without Replication
- Correlation
- Covariance
- Descriptive Statistics
- Exponential Smoothing
- F-Test Two-Sample for Variances
- Fourier Analysis
- Histogram

OK   Cancel   Help

Descriptive Statistics

Input
Input Range: $J$1:$K$197
Grouped By: ⊙ Columns ○ Rows
☑ Labels in First Row

Output options
○ Output Range:
⊙ New Worksheet Ply:
○ New Workbook
☐ Summary statistics
☐ Confidence Level for Mean: 95 %
☐ Kth Largest: 1
☐ Kth Smallest: 1

OK   Cancel   Help

GAFS_M		MED._COM	
Mean	50.63776	Mean	6.18
Standard Error	1.110052	Standard Error	0.19
Median	50	Median	7
Mode	60	Mode	9
Standard Deviation	15.54073	Standard Deviation	2.62
Sample Variance	241.5143	Sample Variance	6.87
Kurtosis	-0.18418	Kurtosis	-0.39
Skewness	-0.23569	Skewness	-0.79
Range	84	Range	9
Minimum	1	Minimum	0
Maximum	85	Maximum	9
Sum	9925	Sum	1212
Count	196	Count	196

Microsoft Excel's Data Analysis Tool for Statistical Analysis.

1. Open the tool by selecting Tools in the Menu bar, select Data Analysis.
2. In the window Data Analysis, select Descriptive Statistics.
3. In the window Descriptive Statistics, specify the Input Range and Output option.
4. The table to the left contains the results.

FIGURE 4.7   Descriptive Statistics Produced with Spreadsheet Data Analysis Tools

SPREADSHEET EXHIBIT 4.6   Descriptive Statistics Produced by Excel's Data Analysis Tool

	A	B	C	D
1	GAFS_M		AGE	
2	Mean	50.64	Mean	45.81
3	Standard Error	1.11	Standard Error	0.93
4	Median	50.00	Median	44.00
5	Mode	60.00	Mode	52.00
6	Standard Deviation	15.54	Standard Deviation	12.99
7	Sample Variance	241.51	Sample Variance	168.84
8	Kurtosis	−0.18	Kurtosis	−0.78
9	Skewness	−0.24	Skewness	0.27
10	Range	84.00	Range	59.00
11	Minimum	1.00	Minimum	19.00
12	Maximum	85.00	Maximum	78.00
13	Sum	9925.00	Sum	8979.00
	Count	196.00	Count	196.00

a comprehensive array of descriptive statistics, perhaps more than many users find necessary, informative, or essential. In such a case, rows in the resultant table in the spreadsheet may be deleted in order to use only those statistics germane to the task at hand.

Bivariate Analysis

The purpose of bivariate analysis is examination of the relationship between two variables. Spreadsheets provide a number of powerful tools for bivariate analysis. These tools include tables, statistics, and visual representations of the relationship between variables. In this section we examine the statistics and methods for production of tables that can specify bivariate relationships. Chapter 6 details the procedures to visually represent bivariate relationships with charts and graphs.

Tables are a means to collapse and summarize data in order to understand the relationships between variables (Weinbach & Grinnell, 1991). Tables are a useful way to communicate to interested parties how two factors (variables) relate to one another. For instance, a treatment facility might want to know if there is any difference in the racial composition of two groups of clients who were assigned to different treatment programs. To answer this question, we construct a table based on two variables, race and treatment group. These tables are sometimes referred to as contingency tables or cross tabulation tables. For reasons that are not readily apparent from reading the manual, Microsoft Excel refers to them as Pivot Tables. Most other spreadsheet programs call them cross-tab or cross tabulation tables. Whatever the name, spreadsheets offer tools for the rapid creation of tables. To find the table generation tool in most spreadsheets, simply click on the Help button and type "cross-tab" in the search or find function.

Figure 4.8 depicts the steps in creating a table with the Pivot Table Wizard in Excel. In the Menu Bar under Data, select Pivot Table Wizard. Selecting Pivot Table Report causes a series of screens to appear requesting information. In Step 1, select the source of the data for analysis. In this case, the data are in a spreadsheet. In Step 2, provide the range of the data. The range of data is the columns and rows containing the two or three variables intended for summarization in the cross tabulation table. If the range of the data is selected before opening the Pivot Table Wizard, this data range will appear in the Range box. The variables specified in the data range need to be in adjoining columns. In other words, a variable in column A and column D cannot be selected for the data range. If the variables are not adjoining, insert a column beside one of the variables, then cut or copy the second variable and paste it into the newly inserted column. If the data range is not selected prior to starting the Pivot Table Wizard, then in Step 2, click the icon to the right of the Range box. The Step 2 window will disappear and the spreadsheet containing the data becomes visible. Select the columns and rows (range) containing data intended for summarization in the table. Click the Range icon and the Step 2 window reappears. Click Next and the Step 3 window appears. In Step 3, drag the field buttons (variables names) on the right side of the window into the diagram indicating whether the variable is to be in a row or a column in the table. Drag into the Data section of the diagram the field button (variable name) to be summarized. In Step 4, specify the intended location of the resultant cross tabulation (Pivot) table in either a new worksheet or in an existing worksheet. If the existing worksheet option is selected, click the Range icon and then indicate where in the existing worksheet to place the table.

Note that in Step 3 there are several options for summarization including sum, count, and average. The summarization option selected is dependent on the intended purpose of the summarization. Using Count provides the observed frequencies in the respective categories. In Figure 4.8, two methods for displaying summarized data, as frequency counts and as column percentages, are outlined. We are now able to answer the question posed earlier as to whether there were any differences between programs in terms of their racial composition. Examination of the column percentages of the second table in Figure 4.8 shows there were no noteworthy differences between the two treatment programs in racial make up.

The bivariate tables in Figure 4.8 are composed of two variables with nominal level data. Nominal data classifies attributes into two or more categories that are mutually exclusive (Weinbach & Grinnell, 1991). There are times when it is informative to create tables composed of one nominal level variable, such as treatment group, and a variable that measures some form of ranking, such as degree of medication compliance. Variables that measure ranking are referred to as ordinal variables. Tables composed of a nominal and ordinal variable allow for the comparison of group differences across ranking. Spreadsheet Exhibit 4.7 displays a comparison of differences between treatment

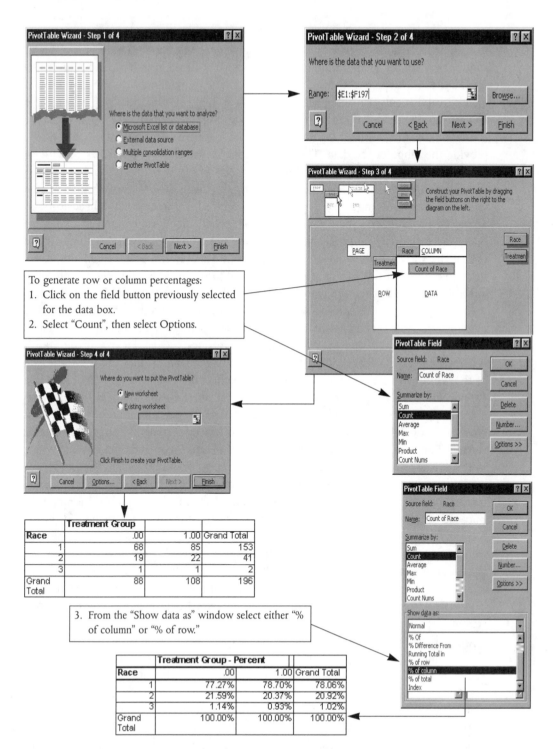

To generate row or column percentages:
1. Click on the field button previously selected for the data box.
2. Select "Count", then select Options.

3. From the "Show data as" window select either "% of column" or "% of row."

	Treatment Group		
Race	.00	1.00	Grand Total
1	68	85	153
2	19	22	41
3	1	1	2
Grand Total	88	108	196

	Treatment Group - Percent		
Race	.00	1.00	Grand Total
1	77.27%	78.70%	78.06%
2	21.59%	20.37%	20.92%
3	1.14%	0.93%	1.02%
Grand Total	100.00%	100.00%	100.00%

FIGURE 4.8   Cross Tabulation Table Production

SPREADSHEET EXHIBIT 4.7   Degree of Medication Compliance across Treatment Groups

	A	B	C	D
1		Treatment Group		
2	Medication Compliance	.00	1.00	Grand Total
3	.00	3.41%	4.63%	4.08%
4	1.00	5.68%	0.93%	3.06%
5	2.00	6.82%	2.78%	4.59%
6	3.00	13.64%	0.93%	6.63%
7	4.00	7.95%	5.56%	6.63%
8	5.00	5.68%	12.04%	9.18%
9	6.00	11.36%	11.11%	11.22%
10	7.00	13.64%	11.11%	12.24%
11	8.00	13.64%	25.00%	19.90%
12	9.00	18.18%	25.93%	22.45%
13	Grand Total	100.00%	100.00%	100.00%

groups across levels of medication compliance. In this table, zero means nonapplicable (not on medication), 1 is the lowest level of medication compliance and 9 the highest. By examining the column percentages in this spreadsheet generated cross tabulation table, we quickly see that the treatment group labeled 0 has lower levels of medication compliance than the treatment group labeled 1.

Bivariate Statistics

CHI-SQUARE.   One of the most frequently used bivariate statistics in the social services profession is chi-square (Weinbach & Grinnell, 1991). Chi-square is used with cross tabulation tables to determine if the values in the table (observed values) are significantly different than would be expected by chance. Returning to the question addressed in Figure 4.8, we might want to statistically test whether there is a significant difference between the two different treatment programs in their racial composition. We conduct a chi-square test to refute chance as an explanation of the distribution of values in the cross tabulation table and establish whether a relationship exists between treatment programs and the distribution of racial groups in their client population.

Unlike the other bivariate statistics we will survey in this section, we cannot use the spreadsheet data analysis tools previously described. As such, the process of conducting a chi-square test requires a series of steps. First, to use chi-square, the two variables of interest must be nominal level variables. Tests of the relationship between two variables measured at the ordinal, interval, or ratio level require other statistical procedures. Once it is determined that the two variables of interest are nominal variables, the next step is to produce a cross tabulation table. Follow the steps in Figure 4.8 to construct the table of the two variables.

The next step is to find the expected values for the cells in the table. The chi-square formula (CHITEST) in both Excel and Quattro Pro requires insertion of the expected values. The formula to find the expect value for each cell in the table is (R * C)/N, where R equals the sum of all values in the cell's row and C equals the sum of all values in the cell's column (Weinbach & Grinnell, 1991). In Spreadsheet Exhibit 4.8, the expected values for the Treatment Group by Race table were found by applying the expected values formula to a two-by-three block of cells below the Observed Frequency Table using the row and column totals from the Observed Frequency Table. For instance, in cell B11 the following formula was inserted: =(D3*B6)/196. In essence, this formula means to find the expected value for the cell B3, multiply the row total (153) by the column total (108), then divide by the total number of clients (196). In Spreadsheet Exhibit 4.8, the formulas to calculate the expected value for each of the cells in the Observed Frequency Table are in bold and the actual expected frequency is the value in the cell that is not in bold. Normally, once the formula is entered into the cell, only the returned value of the formula is present. The formulas are included here for illustrative purposes. In examining the formulas computing the expected frequencies, it is important to attend to the fact that the formula in each cell is different. Each for-

SPREADSHEET EXHIBIT 4.8 Chi-Square Test			
	A	B	C	D
1	Observed Freq.	Treatment Group		
2	Race	1.00	2.00	Grand Total
3	1	85	68	153
4	2	22	19	41
5	3	1	1	2
6	Grand Total	108	88	196
7				
8				
9	Expected Freq.	Treatment Group		
10	Race	1.00	2.00	
11	1	84 =(D3*B6)/196	69 =(D3*C6)/196	
12	2	23 =(D4*B6)/196	18 =(D4*C6)/196	
13	3	1 =(D5*B6)/196	1 =(D5*C6)/196	
14				
15		Chi-square		
16		Probability	0.97	

mula refers to the row and column totals of the Observed Frequency cell for which it calculates the Expected Frequency.

The final step in computing the chi-square is inserting the CHITEST formula in the spreadsheet and specifying the range for the observed frequencies and the expected frequencies. For instance, the formula for chi-square in Spreadsheet Exhibit 4.8 is =CHITEST(B3:C5,B11:C13). In the formula, B3:C5 refers to the observed frequencies and B11:C13 designates the range of the expected frequencies. The CHITEST formula computes the probability that the two variables are independent. In Spreadsheet Exhibit 4.8 the chi-square probability is 0.97, indicating differences in the two treatment programs in racial composition are likely due only to chance. It is important to note that CHITEST does not return the actual chi-square value, nor the degrees of freedom. Instead, the chi-square value and the degrees of freedom are calculated and the chi-square probability is displayed. This saves the step of having to look in the chi-square value and degrees of freedom in a Chi-Square Table to find the probability value.

PEARSON'S r. A second bivariate statistical procedure of common utility in the social services is the Pearson's product moment correlation coefficient. Generally referred to as the Pearson's r, it is a measure of the degree to which two variables are related or correlated in a linear fashion. Values of the Pearson's r range from -1.0 to 1.0, with negative values indicating a negative correlation and positive values indicating a positive correlation. Pearson r values approaching 0 indicate a weak to nonexistent association or correlation between variables while values approaching either -1.0 or 1.0 suggest a strong correlation. Variables used in a Pearson's r correlation test must be either interval or ratio level variables (Weinbach & Grinnell, 1991). Interval data are "a type of data that has all three properties of numbers: identity, order, and additivity. Interval data have known and equal distances between score units and also have an arbitrary zero" (Drew & Hardman, 1985, p. 294). Examples of interval data include temperature measured on the Fahrenheit (F) or centigrade (C) scale, the numbering of years in calendar time, or IQ. Ratio data, on the other hand, is defined as having the three properties of interval data, identity, order, and additivity, in addition to having a zero point that is not arbitrary. Examples of ratio data are age, height, weight, and time as measured from a specified starting point (time zero).

To compute the Pearson's r for two interval or ratio level variables, click on an empty cell in which to insert the formula. In the spreadsheet's menu bar click on Insert, Function and in the Paste Function window, select Pearson from the Statistical category of functions. In the dialog window that appears, specify the ranges of the two variables. Excel uses the term "array" for range, but the function of defining the cells from which to compute the statistic is the same. Spreadsheet Exhibit 4.9 displays the bottom of a spreadsheet, the last 13 cases (N=196), in which the Pearson's r is calculated for two variables. In this example, Pearson's r measures the correlation between the number of months case managers worked with clients and the clients' level of social and occupational functioning as measured by the global assessment of functioning

SPREADSHEET EXHIBIT 4.9   Pearson's r, R^2 and F-Test Probability

	A	B	C	D
1			5.00	50.00
2			18.00	30.00
3			7.00	30.00
4			4.00	75.00
5			6.00	70.00
6			12.00	60.00
7			12.00	75.00
8			28.00	50.00
9			4.00	40.00
10			4.00	39.00
11	Pearson's r	0.12	8.00	35.00
12	r^2	0.014	14.00	45.00
13	F-test probability	0.03	4.00	55.00

scale-modified (GAFS-M) (Goldman, Skodol, & Lave, 1992). The formula is =PEARSON(D2:D197,E2:E197). In this formula, PEARSON is the statistical procedure, D2:D197 is the range of values for the variable Months of TX (treatment) and E2:E197 is the range of values for the variable GAFS-M. The formula produces a Pearson's r correlation coefficient of $r = 0.12$, a small level of correlation in social service research (Cohen, 1977).

Beyond determining the extent of correlation between two variables, we often want to know the amount of variance in a dependent variable explained by an independent variable. The independent variable is the variable that is believed to influence or act upon the dependent variable. The dependent variable, conversely, is the variable that is acted upon or influenced by the independent variable or variables. In this case, we wish to determine the amount of variation in social and occupational functioning as measured by GAFS-M that is explained by Months of TX (treatment) with a case manager. If we square the Pearson's r, the resulting r^2 represents the proportion of the dependent variable's variance explained by influence of the independent variable. In this case, the r^2 was calculated with the formula =(0.12*0.12). Alternatively, the formula =(D199*D199), where D199 is the cell reference for Pearson's r in Spreadsheet Exhibit 4.9, produces the same result $r^2 = 0.014$. This r^2 is interpreted to mean that only 1.4 percent of the variance in social and occupational functioning of this group of clients is explained by the number of months of treatment they have received from their case managers.

In order to know if the correlation between Months of Tx and GAFS-M is statistically significant, we use the F-test formula to determine the probability that the observed relationship is not due to chance. From the Insert command in the menu bar, Function is selected, and then in the Paste Function window, FTEST is selected from the Statistical category. In Spreadsheet Exhibit 4.9, the resultant formula is =FTEST(D2:D197,E2:E197), where FTEST is the statistical procedure and D2:D197,E2:E197 designates the ranges of the tested variables. In this example, the formula yielded an F probability of 0.03, indicating that the probability that the observed correlation between the two variables was due to chance is less than or equal to 3 percent.

t TEST.   The t test is a widely used procedure that is applicable in determining if there are statistically significant differences between two groups. A slightly different form of the *t* test is used with one group to test change from pretest to posttest and other paired data (e.g., husband/wife). To use the *t* test, one variable must be a dichotomous level variable, such as Group 1/Group 2 or Pretest/Posttest. The second variable must be measured at either the interval or ratio level, such as level of social and occupational functioning, or days to rehospitalization. One of the strengths of the *t* test is that it can be used with samples as small as 20 (Weinbach & Grinnell, 1991). Drew and Hardman (1985) suggest the *t* test can be used with samples as small as 12. It should be noted that so small a sample dramatically limits the ability of the statistic to detect a significant difference between the two groups. Despite this limitation, a second strength is that when comparing two groups, the *N*'s of the groups do not have to be equal.

Quattro Pro and Excel offer three methods to compute a *t* test: (1) Paired Two Sample for Means, (2) Two-Sample Assuming Equal Variances, and (3) Two-Sample Assuming Unequal Variances. The selection of the proper method depends on the type of data intended for analysis. The Paired Two Sample for Means is used when a sample group is measured before and after some type of treatment, test, or other event in which pre- and postmeasurement is conducted. This test is often referred to as the *t* test for nonindependent means (Drew & Hardman, 1985). For instance, in a group psychotherapy training group, one might measure the level of group satisfaction at the beginning and end of the group to evaluate the extent of change. The Two-Sample Assuming Equal Variances is used when testing the difference in means of two groups when the sample size is less than 30 (Kachigan, 1986). This type of *t* test is often referred to as a small sample *t* test for independent means. This test might be applied if one wished to determine whether two treatment groups differ in terms of their mean level of group experience satisfaction after 15 weeks of sessions. The third method of computing the *t* test is the Two-Sample Assuming Unequal Variances. This test also is a *t* test for independent means. It is used when the sample size is greater than 30. An example of this method's application is determining if the social and occupational functioning as measured by GAFS-M of two treatment groups is significantly different.

All three of these methods of computing *t* test are available in both Quattro Pro and Excel through their Data Analysis Tools. The procedure for conducting a Paired Two Sample for Means *t* test is illustrated in Figure 4.9. In this example, data were collected in a group psychotherapy training group using an instrument that measures group member satisfaction across a number of dimensions including trust in the group, honesty, group cohesion, leader involvement, and respect. The Paired Two Sample for Means *t* test is employed here to determine if there was a significant change in group members' overall satisfaction with the group from the end of the first group to the end of the last group.

The steps to compute the *t* test for Two-Sample Assuming Equal Variances and for the Two-Sample Assuming Unequal Variances are the same as those specified in Figure 4.9. Unlike the Paired Two Sample for Means, these two *t* tests are appropriate for comparing two different groups on a common measure, such as social and occupational functioning. The only difference in the steps for computing either of these two measures is selecting the appropriate *t* test in the Data Analysis window. Remember, the Two-Sample Assuming Equal Variances is used when the sample *N* is equal to or less than 30.

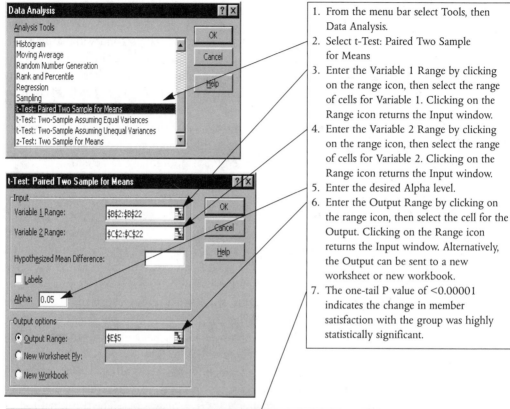

1. From the menu bar select Tools, then Data Analysis.
2. Select t-Test: Paired Two Sample for Means
3. Enter the Variable 1 Range by clicking on the range icon, then select the range of cells for Variable 1. Clicking on the Range icon returns the Input window.
4. Enter the Variable 2 Range by clicking on the range icon, then select the range of cells for Variable 2. Clicking on the Range icon returns the Input window.
5. Enter the desired Alpha level.
6. Enter the Output Range by clicking on the range icon, then select the cell for the Output. Clicking on the Range icon returns the Input window. Alternatively, the Output can be sent to a new worksheet or new workbook.
7. The one-tail P value of <0.00001 indicates the change in member satisfaction with the group was highly statistically significant.

FIGURE 4.9   Steps in Creating a *t* Test for a Paired Two Sample for Means

In order to conduct a *t* test comparing two groups it is sometimes necessary to copy the variable identifying the two groups (the nominal variable) and the variable of comparison (the interval or ratio variable) from the larger data set in which the information is compiled. For example, we may wish to compare the level of social and occupational functioning of mentally ill clients in two treatment programs, intensive case management (ICM) and general outpatient care (GOC). The two variables of interest are Treatment Program (1 = ICM, 2 = GOC) and level of social and occupational functioning, which has the variable name GAFS-M. These two variables are contained in a larger data set of clinical information on 196 outpatients served by a community mental health center.

Since the *N* of the sample is greater than 30, the Two-Sample Assuming Equal Variances *t* test is the appropriate statistic. To conduct this analysis, we must first extract the two variables from the larger data set. To do this, we open the spreadsheet containing the data set. Select the variable Treatment Program by clicking on the letter at the top of the column. This highlights the entire column. Copy the column with the Copy command found under Edit in the menu bar. As previously stated, both Excel and Quattro Pro have multiple spreadsheet (worksheet) pages available in an open workbook (spreadsheet) file. Click on one of the lettered tabs at the bottom of the page to display another worksheet. Paste the variable into the sheet by clicking on the first cell in the first column of the first row (cell A1) and then selecting the Paste command from Edit in the menu bar. Return to the data set by clicking on the tab for it. This is generally Sheet 1. We repeat these steps and copy the second variable, in this case GAFS-M, into the worksheet where we deposited the first variable. Essentially, what we are doing here is copying the variables out of their original data set in order to conduct the *t* test without risking inadvertently sorting or altering the original data set.

The next step is to select the two variables, then using the Sort command, described above, sort the two variables on the variable that identifies the two groups, in this case Treatment Program. Sorting the variables in this way results in the GAFS-M (social and occupational functioning) scores for the clients in the Intensive Case Management being grouped together in the GAFS-M variable and the scores of the clients in General Outpatient Care being grouped together. This sorting of scores into the two client groups is necessary in order to specify the appropriate ranges of the scores of the two groups when conducting the *t* test with the Data Analysis tool. As is evident in Figure 4.9, in the third step, we input the range of scores for the first variable. In this case, since the scores are all in the same variable, but sorted by group, we input the range of scores for the first group. In the fourth step, for Variable 2, we input the range of scores for the second group. To complete the *t* test, we follow the remaining steps as described in Figure 4.9. Spreadsheet Exhibit 4.10 contains the results of this *t* test which indicate, based on the one-tail P value of $< = 0.002$, that there is a strong statistically significant difference between the two treatment groups in social and occupational functioning.

ANOVA.   There are times when we wish to compare the means of three or more groups. In such situations, a *t* test is inappropriate as it is limited to use with two groups. The

SPREADSHEET EXHIBIT 4.10 *t* Test:
Two-Sample Assuming Unequal Variances

		A	B	C
			GOC	*ICM*
1				
2	Mean		46.69	54.31
3	Variance		212.81	217.71
4	Observations		88	108
5	Hypothesized Mean Difference		0	
6	df		187	
7	t Stat		−3.62	
8	P(T< = t) one-tail		0.0002	
9	t Critical one-tail		1.65	
10	P(T< = t) two-tail		0.0004	
11	t Critical two-tail		1.97	

alternative is an ANOVA, or analysis of variance. The ANOVA is used to test the relationship between a nominal level independent variable, such as diagnostic group, and a dependent variable, for instance, social and occupational functioning (Rubin & Babbie, 1997; Weinbach & Grinnell, 1991). We use an ANOVA when we want to know the probability that the observed differences between groups on the dependent variable are due to chance.

When the data analysis question of interest involves a single independent variable with three or more categories and a dependent variable, a one-way ANOVA is the analysis of variance procedure to use. Let us assume that we want to know if, in a sample of mentally ill outpatient clients, there is a statistically significant difference between individuals in different diagnostic groups in their level of social and occupational functioning, as measured by the GAFS-M. We use a spreadsheet cross tabulation procedure in order to produce a table that displays mean level of social and occupational functioning for each group. Spreadsheet Exhibit 4.11 contains the results of this cross tabulation. Examining Spreadsheet Exhibit 4.11, it is apparent that there are differences between the groups in GAFS-M levels, however the cross tabulation does not reveal if these differences are greater than would be expected by chance. To determine this we will use a one-way ANOVA.

Both Quattro Pro and Excel provide in their data analysis tools, procedures for conducting one-way ANOVAs. However, two separate tests of the results of a one-way ANOVA conducted with both of these spreadsheets compared to the findings of the same analyses using SPSS 7.5 revealed output errors for both spreadsheets. These errors may be due to the fact that neither spreadsheet allows for the specification of

**SPREADSHEET EXHIBIT 4.11   Cross Tabulation
of Social and Occupational Functioning
by Diagnostic Group**

	A	B	C	D	E	F
1		Diagnostic Group				
2		1.00	2.00	3.00	4.00	Overall Mean
3	Mean GAFS-M	49.84	52.88	54.62	52.10	50.89

1 = Schizophrenia, 2 = Depressive Disorders, 3 = Organic Disorders, 4 = Other

the dependent variable, in this case GAFS-M. As a result, there were output errors in all values including degrees of freedom (df). Readers choosing to use the one-way ANOVA from the analysis tools in either spreadsheet may want to compare their results with the results of running the one-way ANOVA in a statistical package.

The following is an alternative computational method for running a one-way ANOVA. The Regression Tool, in the data analysis tools, produces an analysis of variance as part of its output. Before using the Regression Tool some consideration of how the independent variable is coded is required. In order for the regression analysis procedure to properly compute the analysis of variance and regression statistics, the single independent variable that labels three or more groups must be converted to dummy variables. A dummy variable is a dichotomous (1 or 0) representation of an attribute in a categorical variable. In this case, our independent variable is a diagnostic group, where the coding of four categories is 1 = schizophrenia, 2 = affective disorders, 3 = organic disorders, and 4 = other. For the purpose of conducting the regression analysis we convert in the spreadsheet these four categories into three dummy variables. The rule for deciding how many dummy variables to create is $n - 1$, where n is the number of attributes or categories in the original variable.

To create the dummy variables, insert a column into the spreadsheet adjacent to the original categorical variable for each dummy variable to be created. In this example, three dummy variables are needed, so three columns are inserted. Next type a label into the top row of each dummy variable assigning a name to the variable. In this case DxGroup1, DxGroup2, and DxGroup3 are used. Next, in order to assign the proper value (0 or 1) to each cell in the three variables, we create three formulas using a logical function. A logical function evaluates whether a condition is true or false and then returns a specified value. In the first cell of the first dummy variable (B2) insert the formula =IF(A2=1,1,0). In essence, this formula makes the following logical argument: If the value in cell A2 is equal to 1, then return the value 1 to this cell (B2), but if the value in cell A2 is not equal to 1, then return the value 0 to this cell (B2). This formula in B2 is now copied and pasted into cells C2 and D2, appearing in the cells as =IF(B2=1,1,0) and =IF(C2=1,1,0), respectively. In order for the formulas to properly assign the correct values to their cells, they must be modified to reference column A, where the value of interest is, and their logical arguments must be adjusted so each formula discerns the proper critical value for each column (dummy variable). In this case the formula in cell C2 becomes =IF(A2=2,1,0) and for D2 the formula becomes =IF(A2=3,1,0). Note that both formulas evaluate the value in column A, the original nominal level variable, returning 0 or 1 depending on whether the condition in the argument is met. The final step in this procedure is to copy cells B2:D2 and paste these formulas into all the cells adjacent to the values in the original variable. In this case, the formulas are pasted into the following range, B3:D197. In doing this, the spreadsheet automatically performs the logical function in the formula and assigns the proper value to each cell. Spreadsheet Exhibit 4.12 contains the results of this procedure for

SPREADSHEET EXHIBIT 4.12   Dummy Variables for Diagnostic Group

	A	B	C	D
	Dx Group	Dx Group 1	Dx Group 2	Dx Group 3
1	Dx Group	Dx Group 1	Dx Group 2	Dx Group 3
2	2	0	1	0
3	1	1	0	0
4	1	1	0	0
5	1	1	0	0
6	1	1	0	0
7	1	1	0	0
8	1	1	0	0
9	1	1	0	0
10	1	1	0	0
11	2	0	1	0
12	1	1	0	0
13	1	1	0	0
14	4	0	0	0

cells B2:D14. Note that cell A14 that has the value 4 is represented as 0 in row 14 of columns B, C, and D. We create only three dummy variables to represent four categories because the Regression procedure will recognize in its calculations the absence of 1 in any of the three dummy variables as a fourth category, as in row 14 of Spreadsheet Exhibit 4.12.

To begin the Regression analysis in Quattro Pro, from the menu bar select Tools, Numeric Tools, Regression. In Excel's menu bar select Tools, Data Analysis, then Regression. In both spreadsheets, the user is required to specify the Input Y Range, which is the range of the dependent variable: in this case GAFS-M. The next step is to enter the X input range, which is the range of the independent variables. For the purpose of this analysis of variance with the Regression tool, select the range of the dummy variables just created. If the first row containing the variable labels (names) were included in either the Y or X input range, click Labels so the spreadsheet recognizes the first row in the range as a variable label. The output range can be specified as a range of blank cells in the spreadsheet containing the data. Clicking a single cell is sufficient if there are no other values nearby. The two other options are to click New Worksheet ply, which sends the results to another worksheet, and New Workbook, which sends the results to a new spreadsheet.

SPREADSHEET EXHIBIT 4.13   One-way ANOVA of Diagnostic Group (DX Group) by Social and Occupational Functioning (GAFS-M)

	A	B	C	D	E	F
1	ANOVA					
2		df	SS	MS	F	Significance F
3	Regression	3	627.83	209.28	0.91	0.44
4	Residual	192	43991.70	229.12		
5	Total	195	44619.53			

Spreadsheet Exhibit 4.13 contains the results of the one-way ANOVA testing the difference in social and occupational functioning of clients in the four diagnostic groups of our sample. The P value of 0.44 indicates that the differences between the four diagnostic groups in their level of social and occupational functioning likely is due to chance. Stated another way, for this group of clients it appears that the type of mental illness they are diagnosed with is not related to their social and occupational functioning (Patterson & Lee, 1995).

Single System Designs

Single system designs are technically not a statistical procedure, but instead a research design for evaluation of practice (Bloom, Fischer, & Orme, 1999; Rubin & Babbie, 1997). They are included in this section on bivariate analysis because in their most fundamental form all single system designs require repeated measurement of an identified phenomenon over time. Time, therefore, is one variable and the identified problem, behavioral change objective, or experience constitutes the second variable. Single system designs can involve the collection of data on more than one phenomenon and as such move beyond the bivariate level to multivariate. At this point, we will confine our consideration of application of spreadsheets in single system data analysis to the bivariate level.

Spreadsheets offer four key features for conducting practice evaluation using single system designs. First, data are readily compiled in spreadsheets. A client or group's daily, weekly, or monthly scores on the outcome measure can be entered and stored in a spreadsheet. Second, a critical feature of single system designs is the visual display of data points over time in order to discern change in the target outcome. Spreadsheets now have graph production tools that make production of single system design graphs uncomplicated and readily updateable. Moreover, it is increasingly important in many social service practice environments to provide treatment progress updates for managed care purposes. Graphs, produced in spreadsheets, of single system designs evaluating client outcomes have a far more professional appearance than graphs produced by hand on graph paper. The third feature spreadsheets bring to single system designs is statistical analysis. Both Quattro Pro and Excel have trend line and moving average functions that are applicable to analysis of single system designs. Fourth, spreadsheet graphs and accompanying statistical analysis are readily integrated into word processing documents for the purpose of managed care reporting.

Spreadsheets offer a number of options for the collection of data in single system designs. The most straightforward method is to use two columns. In the first column record the time interval on which data are collected—hour, day, week, month, year—and in the second column record the designated outcome measure. Figure 4.10 illustrates the steps in collecting and charting a single system design. Note that the spreadsheet at the bottom of the figure has two columns in which data are entered, Week and Anxiety Self-Rating Scale. Review of the range of outcome measures applicable for single system designs is beyond the scope of this discussion. For thorough reviews of outcome measures see Bloom, Fischer, and Orme, 1999; and Rubin and Babbie, 1997. Once an appropriate outcome measure is selected, data collection becomes simply a matter of opening the spreadsheet and entering the score or count from the outcome measure. Note also that the name of the client (a pseudonym) is on the tab of the worksheet. Names are entered

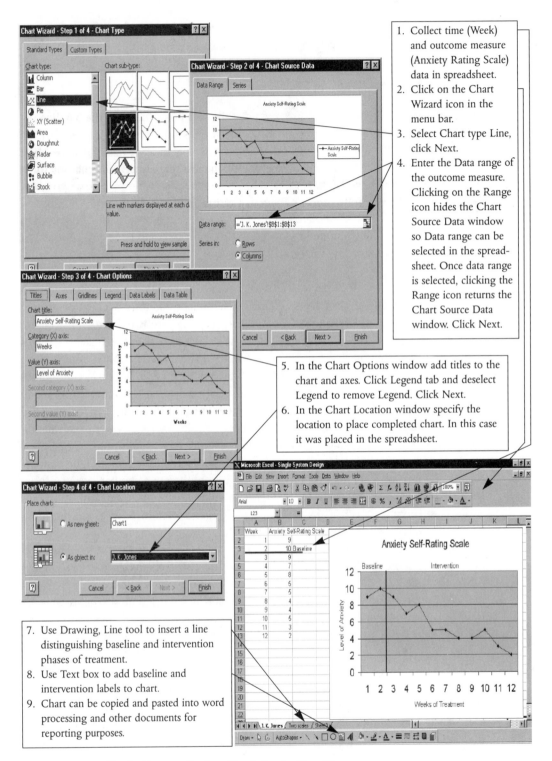

1. Collect time (Week) and outcome measure (Anxiety Rating Scale) data in spreadsheet.
2. Click on the Chart Wizard icon in the menu bar.
3. Select Chart type Line, click Next.
4. Enter the Data range of the outcome measure. Clicking on the Range icon hides the Chart Source Data window so Data range can be selected in the spreadsheet. Once data range is selected, clicking the Range icon returns the Chart Source Data window. Click Next.

5. In the Chart Options window add titles to the chart and axes. Click Legend tab and deselect Legend to remove Legend. Click Next.
6. In the Chart Location window specify the location to place completed chart. In this case it was placed in the spreadsheet.

7. Use Drawing, Line tool to insert a line distinguishing baseline and intervention phases of treatment.
8. Use Text box to add baseline and intervention labels to chart.
9. Chart can be copied and pasted into word processing and other documents for reporting purposes.

FIGURE 4.10   Single System Design Chart Production Steps

on the tabs by double clicking on the tab and then typing in the name. One could, for instance, in a single spreadsheet using multiple worksheets collect data for a number of clients in a caseload.

In Figure 4.10, the single system design used an AB design in which there is a pre-treatment baseline period in which data are collected and no intervention is provided. Typically texts on single system design note that the data points between the baseline (A) and the intervention (B) should not be connected by lines. Moreover, vertical lines are inserted in the chart between treatment phases. This is done in order to distinguish between treatment phases (Bloom, Fischer, & Orme, 1999). In most spreadsheets the charting tools do not provide a means to break the line connecting data points. However, many spreadsheet programs have graphics tools to augment charts. In Figure 4.10, vertical lines were added to the chart to distinguish treatment phases and text labeling the phases were added. Though this procedure does not fully comply with historically specified procedures for visual representation of single system design data, the ease of data collection and charting provided by spreadsheets would seem to be an acceptable trade-off.

Another method for creating a chart to show treatment phases is to enter the data for each phase in a separate column and then plot all the columns. Figure 4.11 displays a spreadsheet in which data from the baseline phase is recorded in column B and the data from the intervention phase is recorded in column C. A line is drawn with the Drawing Tools to indicate the change of treatment phase.

SINGLE SYSTEM DESIGN FOR GROUPS.   Implicit in the notion of single system designs is the fact that individuals, groups, organizations, or any system may be evaluated/studied

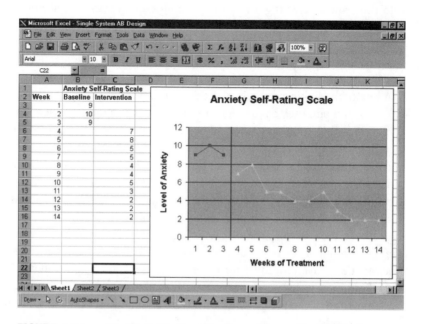

FIGURE 4.11   AB Single System Design—Alternative Method

with these methods. For instance, a spreadsheet can be configured to collect data on a group so that both the changes in the group as a whole and changes for individual group members can be separately graphed. The utility of this procedure is in the resultant capacity to provide distinct feedback over the course of the group's life to both the group and to each group member.

To create a single system design spreadsheet for a group, start by labeling the first sheet with the group's name, such as Parents' Group or Anxiety Management Group. In both Quattro Pro and Excel, after double clicking on a tab, type in the group's name. This group worksheet will serve to compile the data from group members' individual worksheets. To create the individual worksheets assign individual group member's names or identification numbers to worksheet tabs in a spreadsheet. Once this is done, click on the group worksheet and type in the top row of the first two columns the names of the time interval on which data will be collected (e.g., week) and the name of the outcome measure to be used (e.g., Overall Group Cohesion). For more information on outcome assessment in groups, see Richard M. Tolman's chapter "Measuring and Evaluating Individual Achievements and Group Process" in Rose (1989). We will assume for the moment that this is to be a time-limited group that will meet for 12 weeks, so the time variable becomes weeks and in the first column we enter 1–12. Now copy the first 13 rows of the first 2 columns and paste it into each of the worksheets for the group members. The worksheets of the group members now are ready for data entry. Each week, after the group, data from each member's outcome measure can be entered in their worksheets.

The next step is to create a means to compile the data from the individual worksheets in the group worksheet in order to measure changes in the group over time. To do this requires creating a formula in the group worksheet that links it to the worksheets of the group members. This is actually far simpler than it initially sounds. Moreover, once the formula is created in the first cell of the outcome measure, it can be copied to the rest of the cells in the column of the outcome measure for the 12 weeks of the group. If the group is an ongoing group or lasts more than 12 weeks, just copy and paste the linking formula into the necessary cells.

For the purposes of this demonstration, let's assume that there are eight students in our 12-week training group and our outcome measure is group cohesion. Group cohesion is the group's sense of "we-ness," its sense of solidarity, the attraction members feel for the group (Yalom, 1995). The intention here is to create a formula in which we create a group mean level of group cohesion by adding each individual's rating of the group's cohesion and dividing by the total number of group participants. One drawback of calculating the mean level of group cohesion for the group each week is that an appreciation of variance of the ratings is lost. In other words, we do not see the range of opinions of how cohesive the group members are experiencing the group to be. An alternative procedure for representing this information follows.

Returning to how to construct the formula to capture the group's mean rating of group cohesion, we will type in cell B2 of the group's worksheet, the following start of a formula, =(. Note that the period at the end of the formula denotes the end of the sentence and is not part of the formula. Next, we click on the worksheet tab of Student 1 and click on cell B2 of that worksheet. Now type a + sign and then click on the worksheet of Student 2, and click cell B2. Once again the + is added. In essence, the formula is constructed by adding all the cell B2's of the group members. Once all members' worksheets have been included in the formula, enclose it in a closed parenthesis,), add a divide sign, /, and a value representing the total number of group members. The final formula is =('Student 1'!B2+'Student 2'!B2+'Student 3'!B2+'Student 4'!B2+'Student 5'!B2+'Student 6'!B2+'Student 7'!B2+'Student 8'!B2)/8. This formula returns the mean of the values in cell B2 of all eight worksheets. Once the formula is constructed in cell B2 of the group worksheet, copy it and then paste it into the cells of the outcome measure column corresponding to the number of weeks the group will be conducted. The formula in each of the cells it is pasted into is adjusted to add values from the same cell location in each of the worksheets. In other words, the formula pasted into cell B12 in the group worksheet will calculate the mean for all the values entered into cell B12 in all the group members' worksheets. To adjust the formula for absent members, click on the formula in the group worksheet for the week and change the denominator (8) to represent the number of members present. In the absent member(s)' worksheet(s) enter 0 for the week.

Once the formulas are entered in the group worksheet, the next step is constructing the group single system design chart. To do this follow steps 1 through 6 in Figure 4.10. Most groups do not have a no-intervention baseline period, therefore an intervention only single system design, generally referred to as a B design, is employed. In completing steps 1–6, it should be immediately apparent that there are no data in the outcome measure column for the 12 weeks of treatment, therefore the chart will be blank. This is because the formulas have found no data entered in the group members' worksheets and the chart has no data to plot. Try entering values from 1–10, for three weeks, in each of the group member's worksheets. The group chart will automatically plot the group mean for each week as data are entered. Therefore, once the procedure described here to set up the group single system design spreadsheet is completed, monitoring group progress only requires entering the outcome measure data for each group member each week. In this case, only eight values have to be entered to track the group's progress. To chart the process of each group member, construct a chart in each group member's worksheet, again following the procedure in Figure 4.10, steps 1–6.

Figures 4.12 and 4.13 show two charts from a graduate student group psychotherapy training group. Over the course of 12 weeks, students in this group completed at the end of each group an instrument measuring their rating of the level of cohesiveness they experienced in the group. Each of the two charts represents alternative ways to examine change within the group over time. The chart labeled Group Cohesion at the top of Figure 4.12 displays the mean level of group cohesion across the 12 weeks. Group cohesion is ranked by the group members on a 1 to 9 scale with 1 being extremely noncohesive and 9 being extremely cohesive. There are two additional

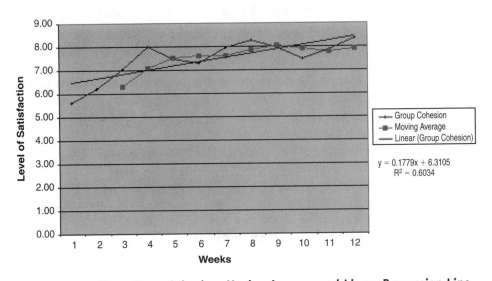

FIGURE 4.12   Mean Group Cohesion, Moving Average, and Linear Regression Line

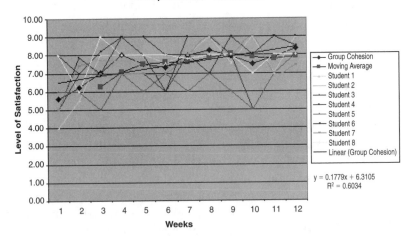

FIGURE 4.13   Group Single System Design for All Students

lines on the graph, the moving average and a linear regression line, referred to in the graph's legend as Linear. The moving average is generally used when there is wide variation in the data over time as a means of smoothing the data to more clearly see any trend in the data (Bloom, Fischer, & Orme, 1999). In Student 1's graph, the moving average is particularly helpful for seeing the underlying trend of an overall rising sense of cohesiveness despite the fluctuations in this student's rating of group cohesion in the last five weeks of the group.

The moving average is a statistical procedure that is available in both Quattro Pro and Excel in their data analysis tools. To compute the moving average, input the range of the outcome measure and specify the location of the output. In order to include the moving average in a graph plotting the values of the outcome measure, be sure to indicate that the output from this data analysis procedure should go in the column adjacent to the column with the outcome measure values. See Spreadsheet Exhibit 4.14 for an example. Note that in the first two rows of the moving average #N/A is present. This is because the formula for calculating the moving average is set to require at least three values to compute the moving average.

The linear regression line on the graph uses the values of the Y axis (Level of Cohesion) and the X axis (Weeks) to fit a straight line across the data points using the least squares method. This line represents the trend in the data and can be particularly useful in discerning the trend, or lack thereof, in data with considerable variability. When there are limited data points, caution should be exercised in interpreting the linear regression line, particularly if there are a few extremely high or low values.

In Excel, the linear regression line is added to the chart after it is constructed by clicking the chart, then from the menu bar selecting Chart, Add Trendline, then select Linear. Under Options, the linear equation and the R^2 value may be added by selecting those options. Adding a linear regression line in Quattro Pro is a little more complex. Click on the cell adjacent to the first value in the output measure. Then on the menu bar select Insert, Function, and Trend. A window appears directing you to insert the range for the known Y values (the outcome measure) and the range of the known X values (the time interval). Click in the field beside the known Y values, then select the arrow icon in the menu bar. Select the Y values in the spreadsheet and hit Enter. Repeat this process for the X values. The formula will return the values of the linear regression values in the cells adjacent to the outcome measure. Plotting both these variables in a single system design chart will yield a line graph of the actual data over time and the resultant linear regression line.

The Group Cohesion graphic in Figure 4.12 also contains the linear regression equation and the R^2 value for the equation. The linear regression equation is the algebraic expression of the linear relationship between the variables. In the equation, 0.1779 is the slope of the regression line and 6.3105 is the y-intercept where the regression line intercepts the Y axis. As described above, R^2 represents

SPREADSHEET EXHIBIT 4.14 Group Outcome Data and Moving Average

	A	B	C
1	Week	Group Cohesion	Moving Average
2	1	5.63	#N/A
3	2	6.23	#N/A
4	3	7.03	6.29
5	4	8.00	7.08
6	5	7.50	7.51
7	6	7.32	7.61
8	7	7.98	7.60
9	8	8.25	7.85
10	9	7.94	8.06
11	10	7.50	7.90
12	11	7.88	7.77
13	12	8.36	7.91

the amount of variance in the outcome measure that can be explained by the independent variable. In this case, the independent variable is weeks in the group psychotherapy training group. The R^2 indicates that 60 percent of the variance in the rating of the level of group cohesion can be explained by the time in the training group.

Figure 4.13 plots the ratings of all the students in the group over the weeks of the group. The graph also includes the Group Cohesion mean (the average of all students' ratings), the moving average, and the linear regression line. This type of group graph is produced by copying and pasting each of the group member's outcome measure data into a common worksheet, along with the group mean data and the moving average from the group's worksheet. When copying values produced by formulas from one worksheet to another, use the Edit command in the menu bar, Paste Special, Values. This menu option is used to paste the values from the worksheet into the new worksheet. If the formulas in the worksheet are pasted into the new worksheet any other way they will not work. With that caution, once all the data is in the new worksheet, the group graph is created with the procedure illustrated in Figure 4.10, steps 1–6. In step 4, entering the data range, be certain to enter the range of all the group members, the group mean, and moving average.

Upon first viewing, the Group Cohesion—All Students graph is a challenge to interpret. What is evident is the variability in the group members' ratings of the group's cohesiveness over the course of the group. In many ways this type of single system design graph illustrates the complexity of group work. The lines representing the mean group cohesiveness, the moving average, and the linear regression provide visual assistance in seeing the trend in the data. Clinically, distributing on a weekly basis this type of graph that plots the group members' anonymous ratings of dimensions of their group experience represents a potentially powerful means of feedback to the group and material for discussion of the group's process and progress.

This concludes our review of the application of spreadsheets in single system design outcome evaluation. While the examples used in this discussion are primarily clinical, the procedures described are applicable to many dimensions of social service practice. In community organizations, single system designs can be used to track participation/meeting attendance over time. Funds receipts can be tracked by weekly totals to record progress in fund-raising efforts. Charting the number of services provided by an agency on a monthly basis can provide documentation to funding sources of the agency's impact in a community. In each of these examples, the procedures described in this section can find application.

Multivariate Analysis

The purpose of multivariate analysis is examination of the relationships between three or more variables. Multivariate analysis can be performed with spreadsheets using tables and statistical procedures. In this discussion, we extend the application of analytic tools described in the previous section on bivariate analysis. More specifically, the use of cross tabulation tables with three variables is described and the procedure to conduct multiple regression is presented.

The addition of a third variable to a cross tabulation table is an extension of the process for creating a bivariate table described in Figure 4.8. Multivariate cross tabulation tables can often reveal relationships between variables that may go undetected in a bivariate cross tabulation (Rubin & Babbie, 1997; Weinbach & Grinnell, 1991). Rubin and Babbie (1997) describe an elaboration model in which the relationship, or apparent lack thereof, between two variables is studied by testing the effect of other variables on the relationship between the original two variables. The multivariate cross tabulation table production that is possible with spreadsheets can dramatically facilitate the speed and depth with which the multivariate relationships are examined.

In Spreadsheet Exhibit 4.15, three variables, gender, diagnostic group, and monthly income are summarized to display differences in average monthly income by diagnostic group and gender. This table was created with the Pivot Table tool. In Step 3 of the Pivot Tool Wizard, gender was selected as the column variable, diagnostic group was selected as the row variable, and monthly income was inserted into the data section of the diagram. Clicking on monthly income in the data section of the diagram made it possible to then select Average to summarize monthly income data. In the resultant Spreadsheet Exhibit 4.15, it is apparent that there are major differences in the average incomes of males across diagnostic groups and between males and females across diagnostic groups. These differences would not have been apparent had we examined only the bivariate relationship between monthly income and diagnostic group.

Multiple Regression

Multiple regression is a multivariate statistical procedure that was introduced in the discussion on one-way ANOVAs. Multiple regression extends the concept of bivariate regression, in which the extent of the relationship between two variables is examined. In multiple regression the relative importance of two or more independent variables on

SPREADSHEET EXHIBIT 4.15   Average Monthly Income by Gender and Diagnostic Group

	A	B	C	D
1		GENDER		
2	Diagnostic Group	Males	Females	Grand Total
3	1.00	$497	$458	$477
4	2.00	$587	$460	$500
5	3.00	$496	$0	$434
6	4.00	$427	$440	$434
7	Average Monthly Income	$502	$452	$475

a dependent variable is tested. Using multiple regression, we can determine both the strength of the relationship between each of the independent variables and the dependent variable and also determine the amount of variance in the dependent variable that can be explained by cumulative effects of the independent variables. The intricacies of multiple regression are beyond the scope of this book. Rubin and Babbie (1997) provide a brief review of the subject and Kachigan (1986) offers a very readable chapter on regression analysis. The intent here is to demonstrate how multiple regression analysis can be computed with a spreadsheet and to review the output produced by the statistical procedure.

As a note of caution, generally speaking multiple regression is probably best conducted with a dedicated statistical software package such as SPSS, SYSTAT, or SAS. The statistical output from spreadsheets tested here lacked an important statistic, the standardized regression coefficient. The standardized regression coefficient, which is also known as the *beta weight*, is a statistic that allows for comparison of the strength of the relationship between each independent variable and the dependent variable. This makes it possible to rank independent variables on the strength of their relationship to the dependent variable. Given this important limitation, performing multiple regression analysis with spreadsheets should probably be limited to preliminary exploratory analysis.

As an example of a preliminary exploratory analysis, we might wish to examine the impact of three factors presumed to be helpful in assisting mentally ill clients to remain in their communities, thereby avoiding psychiatric hospitalization. The three factors are medication compliance, the quality of the living situation, and the number of referrals to other agencies in the community, an indicator of the engagement of resources to support the client. The outcome (dependent) variable is time in the community and out of a psychiatric hospital, here referred to as community survival. In multiple regression, the dependent variable must be either interval or ratio. Independent variables should be either interval or ratio level variables. If they are nominal level, they must be converted to dummy variables.

To begin the regression analysis in Quattro Pro, from the menu bar select Tools, Numeric Tools, Regression. In Excel's menu bar select Tools, Data Analysis, then Regression. In both spreadsheets, the user is required to specify the Input Y Range, which is the range of the dependent variable. The next step is to enter the X input range, which is the range of the independent variables. The independent variables must adjoin each other in the spreadsheet. If the first row containing the variable labels (names) was included in either the Y or X input range, click Labels so the spreadsheet recognizes the first row in the range as a variable label. The output range can be specified as a range of blank cells in the spreadsheet containing the data. Clicking a single cell is sufficient if there are no data nearby. Excel makes available a number of options for the further analysis of results. These include standardized residuals, residual plots, and normal probability plots. The two other options are to click New Worksheet ply, which sends the results to another worksheet, and New Workbook, which sends the results to a new spreadsheet.

Spreadsheet Exhibit 4.16 contains the results of the exploratory multiple regression analysis of the relationship between medication compliance, the quality of the living sit-

SPREADSHEET EXHIBIT 4.16 Multiple Regression Results

	A	B	C	D	E	F	G
1	Regression Statistics						
2	Multiple R	0.11					
3	R Square	0.01					
4	Adjusted R Square	0.00					
5	Standard Error	349.68					
6	Observations	196.00					
7							
8	ANOVA						
9		df	SS	MS	F	Significance F	
10	Regression	3	301994.39	100664.80	0.82	0.48	
11	Residual	192	23476515.02	122273.52			
12	Total	195	23778509.41				
13							
14		Coefficients	Standard Error	t Stat	P-value	Lower 95%	Upper 95%
15	Intercept	475.29	95.07	5.00	0.00	287.77	662.81
16	Medication Compliance	9.39	9.85	0.95	0.34	−10.05	28.82
17	Agency Referrals	−9.83	11.14	−0.88	0.38	−31.80	12.14
18	Current Living Situation	9.98	14.41	0.69	0.49	−18.45	38.41

uation, the number of referrals to other agencies in the community, and the dependent variable, community survival. Of particular note in Spreadsheet Exhibit 4.16 is the R Square value. R Square indicates the total variance in the dependent variable explained by all the independent variables combined. The R^2 of 0.01 indicates that all three independent variables accounted for only 1 percent of the variance in community survival, an insubstantial amount. The Significance F is 0.48, indicating that the regression model is not statistically significant. Finally, examination of the P-values for the independent variables indicates a nonsignificant relationship between each of the independent variables and the dependent variable. Based on the findings of this exploratory multiple regression, we can conclude that other factors determined community survival in this group of clients.

Budgeting: Managing Fiscal Resources

Our consideration of spreadsheets thus far has focused on their utility in the collection, analysis, and reporting of data. Spreadsheets were initially developed for fiscal data analysis and it is to this function that this discussion now turns. Social service agencies carry out their operations each year constrained by the financial resources available to them. The management of these financial resources requires the planning of a budget that balances the anticipated income of the agency with its requisite expenses. Spreadsheets offer a means to develop budgeting alternatives and to track budget information through the fiscal year.

Spreadsheets offer numerous alternatives for the configuration of a budget. One of the primary advantages of using spreadsheets in budget development is the capacity to create formulas within the budget that automatically recalculate critical components of the budget such as Total Income, Total Expenses, and Grand Total. Once the formulas are in place to calculate these critical values, then exploratory examination of budgetary scenarios can be conducted. These formulas display the impact on the overall budget of allocations, reductions, and the redistribution of resources.

Spreadsheet Exhibit 4.17 contains a simplified example of an agency budget. Budgets often reflect a mix of factual information, projected expectations, fiscal management

SPREADSHEET EXHIBIT 4.17   A Spreadsheet Budget

	A	B	C	D	E	F
1	Maximum Mental Health—Budget for 2000					
2						
3	Income	Actual for 1999	Projected for 2000	Allocated for 2000	Difference	Percent
4	State Contracts	500,000	525,000	510,000	15,000	2.94%
5	Federal Grants	150,000	175,000	155,000	20,000	12.90%
6	Fees	300,000	325,000	305,000	20,000	6.56%
7	Fund Raising	100,000	120,000	115,000	5,000	4.35%
8	Total	1,050,000	1,145,000	1,085,000	60,000	5.53%
9						
10	Expenses					
11	Personnel	850,000	884,000	875,000	9,000	1.03%
12	Rent	60,000	62,400	62,400	0	0.00%
13	Utilities	12,000	12,480	12,000	480	4.00%
14	Telecommunications	10,000	10,400	12,000	−1,600	−13.33%
15	Insurance	12,000	12,480	12,480	0	0.00%
16	Equipment	80,000	83,200	90,000	−6,800	−7.56%
17	Total	1,024,000	1,064,960	1,063,880	1,080	0
18						
19	Grand Total	26,000	80,040	21,120	58,920	

values, and quantifiable relationships. In this example, the actual income and expenses for 1999 of Maximum Mental Health is a known fact that contributes to the decision making process. Moreover, information resulting from tracking income and expenses over time can be used to quantify growth or loss trends that can further contribute to calculations in the budgetary process. Note that at the bottom of both income and expenses there is a row that contains totals. These totals are the products of formulas in the spreadsheet that sum the rows in their respective columns. For example, in the income column, Actual for 1999, the formula is =SUM(B4:B7). This formula is copied and pasted into cells C8:F8 in order to calculate the totals across the five categories. In the Total row under Expenses, formulas to total the categories of expenses have been inserted. In cell B17 the formula =SUM(B11:B16) provides the total for the Actual 1999 expenses. The same formula is copied and pasted into cells C17:F17. Remember that as a formula is pasted into a new column, its column reference changes to the column into which it is pasted. Thus, =SUM(B11:B16) becomes =SUM(C11:C16) when it is pasted into column C.

Recall also that once the formulas are inserted in the cells, they will automatically recalculate the sum once a new figure is entered in the column. As a result, a manager can experiment with a range of budgeting options in the process of developing a final budget. For example, the Projected for 2000 personnel expenses is calculated based on the formula =SUM(B11*0.04)+B11. In this formula, the actual personnel expenses for 1999 is multiplied by 0.04 (4%) and then added to the actual personnel expenses of 1999. In essence, the formula calculates the personnel cost for 2000 by assuming a 4 percent increase in cost. The manager could calculate a range of options for increases or decreases in personnel cost and examine their impact on the Grand Total or "bottom line" of the Mental Health Center's fiscal health. The Grand Total row has a series of formulas in it that computes the difference between Income and Expenses. The formula for Allocated for 2000 is =D8-D17, or simply Income minus Expenses.

This formula example includes columns Projected for 2000 and Allocated for 2000. At first consideration, the need for two columns might not seem apparent. It may be assumed that the Projected for 2000 column reflects the best available estimates for the Income and Expenses for the coming years and no further figures would be necessary. However, the Allocated for 2000 incorporates the fiscal values of the management and reflects the goals of the Center. The variance between the Projected and Allocated is evident in the Difference column, which calculates the difference between the Projected and the Allocated. The Percent column computes the percentage of difference between the Projected and the Allocated with the formula =E8/D8. Because the formula returns the value 0.029412, the format of this column was reset by clicking Format, Cells, Number, Percent. This reformats the column to change values into percentages.

The assumptions and values of the management become evident by examination of the Difference and Percent columns. In most cases the income and expenses Allocated are less than those projected. For income, this suggests a fiscal conservatism reflected in the budgeting decision to plan to have available less income than projected.

This is a hedge against unexpected loss of income. The differences between Projected and Allocated expenses can reflect managerial decisions to find ways to hold down costs in certain areas and to allocate additional resources to other areas. In this example, the additional resources are allocated to telecommunications (telephone and Internet access) and equipment (presumably upgraded computers). This allocation may reflect a goal of the Mental Health Center to continue to enhance the information technology available to the Center's staff.

In considering the use of spreadsheets in developing budgets it is perhaps most critical to appreciate that spreadsheets represent dynamic tools that can facilitate the critical evaluation of alternatives. Preparation of a budget in a spreadsheet allows for the testing of the effects of a range of choices in the budgeting process. Essential to this process is incorporating formulas that link changes in any area of the budget to the bottom line figure. In Spreadsheet Exhibit 4.17, this bottom line figure is the difference between the Allocated Income and the Allocated Expenses, $21,120. The figure $58,920 represents the positive budgetary outcome should the Projected figures prove correct. Changes to any of the figures in this spreadsheet will alter the Grand Totals due to the formulas linking the income and expense domains. We can therefore experiment with the impact on the difference between the Allocated Income and the Allocated Expenses, should there be rises in insurance rates or shortfalls in income. This process of formulating a range of possible fiscal events and investigating their impact on the budget is often referred to as examining "what if" scenarios.

Once a budget is decided on, the next step in applying spreadsheet technology to the budgetary process is configuring a spreadsheet to track expenses and income across the year. In larger agencies, this task may fall on the accountants, and they have their own methods. However, in smaller agencies or in departments it is often incumbent upon the administrator or the department manager to track income or expenses to assess their variance with budgeted amounts. This can readily be accomplished in a spreadsheet by reconfiguring the budget planning spreadsheet. Spreadsheet Exhibit 4.18 contains a spreadsheet demonstrating this income and expense tracking process. This spreadsheet started as a copy of the budget in Spreadsheet Exhibit 4.17. The columns for the Actual for 1999, Projected for 2000, Difference and Percent were deleted, leaving the Allocated for 2000 budget figures. The Average Monthly was created with a formula in cell C4, =SUM(B4/12), that simply divides the Yearly Budgeted amount by 12. This formula was copied and pasted into the cells in the column adjacent to a yearly budgeted amount. Each month a new column is inserted next to the previous month and data for the month is entered. The column Year-to-Date Variance contains in cell G4 the formula =SUM(D4:F4)−(C4*3), which is copied and pasted into the cells in the column adjacent to yearly budgeted amounts. This formula sums each month's income or expenses, then subtracts the product of the budgeted monthly average times the number of months. The result is the variance between actual income or expenses versus the expected or budgeted income or expenses. Each month, after inserting a new column for the month's income and expense data, the formula for the Year-to-Date Variance must

SPREADSHEET EXHIBIT 4.18   Year-to-Date Budget Analysis Spreadsheet

	A	B	C	D	E	F	G
1	Maximum Mental Health—Budget for 2000						
2		**Budgeted**	Average				Year-to-Date
3	Income	Year	Monthly	January	February	March	Variance
4	State Contracts	510,000	42,500	50,000	40,000	45,000	7,500
5	Federal Grants	155,000	12,917	8,000	0	24,000	−6,750
6	Fees	305,000	25,417	30,000	29,000	31,000	13,750
7	Fund Raising	115,000	9,583	8,000	12,000	4,000	−4,750
8	**Total**	**1,085,000**	**90,417**	**96,000**	**81,000**	**104,000**	**9,750**
9		**Budgeted**	Average				Year-to-Date
10	Expenses	Year	Monthly	January	February	March	Variance
11	Personnel	875,000	72,917	74,000	73,000	72,000	250
12	Rent	62,400	5,200	5,200	5,200	5,200	0
13	Utilities	12,000	1,000	1,500	1,200	1,100	800
14	Telecommunications	12,000	1,000	1,050	1,000	1,000	50
15	Insurance	12,480	1,040	1,040	1,040	1,040	0
16	Equipment	90,000	7,500	7,000	8,000	3,000	−4,500
17	**Total**	**1,063,880**	**88,657**	**89,790**	**89,440**	**83,340**	**−3,400**
18							
19	**Grand Total**		**21,120**	**1,760**	**6,210**	**−8,440**	**20,660**	**13,150**

be adjusted to include in its calculations the new month. This entails changing the month column range and increasing by one the multiple for the monthly average. Thus in April, after inserting a new column to the right of March, the formula in cell G4 becomes =SUM(D4:G4)–(C4*4).

Examining the Year-to-Date Variance reveals where income and expenses exceed or fall short of budgeted amounts. Additionally, by comparing the figures in the Total rows for income and expenses to the Monthly Average, monthly variations are trackable. The Total rows for Income and Expenses contain in each cell a formula that sums the range of values across the categories of Income or Expense for each month. For instance, the formula in cell D8 is =SUM(D4:D7). The formula in the Grand Total row simply subtracts expenses from income. The formula for January, contained in cell D19 is =SUM(D4:D7). The formulas for Total Income, Total Expenses, and Grand Total must be copied into the appropriate row cells each month after a new column is inserted for the month's data.

The Year-to-Date Budget Analysis Spreadsheet in Spreadsheet Exhibit 4.18 is only one of many possible configurations of this type of budget analysis tool. One alternative is tracking income and expenses on separate worksheets that are linked by formulas to a worksheet that contains only monthly income and expense totals along with a grand total. These figures can be graphed using the procedures demonstrated in the section on single system design. This type of graphical representation can provide a clear picture to both subordinates and administrators of an agency's fiscal status on an ongoing basis. The principles of budget development and analysis with spreadsheets reviewed here are offered as a starting point for readers to experiment with the creation of spreadsheet budgetary tools that match the needs of their practice setting.

Summary

This chapter demonstrates the utility of spreadsheets for a variety of data management and analysis functions. Spreadsheets have to date been underutilized in social service practice despite their common availability and relatively low cost compared to many statistical software packages. This chapter described how to collect data with spreadsheets, create random samples, and produce data entry forms. Data analytic techniques were detailed, including procedures for data cleaning and descriptive statistics. Procedures for creating frequency distributions and computing measures of central tendency and dispersion were presented. This chapter illustrated the use of spreadsheets in the creation of cross tab tables, computing chi-square, Pearson's r, and t tests. The computation of one-way ANOVAs and multiple regression with spreadsheets was also described, including details on how to use spreadsheets for producing single system design charts for individuals and groups. Finally, the chapter discussed the use of spreadsheets for managing fiscal resources and the examination of alternative financial scenarios.

Exercises

1. Create a mailing list data entry form in a spreadsheet and enter either made-up data or data from your own address book. Try sorting the data on last name, state, or some other variable of interest. Now use the Random Sample procedure to randomly select a subset of names.
2. With a group of peers create a data set or locate an available existing data set. There are publicly available data sets on the Web. Import or enter the date into a spreadsheet. Once it is in the spreadsheet, produce a frequency distribution on a nominal, ordinal, interval, and ratio level variable. Calculate within the spreadsheet the mean, median, mode, and standard deviation for two continuous variables (one interval and one ratio).
3. With a group of peers or alone, use the data set produced in Exercise 2 to create a cross tab table, compute chi-square test, Pearson's r, and at least one type of t test.

4. Create a single system design chart with a spreadsheet. Either use existing data from a practice setting or create a data set for an AB design. Then produce a plot of the data.
5. Create a budget in a spreadsheet using either data from your practice setting or personal financial data. Be sure to include formulas for averaging income and expenses over time. Create formulas for summing income and summing expenses for each time period.

chapter 5

Databases

Information When and
How You Want It

This chapter introduces the use of database software as a tool of social service practice. As an alternative to centralized agency databases or as a complementary method, database software, run on a personal computer, represents a robust means for the collection and management of social service data. This chapter describes and illustrates the five functions of database software: data entry, data storage, data organization, data selection, and report generation.

The potential applications of database software in social service practice are manifold. Frequently agencies have central databases for administrative and managerial functions such as compiling client demographic, diagnostic, service provision, and billing information. These databases are often designed and dedicated to highly specific tasks, and are managed and controlled by database managers, under the administrative control of high-level managers or agency administrators. As a result, access to and use of central computing resources for the collection, management, and analysis of information on projects of departments or individuals within the agency is often severely constrained or prohibited. Moreover, there are numerous data collection and management tasks that cannot be accommodated by centralized agency databases. Nonetheless, these more peripheral tasks or projects can be very critical to the agency's operations. Examples of such information management tasks include development of a donor database to track agency fund-raising, compilation of a resource and referral database, and the construction of surveys and recording of participant responses. At the individual worker level, databases can assist practitioners with tasks such as (a) compiling addresses of resources, colleagues, or referral sources, (b) tracking client contact for reporting purposes, (c) recording and reporting expenses, and (d) noting time and billing. At both the department and individual level in many social service agencies, alternatives to centralized database resources are necessary for information collection and management.

Alternatives to central information management systems are available to personal computer users in the form of database management systems (DBMS) (Fuller & Pagan, 1997). A database is best thought of as a collection of information that is organized logically to facilitate information retrieval. "A DBMS is a computer database software application that helps to store, retrieve, sort, filter, print, and present the information contained in a database" (Fuller & Pagan, 1997, p. 584). As the acronym DBMS is not widely used among nontechnophiles, for the purposes of this discussion *database application* is employed. The term *applications* is commonly used to denote software programs designed for end users or nonprogrammers/software engineers (Margolis, 1996).

Commercially available database applications include Paradox, FoxPro, Lotus Approach, dBase, and Microsoft Access. This chapter will focus on Lotus Approach and Microsoft Access, as they are database applications contained in software suites (Lotus SmartSuite and Microsoft Office). These database applications are well integrated with other software packages in their respective suites. This application integration facilitates the sharing of data between applications. Integration promotes operations such as the two-way exchange of information between spreadsheets and database applications and the sending of information to a word processor in a mail merge operation. Moreover, database applications integrated into software suites now have Internet tools that make it possible to turn a form, report, or chart generated by the database into a Web page (McCracken, 1997; Robb, 1997).

As an alternative to centralized information management systems, database applications are extremely flexible tools. They can accommodate a range of types of information including digitized images (such as pictures of employees), extended notes (applicable for case notes), and a variety of different data formats including dates, currency, text, and numbers. Additionally, database applications available in software suites commonly have the capacity to import information from a wide range of sources including spreadsheets, databases, and the Web. This capacity makes it possible to utilize information extracted from centralized agency databases and other sources. An example of the application of this process would be extracting a list of clients' addresses from a central database in order to examine in a database application the relationship between where clients served by the agency live and the locations of outreach clinics.

Many database applications come with database templates which are adaptable to users' specific information management needs. For instance, Lotus Approach has a survey builder that facilitates the design of a survey, production of questions, administration of the survey, and compilation of a report. As another example, Microsoft Access has a database for collection of information and generation of reports on financial donors, their contributions over time, and progress toward fund-raising goals. These and other database templates are examined and their potential application in social service practice are described in this chapter.

The goal of this chapter is to detail how social service practitioners can create and use database applications for a variety of information management functions. The development of a sophisticated database application is complex and time consuming. Such an enterprise is best left to those intrepid souls who have devoted or wish to devote significant portions of their lives to understanding the intricacies of database operations. The focus here is on description of the basic functions available in database applications, how simple databases can be developed, how to employ already developed database applications in social service practice, and how to use and disseminate information from databases.

Database Basics

The brief introduction to databases in Chapter 3 presents the basic terms describing the parts and functions of a database. Table 5.1 reintroduces and expands on the terminology commonly used in conversing about databases. Gaining a familiarity with these terms facilitates the process of beginning to understand the basic functioning of database applications. Database applications are in many respects unlike more widely used software applications such as word processing programs or spreadsheets. In most interactions, word processors and spreadsheets present the user with a single screen in which the function of the software, word processing or data analysis, is performed. Such is not the case in database applications. Indeed, one of the challenges faced in learning about database applications is understanding the role, functions, and relationships that link the various objects in an application.

One starting point in coming to understand database applications is to recall that the most basic functions of a database are data entry, storage, organization, selection, and reporting. Data entry involves inputting data into the database. It is most commonly entered through a "form" or "data entry form." See Figure 5.1 for an example of a data

TABLE 5.1   Database Terms and Definitions (Fuller & Pagan, 1997; Margolis, 1996)

database table	An object in a database for the storage of data. Resembles a spreadsheet.
field	A column in a database table. Can be thought of as data variable.
file	A collection of records. Generally organized as a database table.
flat file database	A database that stores information in a single database table.
form	An object for data entry and viewing.
index	A unique value in a database table that prevents duplicates and accelerates searches.
macro	A means to automate commands or tasks in the database.
object	A component of a database such as a table or form.
query	Extracts data from database tables based on definable criteria.
record	A row in a database table. Each record represents the total information about the case in the database table.
relational database	Stores data in multiple database tables and links them with data indexes.
report	A means to summarize, disseminate, or print data.

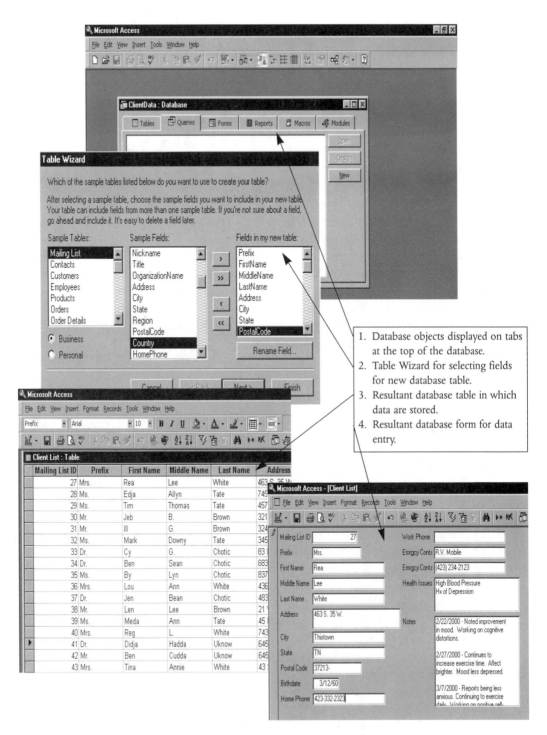

1. Database objects displayed on tabs at the top of the database.
2. Table Wizard for selecting fields for new database table.
3. Resultant database table in which data are stored.
4. Resultant database form for data entry.

FIGURE 5.1   Flat File Database Table and Form Creation in Microsoft Access

entry form. Alternatively, data may be imported into a database application from another software application such as a spreadsheet or as a file extracted from another database.

The second function, data storage, is perhaps most fundamental to databases, their primary use. Information in a database may be organized in a file composed of fields and records. Alternatively, databases can be composed of various types of information, such as text, images, sounds, and numerical information, that are linked to each other. This type of hypertext or hypermedia database makes possible the organization of large quantities of diverse information. The World Wide Web can be thought of as an enormous hypermedia database in which linkages connect related information (Margolis, 1996).

The third function of a database is organization of data. In flat file databases, data are organized in a single file composed of fields and records. In relational databases, data are organized in more than one table and the tables are linked with an index. For instance, in a financial donor database there could be one table that holds information on donors such as names, addresses, and phone numbers. A second table could hold pledge information like the dates pledges are received, pledge amounts, and payment dates. These tables are linked by an index number, which connects pledge information to donors.

Still another way to consider database organization is by how the data are arranged in the database table(s). The organization of the information in a database table is not static. Most database applications have tools for sorting the records in a table on any field. There are times when it is functional and/or informative to identify subgroups within the database. For example, a client contact database on the field "Insurance Type" could be sorted to find all clients in a caseload who are at risk due to Medicaid benefits reduction. Alternatively, a client contact database could be sorted on the field "Date of Last Visit" to find the array of clients in a large caseload with whom there has not been recent contact. Both of these examples represent databases' ability to organize data in ways that facilitate critical information access.

The fourth function of a database is selection, the capacity to choose portions of the data based on certain criteria. A query is a means to request specific information from a database, a way to pose questions to the database. For instance, a financial donor database could be queried to retrieve and calculate the total pledges of each donor in order to select those donors who have contributed more than a specified amount. Or the financial donor database might be queried to sum the total amounts received from each donor or to provide the average amount pledged.

Some database applications have a selection tool called a filter that allows one to select all cases in the database that have an attribute selected (clicked on) in a particular field. Again, think of a client contact database. This database contains a field with information on the type of health care insurance the clients have. To filter the database for all cases with Blue Cross/Blue Shield (BC/BS) insurance, one would simply click on BC/BS in the insurance field, then click the Filter tool in the menu bar. The database application then filters the database and selects all cases with BC/BS insurance. Note that the database has not been sorted, but instead filtered to select a specified group of clients, those with BC/BS insurance.

The fifth function of a database application is report generation. A report is a means to format, organize, summarize, and print information from a database. Reports can select and extract information from one or more database tables. The report writing tools in many database applications include the capacity to generate charts and graphs from the numeric information extracted for the report. Once a report is created, several options exist for its dissemination or further modification. The report can be printed or distributed as an e-mail attachment. Another option is to save the report as an HTML file that can be placed on a Web server. If further modification of the report or analysis of the data is required, some database applications in software suites make it possible to send the report directly to word processing software or a spreadsheet. Reports sent to word processors can be annotated with additional information or included in a larger document. The data in reports sent to a spreadsheet can be further analyzed, augmented with additional data and/or charts, and then printed or sent to a word processor for further modification. Taken together, these options significantly extend the possibilities in analyzing, formatting, and disseminating database application reports.

Database Applications in Social Service Practice

In order to appreciate the range of possible database applications in social service practice it is perhaps necessary to explore the operationalization of the five functions of a database. The construction and testing of a simple database requires implementing each of the five functions: data entry, storage, organization, selection, and reporting. In proceeding through the process of building a database from scratch, we will (a) need to think through the types of information we wish to collect, (b) consider how to organize the collection, storage, selection, and extraction of data, and (c) encounter the tools available in database applications that facilitate these processes.

What Information to Collect

A commonly needed database in social service practice is one in which contact with clients can be documented along with other case-specific information. Procedures for recording client information and client contact notation across agencies are highly varied. In some agencies, client records are maintained in paper-based records while other agencies have developed computer-based client record keeping systems. However, many social service practitioners need a method to collect and manage specific information on clients in their caseloads.

The specific types of information recorded in a client database will likewise vary depending on the agency context, worker role requirements, and client population. In order to build a database, consideration must be given to what information should be collected to improve prescribed employment tasks. Sometimes all that is necessary is name, address, and phone number information. In other situations, additional demographic information such as age, race, and gender is needed for reporting and other purposes. It may be necessary to include diagnostic and medical information or current and past illness, medication, physician to contact, and emergency family contacts. Some practice settings require information on each client contact. Information of this type might include case notes, time and date of contact, fee charged and paid, and data on one or more clinical outcome measures. Still other practice settings could require the collection of more extensive family information such as children and spouse names, addresses, and other demographic information.

Each of these types of information, and likely many more, represent potential fields in which to collect data in a client contact database. Deciding on the specific fields to select for inclusion in a client contact database is a delicate balancing act. One approach is to include all the fields that may possibly ever be needed. This "include everything because it might be needed" approach to database development can create very complete and thorough databases. The downside is that they require considerably more time and effort spent in data entry. Moreover, if unnecessary or inappropriate data fields are included in a database, the likely result is considerable amounts of missing data in the database fields. Large quantities of missing data produce significant problems in subsequent data analysis. Alternatively, some databases are constructed with the fewest possible fields. Data entry in these types of constrained databases is much faster and requires less effort. Clearly, the downside to a field-restricted database is that important information may go uncollected and therefore be unavailable when required.

There is, of course, no easy solution to this dilemma. Practitioners wishing to develop client contact databases may do well to spend time listing the types of information they think they will require. Once this list is developed, consider each type of information (potential database field) with the question, When did I last need to know, find, or report this type of information? Applying this question to each information item can serve to optimize the size of the client contact database eventually developed.

Creating a Database

Upon deciding what information to collect in the client contact database, the next step is to create the database using a database application. The processes for creating a client database in both Microsoft Access and Lotus Approach are described here. This discussion is intended to familiarize readers with the basic tools and steps in creating a flat file database. Both database applications have tools that guide users through the steps to construct a simple flat file database. In Lotus Approach the database development tool is called SmartMaster. In Microsoft Access the database development tool is called Wizard. The basic procedures for both database applications are similar to each other and to the procedures used in other database applications. The product of this process is a database table and a database form, each containing the necessary fields for the data collection tasks the user intends for the database.

In Microsoft Access

1. Start Microsoft Access and select Blank Database.
2. In the New window, select Blank Database and click OK.
3. In the File New Database window, name the database and select the file folder in which to save it.
4. A window with the database name appears, with tabs labeled Tables, Queries, Forms, Report, Macros, and Modules. Click on Tables, then click the New button. (See Figure 5.1.)
5. A window entitled New Table appears with the choices Datasheet View, Design View, Table Wizard, Import Table, and Link Table. Each choice represents a different way to create a new table. To create a database table from an existing spreadsheet, select Import Table, then select the file type and the location of the file. For this demonstration select Table Wizard.
6. In the window entitled Table Wizard, there are three scrollable widows labeled Sample Tables, Sample Fields, and Fields in My New Table. Clicking on each of the Sample Tables will display in the Sample Fields window the field available in the selected Sample Table. (See Figure 5.1.)
7. Clicking any field in the Sample Fields window and then the right arrow will move the field into the window Fields in My New Table. Use this procedure to select fields for the new table. Fields from any of the Sample Tables may be selected and placed into the new table. Fields in the new table are removed by selecting them and then clicking the left arrow. Fields can be renamed by selecting the field in the Fields in My New Table window and then clicking the Rename Field button.
8. Once all of the fields for the new table are selected, a window in the Table Wizard will ask for a name for the new table. After entering a name for the new table, click Next.
9. The next window in the Table Wizard asks if you want to modify the table, enter data directly into the table, or enter data into the table with a form created by the wizard. Select enter data using a form created by the wizard. While not essential, this step creates a form that can facilitate data entry.
10. Access next creates the new database table and the data entry form. (See Figure 5.1.)

The steps in this process result in a database table for data storage and a database form for data entry and viewing. The data form allows for viewing of the records in the database one case at a time. All information entered in the database form is stored in the database table. The form in Figure 5.1 contains two scrollable fields, Health Issues and

Notes, for entering large quantities of text-based information. The scrollbar becomes visible upon clicking on the field. The Notes field in Figure 5.1 is used for case notes. The Notes field scrolls down to accommodate each new entry, just as a word processor screen scrolls when additional text is entered. Access also makes possible the creation of reports in which the information from selected fields in the database table can be extracted and printed or otherwise processed. It is thereby possible to create a report with client names and case notes.

Another important feature of this database application is the capacity to insert new fields into the database table. Remember that the database form here was created by Access based on the fields in the database table. If the database form in Figure 5.1 is closely examined, it is apparent that fields for client home and work phone numbers were not included in the database table or in the subsequently created database form. It is not unusual to create a database table or form and then realize one or more necessary fields were inadvertently omitted. To rectify this omission, first delete the database form. To do this, in the screen displaying the database objects, click the Forms tab and select the database form to be deleted. In the menu bar under Edit, select Delete. The program will ask if you really want to delete the Form. This is a safeguard to prevent accidental deletion of forms. Respond yes. Note that despite the fact that the form is deleted no data are lost, as data are stored in the database table.

The next step is to add the necessary fields to the database table. Fields are added to the database table by inserting new columns. To do this, click on the Tables tab in the screen displaying the database objects and then click the database table into which the fields are to be inserted. Select the location in the database table where the additional fields, such as home and work phone numbers, will be added, and click on the field to the right of the intended point of insertion. From the menu bar select Insert and Column. To add another field, repeat this step. To name the field, click on the top of the column and type in the new field name.

To create a new database form that will include the new fields, click on the Forms tab in the screen displaying the database objects. Click the New button and select form wizard. The form wizard presents a set of choices for creation of the database form. The first choice is to name the table or tables from which to create the form. This option allows for the inclusion in the form of fields from one or more tables. In this present example, only one database table has been created and the purpose of creating this form is to input data into the existing database table. So select the existing database table and all of its fields for inclusion in the form.

After clicking Next, the form wizard asks for a choice about the layout or arrangement of fields on the form and displays a preview of the various options. Select a layout option and click Next. The form wizard now asks for a choice about the background style of the form and again displays a preview of options. Select a style and click Next. Finally, form wizard requests a name or title for the newly designed form. Type in a name and click Finish. With completion of this step, there now exists a newly modified database table for data storage and a database form for data entry.

In Lotus Approach

1. Upon starting Lotus Approach, a window entitled Welcome to Lotus Approach appears.

2. Novice database users may want to first click the button at the bottom left of the window entitled Take a Tour. This is an interactive educational program that offers a wide range of information about using Lotus Approach and developing a database.

3. Next click the tab at the top of the window labeled Create a New File Using a SmartMaster.

4. On the left side of the window, another window offers a range of choices of database templates. Select Blank Database. (See Figure 5.2.)

5. In the New window, name the database and select the file folder in which to save it.

6. Next a window entitled Creating a New Database appears. (See Figure 5.2.) Create each field for the database by typing in the name of the field, for example, First Name. Specify the type of data that will be held in the field. The choices are Boolean (yes or no; 1 or 0), calculate (stores the result of a formula), date, memo (for notes), picture, text, time, and variable (stores intermediate values for macros). Then specify the size (number of characters) of the field. Once all fields have been defined, click OK.

7. Lotus Approach then creates a database form entitled Blank Database and Worksheet 1. Worksheet 1 is the database table in which data are stored. See Figure 5.2 in which there is a worksheet and a database form.

8. Note that on the upper left side of the worksheet and database form in Figure 5.2, just above the tabs labeled Form 1 and Worksheet 1, there are two buttons labeled Browse and Design. Upon clicking the Design button, one can modify the location and size of any of the fields in the database form. For instance, the fields Health Issues and Notes were enlarged within the Design view. Additionally, the name of the database was changed from Blank Database to Client Database.

9. To add fields to the worksheet (database table), in the menu bar under Worksheet, select Add field.

10. To create a new database form with the new fields in the worksheet, select Create in the menu bar and then choose Form. Specify the desired layout and fields for the new form and then click Done.

Comparing the procedures for creating a flat file database in Access and Approach, it is clear that there are commonalties between the two database applications. Both programs (a) offer database development tools (SmartMaster and Wizard), (b) require users to create a new file and save it, (c) name and define new fields, (d) create database tables composed of the specified fields, and (e) have a means for producing a data entry form. The end result of either of the procedures described here is a flat file database

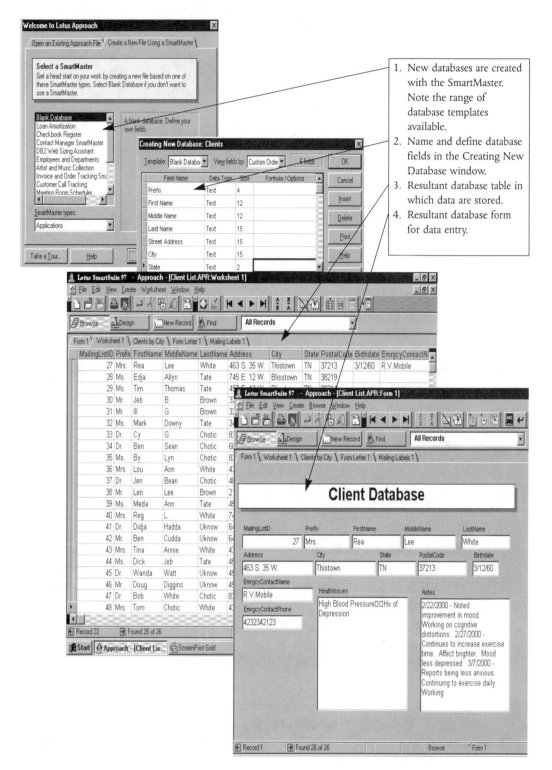

1. New databases are created with the SmartMaster. Note the range of database templates available.
2. Name and define database fields in the Creating New Database window.
3. Resultant database table in which data are stored.
4. Resultant database form for data entry.

FIGURE 5.2   Flat File Database Table and Form Creation in Lotus Approach

for the collection and storage of information: in this case, a client contact database. In creating the database table and data entry, we produced two database objects that make possible two of the basic functions of databases, data entry and storage. Before considering the other three functions—organization, selection, and reporting—we will examine another commonly used method for data entry and creation of a database table for data storage: importing an existing database.

Importing a Database

In personal computing the term *import* refers to the use in one software application of data created in another software application (Margolis, 1996). The ability to import data adds utility to a software application and allows applications to complement each other in their functionality. Database files are imported into database applications from a variety of sources and for a wide range of reasons. Importing of external data into database applications has application in developing mailing lists, examining client services (Patterson & Lee, 1995, 1998), analyzing and reporting financial transactions, compiling social service resources from multiple sources, and creating new databases from Web-based databases.

Imported data from existing databases can form the foundation of new databases with utility extending beyond the original database. For example, consider the possibilities available after importing a database file from one's agency's central database containing a list of all of one's clients, along with address and demographic information. Once the file is opened in a database application, additional fields, such as health issues and case notes, could be added to capture data for a client contact database. Consideration of this possibility is predicated on the assumption that necessary precautions are taken to protect the security and confidentiality of the client information.

In Chapter 4, an example was offered of extracting a flat file of clients' names and addresses from a mental health center's database which was subsequently imported into a spreadsheet. Such a file could also be imported into a database application. Once in the database application, sorting and selection of client records along numerous dimensions and for various applications is possible. For instance, the mental health center may wish to survey clients in a particular geographic area to identify any service delivery problems. Once the data are extracted from the center's central database, they can be imported into a database application. With the file in the database application, all clients receiving services in a particular geographic area could be selected based on Zip code. This subgroup's name and address information could then be used in a mail merge to create a personalized customer satisfaction survey and address labels.

Data files are importable into database applications from spreadsheets, other personal computer applications as well as from mainframe databases, network file servers, and from Internet sources. The importation of data from any of these sources saves the time and effort that otherwise would be required if the data were to be input into a new database file by retyping. This is a nontrivial consideration given the expense of data entry and the relative ease with which most database files are imported into present-day database applications.

Both Microsoft Access and Lotus Approach will import a wide range of data file formats. Table 5.2 is a list of widely used file formats that Access and Approach will import.

Despite the range of file formats that these two database applications purport to import, two notes of caution are necessary. First, the drivers (small programs) necessary to open all of these file formats are not always installed by the database applications at the time the programs are first loaded onto the hard drive of a personal computer. In fact, it is sometimes necessary to visit either the Microsoft or Lotus Web page in order to download the appropriate driver. Given this importing obstacle, it is generally advantageous to save the file intended for importing in a commonly used file format such as Access or dBase. Better still, saving the file from the original database as an Excel or Lotus 1-2-3 file will further facilitate the ease with which it is imported. A second related caution is that it is often much easier to open a spreadsheet file that is native to the software suite of the database application than to open a spreadsheet file from another software suite. For instance, a file saved in Microsoft Excel file format is less complicated to open in Microsoft Access than a Lotus 1-2-3 file. Conversely, Lotus Approach seems to have far less difficulty opening a Lotus 1-2-3 file than an Excel file. Therefore, when possible, save spreadsheet files for exporting in the spreadsheet format that is native to the software suite of the database application that will be used to open it. Both Excel and Lotus 1-2-3 will save files, under Save As, Type, in the other's file format. This small step can often save considerable time and effort in importing a file.

The essential task in importing a data file into a database application is to create a database table with which other database objects can interact and other database functions are possible. The basic steps in importing a file into either Access or Approach are very similar. In Access, open a new database and from the database screen select

TABLE 5.2   Access and Approach Importable File Formats (Fuller & Pagan, 1997)

Microsoft Access Importable File Formats	Lotus Approach Importable File Formats
dBase III, III+, IV, and 5	Access
FoxPro	dBase III, IV
HTLM lists and tables	File delimited
Lotus 1-2-3	FoxPro
Microsoft Excel	Lotus 1-2-3
ODBC (Open Database Connectivity)	Oracle
Older Access databases	Paradox
Paradox	Text delimited

Tables, then Import Tables. This starts the Import Spreadsheet Wizard, which leads the user through the process of importing a spreadsheet. The Wizard will ask:

1. for the location of the spreadsheet to be imported,
2. whether the first row contains the column headings (field names),
3. whether to store the data in a new or existing table,
4. if one wishes to specify the type of data in each field, add a primary key (index), and
5. the name of the file.

Once this process is completed, the spreadsheet will exist in a database table.

If one is working with an already existing database, data are imported into Access under File, Get External Data, Import or Link Tables. If Import is selected, the Import Wizard is started and the steps are similar to the steps described for importing a spreadsheet. The Link Tables option is a more advanced form of database creation. Importing of a database file is much like taking a snapshot of the database at one moment in time. This is particularly true if the database is being continually updated with additional information (Fuller & Pagan, 1997). In importing the data, a copy of the database at that moment in time is created. Linking, on the other hand, uses the data in the original database. The complexity in this process arises from issues of gaining access to an active database—this is usually done over a computer network—and whether the developer of the Access database can update or alter the original database. Readers interested in this option should see Fuller and Pagan (1997) for a more detailed discussion of the matter.

The steps for importing data files into Lotus Approach and creating a new database table (worksheet) are very similar to those in Access. Before starting Approach, be sure to know the location and file format type of the data file that is to be imported into Approach. Upon starting Approach, the Welcome to Lotus Approach window appears. Click Cancel. From the menu bar, select File, Open and the Open window will appear, which displays the files in the selected folder. In Files of Type, select the file format type of the file being imported, then click on the file and hit Open. Approach will open the file into a database table (worksheet) and create a form for it.

The top image in Figure 5.3 displays an Approach database table created by importing a Lotus 1-2-3 spreadsheet. These are the same data that appeared in the Excel spreadsheet in Chapter 4. The Excel spreadsheet was saved as a file in Lotus 1-2-3 format. The Lotus 1-2-3 spreadsheet was imported into Approach with the process described in the previous paragraph. The Client Database form in Figure 5.3 was created by Approach as the data were imported. The Health Issues and Notes fields were enlarged by clicking the Design button, which changes the form from the Browse view, in which data entry/data display occurs, to the Design view, in which changes can be made to the form. To enlarge a field, click on the field and move the cursor to the bottom right or left corner. The cursor will change from a hand shape into a bidirectional arrow at which point the field can be clicked on and expanded to the desired size. To

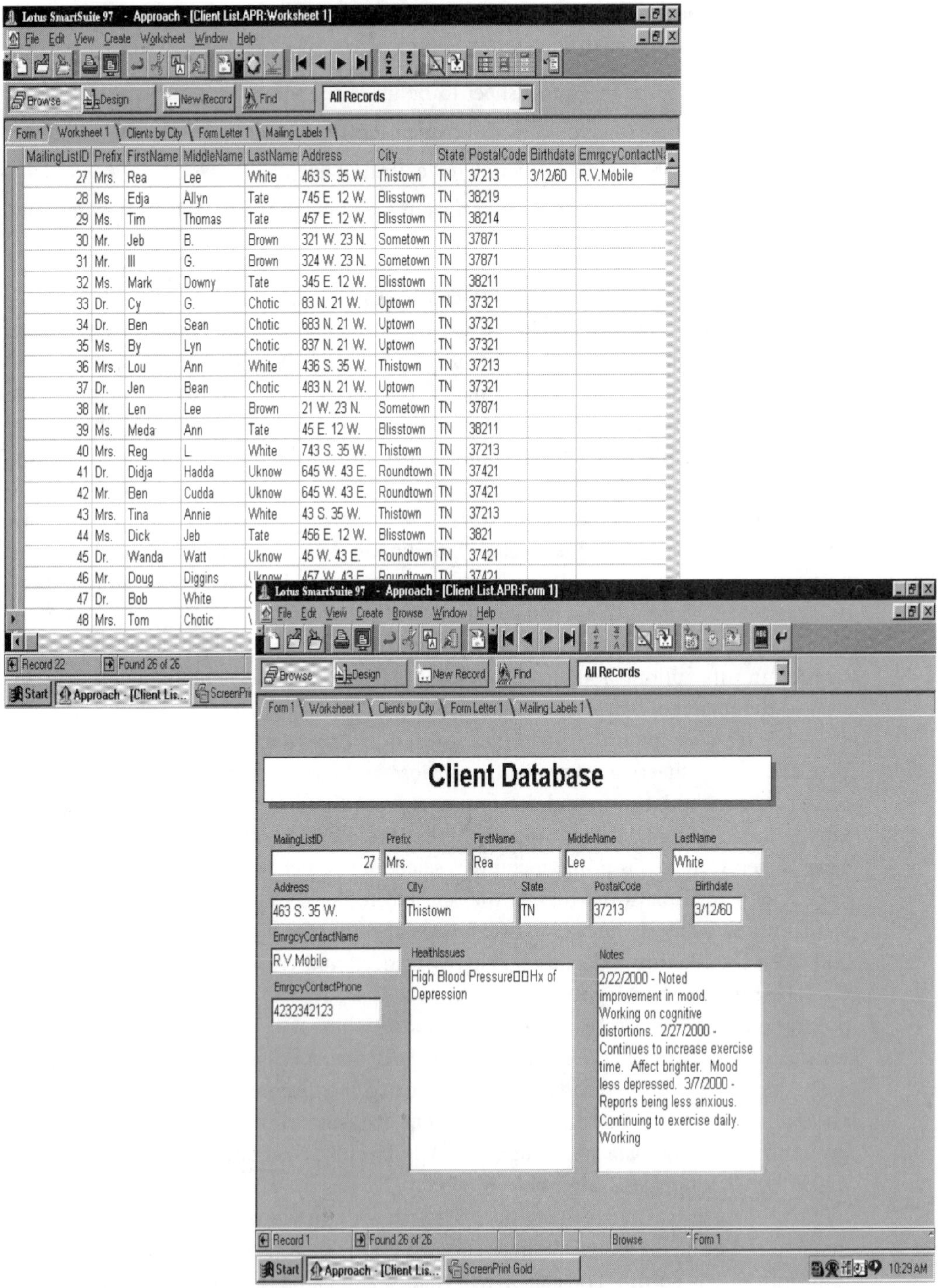

FIGURE 5.3   Data from a Spreadsheet Imported into a Lotus Approach Database

change the location of a field, click on it and drag it to the desired location on the form. Once the desired changes are made in the data entry form, click the Browse button. The modifications to the database table will then appear in the Browse view.

There are times, after creating a database, when it is necessary to import additional data from an external source. This is done in Approach by clicking File, then Import Data. The Import Data window appears, which requires designating the location from which the file will be imported, the name of the file, and the file format type. After providing this information and clicking OK, the next window to appear is Import Setup. This window displays the names of the field in the database file being imported and the names of the fields in the existing (or receiving) Approach database. The fields in the Approach database can be dragged up or down to match the fields in the external database (the one being imported). Between the list of external file fields and the list of the existing database's fields there is a column. Clicking in this column will cause the display of an arrow indicating that the external field is to be imported. Figure 5.4 displays the Import Setup window. Once the links between the external data and the existing database are created, click OK to import the external data.

The fundamental point of the preceding discussion is demonstration of the capacity and relative ease with which data files from various sources and types of applications are importable into database applications. This ability to draw data from numerous sources makes it possible for social service workers to create small, custom databases

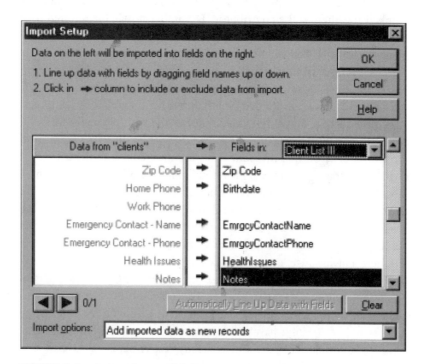

FIGURE 5.4   Lotus Approach's Import Setup Window

applicable to their specific employment tasks. Once the functions of data entry and data storage are activated in a database, the next logical question that arises is what to do with the data. It is toward this issue that the discussion now turns.

Data Organization

The ability to use data in a database is partially contingent on how the data are organized. The organization of data in a database is a function of how it is stored and how it is arranged after it is stored. The construction of database tables for data storage requires decisions regarding what types of information will be stored in what order and in how many tables. As described previously, data in flat file databases are organized in a single database table whereas relational databases organize data in two or more tables that are linked to each other.

The organizational advantage of a relational database is that the storage of data in two or more tables introduces considerable flexibility into the capture, selection, and retrieval of information. Take, for example, a financial contributors database in which there are two database tables, Contributors and Pledges. The Contributors table holds contributor ID number, name, address, and phone information on all contributors. The Pledges table holds contributor ID number; pledge information including date, amount pledged, whether the pledge was paid; and credit card information. The two tables are linked together by the contributor ID number in what is referred to as a one-to-many relationship (Fuller & Pagan, 1997). In this example, the one-to-many relationship means that each contributor in the Contributors table can have many records (pledges) in the Pledges table. Conversely, each pledge in the Pledges table can have only one contributor (matching record) in the Contributors database. This organization of the relationship between the two tables allows for the collection and reporting of data on multiple pledges by a single contributor or the multiple pledges of all contributors. The contributor ID number that links the two tables ensures that contributions made by contributor A on five different dates are all credited to contributor A. Consequently, when generating a report on the total amounts pledged by all contributors, the database application finds each contributor's name in the Contributors database table and sums the total pledges with data drawn from the Pledges database table.

This organization of one-to-many relationships in a relational database has many potential applications in personal computer databases used by social service practitioners. For instance, a client contact database can store client demographic and diagnostic information in one database table and contact dates, charges, payments, and notes in another database table. The advantage of this organizational arrangement in a client contact database is that once the client demographic and diagnostic information is entered, it does not have to be reentered with each visit or contact. Instead, visit or contact information such as dates, charges, payments, and notes is stored in another table linked to the table containing the client demographic and diagnostic information.

It is then possible to create reports that combine client information with contact and billing information.

Detailing the steps in creation of a relational database is beyond the scope of this book. Both Microsoft Access and Lotus Approach have extensive integrated Help files that can assist the users interested in creating a custom relational database. Users considering embarking on developing a relational database should understand that such a course can be time consuming, complex, and may require informational resources beyond the scope of the database application's online Help. Moreover, there are often alternative forms of databases that will organize data in ways consistent with their data requirements.

Both Access and Approach offer template databases that organize data in relational databases. Figure 5.5 displays the main menu screen of an employee and department database available in Lotus Approach. This is a relational database in which there are links between the database tables for employees, departments, and managers. The data are organized so that when examining information on each department, data on the employees in the department is accessible, indicating the presence of a link between the departments database table and the employees database table. The utility of this form of organization is that it allows the user to access a much greater level of informational detail. If there was not a linkage between the departments database table and the employees database table the user could view whatever data were available for the department, but could not see detail on the employees in the department. This employees and departments database template is but one example of the relational database templates available in Access and Approach. Other database templates include

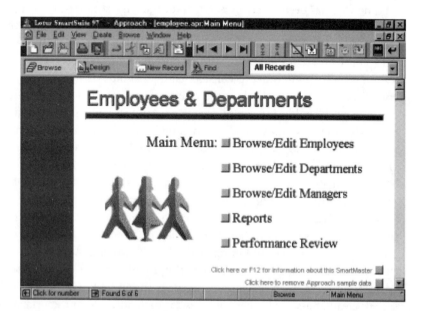

FIGURE 5.5   Main Menu Screen of a Lotus Approach Relational Database

donations, contact management, order tracking, asset tracking, expenses, inventory control, and time/billing.

The second dimension in organization of data in a database is its arrangement. The arrangement of records in a database table is alterable by sorting. The database applications' capacity to sort records is a powerful tool for evaluating and understanding data in the database. Any field, text or numerical, in the database table can be sorted in ascending or descending order. In a spreadsheet, when a column is sorted, only that column is sorted unless all the columns are selected, in which case the entire spreadsheet is sorted. In database applications, sorting any field (column) does not simply sort that field, but instead sorts the entire database on that field so the information in each record remains intact.

The utility of sorting a database field is that it makes it possible to examine the data from multiple perspectives and to find individuals or subgroups of interest within the data. Returning to the data from Patterson and Lee's (1998, 1995) studies of intensive case management, we will explore how the sorting of this database can reveal new information about the data. To start, the database was imported into both Microsoft Access and into Lotus Approach to create databases in each of these applications. It is worth noting as a follow-up to the previous discussion on the importing of data that in order to open the file that was in an Excel spreadsheet in Lotus Approach, it was necessary to first save a copy of it in Lotus 1-2-3 format. However, once the file was converted to Lotus 1-2-3 format, Approach readily created a database with it.

The utility of sorting a database is partially predicated on what questions one has about the data. A user may wish to sort cases on length of treatment in order to determine who has been receiving services for the longest time. Or sorting a database on numbers of hospitalizations will identify clients who need special outpatient care to prevent hospitalization. Each sort of the database represents a new question about the data. For instance, we might want to identify the cases with the lowest levels of medication compliance in order to consider additional interventions to support medication compliance. Figure 5.6 displays the results of sorting the intensive case management database on the field MedCompliance (medication compliance). Identified there are all the cases of clients whose medication compliance is rated under 2 on a 0 to 9 scale with 0 being not applicable and 9 being the highest level of medication compliance. Using the vertical scrollbar makes it possible to examine the rank ordering of the cases. The horizontal scrollbar allows for reviewing across the database fields any other noteworthy attributes of the medication noncompliant clients.

The procedure for sorting a database in Approach is described in Figure 5.6. The procedure is the same in Access. One notable difference between the two database applications is that Access allows for multiple sorts whereas Approach does not. A multiple sort is a sort within a sort. To clarify, a multiple sort can only be done on two adjacent columns, with the leftmost column sorted first. The second column is then sorted, creating a sorted subset of cases for each attribute in the primary sort column. Figure 5.7 illustrates the results of a multiple sort. Note that MedCompliance is the primary field sorted and that the adjacent column Access-A (ability to access and use trans-

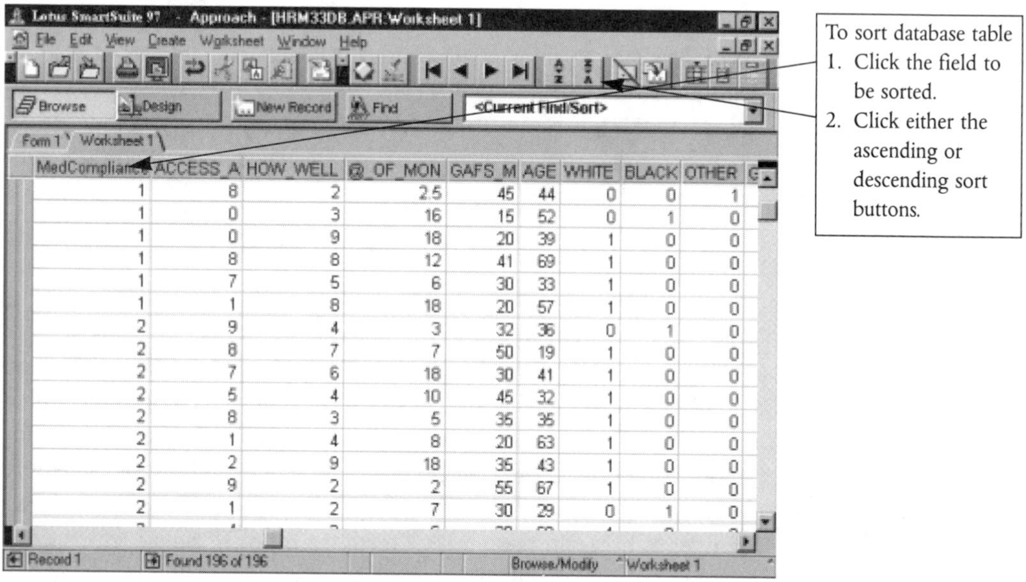

FIGURE 5.6   Intensive Case Management Database Sorted on Medication Compliance

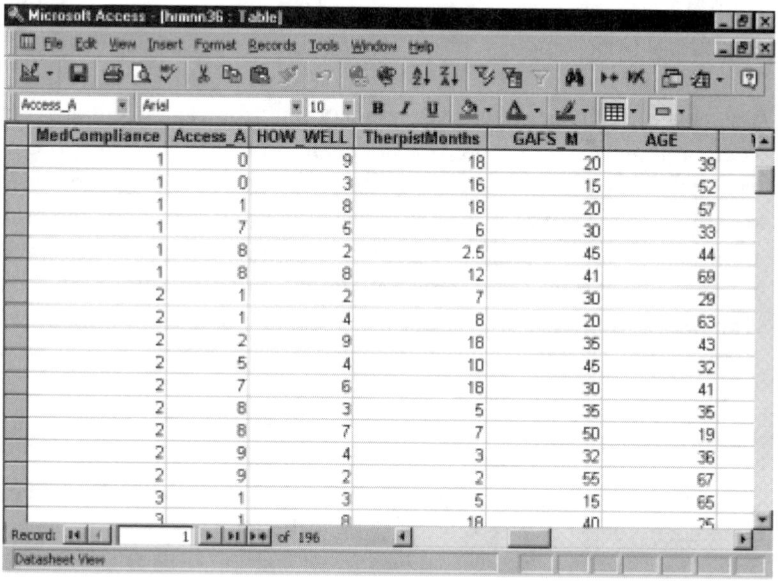

FIGURE 5.7   An Access Database Table with a Multiple Sort

portation) is within each level of MedCompliance. Comparing Figures 5.6 and 5.7, it is apparent that although MedCompliance with both database applications is ranked the same way, the cases within each level of ranking are arranged differently in the two figures. This type of multiple sort is of particular benefit in large databases in which many cases hold the same attribute, such as diagnosis of depression, and one is interested in identifying subgroups, such as clients with a secondary diagnosis of alcohol dependence. A multiple sort on the field Primary and Secondary Diagnosis would quickly identify all clients with a diagnosis of depression and alcohol dependence. In essence, by using the multiple sorts we have reorganized the data to identify a subgroup of clients of particular interest.

Data Selection

The data selection functions in database applications enable users to find information within the database. Whereas the sorting of a database reorganizes the information so subsets of the data are identifiable, data selection represents a number of procedures for the extraction of information from the database. For instance, one might want to identify clients without a high school diploma or GED in a program to provide self-sufficiency skills to clients in danger of becoming homeless. Creating a list of all clients with a GED or high school diploma from the agency's database is accomplished by querying the Education Level field in the database for all clients with a GED or years of school greater than 12. This query results in a copy of all cases meeting the specified criteria. As is demonstrated in the next section, data selection offers considerably more power and flexibility for finding complex categories of information than database sorting.

The procedures for data selection in Microsoft Access and Lotus Approach are considerably different, although the resultant selection capabilities are comparable. To add to the complexity, these two database applications use different terms for essentially the same selection procedures. Despite this variance in language, the selection procedures described in the next sections essentially allow users to pose complex selection questions of databases in order to extract specific information. This refined selection capacity represents a robust tool for social service practitioners wishing to better understand data drawn from their area of practice. More importantly, it is a powerful means to understand and serve the clients and consumers from whom the data come.

In Lotus Approach

Lotus Approach refers to its set of tools for data selection as the Find environment. The Find environment is accessed by clicking the Find button in the toolbar at the top of the screen. Doing so opens a screen in which the fields in the database are displayed along with an "action bar" which displays a number of buttons representing various selection operators. These selection operators include equal to, less than, greater than, less than or equal to, greater than or equal to, and items matching a specified range. Selections are performed by clicking a field or fields and applying an operator.

Figure 5.8 displays the Find environment with fields from the intensive case management database. Note the buttons with the selection operator icons in the toolbar be-

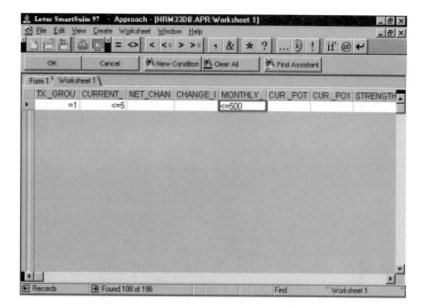

FIGURE 5.8   Lotus Approach Find Environment

neath the menu bar. In this figure, operators are applied to the fields TX_GROU (treatment group), CURRENT_ (current living situation), and MONTHLY_ (monthly income). These selection criteria will find every case in treatment group 1 (intensive case management) whose current living situation was rated as less than or equal to 5 (on a 1 to 9 scale) and with an income less than or equal to $500. When the selection criteria are applied, 42 cases of clients in the intensive case management program and meeting the living situation and monthly income criteria are found. The ability to apply multiple selection criteria across multiple fields dramatically increases the selectivity available for finding required information.

There are times when it is necessary to find a range or group of cases based on exclusion or inclusion criteria. One might want to find all cases within a certain monthly income range. The range icon is three periods (. . .) and is used to make this type of selection possible. To apply it, select the field of interest, in this case monthly income, then specify the high and low values of the desired range. To find all cases with income between $400 and $600 per month, type 400 into the monthly income field, click the range icon, and then type 600. The selection criteria appear in the cell as 400 . . . 600 and when the Enter key is pressed, 146 cases are identified. The opposite selection problem is to identify cases outside of a particular range of values. For instance, one may wish to find all cases with monthly incomes less than $400 and greater than $600. To accomplish this selection, click the monthly income field, then click the "less than" icon, and type 400. Next click the "either condition" icon, which is a comma. Finally, click the "greater than" icon and type 600. The resultant selection criteria appear in the cell as

<400,>600 and identify all cases meeting either of the two criteria. This type of selection is particularly useful for finding outliers, or atypical cases, within a database.

Lotus Approach has a Find Assistant that guides a user through defining criteria for record selection and display. The Find Assistant is activated by clicking the Find Assistant button in the Find environment. Once the Find Assistant is activated, a window labeled Find/Sort Assistant appears which has four tabs, representing steps the Find Assistant procedure moves through. The labels on the tabs vary depending on the type of Find selection one wishes to perform. The choices are "Basic find," "Find duplicate records," "Find distinct records," "Find the top or lowest values," and "Find using query by box."

The Basic find option guides the user through find and sort procedures described in the previous paragraphs. Selection on multiple field criteria can be established to select cases meeting specified conditions. In the next step in the basic find procedure, the user may choose to sort the selected records on a specified field. The final step is to name the Find procedure. Naming the procedure saves the steps in the process. The named selection process runs automatically when the find procedure is activated by selecting it from a drop-down list in Approach's toolbar. The Find Assistant has in essence created a selection command statement which can be rerun as the database expands or whenever it is necessary to find the cases specified by the parameters selected in the Find Assistant procedure. In this case the selection command statement is . . . "In database "HRM33DB", find all records in field "MED._COM" that are greater than (>) "5" AND in database "HRM33DB", find all records in field "CURRENT_" that are greater than (>) "5". Sorted in ascending order by MED._COM." This type of automated selection procedure is applicable for regularly searching for cases in a client contact database with a volatile or at-risk condition who have not been contacted within a specified length of time.

Four other types of Find procedures are available in the Find/Sort Assistant. Find duplicate records is useful in locating records inadvertently entered more than once. Find distinct records is applicable for finding unique records in databases where there are multiple entries for each case. It is useful, for instance, in developing a mailing list. Find the top or lowest values applies in selecting outlier cases in the database. The Find using query by box is a more sophisticated selection tool functional in situations in which complex AND or OR statements are required. The use of AND in the selection process indicates that multiple conditions or criteria must be satisfied: for instance, select all cases in treatment group 1 AND all cases with a medication compliance rating less than 4. This selection statement finds all cases that meet both criteria treatment group 1 and medication compliance less than 4. The OR statement is used to find records that meet one of several criteria. For instance, GAFS-M (social and occupational functioning) less than 40 OR a current potential for violence greater than 7 (on a 1–9 scale). Figure 5.9 displays an elaborate set of selection criteria developed in the Query by Box selection tool. Note that the selection criteria will result in the selection of all cases from the database that are in treatment group 1, have a level of medication compliance less than or equal to 4, a GAFS-M score less than or equal to 40, are male OR have a current potential for violence greater than or equal to 7.

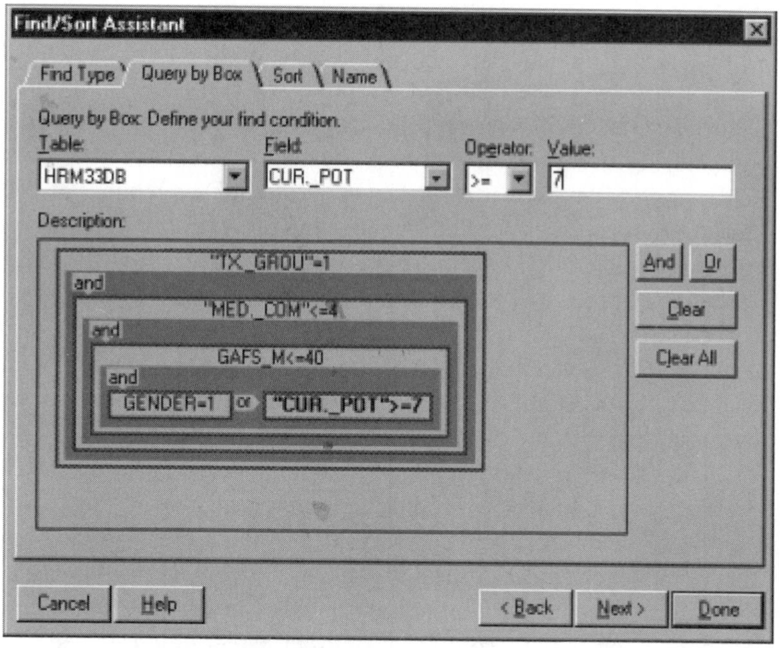

FIGURE 5.9   Lotus Approach Query by Box Assistant

All of the Find types available in the Find/Sort Assistant can be produced and saved for selection tasks that are regularly performed. Moreover, it is possible to save or print the records found through any of the selection procedures of Approach described here. Using the Save View As command, under the File command, selected records are savable in a variety of formats, including HTML which is used for World Wide Web files. Additionally, records selected by these procedures can be imported into reports using the report creation tool which is described later in this chapter. For now, it is sufficient to say that the intricacies of database record selection detailed here produce not only on-screen information, but can be imported into electronic and hard copy output through a variety of means.

In Microsoft Access

The procedures for data selection available in Microsoft Access are extensive and in many ways parallel those of Lotus Approach. These procedures include a simple find operation, database filtering, and queries. From the former to the latter there is a marked increase in the power of the procedures and the complexity of information that is retrievable using them.

The most fundamental means to locate information in a database table is the Find tool. The Find tool is useful in seeking a particular value or finding the record(s) of a person or object in the database table. It will find the first occurrence of the sought information and will continue to seek out other occurrences if prompted by clicking the Find Next button. The Find tool is represented in the Access Toolbar with an icon of binoculars. It is also available in the menu bar under Edit. To search a field for a specific value or string of text, first click the field, then activate the Find tool through the Edit command or Toolbar icon. The Find tool offers a number of choices with which to expand or constrain the search. There is a box to check if one wishes to search only the specified field. Removing the check opens the search to the entire database table. It should be noted that the Find tool can be used with both database tables and with data entry forms. When entering client data in the data entry form, the Find tool is very convenient in searching for a specific client. Moreover, when examining records in the data entry form, it is much more efficient to find specific cases with the Find tool than by paging through the data case by case.

The next set of data selection procedures available in Access is data filtering (Fuller & Pagan, 1997). In many ways data filtering is similar to the Find environment of Lotus Approach previously described. Data filtering finds and segregates requested information from the remainder of the database. In essence it filters the sought information out of the rest of the information in the database. For instance, one might want to filter a database to locate the record of every foster parent on a caseload who currently does not have a foster child. Applying a data filter to a foster parent database is a fast and efficient way to locate a potential home for a foster child.

The first data filtering procedure for consideration is the Filter by Selection button which is represented in the Access Toolbar by an icon with a funnel and a lightning bolt. The Filter by Selection tool is also available in the menu bar under Records and by using a right click of the mouse. To activate the Filter by Selection tool, first open the database table or data entry form containing the data of interest. Within the field containing the data of interest, click on the attribute for which to filter records. For instance, if we wished to locate all foster parents who currently do not have a child in placement, we locate the field Child Currently in Home, and click on a case with "No" entered. We then click the Filter by Selection tool and Access displays all foster families in the caseload who currently do not have a foster child in placement. In this process, clicking the attribute within the field indicates to the database application the attribute to filter for and activation of the Filter by Selection tool either through the Toolbar icon, the menu bar, or by right clicking the mouse, results in the application of the data filter.

The opposite selection procedure to Filter by Selection is Filter by Exclusion, which finds all records without the selected attribute. This type of selection procedure is particularly helpful in fields that contain categorical data such as race, diagnosis, or insurance type. It makes possible the selection of all cases without a particular attribute. For example, in order to make a special-needs foster care placement, one might wish to identify in a foster parent database all nonwhite foster parents. To employ the Filter by Exclusion tool, click on the attribute to exclude for in the data field of interest. Now either right click the mouse and select Filter by Exclusion or from the menu bar under Records select Filter by Exclusion. Access will display all records that do not have the excluded attribute.

A third filtering procedure available by right clicking is the Filter For tool. This selection procedure allows the information seeker to employ wild cards and masks. *Wild cards* are special symbols that represent values or text (Internet.com, 1998). The asterisk symbol (*) is commonly used to indicate any combination of letters or values (Margolis, 1996). A wild card is applicable in the Filter For tool when searching for all cases with, for instance, last names starting with the letter T. To find this subset of cases, click in the field to search in, then right click and beside the Filter For tool type T*. After hitting Enter, all cases with a last name starting with T are displayed.

A *mask* is a type of filter that selects for or excludes certain values (Margolis, 1996). They are essentially the same as the operators used in Lotus Approach for selection. These symbols that indicate a particular mathematical operation include =, >,<, =>, =<. Unfortunately, neither Access's Help file nor its manual specifies the full range of masks available. The range operator (. . .) does not function in the Filter For selection tool. Nonetheless, the Filter For tool has utility in finding values that can be limited by the identified masks (=, >, <, =>, =<).

A fourth filtering procedure is Filter by Form, which is represented in the Toolbar as an icon with a funnel and a form. It is also available in the menu bar under Records. Upon activating the Filter by Form tool, the screen changes to a blank filter form with each field of the database table displayed and a set of tabs at the bottom of the form. Clicking on the cell beneath any field name creates a button with a down arrow, which when clicked opens a drop-down list of each of the attributes in the field. For example, clicking Group (treatment group) lists 1 and 2 as attributes. An advantage of the Filter by Form tool is that selection criteria can be applied to multiple fields, with the specification of filtering criteria on each field further refining the record selection. The use of masks or operators will add specificity to the search. For instance, Figure 5.10 displays a Filter by Form tool to select all cases that meet the criteria of being in Group 1 AND having a current living situation greater than or equal to 5, AND with a monthly income less than

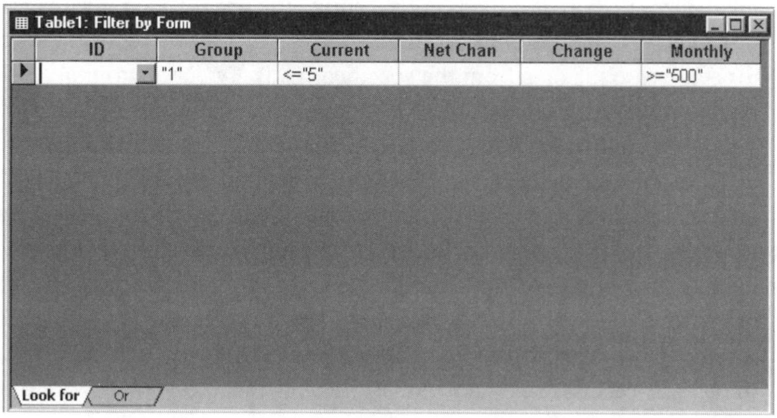

FIGURE 5.10   Microsoft Access Filter by Form

or equal to $500. The use of the capitalized AND here indicates the application of multiple selection criteria. Note the OR tabs at the bottom of the form. They are used to add inclusion criteria that will add additional records to the selection. For instance, after specifying the selection criteria for group status, living situation, and monthly income, clicking on the OR tab and adding the criteria GAFS-M $< = 40$ will pull into the selected cases the additional cases that did not meet the first three criteria but do meet the OR criteria. Once the selection criteria are specified, the Filter by Form tool is activated with the Filter icon in the Toolbar. Filter by Form procedures may be saved under File, Save As Query (Fuller & Pagan, 1997). This is a particularly useful feature when developing complex filtering procedures that will be run on a frequent basis.

Queries are a versatile and powerful set of data selection tools available in Access. In many ways Queries are similar to the Find Assistant in Lotus Approach. Both will find records with duplicate values, unique or matched records, draw records from one or more databases, and can be configured and saved as a custom search and selection tool that can be regularly reapplied as the database grows. Queries are found in Access as one of the database objects of the database application's environment. As can be seen in Figure 5.11, clicking the Queries tab accesses Queries.

The creation of a new query is initiated by clicking the New button which opens a window offering five choices for a new query. The first choice is Design View, with which queries are constructed from scratch. With this tool one may specify the tables and/or fields from which to select records and the sorting order and criteria with which to select records. Designing a query from Design View requires some familiarity with the querying process in Access and is likely best used when one has multiple tables and existing queries from which it is necessary to select information. Utilization of the Design View tool to construct a query should be reserved for data selection problems that cannot be accomplished with queries that may be designed with the Simple Query Wizard described next.

The second choice available in the New Query window is Simple Query Wizard, which will create a query for one or multiple tables. The wizard directs the user through the process of selecting database tables and fields from which it will extract data. Once the database tables and fields are specified, the wizard then asks whether record detail or summary information is required. Answering "detail" will cause the query to select for every case the data from the specified fields. Operators to limit the record selection are added in a subsequent step in this process. Choosing "summary information" instead of "detail" results in being presented with the option to summarize fields on one or all of four parameters: sum, average, minimum, or maximum. The "summary information" option is particularly useful for client service utilization data such as total (sum) treatment delivered, average length of stay, minimum and maximum fees paid, and so forth. In the next screen of the Simple Query Wizard the user selects a name for the query so that it is saved with the database and can be used to query the database again whenever necessary without having to construct the query again. On the same screen the user selects the next step, either opening the query to view information or modifying the query design. Opening the query to view information causes the query to select from the database table(s) the specified information and display it on screen.

The second option of modifying the query design produces the screen illustrated in Figure 5.11, the Design View. Notice that the upper half of the screen shows a window for the database table (hrmnn36) from which the data are selected. If the query pulls data from more than one database table or another query, they also are displayed in this half of the screen.

The lower portion of the screen shows the selected fields and the name of the database table that contains the field. Clicking a cell in the Sort row opens a drop-down box in which the order of sorting is selectable (ascending or descending). Selection of sorting order is not required. In the Show row, a click box makes it possible to indicate whether the field is to be displayed in the results of the query. At times, one or more fields are used to calculate a new field and the query designer may wish to display in the results only the calculated field, electing to hide the fields that are used in the calculation. For instance, a database may contain fields for Appointments Scheduled and Appointments Kept. In the design view, a third calculated field for Missed Appointments shows the results of Appointments Scheduled minus Appointments Kept. In such a case it is unnecessary to display Appointments Scheduled, therefore the query designer can elect to not click the field show box.

In the row labeled Criteria, selection criteria using operators can be designated. Selection criteria may be added to each field shown on the screen. The addition of each criteria adds specificity to the search and further delimits the records selected. The Criteria row has the added feature of being able to query by example. So for instance, if seeking all records of financial contributors from Ohio, typing in the Criteria cell of a database field State, "Ohio OR OH" would return all cases with either state designation

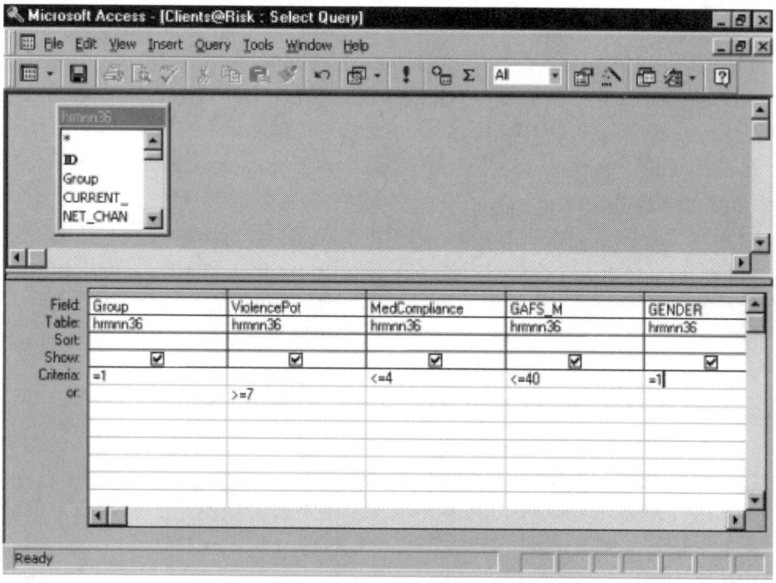

FIGURE 5.11   Microsoft Access Query Design View

(Fuller & Pagan, 1997). This feature is particularly useful in fields with text-based information in which there has been variability in the way an attribute is specified during data entry, for example, Ohio or OH.

Notice that in Figure 5.11, the same set of selection criteria that were used in Figure 5.9 with the Lotus Approach Query by Box Assistant are applied. The same database was imported into both Approach and Access and using the same criteria with the two different query tools produced the same selection of records. It is important to reiterate that these two database applications employ different user interfaces to achieve the same ends in data selection. What is perhaps most important to recognize is the similarities that underlie both procedures. Both require designation of the database tables and fields from which to select data and specification of the criteria for record selection.

Returning to consideration of Figure 5.11, although the fields for the record selection were selected with the Simple Query Wizard, additional fields may be added to the query in the Design view. To add a field to the query, select it from the database table window in the upper portion of the screen and drag it to the grid in the lower portion of the screen displaying the other fields in the query. Fields may be added to the query during its initial design or later by selecting the query from the Queries tab and clicking the Design view button. This capacity to edit queries allows for refinement of search parameters to meet evolving information requirements.

In Figure 5.11, note in the Toolbar there is an icon of an exclamation mark. Once modifications of the query are completed in the Design view, the query is activated by clicking this icon. To run the query again at some later point, click on the name of the query in the Query tab. In many situations, a query is run on the database on a regular basis in order to select information for the generation of reports. It is important to note that as a database grows and changes, the results of queries can summarize and reflect those changes.

Once the results of the query are displayed on the screen, they may be distributed electronically over a network in a variety of file formats with the Send command. The Send command is available in the menu bar under File. A second option also under File is Export. Export allows for the exporting of query results to an external file or database, or saving results as a new table within Access. The use of query results in report generation is described below in the section on report generation.

Three other options for generating new queries are available under New Query in the Query Tab of an Access database, Crosstab Query Wizard, Find Duplicates Query Wizard, and Find Unmatched Query Wizard. Each of these Query Wizards directs the user through the requisite steps to create a specialized query. The Crosstab Query Wizard guides the user through the process of creating a cross tabulation table from data in one or more database tables. As discussed in Chapter 4, a cross tabulation table is a means to collapse and summarize data.

To create a cross tabulation table with the Crosstab Query Wizard, in the Query Tab select New Query, then Crosstab Query Wizard. In the first step of the Crosstab Query Wizard, select the table or query containing the fields that will be summarized in the cross tabulation table. It is possible to draw data from multiple tables and queries by first creating a single query that extracts the requisite fields for the cross tabulation table from the multiple tables and queries. Once that query is created or an existing database table or query holding the necessary fields is selected, the second step is selecting the fields for row headings. Up to three row headings may be chosen, selecting them in the order in which the data are to be sorted. Using two or three row headings allows for the examination of increasingly finer levels of detail of the relationship of the fields (variables) to each other. Spreadsheet Exhibit 5.1 is a cross tabulation table with two row fields produced with the Crosstab Query Wizard. The row fields are treatment group and diagnosis of personality disorder. The column field is gender and the number calculated in the cells is average length of hospitalization in a state psychiatric hospital (Patterson & Lee, 1998). The addition of a second row field (diagnosis of a personality disorder) reveals the dramatic differences in lengths of hospitalization for clients without a diagnosis of personality disorder and those with the diagnosis.

The third step in the Crosstab Query Wizard is selection of the field for the column heading. In the previous example, gender is the field for the column heading. The fourth step is selecting the field for calculation in the cells of the row and column intersections. In Spreadsheet Exhibit 5.1 average days of state psychiatric hospitalization are computed for each intersection. Available functions include average, count, first, last, maximum, minimum, standard deviation, sum, and variance. The fifth step is naming the query and deciding whether to view the results or modify the query further in the Design view. If viewing the results is selected, the cross tabulation query is run and appears on screen. Having named the query, it is listed on the Query Tab and may be rerun as the database is updated. The query results that appear in Spreadsheet Exhibit 5.1 were exported to Excel with the Export command and saved with the Excel file format. Opening the exported query file in Excel allowed for modifications of the format and appearance of the file. Once a query has run, it can be exported, printed, or saved as an HTML file for placement on a Web server.

The two remaining types of queries are the Find Duplicates Query Wizard and the Find Unmatched Query Wizard. The Find Duplicates Query Wizard, obviously from its name, locates for removal redundant records in a database table or query. It is especially appropriate for large databases and is generally used for database housekeeping as it removes unnecessary information. The Find Unmatched Query Wizard is used

SPREADSHEET EXHIBIT 5.1
Cross Tabulation of Average Length of State Psychiatric Hospitalization

	A	B	C	D
1			Gender	
2	Treatment Group	DX of P.D.	Males	Females
3	0	0	683	431
4	0	1	319	334
5	1	0	1164	735
6	1	1	273	101

Note: Treatment Group 0 = general outpatient care, 1 = intensive case management; DX of P.D. (diagnosis of a personality disorder) 0 = no, 1 = yes.

when a database consists of two or more database tables. It is used to find records in one table that are not related to records in other tables. Again, this query is best thought of as a database housekeeping tool for cleaning up databases. Both of these housekeeping queries represent a more advanced level of database management and generally have limited utility in the types of small databases described here.

This discussion of data selection procedures reviewed a wide range of tools for locating, summarizing, and extracting information from a database. This collection of procedures makes it possible to find, discern, and understand phenomena contained in the data. Described here are a number of ways in which the selected information may be exported to other databases or other applications, printed, saved for publication on a Web server, or imported into other applications for further analysis and processing. We will now turn our consideration to the report generation capacity of database applications.

Report Generation

The capacity to generate reports makes possible the dissemination of select information from the database. It is the fifth and final function of a database application that we will consider. The ability to organize and summarize information in the creation of reports from data accumulated in a database is a critical function. Depending on the type and sensitivity of the accumulated data, report generation serves to inform both the database owner and interested parties such as supervisors, administrators, clients, customers, and contributors. Reports generated in both Microsoft Access and Lotus Approach are distributable in printed hard copies, e-mail attachments, HTML format for Web servers, or exportable to other software applications for further modification, enhancement, or inclusion in larger documents. This linkage between report generation and flexible dissemination options optimizes the capacity of the database owner to communicate with parties slated to receive reports.

A major consideration in developing a report is identifying the intended audience of the report (Fuller, 1997). Knowing who will use a report and for what purpose shapes the process of deciding what types of information to include in the report, at what level of detail or summary, and in what format to create maximum clarity in the communication. Once the intended audience of the report is specified, it is often a good idea to speak with either the individual who will receive the report or, if the report is intended for a group of individuals, the representatives of the group. The purpose of such a conversation is clarification of what types of information are available in the database and what types of information the intended audience needs to receive and with what frequency. Reports that do not match the information needs of the recipients seldom receive close attention. Such reports often end up in either the physical or electronic wastebasket. Avoidance of this fate necessitates thoughtful examination of the intended recipients' data needs and wishes along with planning and experimentation in report development. Cognizance of the options in report design is therefore essential in this endeavor.

In Lotus Approach

Lotus Approach offers a wide range of options in report design and considerable interactive assistance in their development. This discussion of report design is predicated on the assumption that one has already developed a database from which a report will be developed. To create a report, first open the database and then under Create in the menu bar select Report. Approach opens a Report Assistant, which like the other interactive tools described in this chapter, guides the user through a series of decisions in creating a report. In Step 1, the layout of the report is designated along with a name for the report. The Report Assistant offers six different report layouts that are displayed in a scrollable box. An example of the appearance of each report layout is shown to the right of the scrollable box making it possible to preview the layout options before selecting one. Layout options include Blank, Columnar, Columnar with grand total, Columnar with groups and grand totals, Standard, and Summary only. The number of subsequent steps and choices offered by the Report Assistant vary with the type of report selected. For this example, Columnar with groups and grand totals was chosen as it provides for the creation of subgrouping of data within the report. In the second step, select the database to draw data from along with the fields of data for inclusion in the report. The fields selected for inclusion in the report are dependent on the purpose of the report. In many cases, data from a select few fields provide the requisite information for a report, but some reporting purposes require highly detailed and specific information and thereby draw upon multiple fields in the database. Step 3 asks for designation of the field(s) with which to group the report data. The grouping field usually contains some type of categorical data such as city, diagnostic group, or agency department. The purpose of the grouping field is organization of the data in some manner germane to the intent of the report. The fourth and final step in creating the Columnar with groups and grand totals report is selection of the field on which to calculate the subtotals and grand totals along with the calculation to perform. The choices for calculation are average, count, maximum, minimum, standard deviation, or sum. The field appropriate for selection depends both on the purpose of the report and the type of data in the fields. For instance, one may wish to count the number of clients in each city represented in the database or one might want to sum the cost of services for each diagnostic group. The decision of what field and what calculation to select is contingent on the type of data and the purpose of the report.

Once the report construction choices are made in the Report Assistant, click Done to produce the report. Approach compiles and calculates the report, subsequently displaying it in the Design view. Modifications to the appearance of the report are made in the Design view. Select the Print Preview icon from the Toolbar menu to see how the report will look when printed or distributed in some other electronic format, such as HTML.

Figure 5.12 displays a Columnar with groups and grand totals report created from a client mailing list database. Notice the names are grouped by city and there is a subtotal count at the bottom of the first group. Subtotal counts appear at the bottom of each city group and a grand total count appears at the bottom of the report. The report is now ready for printing or electronic distribution.

In Microsoft Access

Reports are created in Access with the Report Wizard, which is activated under the Reports tab by clicking the New button. Upon clicking the New button, a New Report window appears that offers six choices in types of reports. The first is Design View that allows a user to create a report from scratch without the assistance of a wizard. The second is the Report Wizard, which is very similar to other Access Wizards described in this chapter. It guides the user through the process of generating a report.

The third type of report available is AutoReport: Columnar, which is a simple report generation tool for producing a report containing every field from the selected database table. Information from each record is displayed in a column, and its arrangement is modifiable in the Design View. The fourth report is AutoReport: Tabular, which again is a simple report that compiles all the data from a database table into a report that displays the data in a table format. The appearance of this report also is modifiable in the Design View.

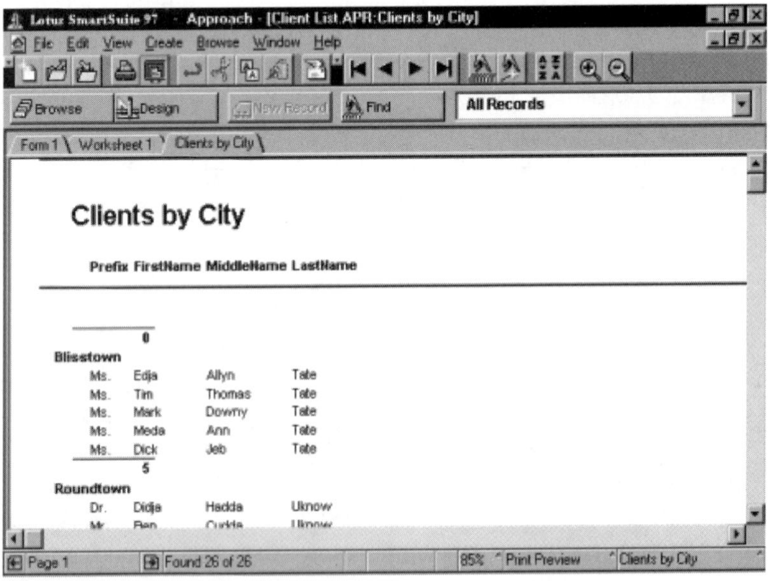

FIGURE 5.12   Lotus Approach Columnar with Groups and Grand Totals Report

Interestingly, both of these auto report tools are applicable to database tables on which a filter or sort is currently applied. For instance, after filtering a client caseload database for all clients with a current potential for self-destructive behavior greater than 6 (1 = absent; 9 = high), reports generated with either the AutoReport: Columnar or AutoReport: Tabular will include only those cases selected by the filter. Both of these report tools also produce reports based on queries. These two reporting tools are particularly suited to generating reports from queries as queries allow for the specification of fields from one or more database tables. As a result, a report from a query based on key fields in a database is readily and simply created with either of these auto report tools. Thus these two report tools are good choices for quickly producing updated reports from regularly run database queries.

The fifth option available for generation of a new report is the Chart Wizard. The Chart Wizard leads the user through the steps of creating a chart in a report based on data in fields from a database table or query. After selecting Chart Wizard from the New report choices, select the database table or query containing the data to be charted. Next choose the fields to be charted. In order to generate a chart, at least one of the fields must contain numeric data. The third step requires picking a type of chart; the choices include column, bar, area, and pie. For a discussion of the applications and relative advantages of various chart types see Chapter 6. The fourth step necessitates choosing the layout of the data fields in the selected chart. In the fifth step, the chart is titled and a legend to describe the meaning of the chart elements is selected or removed. If examined in the Form View or the Design View, the chart will contain only sample data. Modifications to the chart's layout on the page are made in the Design View. The completed chart report is viewable in the Print Preview. From the Print Preview screen it can be sent to Microsoft Word and incorporated in another document or sent to Excel for further modifications. Other alternatives for the completed chart report include printing, saving as an HTML file for Web publication, or sending as an e-mail attachment.

Mailing Labels and Mail Merge

The sixth report generation option in Access is Label Wizard, which is extremely useful for sending frequent or large mailings. This specialized report is used to print name and address information on Avery-type mailing labels. Avery is a large manufacturer of printing labels, many of which can be peeled off a sheet and stuck on an envelope. Microsoft configured Access to support a wide range of sizes of Avery labels, and other manufacturers will also use Avery standards sometimes (Fuller, 1997). The Label Wizard also offers choices for customizing the printing of labels.

To create a mailing labels report, select Label Wizard in the New report choices. The first step of the wizard requires choosing the type of label on which the report will be printed. Check the box of the label paper for the Avery number and select that number from the available choices. In the second step, pick the font, font size, font weight, text color, and font format (italic and/or underline). Remember, the font must be small enough to display the text for the label in the space available on the label. The third step requires constructing the layout of the label in the prototype label space. This step necessitates selecting the fields for the label in their appropriate order and placing them in the appropriate arrangement. Remember to include spaces between fields on the label such as first name and last name. Also, place a comma between city and state. The program does not automatically do this. The fourth step is to pick a field on which to sort the labels, such as last name, city, or state. It is helpful to sort the report on the same field that the mail merge is sorted on to facilitate the ready matching of letters to envelopes. In the fifth step, name the report and click Finish. At this point the report may either be printed on labels or sent to Microsoft Word for further modification. Figure 5.13 displays the result of a Label Wizard report that was exported to Microsoft Word.

The process for creating mailing labels in Lotus Approach is very similar to the procedure described for Microsoft Access. From the menu bar select Create, then Mailing Label. Like Access, Approach lets the user select the address layout from a display of several choices and the type of Avery label being used. In the Mailing Label Assistant's Basics screen, the user designates the database and fields from which data for the mailing labels will come. Once these are selected, the user specifies the placement of each name and address field within the already chosen address layout. An Options tab at the top of the Mailing Label Assistant makes available a number of tools for those intrepid souls who wish to venture into the realm of designing their own custom mail-

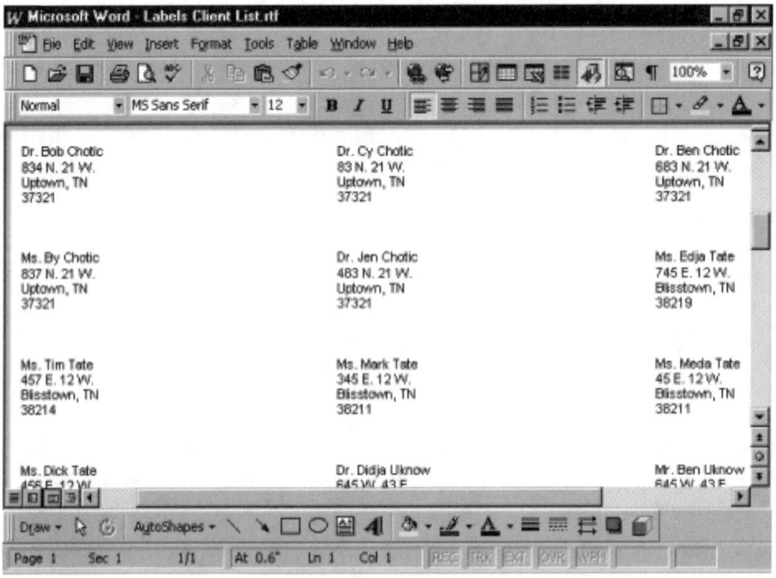

FIGURE 5.13   Mail Label Report from Microsoft Access

ing labels for nonstandard label paper. Once the required choices are made in the Basic screen, clicking Done results in the mailing labels displayed in the Browse View. To see how they will appear on the mailing labels paper, select Print Preview.

MAIL MERGE IN LOTUS APPROACH.   A specialized and widely used form of database report is a mail merge (Eddy, 1997). Name and address data stored in a database are useable in form letters. In a mail merge, data from fields in the database are inserted into specified locations in the form letter. Prior to starting a mail merge, the form letter contains the information content for the intended recipients, but omits personal information such as name and address. These unique bits of information are drawn from the database fields and inserted into the letter in the process of a mail merge. Mail merges can include other personal information such as date of last appointment, date of next appointment, and current balance. Utilization of a database containing name and address data with a mail merge procedure is an efficient and effective way to communicate via standard mail with audiences ranging from a limited client caseload to a broad spectrum of contributors to a local community service organization.

Modern database applications have made mail merge procedures far less complex than earlier predecessors. This section describes how mail merges are created in Lotus Approach. Mail merges in Microsoft Office are initiated from Microsoft Word, drawing name, address, and other personal information from an existing Access database. As such, mail merges in Microsoft Office are described in Chapter Seven, which addresses a range of advanced word processing procedures.

The creation of a mail merge document in Lotus Approach is initiated by first creating or opening a database containing the name, address, and other pertinent information intended for the form letter. In the menu bar under Create, select Form Letter. This starts the Form Letter Assistant, which directs the user through a series of steps in the letter's creation. In the first step the appearance of the letter is defined by selecting a name for the document, a layout, and a style. Layout choices include block, letterhead, modified block, and personal. Each layout is displayed in an adjoining box. The number of steps necessary to create a form letter varies with the letter selected. For the purpose of this example, the block layout, which has six steps, is chosen. In the second step, space to type in a return address for the letter is provided. The third step requires selection of the database from which information for the letter is drawn. The name of the currently open database appears in this field by default, but another database can be selected. Step three also requires a choice of how to lay out the addresses of the recipients to accommodate the name and address data fields. Once the layout is selected, the name and address fields are added to the form. In the fourth step, choices are made regarding the salutation of the letter. The fifth step requires specification of the close of the letter including closing, name, and title. In the sixth step, one can elect to format an envelope for printing. Once this choice is made click Done. Figure 5.14 displays a resultant form letter as seen in the Design View. Note in the top image, there

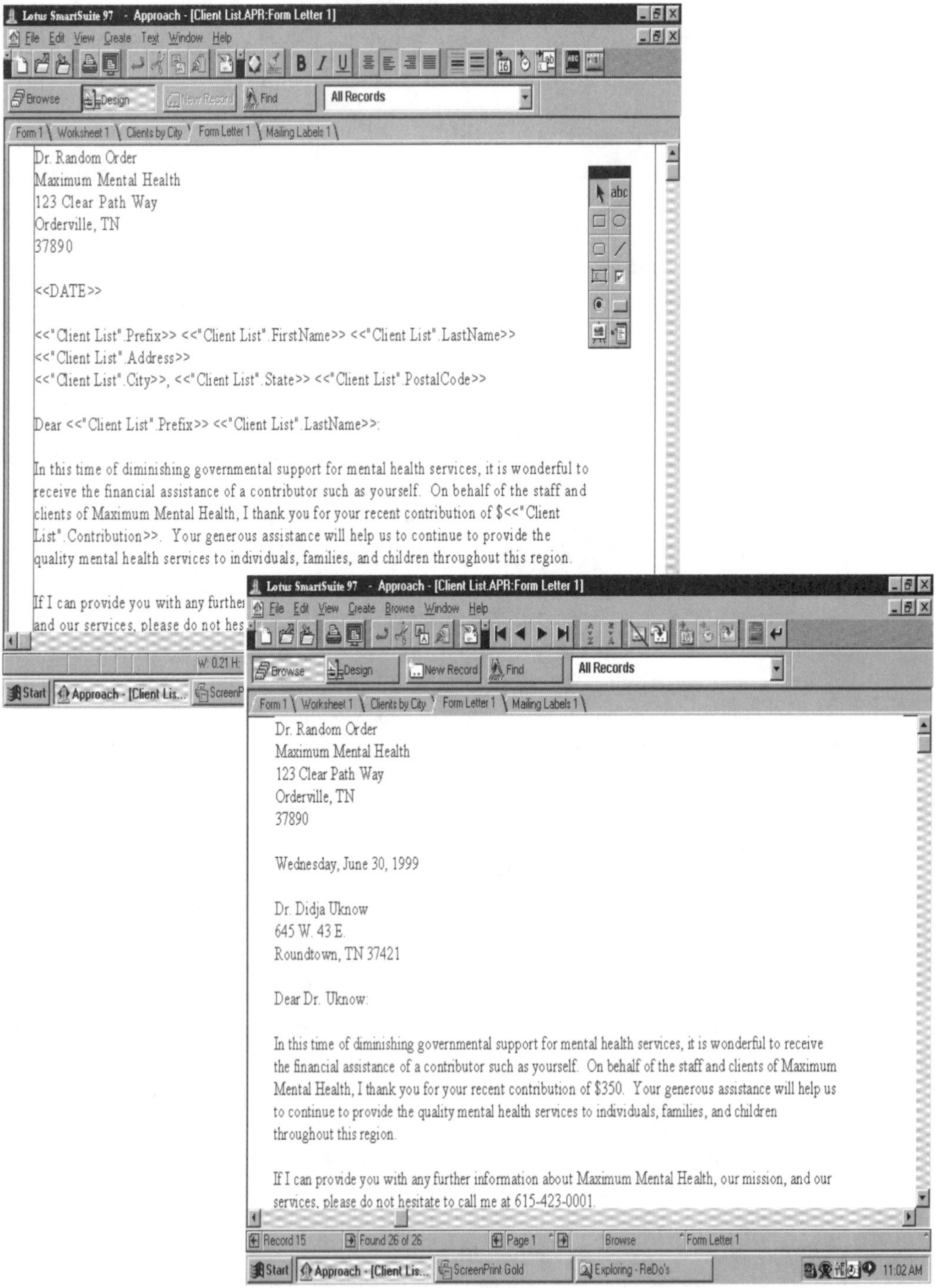

FIGURE 5.14   Form Letter Created in Lotus Approach

is no text in the letter, only the return address and the symbols indicating the placement of the mail merge fields. The text of the letter can either be typed directly into the Design View or composed in a word processor and pasted into the Design View. In this example, the text was typed in the Design View along with the field indicator <<"Client List".Contribution>> which tells the form letter where to find the financial contribution information of each addressee. The bottom image in Figure 5.14 shows the final letter as seen in the Print Preview screen. Note that the contributor information along with the dollar amount of the contribution is contained in the resulting individualized form letter.

Summary

This chapter focused on how social service practitioners could employ personal computer database applications, specifically Lotus Approach and Microsoft Access, in the development and use of databases as tools of practice. This chapter has examined in detail the five functions of database applications: data entry, data storage, data organization, data selection, and report generation. The emphasis here was on the utility and flexibility of personal computer database applications in a wide range of data management tasks. Database applications historically have been avoided by social service practitioners because of a lack of information about their functionality and apprehension about their complexity. This chapter has endeavored to correct both of these impediments to the application of personal computer database applications in social service practice.

Exercises

1. With a group of peers discuss your experiences in using or requesting information from databases in your practice settings. What have been the obstacles to obtaining needed information? How readily available is information that has direct practice application? What types of information do you need that are not currently available?
2. Using a data set created in the exercises in Chapter 4, import that data into a database application, creating a database table. From the database table, create a database form for data entry.
3. Open one of the database templates in either Microsoft Access or Lotus Approach that might have application to your practice setting. Is it a flat file database or a relational database? How do the fields in the database match the data needs of your practice setting? How would you modify it to better fit the data needs of your practice setting?

4. Using the database created in exercise 2, sort the database table on one or more variables. Now use a data selection tool to find a limited set of cases within the database corresponding to selection criteria you specify.
5. Use the report generation function in your database application to create a report from a database table already filtered on a set of selection criteria.
6. Either import a mailing list from a spreadsheet or create a mailing list database and then generate a mailing label report.

chapter 6

Graphics
Visual Representation
of Practice Information

The intention of this chapter is to convey the usefulness of personal computer generated graphics in social service practice. It describes and demonstrates multiple graphics tools for describing, analyzing, and communicating practice information. A central theme of this chapter is the necessity of matching the intended message of a graphical representation to the anticipated audience. It details how to use spreadsheets to create charts and graphics and how to apply their drawing tools in the generation of eco maps, genograms, organizational charts, and flow charts. This chapter lays the foundation for the application of other graphics tools in subsequent chapters.

One of the most remarkable advances in personal computers in their brief history is their expanding capacity to manage images and the visual representation of information.[1] The introduction of the Apple Macintosh computer in 1984 opened vast possibilities of computer generated graphics to the imaginations of a broad spectrum of first-time computer buyers. It ushered in the age of graphical computing in which the potential to express ideas and represent information is continually spurred by the growing facility of both hardware and software to produce images and graphics. As a result, present-day computing is characterized by a graphical user interface in all widely used operating systems; manuscripts and reports are seeded with diagrams and charts, e-mail arrives with accompanying animation, and Web pages are filled with digital images and graphics.

The application of graphics in social service practice to date has been limited. Three noteworthy exceptions are the use of graphs in single system designs for practice evaluation (Bloom, Fischer, & Orme, 1999), eco maps for the representation of clients in social contexts (Hartman, 1978), and genograms for representation of the

---

[1]For the purposes of this discussion the term *image* is used to denote drawings, illustrations, and digitized photographs. Following the convention of Henry (1998), the terms *graph* and *chart* are used interchangeably. The term *diagram* refers to a drawing that shows a relationship or arrangement. The term *graphics* is used in a more general sense to refer to images, charts, diagrams, graphics, and other visual representations.

intergenerational structure of families (Hartman, 1978; Mattaini, 1993). This constrained use of graphical information as a tool of social service practice exists as a result of a reciprocally determined interaction. Until recently there has been an absence of tools for ready production of graphics, little social service educational emphasis on use of graphics in practice, and limited theory to guide experimentation with graphics applications. These interacting impediments are showing signs of erosion. Although there has been virtually no discussion in the social service education literature specifically related to the expanded use of graphics in social service practice, texts on practice evaluation increasingly emphasize the importance of visual representation of client/system change data (Alter & Evens, 1990; Bloom, Fischer, & Orme, 1999; Nurius & Hudson, 1993; Royse, 1992). Mattaini (1993) describes and illustrates multiple applications for the use of graphics in social service practice. A number of researchers have created assessment instruments and packages that employ graphics to illustrate client social/behavioral status and change. (Benbenishty, 1991; Hudson & McMurtry, 1997; Lachiusa, 1996; Ogilvie, 1996). Software application suites now commonly provide an array of tools in word processing programs, spreadsheets, databases, and presentation programs for the production and manipulation of graphics and images.

Despite the heretofore constrained use of graphics in social service practice, the potential applications are numerous. The use of single system design graphs for individuals, groups, and systems is described in Chapter 4. Many practice situations call for the development of educational materials for clients and families. The infusion of such materials with carefully selected graphics both captures the reader's attention and conveys the core message of the pamphlet or brochure. The use of charts and graphs in reports to supervisors or for supervises can concisely summarize service delivery data. Agencies' newsletters and public relations releases employing diagrams, clip art, and digital images convey far more information than simple text-based materials. Computer-based slide show presentations containing graphical materials can engage and hold an audience's attention. Web pages with graphics, images, and animations are far more likely to be reviewed than are those relying solely on text for communication. In each of these examples, personal computer generated graphics are employed with the intention of capturing attention and conveying information.

This chapter describes and provides illustrations of the use of graphics tools in the visual representation of social service practice information. More specifically, this chapter addresses how to use spreadsheets for the production of graphs and the application of spreadsheet drawing tools to create diagrams and illustrations. Many of the drawing and graphics tools available in spreadsheets also are found in the companion word processors of their respective software suites. This review of drawing and graphics tools lays the foundation for the use of graphics, including clip art and digital images, in word processing addressed in the next chapter. Each of these types of graphics is applied in other applications in subsequent chapters.

■ Thinking Visually

At the core of most social services education and professional development is listening. We are trained to listen accurately, to listen empathetically, to listen for the subtext or underlying meaning in verbal communication. Along with the development of listening skills, but perhaps to a lesser degree, social service practitioners are taught to visually observe behavior, body language, and social setting. Historically, much of our reporting of what we have heard and observed is conveyed in text, in written reports. Managers and administrators also are trained to varying degrees to listen, observe, and communicate findings in written format. The use of graphical information and images for communication has not played a major role in the training of most social service professionals. Therefore, before embarking on a description and demonstration of how to use personal computers in the generation and display of graphics and images, we will first consider the role of graphics in communication.

Meyer (1993) points out that throughout history, images have played a major role in communicating our understanding of the world, others, and ourselves. The use of images, of course, predates the written word. Images have been used over time by humankind to communicate about both real events and to symbolically represent experiences from the corporal to the transcendental. Images evoke emotions, tell stories, and provoke thought. Images make it possible to communicate complex information in a simple and direct way. One of the enduring images of the 1989 Tiananmen Square uprising in Beijing, China, was the photograph of a single student standing in front of a line of tanks. For many in Western democratic countries, this photograph is deeply symbolic of the struggle of the pro-democracy movement in China at that moment in history. The same image likely elicits an entirely different response from Chinese leaders.

The precarious balance in the use of images is always between the message or experience the creator wishes to communicate or evoke and the interpretation of the viewer. The use of words in communication allows for the careful crafting of a precise message. Images are open to greater interpretation (Meyer, 1993). Images can reflect the cultural tradition and biases of the creator and, conversely, images are commonly interpreted through the lens of the viewer's cultural world view. For instance, a child raised in the religious traditions of India drew a picture of Lakshmi, the goddess of beauty and abundance. In the picture, Lakshmi appears with four arms, as she is traditionally represented in Indian art. A clinical social worker who looked at the picture without any information about the child or her cultural tradition, concluded the image was suggestive of possible sexual abuse, the four arms symbolizing unwanted touching. In this example, a single image evokes two dramatically different responses as a result of differences in cultural backgrounds and the social worker's professional training. As such, the continuing struggle in graphical representation is the selection of images that carefully match the intended message with consideration of the anticipated audience.

Graphical Representation

While the expression of human experience through drawings, paintings, and other media predates recorded history, the use of charts and graphs to symbolically represent quantitative information developed only in the last 400 years (Holmes, 1984). Perhaps most noteworthy is the work of René Descartes (1596–1650) whose development of the "Cartesian grid" laid the foundation for plotting numerical information on a grid in the form of graphs and charts. The use of graphs and charts for the expression of financial and other information was left to William Playfair (1759–1823) who is credited with the invention of the line graph, the bar chart, and the pie chart. In doing so, he devised a means of making the abstract visible, as in the relationship between time and rising national debt. According to Holmes (1984) wide interest in the use of graphs in the United States did not develop until the late 1920s, concurrent with the crash of the stock market.

Prior to the advent of personal computer software for the production of charts and graphs, they were created by hand with drawing tools, a time-consuming and exacting endeavor. The ease with which charts and graphs are produced with software can lead to quick creation of graphics that are visually compelling without adequate consideration for the accuracy or the parsimony of the message they convey. Poorly designed graphs can confuse and frustrate viewers' attempts to decipher the data expressed in the graph (Henry, 1998). Conversely, when graphs are carefully planned and well designed, they reveal information to viewers. Henry (1998) argues that the visual representation of quantitative information in a well-executed graph draws upon viewers' spatial intelligence and conveys information more directly than text-based material.

The question that then arises is what are the characteristics of a well-designed and useful graph? White (1984) proposes six characteristics evident in the design of a useful graph.

1. Elegance—The graph should express the information present in the data in a simple and direct manner. The graph displays the essence of the idea or finding present in the data.

2. Clarity—The meaning of the graph should be clear to the viewer. The graph should be designed to facilitate the transmission of information. The graph's title, axis labels, and legend should use unambiguous language that requires no further explanation.

3. Ease—A well-designed graph is easy to understand. It engages and stimulates viewers' interest. Text and graphics should be easy to read, their respective sizes balanced with each other.

4. Pattern—Use the same type of graph when presenting the same type of information to an audience. Once an audience understands the information contained in a particular type of graph, changes in the style or format will likely produce only confusion. Mixing bar charts and column charts without a reason directly related to the data does not enhance comprehension.

5. Simplicity—Design the graph to focus viewers' attention on the information evident in the data. While many software applications have tools to add visual bells

and whistles to graphs, their parsimonious application is recommended. Any element added to a graph should be used in the service of enhancing the conveyance of the intended message. Too much information on a single graph may confuse the audience. Sometimes the use of multiple, simple graphs to convey elaborate information is far better than a single, visually complex graph.

6. Validity—Graphs should accurately portray the relationships present in the original data without distortion. Distortion can occur, for instance, through the use of scales in a graph that create overly steep upward or downward slopes.

Henry (1998) emphasizes the necessity to give primacy to the data. Comparisons are the primary means by which graphical information is understood. Therefore, viewers should be able to clearly see differences and similarities between groups as displayed in a chart. They should be able to detect trend changes in a measured behavior or attitude over time. Graphs should display the relationships that exist or do not exist between subjects or variables. Patterns and trends in the data should be emphasized in the design. Consideration must also be given to the intended audience of the graph. Viewers vary in their experience and sophistication in understanding charts and graphs. Some viewers are better prepared to appreciate complex relationships displayed in graphs, while for others communication is maximized by parsing complex data into two or more graphs.

The best graphs both answer questions for viewers and stimulate the desire to know more (Henry, 1998). The questions raised by a graph should not be related to its meaning, but instead should be in response to the ideas conveyed in its representation of data. This resultant aroused viewer response is facilitated by having clear intention about the information one wishes to express with a graph. Development of a clear intention for a graph by using preliminary graphs as tools for considering what the data show (Drew & Hardman, 1985). This preliminary graphing is a thinking tool used to contemplate the relationships, or lack thereof, in the data. Visual examination of the data in preliminary graphs can stimulate further ideas about the information present in the data. This visual inspection of the information can further clarify how to display its maximum information transmission. This iterative process results in refining a graph's communicative effect through the creation of multiple versions. This process is facilitated by modern software applications, which make possible the ready generation of multiple versions of a graph along with an enhanced capacity to edit many of the elements composing a graph.

Tools for Graphical Representation of Information: Spreadsheets

As reviewed in Chapter 4, spreadsheets are robust tools for the collection and analysis of quantitative information. Commonly available spreadsheet applications such as Corel Quattro Pro, Microsoft Excel, and Lotus 1-2-3 have graphing tools for the generation of a broad spectrum of charts and graphs. The approach of these spreadsheets to graph production is remarkably similar. Figure 6.1 displays graphing tools from each spreadsheet.

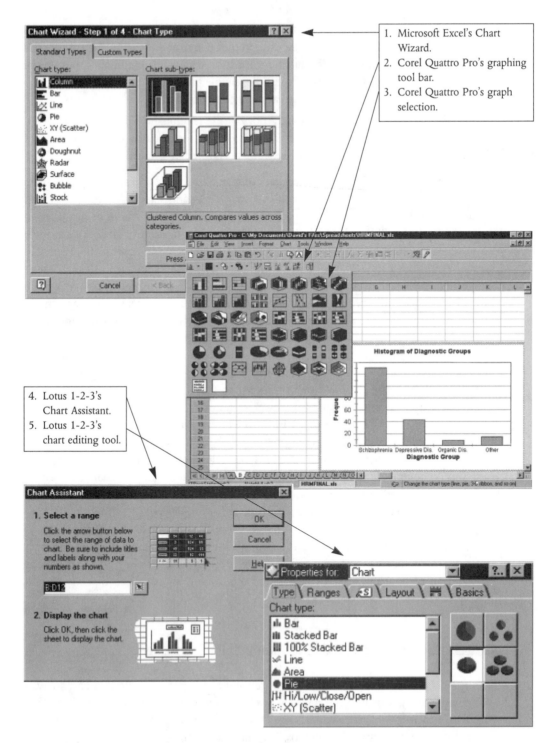

FIGURE 6.1 Spreadsheet Graph Production Tools

Notice that each of the spreadsheets provides icons that pictorially represent the available choices in chart type. The essential process common to all three applications is (a) select the data to be graphed, (b) choose a type of graph, (c) specify title and labels for the graph and, if desired, (d) modify formatting and appearance. Each of these steps is described and illustrated in the following pages. Readers unfamiliar with graphing are encouraged to review the terms in Table 6.1 to prepare for the ensuing discussion.

TABLE 6.1 Graphing Terms

Area graph	Displays one or more series of data points over a time period. By stacking data series on each other it shows the sum of the combined series over time.
Bar graph	Used to horizontally or vertically represent quantitative information on two or more categories. Usually has space between the bars.
Column graph	Used to vertically represent quantitative information on two or more categories. Usually has space between the bars. AKA bar graph.
Data series	Variables plotted in the graph.
Fever chart	Plots quantities over time as a rising and falling line.
Grid line	A line extending vertically and/or horizontally from points of measurement on the x- and/or y-axis.
Histogram	Chart used to represent a frequency distribution of interval or ratio data. The bars must be joined.
Legend	A key that indicates name and/or pattern of each data series.
Line chart	Plots trends or changes over time or frequency distributions on which the x-axis represents some quantity, e.g., age or income.
Pie chart	Displays proportions of a whole, e.g., ethnic composition of a city's population. Used with nominal level data.
Plot	The body of the graph in which the data are graphically displayed.
Scattergram	Displays the paired observations of two variables as single points on a two-dimensional graph. Used to represent the relationship between two variables.
Series	A set of data plotted on a graph.
Table	The columns and rows containing the data for the graph.
Tick mark	Short line identifying a value on a graph.
Time-series	A line graph representing the repeated measurement of some phenomenon over time.
Title	The name or heading given to a graph.
Trend	A line graph on which time is measured on the x-axis and a dependent variable is measured on the y-axis.
x-axis	The horizontal axis (abscissa) used for the independent variable.
y-axis	The vertical axis (ordinate) used for the dependent variable.
z-axis	The vertical axis present in three-dimensional graphs. Often indicates a frequency count.

(Boyce et al., 1997; Drew & Hardman, 1985; Eddy, 1997; Holmes, 1984; Lefferts, 1981; Weinbach & Grinnell, 1991)

Data Selection Prior to Graphing

The first step in creating a graph with a spreadsheet is to have the data ranged in a table of columns and rows. At times the data are already in a format from which they can be graphed. For instance, data on the number of people attending a weekly support group might be entered in two columns of a spreadsheet, week number and attendance, as in Spreadsheet Exhibit 6.1. In Figure 6.2 this data table is converted into a bar graph displaying a frequency count (attendance) over time (weeks).

Another example of creating a graph directly from unsummarized data is a scattergram. A scattergram represents the relationship between two interval or ratio level variables as single points on a two-dimensional graph. Scattergrams are useful in displaying the strength of association or correlation between two variables. The strength of the relationship between the two variables is evidenced in how tightly the points are grouped together. Widely dispersed points on scattergrams indicate a lack of relationship between the plotted variables. In Figure 6.3, there appears to be a strong, positive relationship between age and GAFS-M (social and occupational functioning) scores. The relationship is said to be *positive* if the data points move in an upward slope from left to right. A *negative* relationship between two variables forms a downward slope from left to right. In a negative relationship the values of one variable increase as the values of the second variable decrease. A regression line is displayed in Figure 6.3 to emphasize the apparent linear relationship between the two variables in this hypothetical example.

Line graphs used in single system designs, as described in Chapter 4, are yet another example of graphs that require no prior summarization of data. Line graphs plot the change over time of one or more outcome measures. The use of two or more outcome measures in the same graph requires that the outcome measures have the same scale. The use of the same scale is necessary in order to detect differences and have a

SPREADSHEET EXHIBIT 6.1
Support Group Attendance
Data Table

	A	B
	Week Number	Attendance
1		
2	1	15
3	2	13
4	3	16
5	4	12
6	5	15
7	6	16
8	7	17
9	8	16

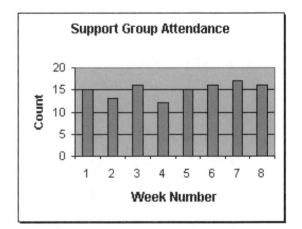

FIGURE 6.2   Bar Graph of Support Group Attendance over Time

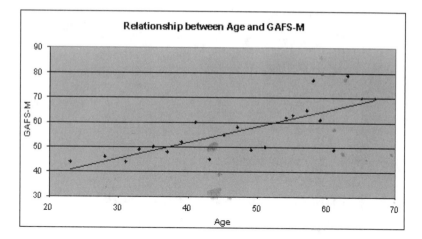

FIGURE 6.3   Scattergram of the Relationship between Age and GAFS-M Scores

common means of comparison of the two or more measures. For instance, an agency that aids former welfare recipients in securing and holding jobs wishes to measure on a weekly basis each client's overall satisfaction with their job and the client's perception of their supervisor's supportiveness. The first measure uses a 0–100 scale to measure job satisfaction and the second measure uses a 1–10 scale to measure perceived supportiveness of a supervisor. When these two measures are plotted on the same line graph, changes in the smaller scale are dwarfed by the larger scale, despite the fact that both of them may be of equal significance in job retention. Therefore, if multiple measures are to be used in construction of a line graph for a single system design, careful consideration must be given to the selection of measures in order to make appropriate and meaningful comparisons. Figure 6.4 displays data from two self-rating measures that use the same scale (1–10) measuring anxiety and relaxation. Notice that because the measures use the same scale, a visual comparison of the relationship between the two scales over time is possible.

In some situations summarization of data sets in some manner before attempting to graph the information is necessary. For example, in order to depict graphically the relative proportion of clients in an agency's different treatment programs, it is first necessary to have a frequency distribution of the number of clients in each program. Once a frequency distribution is produced (see Chapter 4 for the procedure), the data are arrayed in two columns, one column containing either a label or number for each attribute (e.g., the different treatment programs) and a second column with a frequency count of each attribute. The summarized information in these two columns may then be graphed in a pie chart or bar graph.

A second means of summarizing two or more variables is a cross-tabulation table. The use of a cross-tabulation table makes possible the reduction of complex information

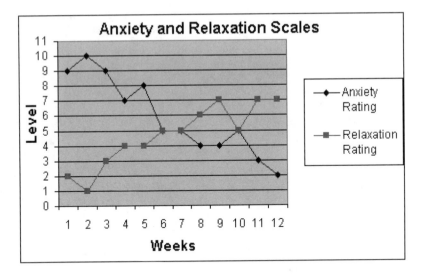

FIGURE 6.4 Single System Line Graph Plotting Anxiety and Relaxation Ratings

in two or more variables into a table, which can then be graphically represented. In Chapter 4, Spreadsheet Exhibit 4.7 reports the level of medication compliance for clients in two treatment groups, general outpatient care (GOC) and intensive case management (ICM). The data contained in Spreadsheet Exhibit 4.7 were compiled with a cross tabulation procedure. Figure 6.5 displays the first three columns of Spreadsheet Exhibit 4.7 in a bar graph. The resultant bar graph enables the viewer to readily discern the fact that medication compliance was higher for the ICM group, while noncompliance was higher for the GOC group. Another way to think about Figure 6.5 is that it represents the summary of information contained in 196 cases across two variables, treatment group and level of medication compliance. For most viewers the relationship apparent in the bar graph is much more quickly understood than it would be through examination of Spreadsheet Exhibit 4.7.

In summary, the first step in creating a graph with a spreadsheet is compiling the data into columns representing the variables and rows representing the cases. Data are either entered directly or summarized with a frequency distribution or cross tabulation table. To graph these data, select the columns and rows containing the information. Corel Quattro Pro, Microsoft Excel, and Lotus 1-2-3 each have a toolbar icon for graphs to click in order to initiate graph creation.

After selecting the data in Lotus 1-2-3 and clicking the graph icon in the toolbar, the cursor becomes a graph icon. To place the graph on the spreadsheet, click once to establish the top left-hand corner of the graph, then drag the cursor across the screen to establish the desired size of the graph. The graph appears in the area created by this click and drag procedure. To change the type of graph appearing in the newly created graph box, select the desired type of graph from the toolbar icon.

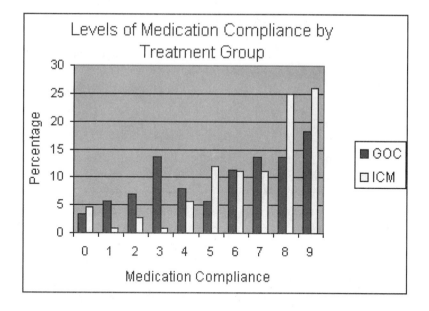

FIGURE 6.5   Bar Graph Produced from Cross Tabulation Table

Selecting data and clicking the graph icon in Microsoft Excel activates a Chart Wizard. The Chart Wizard walks the user through the four steps in creating a graph, (a) specification of chart type, (b) designation of the location of the data source for the graph, (c) selection of options for the appearance of the graph, and (d) location of the final chart. The location options are in the spreadsheet or on a new worksheet.

Graphs are produced in Quattro Pro in much the same way as in Lotus 1-2-3. After selecting the data for graphing, click the graph icon in the toolbar, then click in the spreadsheet to set the location of the top left-hand corner and drag the graph to the required size. To change the type of graph, click the graph icon on the far left of the toolbar, as displayed in Figure 6.1. Each of these three spreadsheet applications readily transforms data in the spreadsheet into its corresponding graphical representation.

Matching Data to Type of Graph

The next consideration is what type of graph to use with what type of data for what purpose. The proper match between the purpose of the graph, the type of graph, and the type of data enhances the capacity of a visual representation to transmit information. Graphs are used to describe data and as analytic tools for understanding complex relationships intrinsic to some data. We will return to the use of graphs as analytic tools later and retain our present focus on graphs as tools to visually describe data. Graphs work best as descriptive tools when they are selected with consideration to the type of data they are to describe. For instance, a pie chart is a good choice for nominal data to illustrate the relative proportions of parts of a whole. Conversely, a pie chart is an inappropriate choice to display the relationship between two continuous (interval or ratio) variables, as is represented with a scattergram in Figure 6.3. The question that now arises is what types of graphs work best with what types of data?

Pie Charts

Henry (1998) suggests that pie charts and bar graphs are frequently used in descriptive displays that represent parts of a whole. These two graphs are commonly employed to illustrate the proportions of a budget allocated to different spending categories, the relative frequency of individuals of different ethnic groups served by an agency, or the percentage of clients served by distinct treatment programs in an agency. However, research has shown that viewers are able to derive information from bar graphs faster and with greater accuracy than from pie charts (Cleveland & McGill, 1984; Simkin & Hastie, 1987). Henry (1998) recommends that a pie chart is appropriate only for presenting the relationship of parts to a whole when there are a limited number of categories (parts) in a variable and their relative proportions are distinct. In other words, it is difficult visually in a pie chart to distinguish between categories of 35 percent and 30 percent. One of the drawbacks of the use of graphing tools in spreadsheets is that they offer multiple possible configurations and enhancements to pie charts that can ultimately result in distorted comprehension. Henry (1998) contends that effects such as pseudo 3-D, contrasting shading, use of legends, and arbitrary pullouts (slice of the pie set apart) all represent possible impediments to comprehension and should therefore be avoided in pie chart production.

The pie chart in Figure 6.6 conforms to Henry's guidelines. It displays budgetary information drawn from Table 4.17 in Chapter 4. This pie chart illustrates the relative proportions of nonpersonnel expenses allocated to expenditure categories. Because actual dollar amounts for the categories are not displayed, it would be necessary to provide an accompanying table with those figures. In this case, the pie chart communicates proportionally where dollars will be spent and raises the question of how much will be spent. This pie chart is intended to capture the viewers' attention, raise the question of how much will be spent, and draw their attention to the table containing the actual amounts.

Bar Graphs

The second and more highly recommended means to visually describe data about parts of a whole is the bar graph. The bars of bar graphs are oriented either horizontally or vertically, in which case they are sometimes referred to as column graphs. Henry (1998) points out that an important advantage of using horizontally arranged bars is that if labels (values or names) are attached to the bars, they are easier to read than labels set at the base of columns. Moreover, attaching values to bars improves the accuracy with which viewers comprehend the graph (Jarvenpaa & Dickson, 1988). Figure 6.7 illustrates the use of a horizontally oriented bar graph with attached values. This graph is

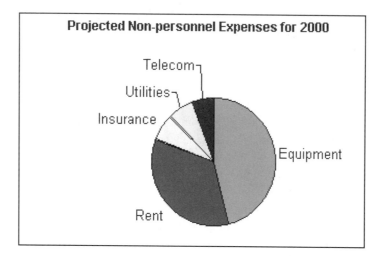

FIGURE 6.6   Pie Chart of Budgetary Expenditures by Category

an alternative representation of the same data displayed in the pie chart in Figure 6.6. The vertical grid lines offer a visual cue to assist in judging the relative lengths of the bars. The use of grid lines is especially important if values are not attached to the ends of the bars. The bars in Figure 6.7 are arranged in descending order to display the relative magnitude of the nonpersonnel expenditures. The arrangement of the bars in ascending or descending order is achieved by sorting the data in the spreadsheet. The choice of ascending or descending order is a matter of the message the graph is intended to convey. It is important to remember that viewers read from top to bottom,

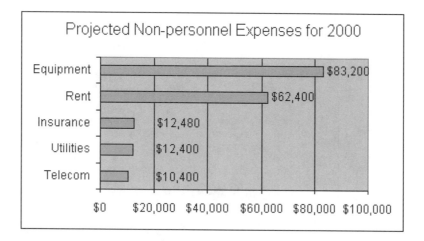

FIGURE 6.7   Bar Graph with Attached Values

so it is important to consider what category the viewer will see first when deciding whether to use ascending or descending order. In the example in Figure 6.7, the bar graph clearly displays the emphasis placed on equipment expenditures in the budget.

Line Graphs

In its most basic form, a line graph depicts the relationship between two continuous (interval or ratio level) variables with a line crossing a plane created by the x- and y-axes. Variants of line graphs include fever charts, trend lines, and time-series graphs. Line graphs are most frequently used as either a frequency distribution or to display change in a dependent variable over time (Lefferts, 1981).

A line graph used as a frequency distribution displays the shape of the distribution that is being counted across a range of values. Frequency distribution graphs also are called frequency polygons (Weinbach & Grinnell, 1991). Figure 6.8 is a frequency distribution of GAFS-M scores for 196 severely and persistently mentally ill outpatients (Patterson & Lee, 1995). Frequency distribution graphs are important for both describing the relative frequency of values in a variable and as an analytic tool in understanding and raising questions about the variable. For instance, the values in Figure 6.8 are not normally distributed in a standard bell curve. Instead, the three major peaks in the frequency distribution occur at 10-point intervals (40, 50, 60), while the remaining minor peaks are generally at five-point intervals. Examination of this frequency distribution suggests that the therapists who provided these ratings of social and occupational function either did not or could not differentiate on this 0 to 100 point scale at increments less than five points. Instead, they relied on five-point increments in rating social and occupational functioning. Applications of frequency distribution graphs in social service settings include examination of lengths of treatment of service recipients, family

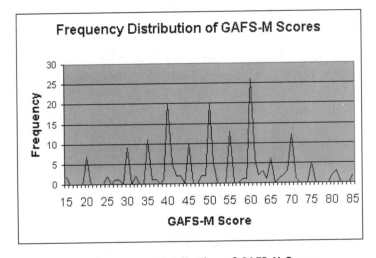

FIGURE 6.8 Frequency Distribution of GAFS-M Scores

income of clients, age of program participants, and lengths of stay in residential care. Frequency distribution graphs are particularly useful in visually describing some client characteristics (age or income) and service use indicators (number of services, length of stay, or cost of treatment).

The second type of line graph displays changes in a dependent variable over time. For the purposes of this discussion, a dependent variable is an event, behavior, or indicator that is repeatedly measured over time, such as income, customer satisfaction, or rate of unemployment. This type of line graph often depicts trends in the dependent variable over time, such as declines in rates of juvenile violence or increases in childhood poverty rates. The line chart in Figure 6.4 displays the relationship between two variables (anxiety and relaxation levels) over a 12-week period. This is a second function of line charts, illustrating the relationship between two or more dependent variables for the purpose of comparison. Corel Quattro Pro, Microsoft Excel, and Lotus 1-2-3 all allow for the display of multiple dependent variables in a line chart. However, as with many software features, just because it is possible to apply it to data, does not necessarily mean the intended message of the graph is served by plotting multiple dependent variables on the same line graph. For instance, in Chapter 4, Figure 4.11 contains a line graph labeled "Group Cohesion—All Students" that depicts the ratings from eight students over the course of the group. The multiple dependent variables (students' ratings) were graphed with the intent of displaying the complexity of group process. The linear regression trend line and moving average line were added so viewers could discern the trend and clarify the message of the graph. Nonetheless, this graph requires the viewer to expend time and energy to appreciate its meaning. Readers are cautioned to carefully consider the intended message and purpose of a line graph before creating a graph with more than one dependent variable. Despite this cautionary note, line graphs, particularly as applied in single system evaluation, remain an important graphing tool for data description and analysis.

Area Graphs

Area graphs display data from one or more variables over time. The filled portion of the graph depicts the relative contribution of each variable to the whole. Area graphs are particularly useful in showing variation over time in the proportion of the sum of a phenomenon accounted for by its parts. For instance, Figure 6.9 displays six months of nonpersonnel expenditures for Maximum Mental Health. Each section of the graph represents a budgetary cost category. Notice how declines in equipment expenditures impact the overall budget while costs in the other categories remain relatively stable. This stability of nonequipment costs over time is evidenced by the lack of changes in the size of the areas of each cost category. This graph shows both the relationship of each cost category to the whole and to the other categories over time. Area graphs are essentially a multivariate form of the line graph. They are useful in displaying data collected over time (a) for categories of fiscal information, (b) population or demographic groups, or (c) for comparing groups on outcome measures.

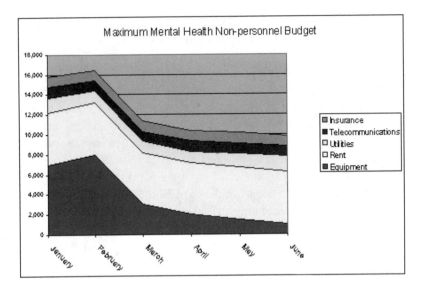

FIGURE 6.9   Area Graph of Nonpersonnel Budget Expenditures

In summary, the graphs reviewed here, pie, bar, line, and area, represent the major types of charts commonly found in the social service literature. Moreover, social service agency audiences such as clients, contributors, and board members likely are familiar with these types of graphs through newspapers, magazines, the Web, and television. These basic types of graphs have become part of a common visual vocabulary for most literate people in the developed world. This visual familiarity aids comprehension of the intended message of these basic graph types. These graphs do not, however, represent the full range of graph types available in the three spreadsheet programs discussed here. A partial list of additional choices available in these spreadsheets includes the doughnut, radar, surface, bubble, and stock. The drawback to using any of these options is that they may be unfamiliar to the intended audience and therefore produce confusion as opposed to communicating a clear message. Henry (1998) urges careful consideration of the ability of an audience to retrieve the meaning of a graph. This caution extends to selection of a graph. The choice of an unfamiliar graph is at times justified by its capacity to display a particular type of data or for the clarity with which it depicts a set of relationships in the data. The use of an unfamiliar type of graph should be supplemented by explanatory text. If used in a presentation, accompanying oral explanation will aid the audience in grasping the graph's meaning.

Enhancing Graphs

Clear communication of an intended message with a graph requires not only preparation of the data in a spreadsheet and selection of an appropriate type of graph, but also careful choices regarding its augmentation. Each of the graphs presented in this chapter contain the basic graphic representation of the data, a title, labels for the axes when necessary, numerical scales or category names on the axes, and in some cases, legends to identify components of the graph. Beyond the graph itself, each of these components conveys information that, when appropriately used, informs viewers and clarifies the intended message of the graph.

Quattro Pro, Excel, and Lotus 1-2-3 each take a slightly different approach to creating and editing the components of a graph. As described previously, graphs are created in both Quattro Pro and Lotus 1-2-3 by (a) selecting in the spreadsheet the data for graphing, (b) clicking the graph icon in the toolbar, (c) then clicking a place at which to locate the graph on the spreadsheet, and (d) dragging the graph to a desired size. In both programs, modification of resultant graphs is accomplished by clicking any component of the graph. This produces a dialog window offering a number of choices about that element of the graph.

Figure 6.10 displays the Lotus 1-2-3 dialog window entitled "Properties for:" in which modifications to the graph are specified. Each of the tabs at the top of the window offers a different set of choices about elements of each graph's components. For instance, the dialog window in Figure 6.10 allows users to specify preferences about (a) type of graph, (b) the data ranges comprising the graph, (c) the styles of the graph's visual elements (bars, columns, etc.), (d) the layout of components such as titles and legends, the colors, patterns and line styles, and (e) other basic decisions about the graph's composition. Note that at the top of Figure 6.10, the field holding the word "Chart" is a drop-down box which, when clicked, will offer other choices on components of the graph to modify. These components include title, legend, x-axis, y-axis, series, series label, plot, note, and table. Selecting any of these components produces a new window with a different set of modification options displayed on tabs across the top of the window. Access to this graph properties window also is available through an icon in the

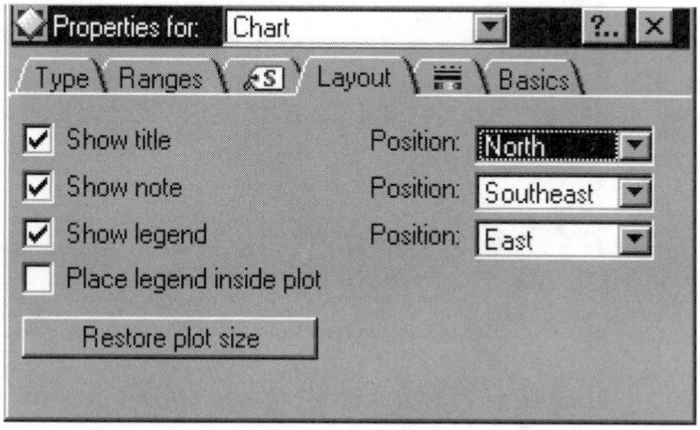

**FIGURE 6.10   Lotus 1-2-3 Dialog Window
for Graph Modification**

toolbar that displays a "Change chart properties" window when the cursor is passed over it. Additionally, clicking once on a chart alters the menu bar, making available the "Properties for:" window by selecting the desired graph component under the menu item Chart. Accessing the chart properties dialog window through any of the three means makes possible a high level of control over the final appearance of a graph. Experimentation with different graphing options aides in learning how each of the tools works. Eddy (1997) provides considerable detail in her discussion of the Lotus 1-2-3 graph modification options.

Quattro Pro's approach to graph modification is very similar to that of Lotus 1-2-3. Clicking on an existing graph alters the menu bar to display a range of tools related to chart manipulation and modification. Appearing under the menu option Chart are choices to modify (a) the type and layout of a graph, (b) the series, (c) titles, (d) legends, (e) axes, and (f) background. Each of these options produces a dialog window in which to refine the modification of that particular component of the graph. Alternatively, clicking on any component of an existing graph produces the same dialog window. Figure 6.11 contains a dialog window from Quattro Pro for modifying the bars of a bar graph. The tabs at the top of the dialog window offer choices for modifying elements of the bar series. This capacity to click on a component of a graph and alter

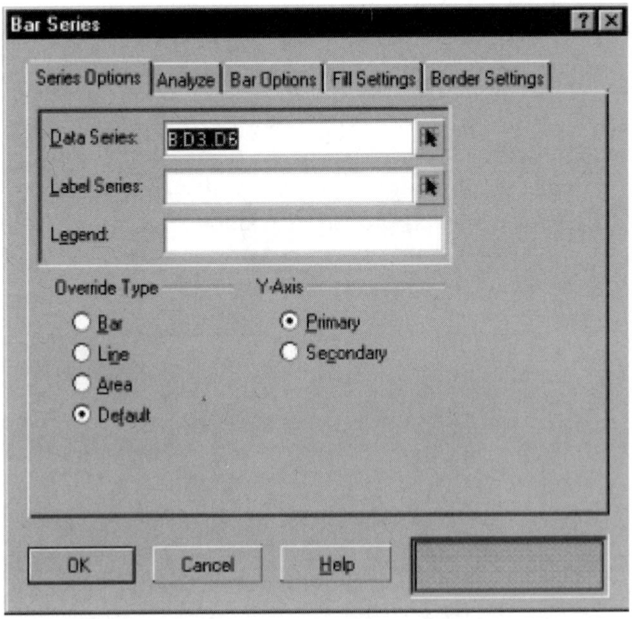

FIGURE 6.11   Quattro Pro Dialog Window for Modifying a Bar Graph

its features makes it possible to modify and enhance a graph in order to hone the clarity of its intended message. For instance, notice in Figure 6.11 that it is possible to specify the range of Label Series. This makes it possible to include in a graph very clearly worded labels from the spreadsheet in order to identify bars of the graph, instead of relying on abbreviated labels or numbers.

Microsoft Excel offers a chart wizard for graph production. The chart wizard has four steps: (1) selection of chart type, (2) specification of source data, (3) choosing chart options, and (4) designation of the completed chart's location in the spreadsheet. The choices in the third step, chart options, include titles, axes, gridlines, legend, data labels, and data tables. Figure 6.12 displays the dialog window for the chart wizard's third step. Again, as with Quattro Pro and Lotus 1-2-3, chart modification options are selected by clicking the tabs at the top of the window. Once created, modifications to a chart are made by clicking on the component of the chart intended for alteration. This produces a dialog window with an expanded array of modification options for the component. In other words, once a graph is produced with the chart wizard, an expanded array of refinements is available by clicking the component of the graph intended for modification. Additionally, selecting the graph alters the menu bar to include a Chart option. Under this menu option, each of the steps in the chart wizard is available, so decisions made in the original graph production with the chart wizard can be revisited.

The judicious application of the graph tools described in this chapter facilitates the conveyance of the graph's intended message. Listed here are several guiding principles for the labeling and enhancement of graphs.

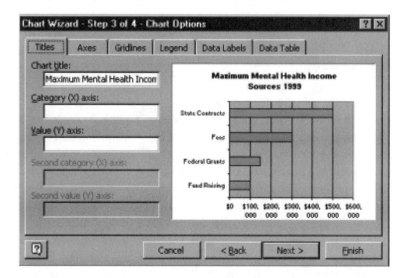

FIGURE 6.12   Microsoft Excel's Chart Options Selection Window

1. Titles should clearly describe what the graph displays so the viewer knows what it represents (Drew & Hardman, 1985; Lefferts, 1981).

2. The label of each axis should be specific and clear. The unit of measurement of each axis should be identified. "Place the axis label parallel to the proper axes. Do not stack letters so that the label reads vertically." (APA, 1994, p. 158).

3. Numbers for the grid points on both axes should be horizontal.

4. Make sure that the scales used on the x- and y-axes on line graphs do not distort the data by creating inappropriately steep slopes.

5. Use a legend to identify symbols used in graphs. The letters in a legend should be of the same font and size as letters used in the graph. Legends can distract the viewer by having to look back and forth between the graph and the legend. Consider using labels with the graph to identify data.

The enhancement of graphs with careful choices regarding components improves the likelihood that viewers will comprehend their intended meaning. Quattro Pro, Lotus 1-2-3, and Microsoft Excel each have an array of options for modification and enhancement of graphs. These tools enable the user to carefully format graphs so the information contained in the data is clearly expressed. The temptation for a user learning the graph enhancement tools is to add extraneous information and formatting to the graph, which can distract viewers' attention away from the core message of the graph. Henry (1998) emphasizes the importance, while developing a graph, of continually asking, "What is the purpose of this graph?" (p. 554). Consideration of this question can both guide the application of enhancements to a graph and further improve its clarity.

Exporting Graphs

The primary purpose of creating a graph is to communicate the information contained in the graph to an audience of viewers. Once a graph is developed in any of the three spreadsheets reviewed here, it may be printed, distributed as an e-mail attachment, published on the Web, and/or used in presentation software. Graphs can be printed directly from a spreadsheet. A second option is to copy and paste the graph into a word processing program where it can be incorporated into a document and subsequently printed or distributed as an e-mail attachment. The use of e-mail attachments is described in Chapter 9. For now it is sufficient to say that an e-mail attachment is a formatted document that is coupled with an e-mail message. When received, the attachment can be opened by the recipient's computer, providing the computer has software capable of reading the format in which the attachment was saved. Before sending attachments, it is advisable to e-mail the potential recipients and determine if they have software to open your forthcoming e-mail attachment.

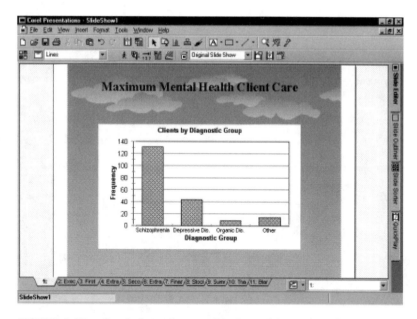

**FIGURE 6.13   Graph from Quattro Pro Pasted into a Corel
Presentation Slide Show**

Exporting graphs into presentation software is facilitated by moving files between
applications in the same software suite. Graphs created in Lotus 1-2-3 are readily imported into Lotus' presentation software, Freelance Graphics, whereas graphs created
and saved in Excel file format create a greater import challenge. Likewise, Excel files
are easily copied and pasted into Microsoft's PowerPoint presentation software. Graphs
developed in Quattro Pro may be copied, then inserted into Corel Presentation with a
Paste command. Figure 6.13 contains a screen from a Corel Presentation slide show
with a Quattro Pro graph. The key point is that graphs created in the spreadsheets reviewed here may be smoothly transferred to presentation applications within the same
software suite. Graphs in presentation software can be combined with descriptive text,
other graphics, and background patterns and coloring to further augment the information they convey. Chapter 8 describes in detail presentation software and its applications in social service practice.

Due to the growing importance of Web-based information, all three software suites
have tools for saving graphs as HTML files (the format of Web files). The procedures
for creation of basic Web pages are presented in Chapters 7 and 8. Figure 6.14 shows
a simple Web page containing a graph produced in Lotus 1-2-3, enhanced in Excel,
copied to Microsoft Word, and then saved as an HTML file. This process again demonstrates the fluidity with which objects such as graphs can flow between software applications. Placing the resultant HTML file on a Web server then makes the information
available to viewers worldwide with Web access.

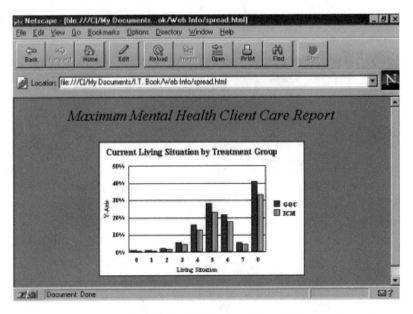

FIGURE 6.14   Lotus 1-2-3 Graph Displayed in a Web Page

Spreadsheet Drawing Tools

Drawing tools are a set of graphic functions used for the creation, coloring, and enhancement of lines, geometric shapes, and text boxes. The drawing tools available in Lotus 1-2-3, Corel Quattro Pro, and Microsoft Excel are nearly identical to the tools found in their counterpart word processors, Lotus Word Pro, Corel Word Perfect, and Microsoft Word. Consequently, the procedures and tools described here also are applicable to the creation of graphics in these word processors. These drawing tools are useful for both adding graphics to charts and for creating graphics with social service practice applications. Described here are the use of spreadsheet drawing tools for the creation of ecomaps, genograms, flow charts, and organizational charts.

Ecomaps

A commonly used graphic tool in social service practice is the *ecomap* (Mattaini, 1993). Hartman (1978) describes the ecomap as a tool to facilitate a worker's thinking about issues of assessment and intervention with cases. An ecomap graphically represents a client's relationships with individuals, family, friends, organizations, and institutions. The relative strength and nature of these relationships or interactions is depicted with choices of types of lines and their relative thickness. Color lines may be used if a color printer is available or the results are to be displayed on a monitor. Mattaini (1993) suggests red lines to represent negative relationships and black lines for positive relationships.

Ecomaps can be developed with the drawing tools in any one of the three spreadsheets discussed here. Figure 6.15 displays a Quick Scan ecomap (Mattaini, 1993) produced with the drawing tools in Excel. The Quick Scan ecomap is a blank ecomap template that Mattaini reports is useful for intakes and crisis situations to produce a quick graphical representation of a client's psychosocial environment. The basic graphical objects of this Quick Scan are circles, text boxes, and bidirectional arrows. Notice in Figure 6.15 that the drawing tools of Excel appear in the toolbar at the bottom of the screen. To use any of these drawing tools, click the tool, then click the location on the spreadsheet where it should appear. Drag the resulting object to a desired size and shape (Gilgen, 1997). Once in place, modifications are made to the object by right-clicking it. This produces a dialog window with a number of options including cut, copy, paste, order, and format auto-shape. The order option is useful when objects are arranged on top of one another, as in the Family or Household circle in Figure 6.15. The order of the larger circle was changed from front to back, to make the smaller circles visible; in other words, the smaller circle now sits on top of the larger circle. The format auto-shape option in the dialog window produces another dialog window in which changes to color, size, and line characteristics are made.

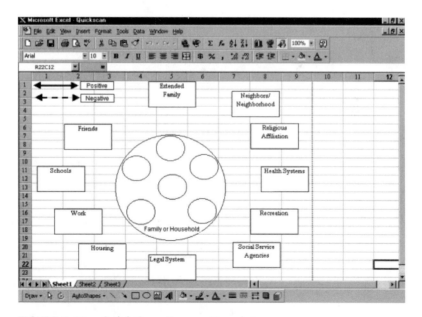

FIGURE 6.15   Quick Scan Ecomap Template
Source: Adapted from *More Than a Thousand Words*, p. 50, by M. Mattaini, 1993, Washington, DC: NASW Press. Copyright 1993, National Association of Social Workers, Inc., *More Than a Thousand Words: Graphics for Clinical Practice.*

The Quick Scan template in Figure 6.15 contains multiple copies of the same text box. This uniformity of size and shape is achieved by creating one box with the desired dimensions, which is then copied. Once copied, repeat the paste command until the requisite number of copies is produced. Use "click and drag" to position the new objects.

After producing a Quick Scan ecomap template, save a back-up copy that will not be used. The Quick Scan ecomap can either be printed and used with clients or completed within the spreadsheet. With each new client, open the template file and immediately use the Save As command to save the new version with some identifier of the client. Use of the spreadsheet version allows for rearranging objects and the addition or subtraction of family members, organizations, social constellations, or institutions. Moreover, if new ecomaps are completed over time, discussion of changes between ecomaps can provide evidence of change (Mattaini, 1993).

Figure 6.16 shows an ecomap produced from the Quick Scan ecomap template. Extraneous social connections were removed from the template in order to produce an ecomap that clearly depicts sources of support and conflict present in the client's life at this time. Note the lines indicating the client reports negativity toward the husband, but is aware of his positive support. The line from friends to the client runs through the husband, reflecting his mediation of contact with friends. What else is evident in this ecomap about the client's other relationships? Note that the size of the line indicates the strength of the relationship.

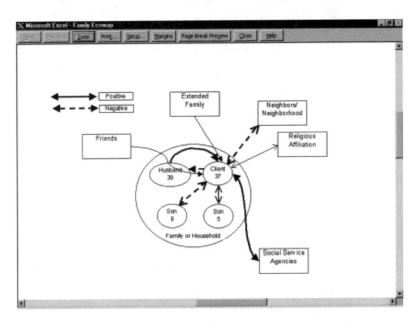

FIGURE 6.16 **Ecomap Developed in Excel from Quick Scan Template**

Genograms

Genograms are a graphic tool used in social work, medicine, and other applied health sciences to create an intergenerational picture of family relationships (Mattaini, 1993; McGoldrick & Gerson, 1985). They are commonly used to represent family functioning and to detect intergenerational patterns in biopsychosocial processes. Figure 6.17 is a screen from Lotus 1-2-3 in which the commonly agreed on symbols of genograms have been created with the application's drawing tools. Notice that the toolbar contains icons representing various graphics such as a line, arrow, rectangle, and circle. The drawing tools are accessed in the menu bar under Create, Drawing. The triangle was created with a drawing tool called a polygon. To create a triangle, select the polygon tool under Drawing. Click once in the spreadsheet to locate the first point of the triangle, then holding the left button down, drag a horizontal line to the desired length of the base. Another single click indicates the end of the first side of the triangle. Continue to hold down the mouse button and create the second side of the triangle. Click a third time to create the third side of the triangle. When the third line connects with the starting point of the first line, double click the left button to complete the triangle.

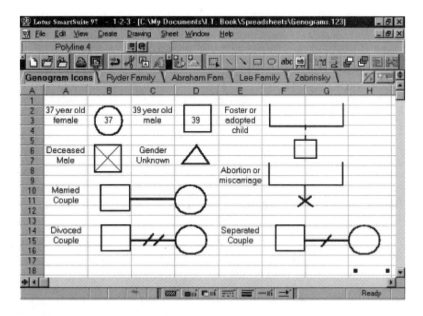

FIGURE 6.17   Genogram Symbols Created in Lotus 1-2-3

Source: Adapted from *More Than a Thousand Words* p. 14, by M. Mattaini, 1993, Washington, DC: NASW Press. Copyright 1993, National Association of Social Workers, Inc., *More Than a Thousand Words: Graphics for Clinical Practice.*

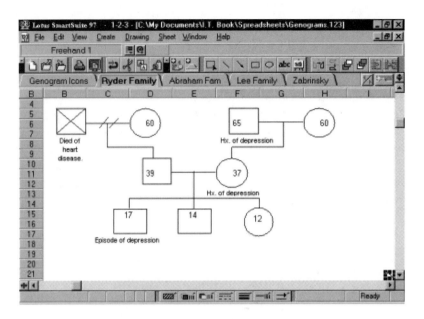

FIGURE 6.18   Genogram Created in Lotus 1-2-3

Once a set of genogram symbols is created and saved in a file, the creation of a genogram in a spreadsheet becomes a matter of copying and pasting the symbols into a new worksheet in the genogram spreadsheet. To copy a genogram symbol in a spreadsheet, select the range of cells beneath the symbol, then click Copy under Edit in the menu bar. As is displayed in Figure 6.17, each family's genogram can be labeled in the spreadsheet on a worksheet tab at the top of the spreadsheet.

Figure 6.18 contains a family's genogram created in Lotus 1-2-3. The grid lines of the spreadsheet were removed by selecting under View in the menu bar, Set View Preferences. In the Set View Preferences dialog window, on the tab View, deselect Gridlines. The text under each symbol is typed in a text box made available by selecting Text under Create in the menu bar. In the menu box, selecting Drawing Properties produces a dialog box. Under the tab with the line icon, the Border Line Color was set to white. This, in effect, hides the text box border. An alternative to hiding the text box in this manner is to type the text into the cells of the spreadsheet. This may require moving genogram symbols to locate them over the text. Either method allows for the inclusion of critical family information in the genogram.

Organizational Charts

Organizational charts are a widely used graphic that depicts the hierarchy of relationships in an organization. They are useful in understanding and communicating the lines of authority and responsibility within an agency. Organizational charts are often used to inform new employees, external constituents, clients, and board members of the structure of an organization. Organizational charts are composed of text boxes containing the names of units, individuals, or positions in the organization. The vertical arrangement of these text boxes indicates the amount of power; positions at the top of the chart hold the most power. The horizontal arrangement indicates units, individuals, or positions with equal levels of power.

Organizational charts are readily created within spreadsheets using their drawing tools. Microsoft Excel offers a tool for constructing organizational charts. From the menu bar select Insert, Picture, Organization Chart. This tool makes it possible to quickly develop custom organizational charts. Figure 6.19 shows a screen from the Organization Chart tool. Notice the buttons below the menu bar labeled Subordinate, Co-Worker, Manager, and Assistant. These components of an organizational chart are added by clicking the appropriate button and then locating it in the chart with another click. Connecting lines are automatically added by the program. Once in place, clicking the body of the cell opens the cell for entering name, title, and other information. Once the organization chart is complete, it is inserted into the body of the document (spreadsheet, word processing, or presentation) that was open when the Organization Chart tool was activated.

Creation of an organizational chart in Lotus 1-2-3 or Quattro Pro requires the creation of each text box and connecting line using the available drawing tools. The basic drawing tools of Lotus 1-2-3 were reviewed previously. The tools and procedures in Quattro Pro are very similar to those of Lotus 1-2-3. Figure 6.20 shows an organizational chart created in Quattro Pro. The grid lines of the spreadsheet were turned off by selecting Active Sheet, under Format in the menu bar. Grid lines, horizontal and vertical,

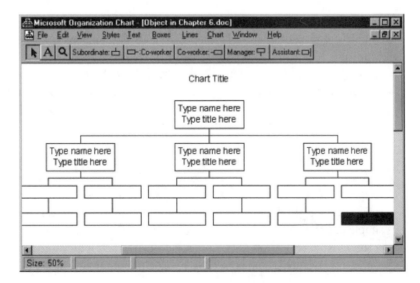

FIGURE 6.19   Microsoft Excel's Organization Chart Tool

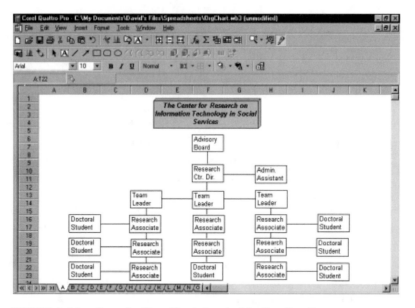

FIGURE 6.20   Organization Chart Created in Quattro Pro

were deselected. Notice that the drawing toolbar is the second toolbar beneath the menu bar. These tools are available also in the menu bar under Insert, Shape. To facilitate text entry, text boxes were used instead of the "rectangle" shape tool.

Flow Charts

Flow charts are a means to visually represent processes, procedures, or steps to an end result. They illustrate the interaction of factors or players in the process. Depending on their intended function and design, they may show a broad overview of a process or provide highly specific detail about each step. Flow charts are an important means of (a) documenting procedures in organizations, (b) planning future events, products, or services, and (c) specifying paths for the flow of information. Flow charts use a common set of symbols; circles indicate the start or end of a process, rectangles indicate an event, step, or process, and diamonds designate a decision point.

Once developed, flow charts are not set in stone, but are commonly modified as previous plans collide with present reality. Beyond the common set of symbols, flow charts are adaptable to a wide range of purposes. In developing a flow chart it is important to (a) clearly designate the beginning or end of the process, (b) keep the chart as simple as possible without discarding essential detail, and (c) make sure there is only one output from each process box, or use a diamond to indicate the necessity of a decision at the juncture (Kimbler, 1998). Once a preliminary flow chart is developed, its review by individuals involved or familiar with the charted process is invaluable in detecting error, omission, and/or excessive detail.

Lotus 1-2-3, Quattro Pro, and Excel each have the requisite drawing symbols and lines for construction of flow charts. Excel has an additional set of drawing tools specifically for the construction of flow charts. When Excel's drawing toolbar is activated, flow chart tools are available under AutoShapes. There are 28 flow chart symbols available, but their specific functions and meanings are not documented. Also available under AutoShapes are flow chart connectors. These connectors link symbols with lines that remain connected to the symbols they are linked to even when the symbols are moved around in the flow chart. This is a very helpful feature. In Lotus 1-2-3 and Quattro Pro, one must redraw or reconnect lines to symbols when the location of a symbol is changed. This inhibits experimentation with the location of symbols in the flow chart due to the extra effort required to redraw or reconnect the lines.

Figure 6.21 was created using the flow chart tools of Excel. Note the two lines with right angles at the bottom of the flow chart. These angled connectors make it possible to link symbols in the flow chart that are not in a direct line. There also are connectors with arcs to create curved connections.

Copying and pasting a flow chart created in Excel with the AutoShape tools into a word processing document or presentation software requires a slightly different procedure than the standard copy and paste. While holding down the SHIFT key, select the spreadsheet cells that encompass the flow chart. Continuing to hold down the

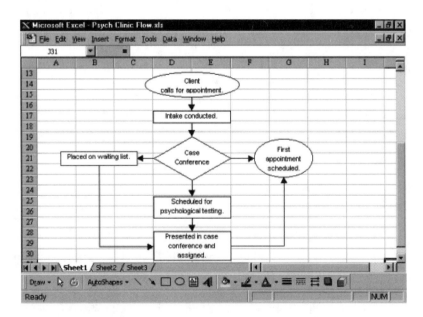

FIGURE 6.21 Flow Chart Created in Microsoft Excel

SHIFT key, under Edit, select Copy Picture. A dialog window will appear. To paste the flow chart without the spreadsheet grid lines, select As Shown When Printed. Open the word processing or presentation software document for which the flow chart is intended and paste it into the desired location. One advantage in developing flow charts in Excel and pasting them into a word processing document is that the flow chart connects described earlier are not available in the drawing tools of Microsoft Word. Flow charts created in Lotus 1-2-3 and Quattro Pro may also be copied and pasted into word processing documents and presentation software. After creating the flow chart, use the object selection tool to select the entire flow chart. In both programs, the object selection tool is an icon of a rectangle with dotted lines. It is found in the drawing tools toolbar. Once the flow chart is selected, choose Edit, Copy. Open the document into which the flow chart will be pasted and then select Edit, Paste in the menu bar. In all three programs, the flow chart can simply be printed from the spreadsheet if it is not going to be incorporated into another document.

Summary

This chapter described the role of visual representation in the presentation of practice information. The core message of the chapter was that social service workers can now employ the multiple graphics tools available in software suites to describe, analyze, and communicate practice information. In this chapter, consideration was given to the balance between the intended message of a graphical representation and the anticipated audience of viewers. The characteristics of well-designed and useful graphs were presented. The use of spreadsheets for graphical representation of information was described. Discussed were the topics of selection of data prior to graphing, matching data to type of graph, the enhancement of graphs, and their subsequent export to other documents. The application of spreadsheet graphics tools for the creation of ecomaps, genograms, organizational charts, and flow charts was reviewed. Many of the tools of graphical representation described in this chapter are further applied in subsequent chapters on expanded uses of word processing, presentation software, and the Internet.

Exercises

1. Use data from your practice setting to create with a spreadsheet a bar graph of the data. Examples of possible graphs include group attendance over time, revenues by day for a week, or clients served in the agency during a week, plotted by day.
2. With a group of peers and using either the spreadsheet data from the exercises in Chapter 4 or from your practice setting, create a cross tabulation table with two nominal or ordinal level variables. Review Chapter 4 for the cross tab-

ulation procedure. Then select an appropriate type of graph for the data and generate the graph.

3. Using an available data set, generate the following types of graphs with appropriate titles and legends: a bar graph with attached values, a line graph, a pie graph, a frequency distribution, an area graph, and a scattergram with regression line.

4. Using the drawing tools available in a spreadsheet, create an ecomap. Create a spreadsheet with genogram symbols on one worksheet and then create genograms for two individuals or families.

5. Using a spreadsheet's drawing tools, create either an organization chart or flow chart for your practice setting.

chapter 7

Beyond Word Processing

The intention of this chapter is to provide an expanded view of the functional capabilities of word processing software. The focus here is on describing how to use word processing software for a range of tasks germane to social service practice, beyond just text manipulation. More specifically, this chapter explains the creation and use of smart notes, interactive documents, collaborative documents, graphics, images, templates, mail merges, and Web pages. The theme that pervades this chapter is that word processing software is extremely versatile and offers many functions directly applicable to a range of practice settings.

Despite the ever increasing use of Internet browsers to explore the World Wide Web, word processing is still the most widely used application of personal computers (Margolis, 1996). Word processing is a fundamental skill of personal computing in which documents are created, formatted, stored, printed or otherwise disseminated. Word processing allows for the creation of documents ranging from the simplest of notes to graphically rich, multicolored, professional-looking brochures.

In their early manifestations, word processors on personal computers were very similar to the text editors found on mainframe computers. Text in documents could be moved, inserted, deleted, searched, aligned, and printed, but few other functions were available. Users of modern word processing software often are initially overwhelmed with the range of features available. Word processing software now commonly includes spell checkers, a thesaurus, graphics tools, multiple fonts and text formats, and tools for creating Web pages and linking documents to the Web. Some word processors, such as Corel WordPerfect and Microsoft Word, even allow for the inclusion of multimedia such as digitized video and sound in documents. Enhanced control in word processing software over document layout and graphics has increasingly blurred the line between word processing and desktop publishing software. The result of these enhanced features in word processing software is the emergence of robust tools for the dissemination of information.

What is not clear is the degree to which social service practitioners and agencies have recognized and extended their use of word processing software beyond the creation and handling of text-based information. This confusion is fostered by a dearth of articles in the social service literature describing the application of advanced word processing tools toward improved service delivery. Several notable exceptions have appeared. Johnson (1994) writing in the journal *Computers in Nursing* suggests the use of modern word processing software for the creation of client information sheets, forms, brochures, and newsletters. Mahler and Meier (1993) examined the effects on client self-esteem and sense of mastery of teaching word processing and other computer skills to severely mentally ill clients. Williamson (1992) has written on how psychiatrists can use word processing and desktop publishing as a part of their practice. Each of these articles suggests the potential of the use of word processing beyond text manipulation.

The purpose of this chapter is to describe and demonstrate the use of word processing software in the creation of information resources for social service practice. The topics covered in this chapter include (a) creating smart documents, (b) applying graphics in word processing, (c) employing templates to facilitate the creation of commonly used documents, (d) producing mail merges, and (e) building Web pages. Each of these skills draws upon the enhanced capabilities of modern word processors.

The three word processors employed in the examples detailed in this chapter are Lotus Word Pro, Microsoft Word, and Corel WordPerfect. They are the word processors for their respective software suites, Lotus SmartSuite, Microsoft Office, and Corel Word-Perfect Office. As integrated components of software suites, they are optimized for the exchange of information, graphs, and graphics within their respective suites. Each of these programs has a wide range of formatting and graphics tools. They also each have tools for the creation of Web pages. Although there is some variation in their approaches to some tasks, each of these three word processors are robust tools that are capable of performing all of the advanced word processing skills described in this chapter.

Smart Documents: Finding and Linking Information

Word processing documents have historically been static, noninteractive documents. They were typed, printed, and distributed. An array of new tools in word processors dramatically expands the range of options now available for organizing, finding, and interacting with information contained and referenced in documents. Of particular interest in this section is the creation of smart notes, interactive documents, and collaborative documents. The term *smart notes* refers to documents organized to facilitate the finding and retrieval of information. It is not a reference to any particular feature of Lotus Smart-Suite, which makes ample use of the term "smart" in its array of features. Interactive documents are hyperlinked electronic documents that have Intranet and Web addresses embedded in them. Collaborative documents contain comments and text markings used for adding commentary and suggestions in collaboratively developed documents exchanged between individuals. It is, of course, possible and sometimes helpful to create documents with all three of these features. For the purposes of explication, these three features are addressed separately in the following sections.

Smart Notes

Documentation is an extremely common and widely varied activity in social service practice. Widely used forms of text-based documentation include case notes, minutes of meetings, and supervisor notes. We reviewed in Chapter 5 ways to create databases for the management of client information, including case notes. Database tools are a robust option for collecting client contact information such as date, financial data, category of service provision, as well as case notes. Depending on the management information systems in their particular agency, some practitioners may prefer to or need to compile case notes in word processing documents. Likewise, there are advantages to collecting the notes from committee or organization meetings into a single document that archives the activities of the body over time. Supervisory notes, like case notes, document the facts and inferences of meetings between supervisors and subordinates. Each of these three documentation tasks can be augmented by organizing the information collected over time with consideration of its eventual retrieval.

The goal of creating smart notes is to organize the information within a document to facilitate finding specified information. Word processing tools that expedite this process include outlines, bookmarks, and document maps. One approach to recording both case notes and supervisory notes is to create them with the outline tools available in each of the three word processors. An *outline* is a hierarchically arranged document in which heading levels are used to organize the content of the document (Boyce, 1997a). For the purpose of writing case or supervisory notes, names are placed in the first heading level and dates of contact are placed in the second heading level. The meeting or contact notes are written in the body text. The *body text* is text that is not formatted as a heading level. In other words, the body text is where the primary content of the notes is typed or inserted. See Figure 7.1 for an example of case notes written in outline form in Microsoft Word. The heading level is set with the directional arrows in the toolbar at the top left-hand corner of the page.

Compiling case or supervisor notes in outline form offers several advantages over simply writing notes in a standard word processing document. First, it organizes the information in a visually distinct way that facilitates both reading and finding information. Second, the use of client or subordinate names in the first heading level allows for the sorting of cases in alphabetical order. As new cases are entered into the document, the file can be resorted to return it to alphabetical order. A third advantage to recording case or supervisor notes in outline form is document mapping. This feature, which is currently available only in Microsoft Word, creates a map of the document's headings in a pane on the left side of the screen. This document navigation tool makes it possible to go to a desired heading (case or subordinate name) by clicking on the heading in the document map pane. Applying this tool to case or supervisor notes makes it possible to quickly locate names and enter notes. Figure 7.2 shows a document in which the document map is activated. The size of the document navigation pane can be adjusted by dragging the line between the two sections. Note also that beside Case 1 and 2 there is

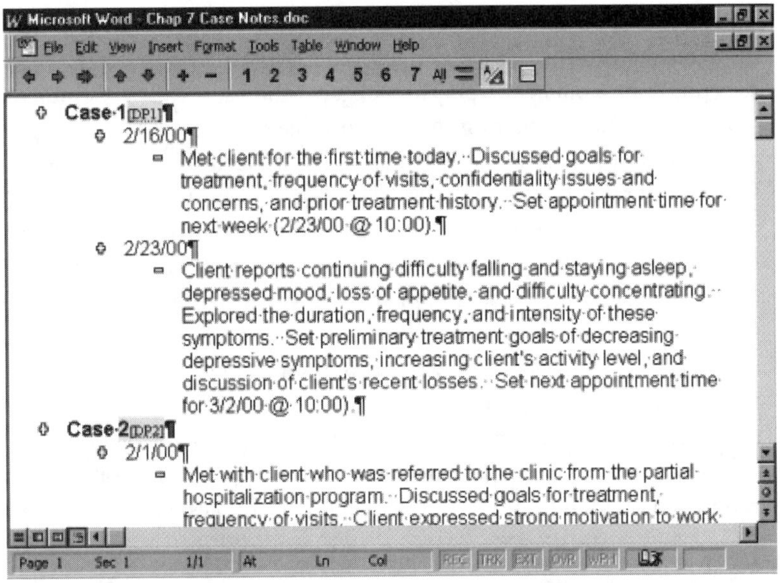

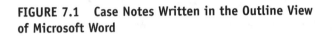

FIGURE 7.1   Case Notes Written in the Outline View of Microsoft Word

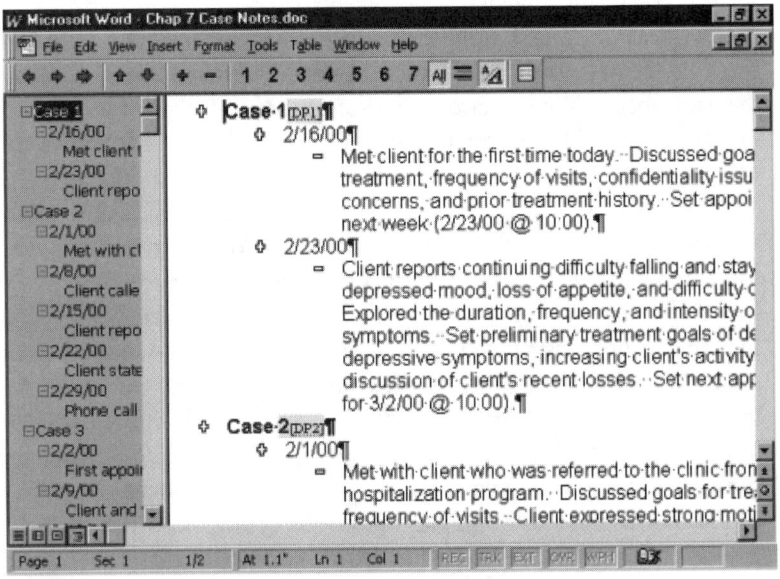

FIGURE 7.2   Case Notes in Outline Format with Document Map Activated

highlighted text (DP1 and DP2). DP are the author's initials and the highlighted text indicates the presence of a Comment note. Right-clicking on the highlighted text and selecting Edit Comment from the pop-up window reveals a Comment note. Comment notes are useful for entering information that will not appear on a printed form of the document. Moreover, if the document is sent electronically to a supervisor for review, supervisory remarks may be inserted with Comment notes.

The creation of smart notes using a word processor outline format is applicable to collecting and archiving committee notes, meeting minutes, and other documents that are issued electronically on a regular basis. For instance, organizations increasingly distribute the minutes from committee meetings as attachments to e-mail. Such documents can be copied and pasted into a smart notes document. The committee name constitutes the first heading level, the meeting date the second heading level, and the minutes of the meeting are pasted into the body text. The advantage of storing notes and minutes this way is that it creates a central document for the collection and retrieval of organizational information. This can help deliberative bodies maintain the focus of their work.

Interactive Documents

Increasingly, information resources are located on agency networks, intranets, or on the Web. Intranets are networks internal to organizations or companies that use Internet software to share information on internal Web sites (James & Jansen, 1998). They can employ standard Web addresses, but limit access to their resources with security measures such as passwords. Interactive documents created in word processors provide readers with a means to access supplemental information resident on a network, intranet, or the Web. Interactive documents have embedded hyperlinks to intranet and Web documents. Hyperlinks are electronic addresses that connect to files, Web pages, e-mail addresses, or FTP (file transfer protocol) servers. Figure 7.3 shows the dialog box in Microsoft Word in which hyperlinks are created. Hyperlinks are referred to in Lotus WordPro as links. The power of an interactive document is derived from the fact that it is informationally enriched with links that allow the reader to access additional information on the Web and/or available on an organization's intranet or network.

The utility of interactive documents is predicated on two facts. First, the interactive document is distributed in electronic format. For instance, the clinical director of a mental health care agency might send a memo to the clinical staff, as an e-mail attachment, with embedded hyperlinks to Web sites reporting on a recent development in the treatment of depression. Upon receipt of the memo, each clinical staff member can click on any of the hyperlinks to read the new information on the treatment of depression. The second fact impinging on the utility of an interactive document is that the functionality of the hyperlink is dependent on the reader's personal computer having access to the location of the hyperlinked document. If the hyperlinked document is on the Internet, then the reader's access to the information necessitates Internet access. However, interactive documents can be created that link to files on a diskette,

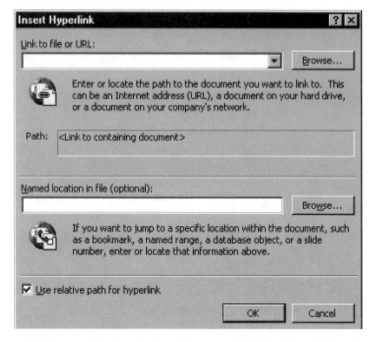

FIGURE 7.3   Window for Creating Hyperlinks in Microsoft Word

CD-ROM, or other portable storage medium. Moreover, if an agency's Internet access is constrained, Internet-based files can be copied to a local network server. The interactive document would then reference the local network file. (Agencies should be careful to not copy copyrighted material and distribute it on a local network server.) The essential point here is that interactive documents need not reference Web-based information to function as informationally enriched resources. An interactive document's value to a reader is derived not from the location of the material that is hyperlinked to the document, but instead from the quality, relevance, and usability of that information.

Figure 7.3 depicts the means for creating hyperlinks in Microsoft Word. In Lotus Word Pro, hyperlinks (links) are inserted into documents by first activating the Web Authoring Tools. The Web Authoring Tools are under File, Internet in the menu bar. The Web Authoring Tools appear as a toolbar on the screen. Clicking Create Link opens the Create Link dialog box displayed in Figure 7.4. The type of link to create is defined in the drop-down menu which offers a range of types of links to create, including links to documents on the Web, bookmarks in the same document, and FTP sites on the Web. The address of the link is specified by either typing it into the Link to text box or by selecting it from a list of existing links shown in the drop-down menu.

Figure 7.5 shows a case notes document in which a clinical supervisor has added a hyperlink to a Web resource on the treatment of depression, thereby creating an interactive Smart Notes document. On reading the supervisor's note, the caseworker can

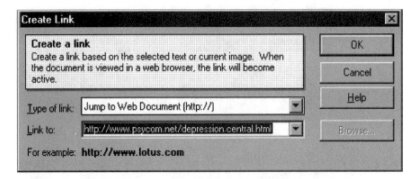

FIGURE 7.4   Dialog Box for Creating Hyperlinks in Lotus Word Pro

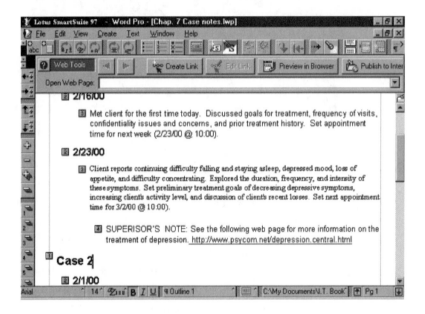

FIGURE 7.5   Smart Notes Interactive Document

link to the cited Web page, assuming that the document is in electronic format and the caseworker has Internet access.

Hyperlinks are created in Corel WordPerfect by selecting Tools, Hyperlinks in the menu bar. A dialog box opens in which the hyperlink is defined by identifying either the location of a document or Web page with which to create the linkage. There is a Browse Web button for finding Web sites for linkage. Again, use of this Browse Web button presumes Internet access. This Hyperlinks tool in Corel WordPerfect, like the other hyperlinks procedures described, makes it very easy to develop interactive documents capable of providing readers with a rich array of information supporting, confirming, or contrasting the information contained in the interactive document.

Collaborative Documents

Agencies and organizations are increasingly relying on teams, work groups, and/or committees to develop problem solving strategies and carry out tasks toward the accomplishment of specific goals. The increasing capacity within organizations to share documents via e-mail has promoted the collaborative development by work groups of documents germane to the group goals. Technologies exist for geographically distributed collaborators to work simultaneously on a document over intranets, networks, and the Internet. However, for present purposes, the term *collaborative documents* refers to electronic shared documents that collaborators interact with sequentially.

The collaborative creation of a document can occur between two individuals who exchange it in an iterative process of development and refinement of its content. Collaborative documents may be developed by work groups in a process in which the document is passed from one member to another with successive additions and editing. Alternatively, a single work group member may electronically distribute a single version to all group members, requesting their contributions and editorial suggestions. The work group members' contributions are made to the collaborative document and subsequent versions are distributed, again in an iterative process. A final document evolves from the successive revisions.

However the collaborative process unfolds, it is crucial that the participants are able to both add comments or contributions to a document and readily determine what changes others made. Corel WordPerfect, Lotus Word Pro, and Microsoft Word each has tools with which to develop collaborative documents. Two of the primary tools shared by all three are the ability to highlight text and add comments.

Highlighting text in a document is much like highlighting text with a highlight marker in a book. Click the highlight tool icon from a toolbar and select the portion of the text to be highlighted. Highlighting text can serve to designate (a) text inserted into a collaborative document, (b) text the reviewer has revised from the original, or (c) text that the reviewer has attached as a comment.

Comments are brief notes inserted into the body of a document that do not alter the text of the document. In collaborative documents comments are a useful means to share suggestions, possible revisions, and other editorial comments. The comment appears as either highlighted text or as a small highlighted box that will display the hidden comment when the cursor passes over the highlighted text or the highlighted box is clicked. In Microsoft Word, audio comments can be recorded and added to a document if the computer has a sound card and microphone. Of course, the utility of this feature is lost if the reviewer's computer does not likewise have a sound card and speakers.

All three word processing programs have toolbars that contain highlight and comment tool icons. In Microsoft Word the toolbar with the highlight and comment tools is referred to as the Reviewing tools and is available from the menu bar under View, Toolbars. In Lotus Word Pro, clicking the small down arrow in the middle of the toolbar opens a drop-down box with choices of toolbars to display. Clicking Comment Tools opens a toolbar with highlighting and comment tools. In Corel WordPerfect, the highlight tool is in the main formatting toolbar. Insert comments in a document by selecting Insert, Comment from the menu bar. A new screen appears in which to type the comment. Once the comment is complete, select File, Close, which will return to the original document. A small text bubble icon will appear in the left margin of the original document (Steward & Perry, 1997). When the text bubble icon is clicked, the comment appears.

Both Microsoft Word and Lotus Word Pro have more advanced tools for collaborative documents. In Lotus Word Pro, selecting File, Versions opens a dialog box that allows for the creation of new versions of a document, the viewing of older versions, and the renaming and saving of the versions into different files. Moreover, it will track who edited which version, date the editing, and display remarks from the editors. This feature makes it possible to track and document the contributions of each author to the collaborative document. Under Microsoft Word's Reviewing toolbar there are tools for tracking and finding changes in collaborative documents. The Track Changes tool marks changes made in a document (Warner, 1997). When activated, changes made in the document are lighted either on the screen, on the printed page, or both, depending on which option is selected. For more detailed information on how to create collaborative documents in Microsoft Word see Warner (1997).

The essential point to understand about collaborative documents, whether they are developed with the advanced tools of Lotus Word Pro or Microsoft Word or with the use of highlights and comments, is that collaborative documents make it possible to pool the intellectual and information resources of a team toward a common goal. Collaborative documents are an integrative and iterative endeavor of a workgroup that may result in a final document far superior to the efforts of any individual team member.

Taken together, the three types of smart documents described here, smart notes, interactive documents, and collaborative documents, expand the utility of word processing for social service workers. Employment of these tools offers social service workers ways to organize documentation, enrich the information content of documents, and work together toward common goals. It is perhaps crucial to understand that these smart documents move word processing beyond the production of a static, paper-based document and toward the creation of dynamic and interactive documents.

Graphics: Beyond Charts and Graphs

Chapter 6 reviews the use of graphics for visual representation of practice information. This section extends the discussion of graphics to their use in word processing documents. How graphics are actually used in word processing documents is dependent on the type of document being produced and its intended use. Generally speaking, graphics in word processing documents serve to capture the reader's attention, save readers time in comprehending the message, make a point, enhance the document's visual appeal, and provide a context for the document's content (White, 1984). This discussion describes the utilization of text art tools, clip art, and images to complement and enhance word processing documents. Each of theses types of graphics is applicable in a wide variety of word processing documents including memos, letters, manuals, newsletters, brochures, and flyers.

Text Art: Text with a Twist

Text art tools are graphics procedures in word processors that make it possible to add special effects to text. These special effects may include shadows, stretching, skewing, and rotating text. Text art effects may also include the creation of 3-D effects and altering the frame and background of the text art. Each of the three word processors discussed in this chapter has tools for text art formatting. One commonality among the three word processors is that they treat text art as objects in the word processing document. *Objects* are items such as graphics, clip art, and images that can be selected and manipulated in software applications (Margolis, 1996). As such, text art in word processors cannot be spell-checked nor will the thesaurus work on text art.

Figure 7.6 displays the range of options for text art available in Microsoft Word under WordArt Gallery. The WordArt Gallery is selected from the Drawing toolbar.

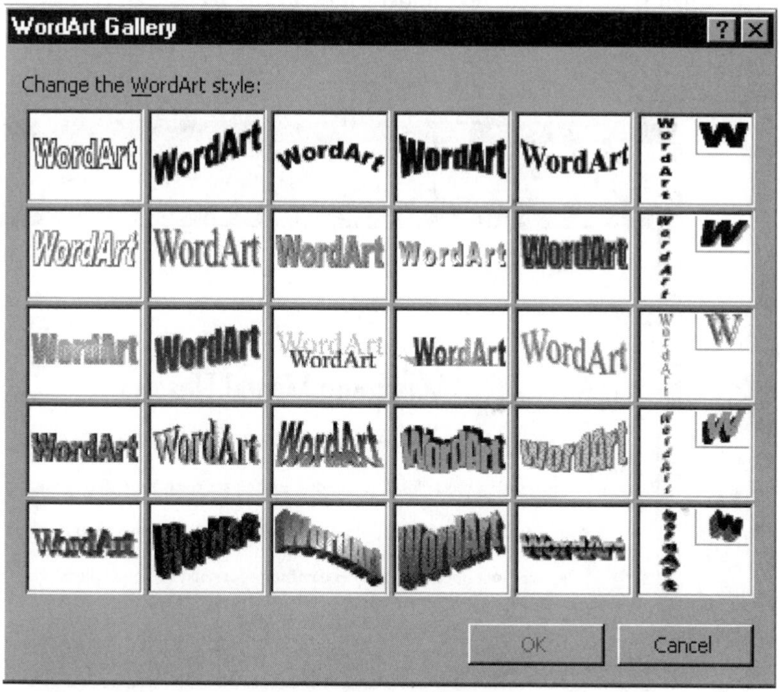

FIGURE 7.6   Microsoft Word's WordArt Selection

Once the WordArt style is specified, an Edit WordArt text window appears in which the desired text is entered, font size chosen, and bold and/or italic formatting is set. The resultant text art appears in the open document. It can be selected and moved to any location in the document. Altering the size of the text art requires only moving the cursor to one of the corners of the object, where it changes into a bidirectional arrow. By clicking and holding down the left mouse button, the text art object's size can be enlarged or decreased.

Right-clicking on the text art object opens a menu from which Format WordArt can be selected. This formatting window offers choices for the text art regarding colors, line, size, position, and wrapping. Wrapping makes available a number of options for wrapping text around the text art object. Wrapping allows text art objects to be embedded into the body of the document's text. It is especially helpful for breaking the monotony of text and holding the reader's attention. Figure 7.7 displays a draft of a flyer using text art to represent the agency's name. The body of the message on the flyer wraps around the bottom of the text art in a way that joins the message and the agency's name. The use of text art in this way serves to fuse the agency's name with the announced activity.

Text art is produced in Lotus Word Pro with the Drawing command, available under Create in the menu bar. The Drawing command opens a resizable drawing frame in which text and geometric figures (circles, rectangles, lines, etc.) are inserted. Once text is typed into the drawing frame, select it with the arrow icon in the Drawing toolbar. Then select Curved Text under Draw in the menu bar. A dialog window appears from which a range of text shapes can be chosen, much like the WordArt Gallery of

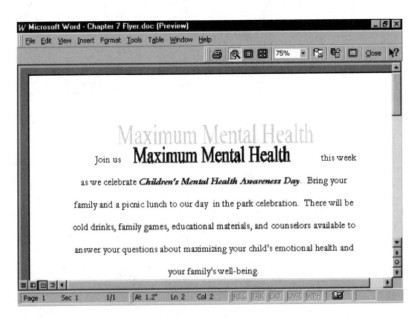

FIGURE 7.7   Text Art with Wrapped Text

Microsoft Word described previously. The primary difference is that in Lotus Word Pro, choices for formatting text color, font size, bold, and italic are made in the toolbar at the bottom of the page. Make choices about the background of the frame by right-clicking the Drawing frame and selecting Frame properties from the menu window.

Creating text art in Corel WordPerfect involves a process very similar to the two already described. Text can be skewed and reshaped. Patterns, fills, and shadows can be added to text in order to create an attention-getting image in the document (Steward & Perry, 1997). To open the TextArt dialog box, select Insert, Graphics, TextArt from the menu bar. Insert into the "Type here" box the text that will be transformed into text art. Select font, justification, text color, and text shape. Once the text art object is complete, right-click it to select styles from the menu to alter borders, add captions, or resize or rotate it.

In summary, while each of the three word processing programs uses a slightly different approach to the creation and modification of text art, the resultant text art objects in documents are very similar. As is often the case with computer generated graphics, just because the software can produce an extraordinary array of images does not mean that a document will benefit from the synergy of software capacity and one's creative impulses. The use of text art in a document must be balanced with careful consideration of its purpose in conveying the informational content of the document.

Clip Art

Clip art is defined by Margolis (1996) as "electronic illustrations that can be inserted into a document" (p. 85). Like text art, the judicious use of clip art in a document can attract and hold a reader's attention, add emphasis to a point, or convey emotive elements of a document such as humor, enthusiasm, or excitement. Corel WordPerfect, Lotus Word Pro, and Microsoft Word each have numerous clip art illustrations available for inclusion in a document. Each of these programs makes it possible to readily insert a clip art illustration into a document, resize and reshape it, and wrap text around it.

Figure 7.8 displays a Lotus Word Pro document in which text art is combined with two clip art illustrations. The result is a document with a simple and clear message. Try this experiment. Cover Figure 7.8 with a book or sheet of paper. Now read the same message without the clip art. "Maximum Mental Health: Working for your well-being." Now remove the object covering Figure 7.8 and again examine it. What does the clip art add to the message? What else is conveyed with the two simple illustrations? How is the meaning of the term "your" altered by the clip art illustration of the three people?

Clip art is added to Microsoft Word documents with the Insert, Picture, Clip Art command series from the menu bar. Figure 7.9 displays the Clip Art Gallery of illustration choices available in Word. A clip art illustration is inserted into a document by clicking on the illustration and then clicking Insert. The clip art will appear in the document at the location of the insertion point. (The insertion point is the point where

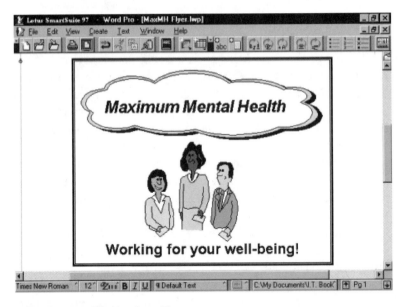

FIGURE 7.8   Clip Art in a Flyer

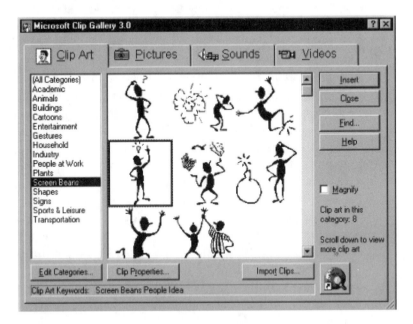

FIGURE 7.9   Microsoft Word's Clip Art Gallery

text characters appear during typing (Margolis, 1996).) Just like text art, once the clip art is in the document, it can be resized and reshaped, as well as relocated within the document. Also, as in the case of text art, the text of the document can be wrapped around the clip art. Word wrapping for clip art is activated in the same way as it was for text art, by right-clicking the image, selecting Format Picture, Wrapping, and then choosing the Wrapping style. This is illustrated in Figure 7.10.

In Lotus Word Pro, a clip art illustration is referred to as a Drawing. A Drawing is inserted into a document by selecting from the menu bar Create, Drawing, Import Drawing, then selecting the desired file. One drawback of this process is that it is not possible to preview a Drawing before inserting it into a document. Consequently, unless one is familiar with the available Drawings by file name, finding the right Drawing in Word Pro is a matter of trial and error. Despite this difficulty, Drawings in Lotus Word Pro can readily be reshaped, resized, and relocated. Word wrapping can be applied and colors of the drawing are easily altered. Right-clicking the drawing and selecting Draw properties opens a Properties dialog box that offers multiple options for modifying the Drawing.

Corel WordPerfect offers two slightly different approaches to accessing and placing clip art in a document. One option is to create a box in the open document by clicking and dragging the mouse until the box is the desired size (Steward & Perry, 1997). Upon releasing the mouse button, a pop-up menu appears in which Clip Art is a choice. Selecting Clip Art opens the WordPerfect Scrapbook in which a range of clip art illustrations is displayed. Figure 7.11 shows the WordPerfect Scrapbook. Note the two tabs at the top of the Scrapbook, Clipart and CD Clipart. The Corel WordPerfect Suite CD-ROM contains additional clip art illustrations. To place an illustration in a document, click the desired illustration in the Scrapbook and drag it to the intended location in the document. An alternative to creating a box for the clip art in the document

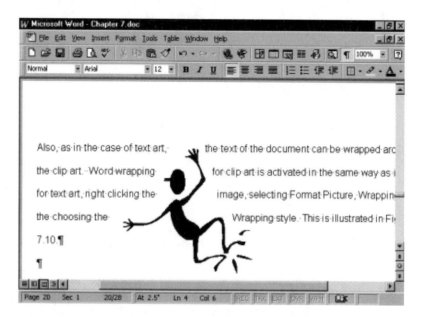

FIGURE 7.10   Clip Art with Word Wrapping Activated

FIGURE 7.11   WordPerfect Scrapbook of Clip Art

is to use the menu bar and the commands Insert, Graphics, Clipart. This sequence opens the Scrapbook and clip art can then be dragged from the Scrapbook into the document. Right-clicking on a piece of clip art opens a pop-up menu with numerous choices for altering the appearance of the clip art, including the capacity to edit the clip art illustration and modify the color, contrast, and rotation of the illustration. Alterations in the size, position, and style of word wrapping are also available. Taken together, Corel WordPerfect offers tools for a high level of control over the appearance of the clip art illustration.

The clip art tools in each of the three word processors provide users with the capacity to enrich documents with illustrations in the service of the document's message. Clip art is particularly useful for flyers, brochures, newsletters, and other types of documents aimed at broad audiences in order to capture and hold attention. Clip art can also be helpful in documents with lighthearted or unassuming messages. Depending on the illustration, clip art can be construed as comic or less than serious. As such, contingent both on the intended audience and the clip art, caution is urged in using clip art in documents intended to communicate a serious message. While it is impossible to offer global rules for the use of all clip art across all possible documents, it is prudent to carefully consider who will likely read a document and what is its message before including a piece of clip art.

Images

The advent of digital cameras and digital scanners has made a boundless range of digital images available for use in documents. Images captured by digital cameras are downloadable to personal computers and readily integrated into word processing documents. Photographs, drawings, and other images scanned by digital scanners are processed into electronic files and saved on personal computers. These image files are then available for use in documents. Furthermore, most digital cameras and scanners come with photo editing software, which makes it possible to crop, enhance, and visually transform digital images. Photo editing software offers a range of filters, which are special effects applied to alter an image. Commonly available filters make it possible to soften, sharpen, polarize, and change the brightness and color saturation of the image. Moreover, inexpensive photo quality printers now allow for the printing of documents with embedded images. Taken together, this hardware and software for image capturing and editing opens tremendous creative possibilities for utilizing images in word processing documents.

Images used in word processing documents are generally saved in one of two file formats: GIF (graphics interchange format) and JPEG (joint photographic experts group). JPEG images will generally have JPG as the extension on the file's name. Both GIF and JPEG images use file compression protocols in order to reduce the disk space required for storing the image. GIF and JPEG images are also the most commonly used image formats on the World Wide Web because of their capacity to provide reasonably good resolution with small file sizes. While this fact is not specifically germane to the topic of using images in word processor documents, it will find application later when we turn our discussion to converting word processor documents into Web pages.

Images are handled by the word processors in much the same way as text art and clip art. They are imported into the document and then resized, reshaped, and repositioned as necessary. Images are imported into Microsoft Word with the commands Insert, Picture, From File. Clearly, it is necessary to have the image one wishes to import in a file on a diskette or the hard drive before starting this command sequence. The Microsoft Office CD-ROM also comes with an array of digital photos. To access these images, insert the Microsoft Office CD-ROM into the CD player, then from the menu bar select Insert, Picture, Clip Art and select images from the Microsoft Clip Gallery. If the selection of photos available on the CD-ROM is not displayed, select Import Clips and then click the CD-ROM icon, open the Clip Art folder, then the Photos folder. Digital photographs in this folder are classified by subject. Selection of a file will add that image to the Microsoft Clip Gallery. From there, it can be selected and inserted into a document.

Figure 7.12 displays the flyer first introduced in Figure 7.7. This is enhanced by a digital image of a child's drawing. The drawing was first scanned and then saved as a JPEG file. The document containing the flyer was then opened in the word processing software—in this case, Microsoft Word. Next the command sequence Insert, Picture, From, was initiated. The drawings file was selected and the image appeared in the flyer document at the insertion point. The size of the image was reduced by moving the cursor to its top left corner. When the cursor changed to a bidirectional arrow, the mouse button was clicked and held down as the image was resized. The result is a flyer that integrates text art, a digital image, and text to convey an invitation to an agency function.

Like Microsoft Office, the Corel WordPerfect Suite CD-ROM contains a large number of digital photographs available for use in documents (Steward & Perry, 1997). These photos are accessed, once the CD-ROM is in the CD-ROM drive, with the menu bar commands Insert, Graphics, From File. A dialog box entitled Insert Image appears. Select the CD-ROM drive from the Look in drop-down menu. Double-click Photos and then double-click the folder containing the category of photos of interest. To preview Photos in this folder, select View, Preview, Use Separate Window. Once a desirable photo

FIGURE 7.12   Flyer with Digital Image and Text Art

is found, double-click the image to insert it into the document. The image can be resized by clicking down on the corner of the photo and dragging to the desired size.

In Lotus Word Pro, images are imported with the Import Picture command found under File in the menu bar. Selecting Import Picture opens a dialog box in which to specify the location of the image file for import (Look in) and file format (Files of type). Once a file is selected, it can be previewed before it is opened if Preview is checked. The selected file is opened and inserted into a Frame in the document when the Enter key is pressed or the Open button is clicked. A Frame is the container within a document for drawings, text art, and images in Lotus Word Pro. The image is resized, reshaped, and relocated by altering the size, shape, or location of the Frame. Once the image alteration is complete, the Frame disappears. Figure 7.13 shows a flyer created in Lotus Word Pro. The image in the flyer was produced by scanning a photograph and then importing the resultant JPEG file into the document using the procedure described here.

It should be noted that Figure 7.13 is a screen shot of a print preview screen in Lotus Word Pro. As a result, there is a considerable loss of clarity in the image. The actual clarity or sharpness of images is referred to as *resolution* (Margolis, 1996). The resolution of an image is a function of the number of dots per inch (dpi) contained in an image. Seventy-two dpi is generally considered low resolution, although it can be sufficient for images on the Web; their small file size requires less time to download to Web browsers. Many scanners capture and printers produce images at 300 dpi or greater. High resolution is generally considered to be 1,200 dpi or greater. Therefore, the appearance of an image in a word processor document depends on (a) the resolution at which the image was captured by either a scanner or digital camera, (b) the resolution it was stored at, and (c) the resolution at which it is printed. A 1,200 dpi

FIGURE 7.13   Flyer with Digital Image Produced in Lotus Word Pro

high-resolution image in a word processor document will have no greater clarity than a 300 dpi image if both are printed on a 300 dpi printer.

In summary, the text art, clip art, and image graphics described in this section extend the functionality of word processing software from mere text manipulation to the production of visually rich and compelling documents. For those wishing to use the graphic riches of modern word processors, there remains the continual struggle to balance creative visual impulses with the centrality of a document's message. The judicious application of text art, clip art, and images can enliven a report, focus the message of a flyer, attract readers to a newsletter, and enhance the delivery of information in a brochure. Excessive use of graphics can distract readers, undermine the document's message, and call into question the authority and judgment of the author. Perhaps one of the best ways to manage the balance between the creative use of graphics and allegiance to the message of a document is to seek feedback on a document from peers and intended audience members. Inviting feedback on a document prior to disseminating it makes it possible to adjust the use of graphics so they facilitate the conveyance of a message instead of impeding it.

Templates: Frequently Used Document Forms

An often-overlooked tool of word processors is the template. A template is a preformatted type of document used for creation of a custom document. One of the chief advantages of using a template to produce a document is the time saving that results from not having to create a document from scratch. Pertinent information is inserted into the preformatted spaces of the template, freeing time and energy to concentrate on the core purpose of the document. Moreover, once a template is modified with custom information such as agency name and sender's address, it can then be renamed and saved as a custom template. Commonly available are templates to produce faxes, memos, business letters, newsletters, and resumes. Figure 7.14 displays some of the templates available in Corel WordPerfect.

Lotus Word Pro, Microsoft Word, and Corel WordPerfect have a selection of templates. In all three programs, templates are accessed from the menu bar, under File, New. In Corel WordPerfect, once the creation of a new document such as a letter is initiated, a PerfectExpert dialog box appears. The PerfectExpert is much like a Microsoft Wizard. It takes the user through a step-by-step process of creating the selected document (Steward & Perry, 1997).

Opening a new document under the File command in Microsoft Word brings up a tabbed window in which a number of document options are available. The tab labels include General, Letters & Faxes, Memos, Other Documents, and Web Pages. Clicking any of these tabs displays the available templates and document wizards. A preview screen on the right side of the window displays a small image of what the document looks like. Document wizards make possible the creation of more complex documents through a step-by-step process. Additional templates and wizards are available at the Microsoft Web site at http://www.microsoft.com (Boyce, 1997b).

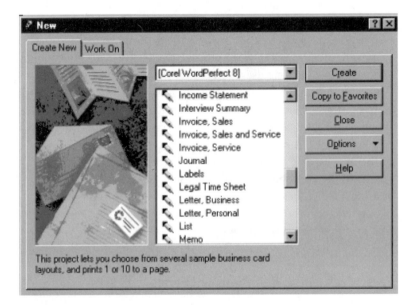

FIGURE 7.14   A Sample of the Template Options Available in Corel WordPerfect

Lotus Word Pro refers to templates as SmartMasters. To produce a memo in Lotus Word Pro from a SmartMaster select File, New. This opens a New Document window where one can select either Create from a Recently Used SmartMaster or Create from any SmartMaster. Selecting the first option brings up a listing of those SmartMasters one might commonly use, whereas the other option provides a complete listing of the available SmartMasters. Figure 7.15 displays the New Document window with Select a recently used SmartMaster selected. Note that choices made in the Select a Look field will display a prototype of the template in the adjacent field of the window. This allows for previewing templates before selecting one.

Figure 7.16 contains a screen image of a memo created in Lotus Word Pro. The information in each element of the memo was inserted into the preexisting fields. The graphic in the center of the top of the page was created with Word Pro's drawing tools. If the agency had an existing logo or graphic, it could have been pasted into the memo. Once the basic information and form of the template is customized to the needs of the agency or individual user, it can be saved as a custom template. Then each time the custom template is used it is only necessary to insert the relevant current information such as the name of the memo's recipient, purpose of the memo, and the body of the message. Once the document is complete, it is important to remember to name and save the new document as something other than the name of the custom template.

There are templates to produce business letters, fax cover sheets, newsletters, brochures, forms, and Web pages. Each of these types of document is widely used in social service practice, especially in agency administration. The time saving that results

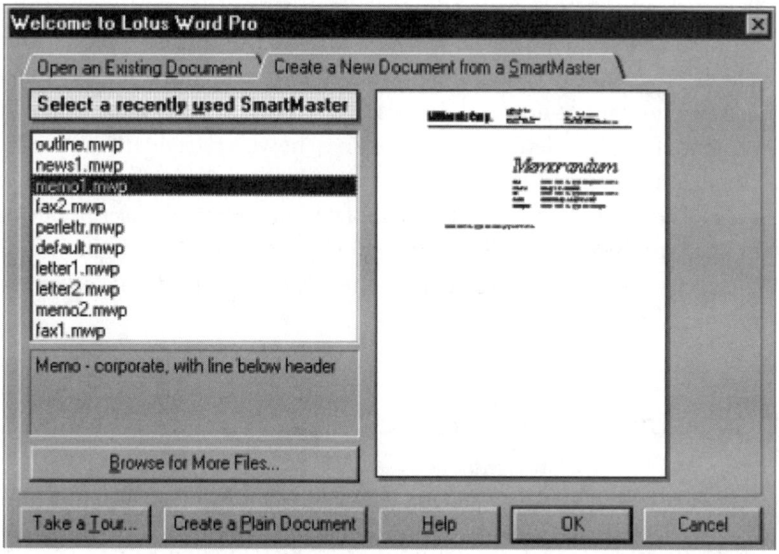

FIGURE 7.15   New Document Window for SmartMasters in Lotus Word Pro

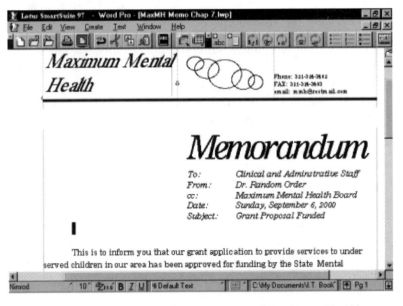

FIGURE 7.16   Memo Created from Lotus Word Pro Memo Template

in the regular use of templates increases staff efficiency and thereby saves already limited fiscal resources. Moreover, the use of templates in combination with graphs, text art, clip art, and/or images further extends the creative and communicative possibilities of agency word processing documents. For instance, many agencies publish newsletters to inform customers and constituencies of the agency's ongoing activities. The use of a newsletter template makes it possible to regularly produce the newsletter by simply inserting text and digital images into a preformatted template. The use of a newsletter template does not do away with the need to produce and edit the *copy* or text content of the newsletter. A template does, however, facilitate the production process by eliminating the need to produce a formatted document from scratch each production cycle. The essential point is that templates are extremely useful, but heretofore underutilized, tools for extending time and productivity. One might well wonder where is the social service agency or practitioner who can afford not to use them for regularly produced documents?

Mail Merge: From One to Many

Dependent on whether one is the recipient or sender, the capacity to create mail merges is either one of the great banes or boons of life in the age of information technology. The shredded remains of trees in the form of junk mail which arrives daily in a steady stream is a reminder of the widespread use of this communication irritant. Receipt of mail merge documents that to varying degrees appear personalized is perhaps an inescapable fate of anyone with an address. On the other hand, social service agencies, as well as capitalist enterprises, derive great benefit from the ability to generate and send letters, billing statements, appeals for financial support, and flyers promoting services. It is toward the use of mail merge tools in word processors and their application in social service practice that we will now turn our attention. We will leave it to the MBAs to contemplate the more pernicious applications of mail merging.

The chief benefit of using a mail merge is the production of personalized letters without investing the time and effort to produce each letter individually. The fundamental process in a mail merge is combining a generic document, usually a letter, with information from a database,[1] usually names and addresses, to create personalized documents for each of the individuals listed in the database. Clearly, the degree of personalization of a mail merge letter is a function of the data contained in the database. For instance, if a database of financial donors contains name, address, and contribution amount, then an agency could readily generate mail merge thank-you letters in which the donor is personally addressed (Dear Mr. Smith) and the amount of the contribution specified (Thank you for your contribution of $500). The names and contribution amounts are automatically inserted into the generic letter in the mail merge. Despite the fact that most donors will recognize the resultant letter as the product of a mail merge, generally they are happy to receive, for tax purposes, a document that specifies their name and the amount of their contribution.

Microsoft Word, Lotus Word Pro, and Corel WordPerfect each have mail merge tools that guide users, step by step, in the creation of mail merge documents. Each of the programs has procedures that require (a) the identification of an existing generic document or its creation, (b) specification of an existing database or its creation, (c) inserting of database (merge) fields into the generic document, (d) merging the database with the generic document, and (e) printing the resultant documents. The programs vary in their sequencing of these steps, the types of databases from which they will draw data, and how the user interfaces with the mail merge tool. Despite these differences, acquisition of skills in using the mail merge tool of any one of these word processors lays the foundation for using either of the other two.

In Microsoft Word

Microsoft Word's mail merge tool is found in the menu bar under Tools, Mail Merge. When selected, it opens a dialog window called Mail Merge Helper in the Main Document (the generic document), the Data Source is specified, and Mail Merge is activated. Figure 7.17 displays a Mail Merge Helper dialog window in which the Merge type and

---

[1]The term *database* here refers to collections of name, address, and other individual information used for mail merge. These data are not necessarily stored in a database application (see Chapter 5). They may be contained in a spreadsheet, electronic address book, or in a database application.

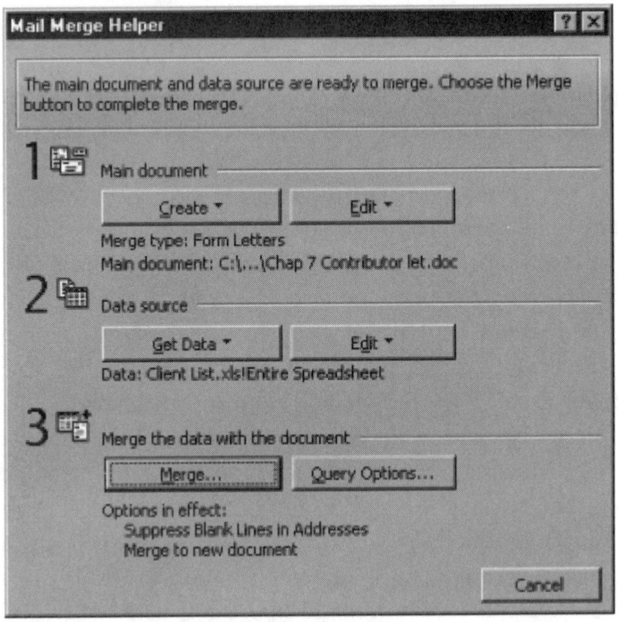

FIGURE 7.17   Microsoft Word's Mail Merge Helper

Main document are identified. Merge type refers to the fact that there are several options for types of mail merges including form letters, envelopes, mailing labels, and catalogs. If for instance, form letter is selected, the user must select the location of the letter or create one in an open document. In the Mail Merge Helper, the location of the data for the merge is specified under Data Source. The Get Data button allows the user to get a data source, create a data source, or get data from an electronic address book. In Figure 7.17, an Excel spreadsheet is selected for use as the data source.

Once the data source is selected, the form letter document is opened with the Mail Merge toolbar activated. It is now necessary to insert the merge fields into the form letter document in the proper locations. Place the insertion point in the document at the location where the first field is to be inserted. Click Insert Merge Field in the Mail Merge toolbar and select the first merge field. If placing more than one field in a location, such as first name and last name, be sure to insert a space between the two merge fields. Figure 7.18 shows a form letter created from a business letter template with the merge fields inserted into their proper locations. Note, in the first line of the body of the letter "<<Contributed>>" appears. This is the name of the field from the database containing information on the amount of money contributed by the donor. This and other personal information is inserted into the document from the database when the mail merge is run. Figure 7.19 shows one of the letters generated from this mail merge. It should be noted that running the mail merge generates a new document containing all the letters in the mail merge. It is then possible to review the let-

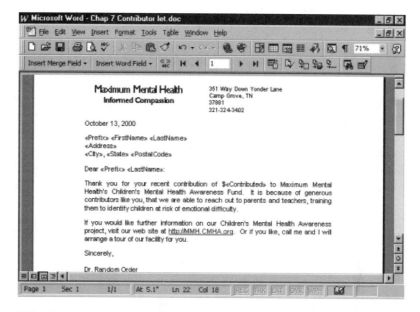

FIGURE 7.18   Mail Merge Document with Inserted Merge Fields

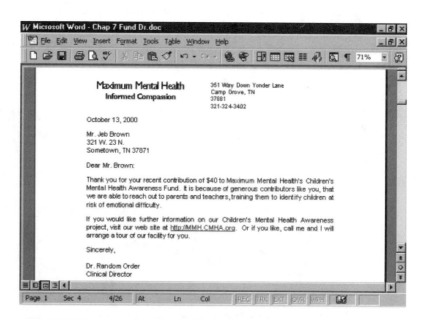

FIGURE 7.19   Completed Mail Merge Letter

ters for errors before sending them to the printer. If errors are found, the document may be discarded. Changes can then be made to the original form letter document and the mail merge rerun.

In Lotus Word Pro

The mail merge tool in Lotus Word Pro functions in much the same manner as the Microsoft Word mail merge tool. From the menu bar, select Text, Merge, and Letter. A dialog window appears from which the mailing list database is selected. Figure 7.20 displays the Mail Merge Assistant dialog box. The second step is to select the Letter to Merge. In this step, the choices are to use the current document, create a new document, or browse for an existing file. Once the Letter to Merge is chosen, the document opens with a merge toolbar from which fields from the mailing list database are selected and inserted into the document. The process is almost identical to the process described for Microsoft Word. When all the required fields are placed in the document, click Close and the Mail Merge Assistant dialog box reappears. Figure 7.21 shows a Mail Merge Assistant dialog box with two of the three steps completed. The final step is to decide where to direct the mail merge file and then initiate the mail merge. The choice of where to direct the mail merge file is described in Figure 7.21.

In Corel WordPerfect

In many ways, the mail merge procedure in Corel WordPerfect is very similar to the two procedures already described. There are differences, however, that make the process somewhat more complicated. To initiate a mail merge, select Tools, Merge from the menu bar. Figure 7.22 shows the Merge dialog box of WordPerfect. Selecting the Create Data button opens a window in which new fields for a mail merge database are

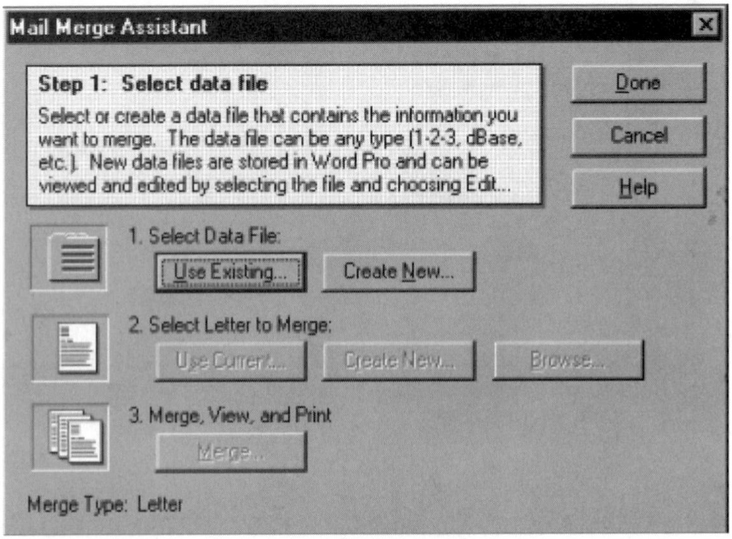

FIGURE 7.20   Lotus Pro's Mail Merge Assistant

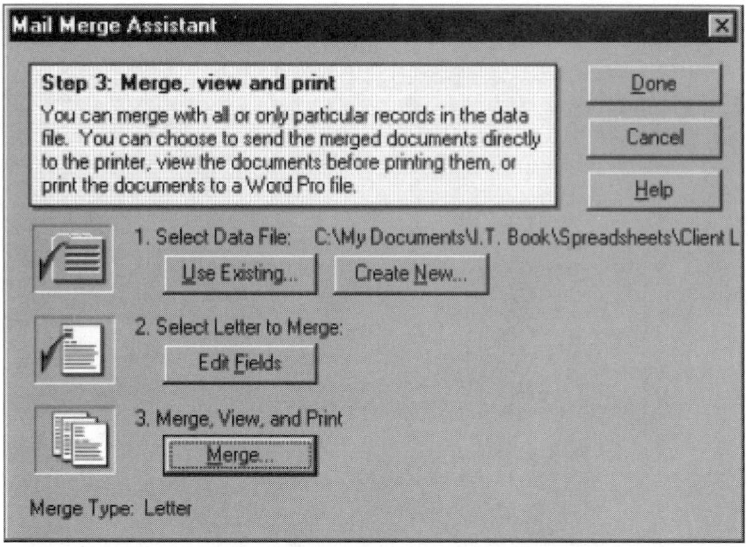

FIGURE 7.21   Lotus Word Pro's Mail Merge Assistant Ready to Initiate Merge

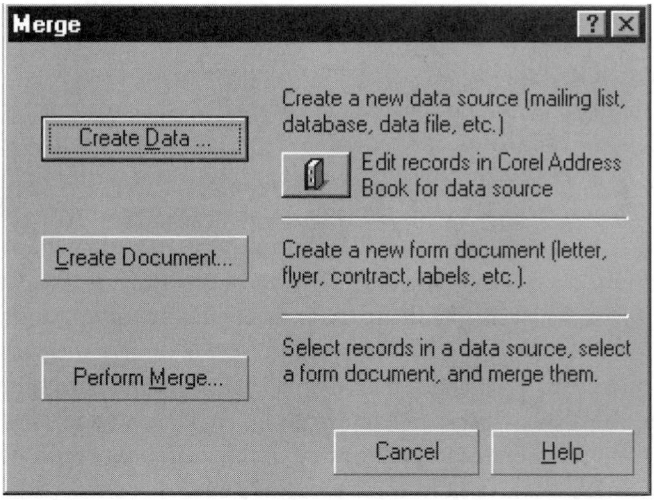

FIGURE 7.22   Mail Merge Dialog Box in Corel WordPerfect

labeled. However, there is no way to import data into the new database. Instead, each entry must be typed into the database.

The other option is to use the Corel Address Book. Data may either be typed into the Address Book or imported from an external database or spreadsheet file. Figure 7.23 shows the Import Expert in which the import file type is specified. DBase, Clipper,

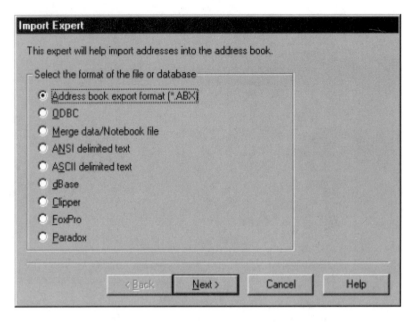

FIGURE 7.23   Import Expert for Data Importation into the Address Book

FoxPro, and Paradox are all database applications from which mailing data is importable. ODBC (open database connectivity) is a protocol for importing Microsoft files. There appears to be no direct way to import files from Quattro Pro, despite the fact that it is the spreadsheet used by the Corel WordPerfect Suite. Data in Quattro Pro can be saved in an Excel format and imported through the ODBC file option.

A second problem is that the Address Book has a limited number of fields. When importing data from a database or spreadsheet file, it is necessary to map (show the connection between) the fields in the file being imported to the existing fields in the Address Book. The problem here is that for mail merges there is often personalized information such as "amount contributed" which has no corresponding field in the Address Book. Nor does there appear to be any way to add new fields to the Address Book. It therefore becomes necessary, in the mapping process, to use existing fields in the Address Book to hold some types of personalized information from the imported database. For instance, a donor database might contain the field "amount contributed." When importing the database into the Address Book, it might be necessary to map "amount contributed" to the existing field "Comments." Figure 7.24 shows a database that was imported into the Address Book from Excel. The Comments field holds "amount contributed" information from the original database.

Once the mail merge data is in the Address Book and the form letter is written, clicking Create Merge in the Merge dialog box (Figure 7.22) opens the form letter with a mail merge toolbar. (See Figure 7.25.) Name, address, and other fields are inserted

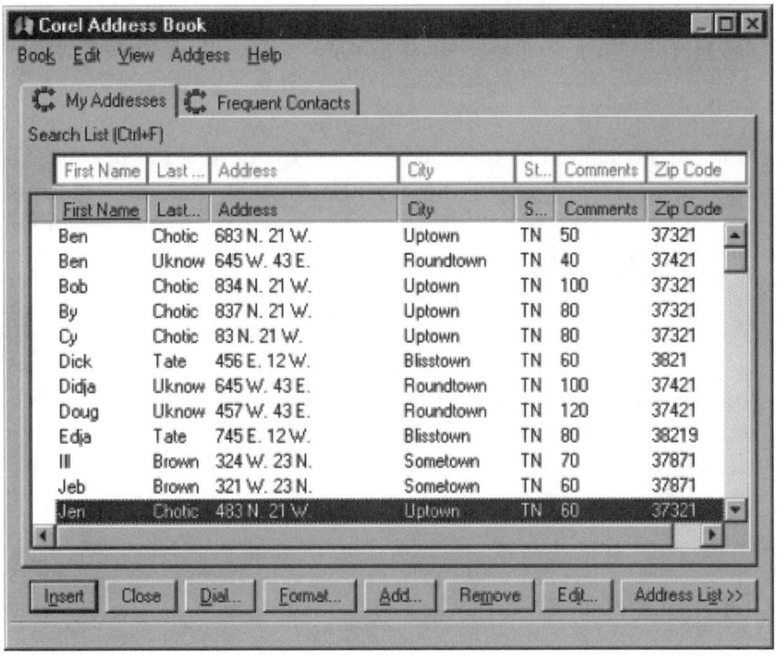

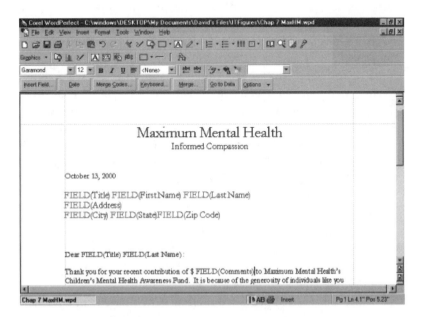

FIGURE 7.24   Corel Address Book with Data Imported from Excel

FIGURE 7.25   Corel WordPerfect Mail Merge Document with Fields Inserted

into the form letter by clicking the insertion point in the desired location in the document, then clicking Insert Field, causing a drop-down list of fields from the Address Book to appear from which fields for insertion are selected. Once the necessary fields are in place in the form letter, clicking the Merge button in the toolbar opens the Perform Merge dialog box in which to select the destination of the resultant mail merge. The options are the printer, the current document, or a new document. It is prudent to choose the current document or a new document, as opposed to sending the output directly to a printer, in case there are errors in the merged document.

In summary, the mail merge procedures of all three of these word processors are robust tools for producing personalized correspondence. Each of them, to varying degrees, works in combination with database and spreadsheet applications to produce customized letters. In many circles, the generation of mail merge documents has been considered the domain of office staff. It was alternatively viewed as either too technical or too labor intensive for professional staff. The preceding review of the mail merge capacities of these three word processors suggests that neither view is any longer true.

Web Page Development

The growing preeminence of the World Wide Web as a medium for the publication of information has pushed software manufacturers to include tools for creating HTML (hypertext markup language) documents in word processors. HTML is the software language used to author documents for the Web. The good news is that it is possible to create interesting and informative Web pages without writing any HTML code. This will come as a relief to most social service workers, as programming languages are usually not part of their course of study in college and graduate school. The further good news is that Corel WordPerfect, Lotus Word Pro, and Microsoft Word all have procedures for creating Web pages without the user having to write HTML code. Although these word processors are generally not considered high-end Web authoring applications, they each have sufficient tools for producing informative and visually compelling Web pages. They are more than adequate to create Web pages for the dissemination of information from a social service agency. Readers interested in more powerful Web authoring tools might consider Microsoft Front Page or Adobe Site Mill. Agencies wishing to build Web pages that work interactively to collect information from site visitors, publish online database information, or exchange financial data for the sale of goods and services should consult an experienced Web author and their Internet Service Provider (ISP). In order to publish a Web page it is necessary to transfer the page and its associated files to a Web server (a computer on the Internet) of the ISP. ISP companies maintain one or more servers on the Internet from which Web pages are displayed.

There are at least three ways to create a Web page with any one of the word processors discussed here. First, Web pages can be developed with templates or wizards that come with the word processor. Second, existing word processing documents may be saved in HTML format and thereby transformed into a Web page. Depending on the formatting of the document and the graphics in it, there can sometimes be a loss or change of formatting with this method. The third way to create a Web page is starting with a blank word processing document and building the page from scratch. This method maximizes both the creative potential in the page development and the work required in realizing this potential. In the following sections we will explore each of these methods.

In Lotus Word Pro

Lotus Word Pro offers a number of templates (SmartMasters) from which to construct one or more Web pages. There are two categories, Internet/Corporate and Internet/Personal from which to select styles of Web pages. Internet/Corporate offers the choice of creating pages that are catalogs of products or services, corporate (agency) home pages, newsletters, and pages with information on products or services. Internet/Personal Web page choices include pages that present biographical information, favorite Web page sites, personal home pages, and Web pages for kids.

To create a Web page from one of these templates, open Lotus Word Pro and select New Document, Create from Any SmartMaster. The New Document dialog box has a preview window with the choices to preview selections. For the purposes of illustration, and to create a home page for Maximum Mental Health, we will select Internet/Corporate home page option. Figure 7.26 displays the SmartMaster template for creating a corporate, or in this case an agency, home page. Note the various "Click

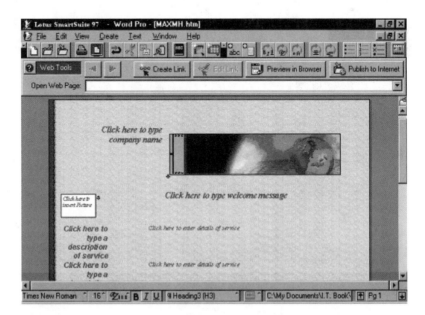

FIGURE 7.26   Lotus Word Pro Web Page SmartMaster

here" sections on the page into which text is inserted to fill in the information provided by the page. The graphic at the top of the page can be replaced with another GIF or JPEG graphic. A Web Tools toolbar appears above the page with options for creating links to other Web pages, editing those links, previewing the page in a Web browser, and publishing the page to the Web. This last option essentially means sending the page to a server from which it will be displayed on the Web.

Figure 7.27 displays a Web page produced by inserting content into the Smart-Master template shown in Figure 7.26. Once the content of the page was entered in the appropriate locations, the Preview in Browser button was clicked, which opened a Netscape browser in which to view the page. Note that the child's art graphic is the same graphic file that was used in the flyer in Figure 7.12. Inserting a copy of the file into the Web page is only a matter of clicking the existing graphic, then clicking File, Import Picture, and then finding and selecting the graphic (JPEG) file. The entire Web page was created without writing a single line of HTML code.

In Microsoft Word

Like Lotus Word Pro, Microsoft Word has templates for creating Web pages. To access these templates in the File menu, click New, then Web Pages. Click the Web Page Wizard to start a guided construction of a Web page. The first choice is type of page. The options include page with 2 or 3 columns, calendar layout, centered, three types of forms, personal home page, simple, and table of contents. Once the type of page is se-

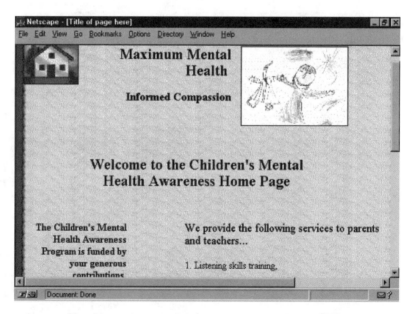

FIGURE 7.27   Web Page Created with Lotus Word Pro SmartMaster

lected, the wizard requires a choice about visual style. The names of the choices here include community, centered, elegant, festive, harvest, jazzy, outdoors, and professional. Any of these layout types or styles may be selected, examined, and then discarded by closing the document and not saving it. This allows the user to experiment with several options before selecting a type and style and adding content to the page.

Figure 7.28 displays a Web page generated from the Web Page Wizard. "Simple" was selected for type of Web page and "contemporary" was chosen for the style. Each of the mental health services listed is hyperlinked to other pages with information about that service. Hyperlinks are created by first selecting from the menu bar View, Tools, and then Web. This opens a toolbar with a number of Web page specific tools. The hyperlink tool is an icon of a globe with a chain link. Clicking this icon opens a dialog window in which the address of file or page on a hard drive, local network, or the Web is entered. There is a browse tool for locating files. Links may also be made to other locations in the same document. In this case, each of the associated Web pages is in the same folder as the home page in Figure 7.28. The graphic at the bottom of the page was added from the clip art files of Microsoft Office. When working on a Web document, the size of fonts is adjusted with an icon of the letter A with up or down arrows. To change the size of a bit of text, select the text, then click the up or down icon. Formatting such as bold, italics, underlining, and text justification are applied with icons in the Web toolbar.

As stated previously, it is possible to convert an existing word processing document into a Web page. The translation from word processing document to Web page is at

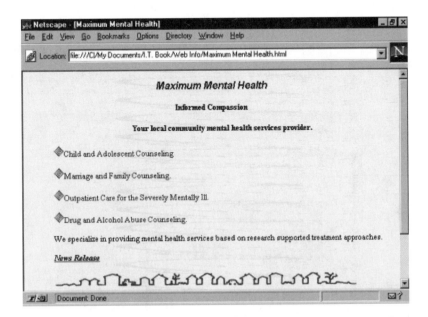

**FIGURE 7.28   Web Page Created with Web Page Wizard
in Microsoft Word**

times perilous due to the fact that some formatting used in word processing documents is not recognized by HTML. One frequently encountered example of this problem is tabs. Tabs are commonly used in word processing documents to align text, indent paragraphs, and sometimes to create tables. When a word processing document is saved as an HTML file, the tabs are lost. Therefore, when creating documents that may be translated into HTML and turned into Web pages, be sure to use the Insert Table icon to create tables in a document.

Figure 7.29 shows a portion of a Web page first created as a document in Microsoft Word and then saved as an HTML file. The most noteworthy feature on this page is the graph. This is the same graph used in Figure 6.5 of Chapter 6. The graph was copied from Excel and pasted into the Microsoft Word document. When the word processing document is saved as an HTML file, the required formatting codes are automatically inserted (Kraynak, 1997). This makes it possible to readily integrate any of the graphs described in Chapter 6 into Web pages. This capacity may be particularly useful in large agencies with intranets for the sharing of graphs depicting service provision data, service outcome data, and financial data. Of course, issues of confidentiality must always be considered before posting any data derived from agency clients. The graph in Figure 7.29 contains no identifying information that could be used to link the data to a particular individual.

The inclusion in Web pages of graphics such as charts, drawings, and images must be balanced with consideration of the file type, size, and characteristics. The two pri-

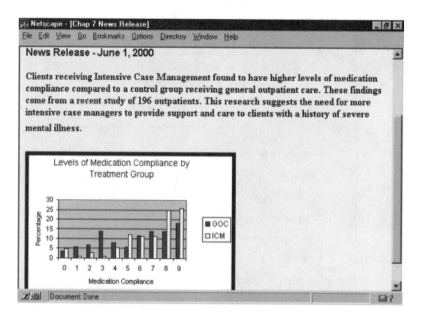

FIGURE 7.29   Portion of a Web Page Created First as a Microsoft Word Document

mary types of graphics files used on the Web are GIF and JPEG (Steward & Perry, 1997). GIF files are generally small in size and do not display color as well as JPEG files. GIF files can be saved as transparent files. Transparent graphics allow the background of a Web page to show through the graphic. For instance, the "community" graphic at the bottom of Figure 7.28 is a transparent GIF file. When closely examined, it is apparent that the background of the page is displayed within the "community" graphic. JPEG files are now commonly used on Web pages where color quality and image clarity are important to the page designer. For use on the Web, an image does not have to be more than 72 dpi. The photo editing software that comes with digital cameras and scanners can set this resolution.

In Corel WordPerfect

Corel WordPerfect has an interactive tool for generating Web pages called WordPerfect Internet Publisher. To access this tool select File, New, Create New, WordPerfect Web Document, Create. Figure 7.30 displays a blank Internet Publisher template. Note on the left side of the page the page formatting options for creating a Web page.

In Figure 7.31 content has been added to the original blank page of the Internet Publisher. A textured background was selected from the available choices under the Change Background button. The title "Maximum Mental Health" was added with the Add a Title button. A title is the name of the Web page that appears in the top line of a Web browser. Web search engines use the title to determine the content of the page.

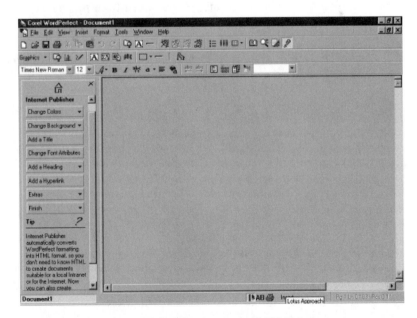

FIGURE 7.30   Corel WordPerfect's Internet Publisher

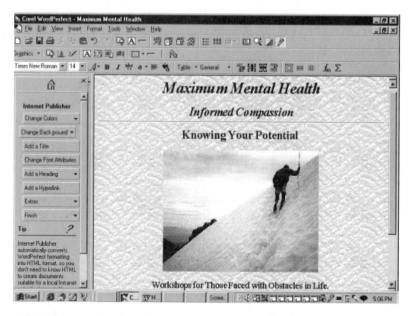

FIGURE 7.31   Corel WordPerfect's Internet Publisher with Content Added

It is therefore important to carefully consider the information given in the title. The headings appearing in the middle of the page were inserted with the Add a Heading button. The line and the JPEG image were added from the choices under Extras. Although there are no hyperlinks on the page in Figure 7.31, hyperlinks may be added with the Add a Hyperlink button.

As a Web page is being constructed it is helpful to examine it from time to time in a Web browser to determine how the page will actually look on the Web. The View in Browser icon in the middle of the top toolbar, launches the computer's chosen Web browser and displays the Web page under construction. Figure 7.32 shows the completed page from Figure 7.31 displayed in Microsoft's Internet Explorer Web browser that was launched with the View in Browser icon. Note that the background of the page was changed and a table was added at the bottom of the page. Tables are added with tools available under the Extras button.

Once the Web page is complete, click the Finish button in the Internet Publisher. The page will be saved as an HTML file. If this page is linked to additional pages created in the Internet Publisher, be sure to save all the files in the same folder. This folder is transferred or uploaded to the Web server on which the page will be published. For further information on how to prepare the folder and its files for uploading, contact the Web server's administrator.

This discussion on Web page creation with word processors represents only the briefest of introductions to Web page authoring. One goal of this section was to in-

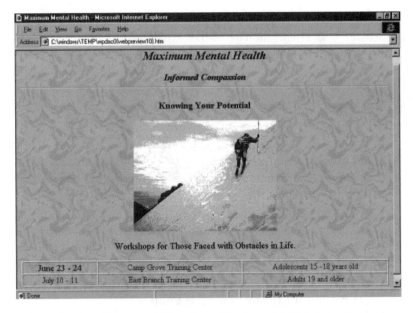

FIGURE 7.32   Completed Web Page Previewed in Internet Explorer

troduce readers to the potentials in developing creative and informative Web pages with the tools available in any of these three word processors. A second goal of this section was to lift the veil of mystery that shrouds the creation of Web pages for many social service practitioners. Building Web pages that inform clients, colleagues, and constituencies of social service agencies need not be left to "Web masters" when the tools for constructing Web pages are at hand. We will return to Web page construction in the next chapter when we describe how electronic presentations can be converted to Web pages.

Summary

This chapter documented a broad array of ways to extend the functionality of word processing software. It described the creation and application of (a) smart notes for collecting case information and archiving other practice information, (b) interactive documents for developing information rich materials, and (c) collaborative documents to facilitate the work of teams. This chapter expanded on the graphics knowledge established in Chapter 6 by describing the use of text art, clip art, word wrapping, and images in word processing documents. The use of templates to create memos and other documents was explained. Mail merges are an important tool in the dissemination of information. This chapter described how to create mail merges using Corel WordPerfect, Microsoft Word, and Lotus Word Pro. This chapter concluded with a discussion of how to create Web pages using the tools available in word processing software. This discussion lays a foundation for further exploration of Web page development and publication in Chapters 8 and 9.

Exercises

1. Use the outline view of a word processor to create a set of case notes or a log of your activities in your practice setting. If creating case notes, be sure to protect any confidential information by excluding any and all identifying information. Embed in the document one or more hyperlinks to Web pages containing information relevant to an issue addressed in the smart notes. Creating the hyperlinks creates an interactive document.

2. With a group of peers, develop, in an iterative process, a collaborative document that is shared either by e-mail or on some storage device (e.g., diskette). Establish a procedure for editing the document that ensures that the document evolves as a team effort.

3. Create a document related to your practice setting that uses text art, clip art, and images to convey a message. This document might be a flyer, newsletter, brochure, or some other document to convey information.

4. Using the address database created in the exercise in Chapter 5, create a mail merge using a word processor mail merge function.

5. With a group of peers, design and create a Web page using word processing software that has application in providing information on the Web about a practice setting. Once the page is created, use a Web browser to open the page and check its appearance.

chapter 8

Presentation Software

Beyond Magic Markers
and Posterboards

This chapter explains and illustrates the creation of slide shows with presentation software. It describes the fundamental features and functions of presentation software and the tools available to create multimedia presentations. It illustrates how to transform slide shows into Web pages, standalone presentations, and interactive training materials. It discusses a number of options for disseminating completed slide shows, including e-mail and Web publication. This chapter provides examples of the specific applications of slide show presentations in social service practice.

Presentation software is a category of software designed to enable users to integrate text, graphics, animation, sound, and video in multimedia, computer-based, slide show presentations. Unlike traditional posterboard or overhead transparency presentations, presentation software has the capacity to engage and hold the attention of an audience with animated screen transitions, the sequential revealing of points on a single slide, and the inclusion of video clips and sound in the presentation. Once created, presentations can be converted to Web pages or saved as portable presentations, or distributed via e-mail or diskette (depending on the file size) for viewing independent of the software on which they were generated. Moreover, these types of presentations are applicable not only for conveying information to groups, but also are useful for creating staff training and client education programs in which a single user interacts with the presentation's content on a personal computer. Each of these potential uses of presentation software is described in this chapter.

Corel WordPerfect Office, Microsoft Office, and Lotus SmartSuite have presentation software integrated into their software suites. The presentation software in Corel WordPerfect Office is called Corel Presentations. Microsoft Office's presentation software is PowerPoint and Lotus SmartSuite's package is Freelance Graphics. As with other applications in these three software suites, each of these three software applications essentially accomplishes the same end: the creation of multimedia presentations. Each employs its own unique interface and methods to accomplish this common end. In this chapter we will learn how to (a) create multimedia slide show presentations,

(b) develop client education and staff training programs, (c) save presentations as portable presentations, and (d) turn slide show presentations into Web pages.

Before turning our attention to presentation software, it is necessary to return briefly to a review of hardware begun in Chapter 2. Presentation software is most commonly used to create slide shows that are presented to audiences of various sizes. While two or five people might be able to view a slide show on a computer monitor, for larger audiences it is necessary to use a large-screen television monitor or an LCD projector to display the slide show. Transferring the video output from a desktop or laptop computer to a television screen requires a scan converter, or what is sometimes called a PC-to-TV device. Essentially, this device transforms the video output signal from the computer to a form of signal that a television can display. Scan converters are generally inexpensive, small, and lightweight. The downside of using a scan converter is that there must be a television monitor available in the location in which the slide show is presented. An alternative to a scan converter is an LCD projector. The video output from a desktop or laptop computer is fed via cable into an LCD projector and then displayed on a screen or blank wall. Many LCD projectors can also accept input from videotape machines, allowing a presenter to readily switch between a computer slide show and videotaped material during a presentation. LCD projectors vary in the resolution of the image they will display, the brightness or luminosity of the image they project, and the distance to which they will "throw" or display an image. One major drawback of LCD projectors is their high cost—usually several thousand dollars. This cost may come down over time with improved technology, increased market demand, and price competition. Social service agencies that do a great many public presentations in a variety of locations could readily justify investing in an LCD projector and laptop.

Presentation Software's Fundamental Features

Slide Layers

Slides created with presentation software are composed of three layers (Gilgen, 1997). First, the *design* or *master* layer sets the appearance of all slides in the presentation. The color scheme, font selection, and background graphics are all fixed at the design layer. This creates a consistent appearance for the slides in the entire presentation. Figure 8.1 displays a screen image from Lotus Freelance Graphics that contains the first slide of a presentation under development.

Each of the three presentation applications offers templates with which to develop custom presentations. The templates define the design layer for the presentation. If one chooses to not use a template and instead create a custom slide show, it is still necessary to select a design layer. The creation of presentations with templates is described later in this chapter.

The second layer of a slide is the *layout* layer. Each of the three presentation applications has a range of slide types, each with its own unique layout. Examples of lay-

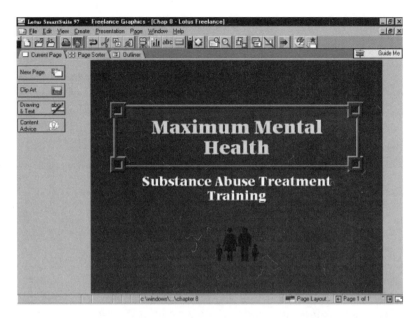

FIGURE 8.1   Title Page of Presentation in Lotus Freelance Graphics

out layers include title, bullet list, text, chart, table, organizational chart, and clip art. Figure 8.1 shows a title page layout with three elements, the title, subtitle, and clip art. The layout layer of a slide determines where and how elements of the slide are arranged. Therefore, any time a slide with a bullet list is added to a presentation, it will look exactly like all other bullet list slides in the presentation. This produces another level of consistency or order in the appearance of the presentation.

The third layer of a slide is the *slide* layer. The content of each slide layer is unique to that slide. The content of a slide may consist of text, graphics, sound, or digitized video clips. In the example of Figure 8.1, the content of the slide is title and subtitle information along with the arrow graphic in the corner.

Slide Views

All three presentation applications offer at least four views of a slide show that enable a user to examine the presentation from different perspectives. Unfortunately, each of the three software companies uses different language to name the same view. Table 8.1 shows the four basic types of views, describes their function, and provides the name for the view used by each of the three presentation programs.

Figure 8.1 shows the Current Page (slide editor) of Lotus Freelance Graphics. In Freelance Graphics, as in the other two applications, the slide editor view is used to add text and graphics content to the slide as well as edit the content of slides. Note that the tabs at the top of the page allow the user to move between the Current Page,

TABLE 8.1 Presentation Software Terms by Application

Presentation Software	Slide Editor (used to add content and edit a slide)	Slide Sorter (display and modification of the structure of a presentation)	Outline View (text content of slides displayed in outline format)	Presentation View (displays a full screen view of slide show)
Microsoft PowerPoint	Slide	Slide Sorter	Outline	Slide Show
Corel Presentation	Slide Editor View	Slide Sorter View	Slide Outliner	QuickPlay
Lotus Freelance Graphics	Current Page	Page Sorter	Outliner	Screen Show

Page Sorter, and Outliner to access different perspectives on a slide show. Above the tabs there is a toolbar for formatting, editing, display, and media insertion functions. In the left margin there are buttons for adding a new page and clip art. The Drawing and Text button opens a window with tools for adding lines, geometric shapes, shapes with text inserted, and connectors for linking objects on the slide. Similar editing and text/graphics tools also are available in Microsoft PowerPoint and Corel Presentation.

Figure 8.2 displays the slide sorter view in Microsoft PowerPoint. This view allows the user to scroll through the presentation and see the overall arrangement of slides. In each of the three presentation applications the location or order of slides in the presentation is rearranged by clicking and dragging the slide to the desired location. Note that on the far right side of the toolbar in Figure 8.2, the number 66% appears. Clicking on the arrow to the right of this "Zoom" control allows a user to set the number of "thumbnail" slides that appear on the screen. When set on 66%, six slides appear on the screen, but when the Zoom is set to 33%, 18 slides are displayed. Both Corel Presentation and Lotus Freelance Graphics have similar zoom features.

Slide Transitions

In the toolbar directly above the slides in Figure 8.2 there are pull-down menus with the words "Uncover Left" and "Spiral". "Uncover Left" refers to the type of "slide transition" used when moving between slides. Slide transitions are special effects in the transitions between slides intended to engage and hold the audiences' attention. Spiral refers to a type of text animation used to present text on a slide. In this case the text of the slide spirals onto the slide, moving from the top left corner to the center of the page. Both Corel Presentation and Microsoft PowerPoint offer several ways to animate the appearance of objects (titles, text, graphics) on the slide.

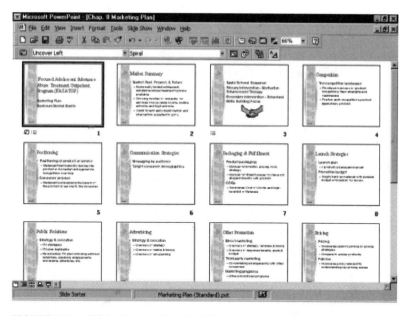

FIGURE 8.2   Slide Sorter View in Microsoft PowerPoint

All three of the presentation applications offer numerous slide transitions. Some commonly included types of slide transitions are (Gilgen, 1997):

1. Blinds—a venetian blind effect in which the first slide disappears with the closing of the slide and the next slide appears with the opening.

2. Checkerboard—a checkerboard pattern appears on the screen revealing the next slide.

3. Dissolve—the first slide dissolves to reveal the next slide.

4. Uncover—the entire slide moves in a specified direction to reveal the next slide, which appears to be underneath the previous slide.

5. Wipe—creates the appearance of the slide being erased and uncovering the next slide.

Slide transitions in Corel Presentation can be added in the Slide Sorter view with a similar pull-down menu in the toolbar. As the cursor is passed over each slide transition option, a small window to the right of the pull-down menu shows the slide transition animation. In Lotus Freelance Graphics, slide transitions are added by clicking a slide in the Page Sorter view and then selecting the Properties icon from the toolbar.

The use of either slide transitions or animated objects, like graphics in word processing documents, should be tailored to match both the contents of the overall presentation and the audience for whom it is intended. There is sometimes a fine line between holding an audience's attention and annoying them with slide transitions and animated objects moving about the screen. Testing a presentation on a trial audience is one way to get feedback on whether the line between interesting and annoying is crossed.

Figure 8.3 shows Corel Presentation's Outline View in which the text content of the slides is displayed in outline format. In either of the three presentation applications the Outline View is a tool to organize the content of a presentation and to view its structure. Presentations can be started in the Outline View, adding text content and additional slides as the presentation develops. Graphics are added in the Slide Editor. The Outline View functions much like the outlining in word processing. Slides may contain titles, subtitles, text, and bullets. Note in Figure 8.3 that there are three levels of headings present: title, subtitle, and text. This capacity to promote and demote the organizational level of a presentation's content is useful in defining and seeing the structure of idea and facts in the presentation. In Figure 8.3, the subtitles in slides 2 and 3 should be demoted to the text level, given their content. In examining the flow of ideas in a presentation in the Outline View, it sometimes becomes evident that slides should be rearranged to improve the organization of the information. The arrangement of slides in the Outline View is alterable by clicking and dragging slides to new locations within the outline.

Figure 8.4 shows an Outline View of a presentation created in Microsoft Power-Point. Note the two windows that appear within the outline. The top one, Color, displays a thumbnail view of the selected slide. The bottom window shows the array of animation effects available for the title and text of slides. The icons in the window display pop-up labels when the cursor is placed on them, making it possible to identify their specific form of animation. Note also the outlining tool bar on the left side of the screen. It makes available a number of outlining options including promoting and de-

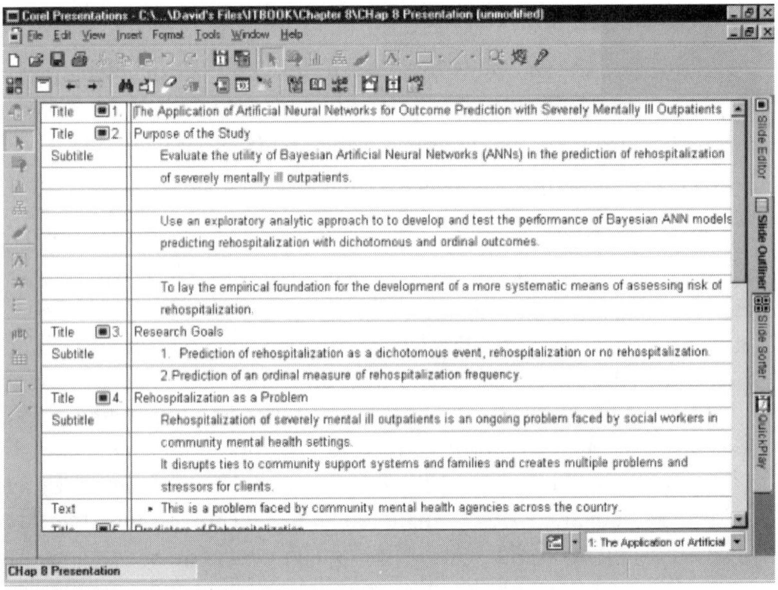

FIGURE 8.3   Outline View in Corel Presentation

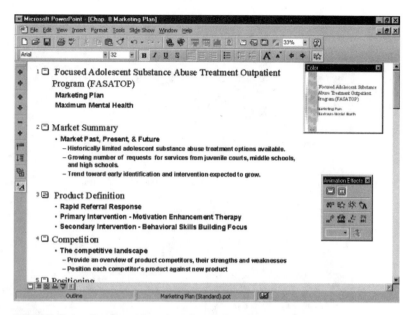

FIGURE 8.4   Outline View in Microsoft PowerPoint

moting headings, moving text up and down in the outline, and collapsing and expanding subheadings to display or hide their content.

The fourth view available in the three presentation applications is the Presentation View. This view displays a full-screen view of the slide show. It is useful in assessing how the slide show will look when it is actually presented. Figure 8.5 (Patterson & Cloud, in press) shows a slide displayed in the Presentation View of Corel Presentation. Note the absence of any menu bars, toolbars, or other extraneous information. Reviewing a slide show in the Presentation View provides a clearer picture of how titles, text, graphics, and animations work, or perhaps do not work, in concert to convey the information contained in the presentation. It is especially important to review a slide show in the Presentation View before presenting it to an audience. In all three programs, the Escape key allows a user to exit the Presentation View and return to the previous view in which they were working.

Templates: Quick Steps to Producing Presentations

Each of the three presentation applications offers templates with which to develop custom presentations. Like templates in other types of applications in these software suites, the presentation templates are preformatted slide shows to which information content and graphics are added. The design and layout layers for slides in these templates are set. Both of these slide layers may be altered, but generally it is more efficient to carefully select a template that matches the intended purpose of the presentation as well as the organization of the content. For instance, if an agency director is presenting an overview of the

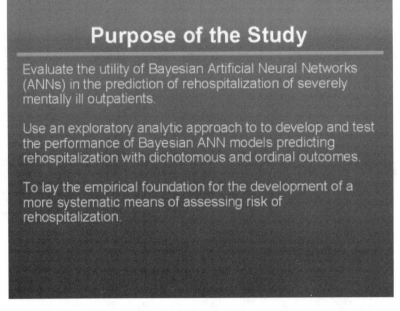

FIGURE 8.5   Presentation View in Corel Presentation

agency's financial status to its board of directors, then a "financial performance" template could be readily adapted to the agency director's intended purpose. Templates sometimes contain slides that are irrelevant to the purpose of a presentation. These slides may be either deleted or modified to match the purpose of the presentation. The modification of slides and the use of templates for Microsoft PowerPoint is described in the following section. The use of templates in Lotus Freelance Graphics and Corel Presentation is described later in this chapter.

To summarize, in this section we reviewed the fundamental features of the three presentation software packages under consideration in this chapter. Common features include all slides having three layers (design, layout, slide), the availability of at least four views (slide editor, slide sorter, outline view, and presentation view) in which to create and view a presentation, slide transition effects, and templates from which to construct slide shows. Having reviewed the common features of the three presentation applications, we now turn our attention to how to develop slide shows in each of the three programs.

Using Microsoft PowerPoint

Templates

Templates in PowerPoint are found under File, New, Presentations. The marketing strategy template is used here for the purposes of this discussion. This template would normally be considered a "business" template, one developed specifically for companies and corporations to communicate a marketing plan to employees and managers. However, in an increasingly competitive and managed care–dominated market, it is necessary for social services agencies to plan marketing of specific services to specific populations. Therefore, it may be fruitful to consider how a marketing plan template can be adapted to communicate a marketing plan for a specific social service "product" in a social service agency.

Figure 8.6 displays the first six screens in the template: marketing plan, market summary, product definition, competition, positioning, and communication strategy. Note that the design layer of each slide is the same. The color scheme, font selection, and background graphics are the same for all the slides. Note, however, that there are differences in the layout layer of the slides—some containing only a title and subtitle, others containing titles and text. The marketing plan presentation content for each slide is entered in either the slide editor view or the outline view.

One advantage of using a template for developing a slide show is that the organization of slide titles in the template can serve as a thinking tool, providing structure around which to shape a unique presentation. The slide titles or topics may provoke consideration of issues, ideas, or problems that had not previously been considered in preparing a presentation. Figure 8.7 shows the first four slides in the marketing plan template before the unique content for the presentation is added. Note the logical presentation of topics evidenced in these first four slides. The product is introduced in the first slide. The market

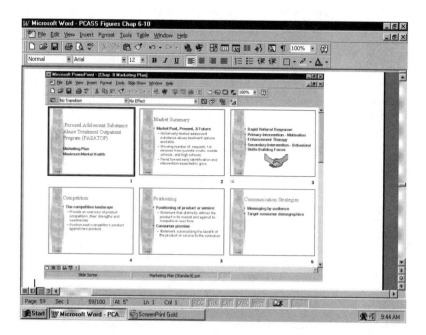

FIGURE 8.6   Marketing Plan Template in Microsoft PowerPoint

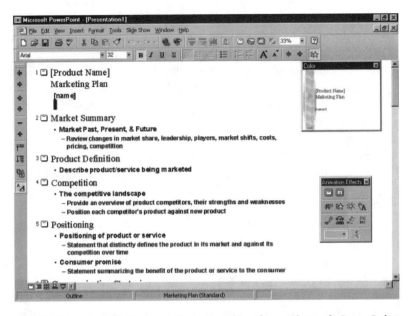

FIGURE 8.7   Outline View of Marketing Plan from Microsoft PowerPoint

for the product is summarized in the second slide. The product or service is more completely described in the third slide and then evaluated in the fourth slide. The user is free to use the existing organization of the template, delete slides, add slides, or rearrange the order of slides to meet the unique structural needs of a particular presentation.

In Figure 8.8 the marketing plan template is infused with content for a particular presentation. Information is added to a template simply by typing or pasting it into the existing sections. Information can be copied and pasted directly from existing word processing document. Note that in the Outline View, only text can be added to the template. Graphics are added in the Slide Editor. Figure 8.9 shows the third slide of the Marketing Plan template with a bit of clip art added to it. Clip art is pasted into a slide in PowerPoint exactly the same way as it is pasted into a word processing document. The menu bar command sequence is Insert, Picture, Clip Art.

Slide Transitions and Text/Graphics Animation

At some point during the development of a presentation, it is necessary to make a decision about the use of slide transitions and text/graphics animation. Slide transitions and text/graphics animations can be added with the development of each slide. Alternatively, slide transitions and animations can be applied once all intended content, text and graphics, is added to the entire slide show. Animation of graphics, text, and titles may be added in the Slide Editor using the Animation Effects toolbar shown in Figure 8.4.

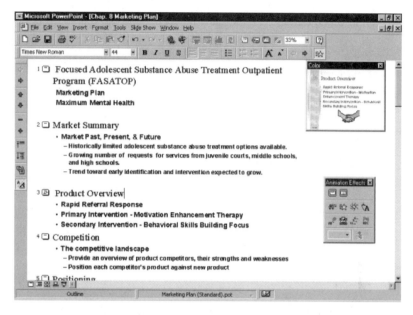

FIGURE 8.8   Content Added to Outline View of Marketing Plan
from Microsoft PowerPoint

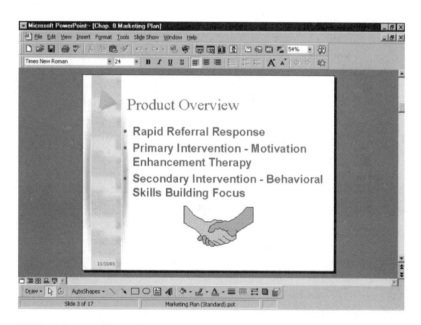

FIGURE 8.9   Slide Editor View in Marketing Plan Template
of Microsoft PowerPoint

When in the Slide Editor, slide transitions are added to one or all of the slides with the menu bar commands Slide Show, Slide Transitions. This opens a dialog window with choices of type of transition and automation of transitions. Normally, slide transition takes place upon a single left mouse click. However, it is possible in the Slide Transition dialog window to automate slide transitions by specifying the number of seconds between slides. This feature is useful in information booths and kiosks where a presentation runs in a loop, unattended on a computer. It is also possible to specify in the Slide Transition dialog window whether the selected transition should be applied to a single slide or to all the slides in the presentation. It is generally better to use a single type of transition for all slides, as too many types of transitions is distracting to the audience (Gilgen, 1997). Slide transitions can also be applied in the Outline View and the Slide Sorter View with the same Slide Show, Slide Transitions menu commands. Since the Outline View does not display graphics, animation effects cannot be added to graphics in the Outline View. However, titles and text may be animated in the Outline View.

Transition Sounds

Like slide transitions and text/graphics animations, adding sounds to a presentation offers the potential of capturing and holding the audience's attention and also creates the risk of shifting their attention from the presentation's content to its special effects. Again, careful consideration should be given to the match between the selected transition sounds, the purpose of the presentation and the intended audience. The "less is more" rule of thumb is probably the best advice regarding the use of sounds for slide transitions. The selective application of sound transitions to a few slides in a presentation may direct the audience's attention to particularly salient information. Alternatively, sounds for each slide transition may lose their novelty after a few slides and thereby their capacity as a stimulus to garner the audience's attention. This discussion is, of course, predicated on the assumption that the personal computer on which a presentation will be presented has a sound card and speakers, so the sound transitions are audible.

Slide transition sounds are added to a PowerPoint presentation by selecting the menu bar commands Slide Show, Slide Transitions, Sounds, which opens a drop-down menu of sounds. The choices of sounds include a camera click, the sound of a car driving by, a laser, a typewriter, a whoosh, and other sounds. Selection of "other sounds" opens an Add Sound window that allows the user to browse for sound files. Sound files are created by digitally recording other sounds and storing them on the computer's hard drive. Many personal computers now come with sound cards and microphones that make it possible to digitize sounds. This makes it possible to create and add to a presentation custom slide transition sounds.

Video Clips

Another type of multimedia file that can be inserted into slide presentations is digitized video clips. Video clips in a presentation can dramatically illustrate a point, give the audience a sense of place or person, or demonstrate a technique or procedure. Digitized video clips are created either by digitizing video from videotape with a video capture card in a personal computer or by downloading digital video files from a digital video camera. The file size of digitized video clips can be quite large, depending on the length of the clip, the compression algorithm used by the video capture card or digital video camera, and whether sound is also included in the file. The addition of video clips in a presentation makes it more difficult to distribute the presentation file via e-mail or on diskette, due to the increase in file size.

Video files are added to PowerPoint presentations from the Slide Editor view with the menu bar commands Insert, Movies and Sound. Find the desired video clip on the hard drive or network server on which it is stored. After selecting the file and clicking Open, a video camera icon will appear on the currently open presentation slide. The icon can be resized and relocated on the slide to match the slide's content and layout. Clicking the icon during a presentation will start the video clip. For more information about using video clips in PowerPoint presentations, see Gilgen (1997).

Video clips are also available on the Web, however, any use of video, images, or sound from the Web without the written permission of the Web page author is likely a violation of copyright law (Gilgen, 1997). Before using any media from the Web, e-mail the Web page's author and ask for permission.

Web Links

Hyperlinks are added to PowerPoint presentations in the Outline View by first highlighting the text in the outline to which to attach the hyperlink. Next, from the menu bar select Insert, Hyperlink. The Insert Hyperlink dialog window (shown in Figure 7.3 of Chapter 7) appears in which to type in the desired Web address. Including hyperlinks to Web sites in a presentation can enrich a slide show with additional information, provided of course that the computer from which the presentation is shown has an active Internet connection. If this condition is met, the presenter can move back and forth between the content of the slide show and the linked resources on the Web to convey the points of the presentation.

If, however, the presentation computer does not have an active Internet connection, it may still be useful to add hyperlinks to a presentation slide show for a number of reasons. First, PowerPoint presentations can be saved as standard PowerPoint files (.ppt), which are viewable on other computers that have PowerPoint installed on them. PowerPoint presentations may then be distributed on diskette, CD-ROM, via e-mail, or as downloadable files from a Web site. Once another user receives the file, it can be opened and viewed. If the computer on which the distributed presentation is opened has an active Internet access, then hyperlinks in the PowerPoint presentation will connect to the linked Web page. Second, it is possible to save PowerPoint presentations as a file that will run on computers that do not have PowerPoint installed on them. This makes it possible to distribute presentations to wider audiences. The Pack and Go Wizard for creating such files is described in the section on dissemination options. Hyperlinks function the same way with these files as they do in standard PowerPoint files. This format is particularly useful for placing PowerPoint presentations on Web sites or sending them as e-mail attachments, and makes the materials available to interested parties who may not have PowerPoint installed on their machines. A third way in which hyperlinks in PowerPoint presentations have utility is when the presentations are saved as HTML files that can be placed on Web servers. Visitors to the presentation's Web pages can use the embedded hyperlinks to access other Web sites. The converting of PowerPoint presentations to HTML files is described in the section, Converting PowerPoint Presentations to Web Pages. In summary, even if the computer on which a PowerPoint slide show is first presented is not linked to the Internet, it may still be very helpful to subsequent viewers of the presentation to include hyperlinks to relevant Web sites and documents.

Slide Shows for Computer-Based Training and Education

Presentation slide shows are typically thought of as being intended for two or more people in the same room at the same time. An alternative use of presentation software is for the creation of computer-based training or education packages in which viewers interact with the presentation's content in a self-directed manner at their own pace. Social service agencies often must provide training to employees and others in new skills and procedures. Likewise, it is commonly necessary and important to inform clients and visitors to an agency about the agency and the services it offers. The development of training and education presentations with PowerPoint is described here. Both of these types of presentations are referred to here as "self-directed," as the viewer controls the pace of interaction with the content of the presentation. Also, depending on the design of the presentation, the viewer controls what material will be examined.

There are three basic design configurations for self-directed presentations: linear, loops, and nonlinear. In linear presentations, the slide show moves from one slide to the next without the possibility of branching off in two or more directions. The viewer has no choice about which slide they view next. This type of design is useful if there is specific content the designer wishes to make sure every viewer sees. For example, a supervisor creates a presentation that clearly specifies the steps in evaluating a client's need for day hospitalization services in a local community mental health center. Each slide of the presentation details each step in the process. Upon completing the presentation, the supervisor saves it as a Pack and Go file (described later), attaches it to an e-mail message, and distributes it to all the case managers she supervises. The case managers can open the file and view the linear presentation slides detailing the evaluation procedure. The case managers can then save the file on their computers' hard drives for future reference.

Loop presentations show slides in a circular sequence. For instance, an agency might set up a computer in the lobby with only the monitor accessible, the rest of the computer stored in a locked cabinet. The educational presentation on the computer could be a linear series of slides with basic information about the agency and the services that it offers. Transitions between slides would be automated to change after a specified number of seconds, and the slide show would *loop,* meaning that the slide show would start again at the first slide after the last slide was shown. The linear presentation becomes a circle or loop. The looping feature is activated from the menu bar commands, Slide Show, Set Up Show, Loop continuously until Esc. The Loop continuously until Esc command means that the slide show will run in a loop, one slide after another, until the Escape key on the keyboard is struck.

Nonlinear or branching presentations offer the viewers some choice as to which slides in a presentation they examine and in what order. Nonlinear slide shows are characterized by two or more branches available to the viewer to explore in the presentation. Figure 8.10 shows a diagram of a nonlinear presentation with three possible branches. The viewer is free to examine any combination of the three branches or simply exit the presentation. Note that each branch leads back to the home page where additional branch choices are available. Nonlinear presentations are useful when a creator wants to maximize the available information in the presentation as well as the viewers' choices about what information they will examine. Readers interested in more information on the theory and application of nonlinear or hypermedia education should see Patterson and Yaffe (1994).

To create a nonlinear presentation in PowerPoint it is necessary to create an Action Button for each path in the presentation. Each Action Button hyperlinks the slide to another slide or series of slides in a presentation. Returning to Figure 8.10, the home page would have four action buttons on it. Three of the buttons would link to one of the paths and the fourth would allow the user to exit the presentation. Figure 8.11 displays

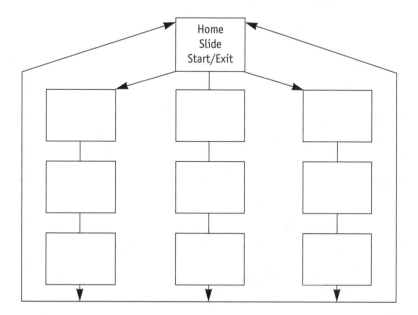

FIGURE 8.10   Diagram for a Nonlinear Presentation with Three Branches

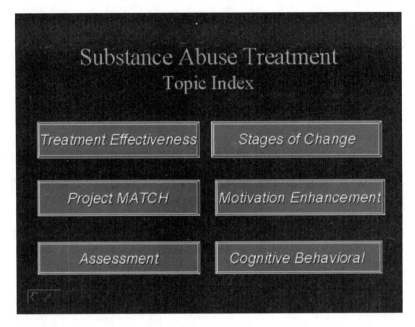

FIGURE 8.11   Nonlinear Presentation in PowerPoint

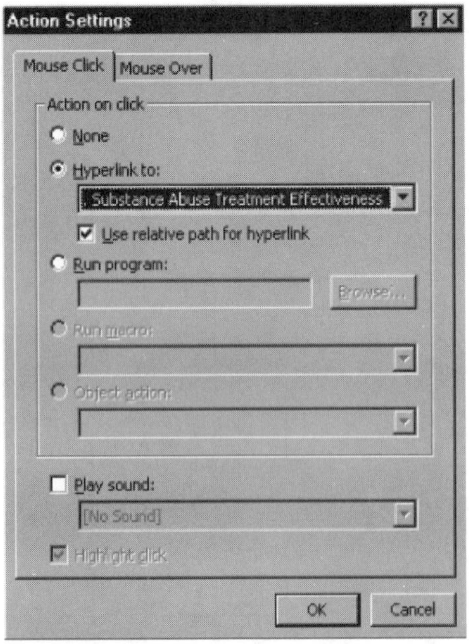

a slide from a nonlinear presentation with six possible paths. Action Buttons are added to a presentation in the Slide Edit view using the menu bar commands Slide Show, Action Buttons. Action Buttons displays a variety of button types to choose from including Home, Help, Information, Beginning, End, Next, Previous, and Custom. The buttons in Figure 8.11 are Custom buttons in which specific slides with which to hyperlink are designated. Figure 8.12 shows the Action Settings window in which a hyperlink is specified. The drop-down menu beside "Hyperlink to" contains a list of all slides in the presentation. This makes it possible to readily find slides and create hyperlinks.

It is important to test each path in a nonlinear presentation to ensure that viewers are able to navigate the path without becoming lost in a maze of slides. It is possible with Action Buttons to create training programs with multiple hyperlinks, much like the World Wide Web,

FIGURE 8.12   Action Settings Window in Microsoft PowerPoint

but on a much smaller scale. The danger in that type of nonlinear presentation is that a viewer may miss important or critical information. The development of nonlinear presentations requires careful advance consideration of the purpose of the presentation, the choices to provide to viewers, and discrimination between what information in the presentation is critical and what is optional. With this forethought, it is then possible to design training and education presentations in which viewers are required by the arrangement of slides to examine certain material and have the option to view other material that may be of interest. Figure 8.13 is an example of a training presentation in which the viewers must examine the three slides beneath the "Home Slide," but also have a number of other training choices. From the slide directly beneath the "Home Slide," viewers may examine slides to either side of the second slide, eventually moving

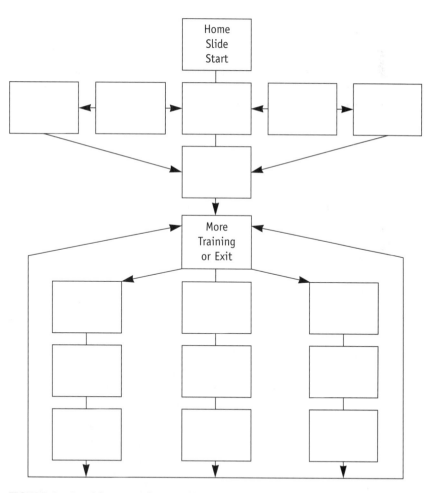

FIGURE 8.13   Diagram of a Nonlinear Presentation with Partially Constrained Navigation

to the third slide in the presentation. Upon arriving at the fourth slide in the presentation, viewers may either exit the training presentation or explore any one or all of the other branches of training information. Despite the apparent complexity, a nonlinear presentation can be an effective tool for providing training and educational information to staff in social service organizations (Patterson, Pullen, Evers, Champlin, & Ralson, 1997; Patterson & Yaffe, 1993).

Slide Show Dissemination Options

Once a PowerPoint presentation is complete, there are several dissemination options available. The first option is to save the presentation as a standard PowerPoint file. This is generally a good first step, even if one intends to save the file in some other format, because it retains the original content and format of the presentation. If one intends to present the slide show on a computer other than the one it was created on, it is necessary to transfer the slide show file over a network to the presentation computer or save it to a portable storage medium such as a diskette or Zip drive. It is also necessary to determine in advance if the presentation computer has PowerPoint installed on it. If it does not, then the slide show should be saved with the Pack and Go Wizard.

The Pack and Go Wizard enables a slide show creator to save a version of the file in a format that can run on a computer that does not have PowerPoint installed on it (Gilgen, 1997). This feature is especially useful when sending presentations via e-mail or placing them on a Web page as downloadable files. To save a slide show with Pack and Go, from the menu bar select File, Pack and Go. This opens the Pack and Go Wizard displayed in Figure 8.14. As is evident in Figure 8.14, the basic steps in the wizard are:

1. Pick the slide show (file) to pack. More than one file may be added.
2. Select a location to save the file. Files can be saved on a diskette, Zip drive, the computer's hard drive, or another computer on a network.
3. Select Include Linked Files to add files linked to the presentation such as sound and video.
4. Select Embed TrueType fonts to ensure that the fonts used in the presentation are displayed when the slide show is opened, regardless of whether the computer on which it is opened has the fonts installed.
5. If the viewers' computers do not have PowerPoint installed on them, then select Viewer for Windows 95 or NT. It is generally wise to include the viewer to avoid the chance that viewers will not have PowerPoint installed.
6. Click Finish. If the slide show being saved on diskette is too large for a single diskette, the program will save the slide show across two or more diskettes.

Sometimes it is helpful to distribute printed versions of a slide show. PowerPoint makes available a number of print format options. Selection of File, Print from the menu bar opens the print dialog window in which the various printing options are available.

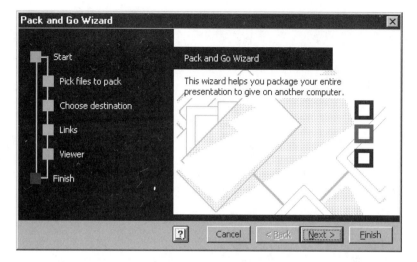

FIGURE 8.14   PowerPoint's Pack and Go Wizard

In this window it is possible to specify the printing of all slides or to designate particular slides for printing. There are options for printing slides, handouts, notes pages, and the outline view. Additional color and formatting options are also available.

An alternative to printing the slides directly from PowerPoint is to send them to Microsoft Word. Select from the menu bar File, Send, Microsoft Word. This option allows for the addition or modification of the material in a slide show within Word. Figure 8.15 displays the five options for page layout when sending slide shows to Word.

Converting PowerPoint Presentations to Web Pages

The World Wide Web is a powerful tool for publishing information. Slide shows transformed into Web pages and uploaded to a Web server are then available for audience members to examine and review after a presentation is delivered. Making a presentation available on the Web may also save the cost of printing handouts from a presentation. An additional advantage of transforming a slide show into Web pages is that the information becomes available to a broader audience than originally attended the presentation.

In PowerPoint, slide shows are converted into HTML files (Web pages) with a wizard that takes the user through a step-by-step conversion process. The process begins with the menu bar commands File, Save as HTML. This starts the Save as HTML wizard shown in Figure 8.16. Note the steps in the process; each offers choices about the appearance and functions of the resultant Web pages. These choices include using either the existing or a new page layout, a page style (frame or no frame), the use of GIF or JPEG graphics, the size and resolution of graphics, author information including e-mail address and home page address, page colors and button look, and button style. The last step is to save the files created by the conversion process into a single folder. This folder

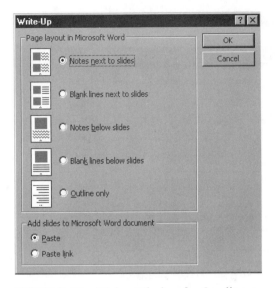

FIGURE 8.15   Dialog Window for Sending a PowerPoint Presentation to Microsoft Word

can then be uploaded to a Web server. If a personal or agency Web page already exists on the server, create a link in that page to the index.htm file in the uploaded folder. This will allow visitors to a personal or agency home page to link to the slide show.

Figure 8.17 shows a Web page created from a slide show. This page uses a "frames" page style in which the page is divided into sections with different types of information or functions in it. Note the navigational buttons in the top frame of the page, the index of pages in the left frame, and the buttons in the top left-hand corner that expand or contract the amount of information shown in the index. This type of Web page allows the user to either move sequentially through the content of the information in the slide show using the navigational buttons at the top of the page or jump to information of interest with the hyperlinks contained in each topic listed in the index. The hyperlinks in the index are automatically inserted.

This section on Microsoft PowerPoint described the use of templates to develop slide shows, the application of slide transitions, text/graphics animation, employment of transition sounds and video clips, inclusion of Web links, development of training

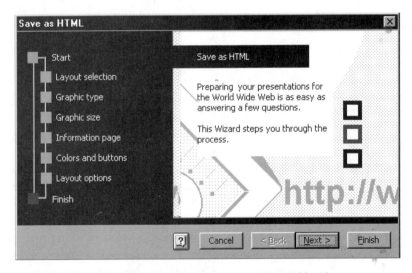

FIGURE 8.16   Wizard for Converting PowerPoint Slide Shows to HTML Files

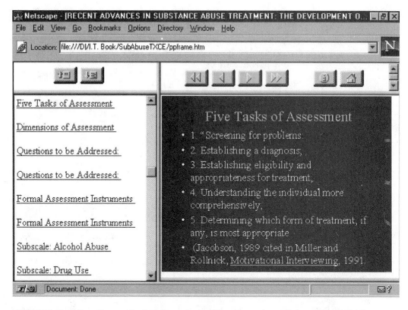

FIGURE 8.17   PowerPoint Presentation Converted into a Web Page

and education slide shows, saving of slide shows, and their transformation into Web pages. In total, application of the skills covered in this section enables a slide show creator to develop a compelling presentation that can be distributed in an array of formats to a range of audiences. The skills demonstrated in PowerPoint are illustrated for Lotus Freelance Graphics and Corel Presentation in subsequent sections. As much of the rationale and utility of these skills was covered here, the following discussion will be limited to the specifics of how to apply them with each presentation application.

Using Lotus Freelance Graphics

Templates

Slide show templates (SmartMasters) in Lotus Freelance Graphics are accessed from the menu bar under File, New. Figure 8.18 shows the New Presentation dialog window. Note the scrollable "Select a content topic" menu from which templates are selected. The window to the right of this menu displays a brief description of the template. In the scrollable "Select a look" menu there are choices for the design layer of the slides in the presentation. To the right of this menu is a thumbnail view of the template. This view provides a preview of both the appearance of the selected template and the available alternatives in the design layer.

Once the desired template and design layer for a presentation are selected, the text content of the slide show can be added. In Freelance Graphics, content is added to each

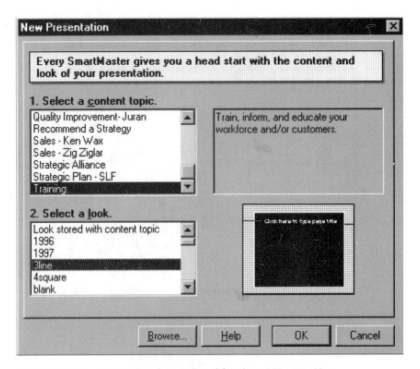

FIGURE 8.18   Lotus Freelance Graphics SmartMaster New Presentation Window

new slide either in the Outliner or Current Page view. Figure 8.19 shows an Outliner screen with two slides present. New slides are added in the Outliner by clicking the icon on the far right side of the toolbar, directly beneath the Guide Me help icon. Clicking the New Page icon opens the New Page dialog window, shown in Figure 8.20. The New Page dialog window offers choices in the type of content and the layout of each new slide in a presentation. Note the tabs at the top of the dialog window that allow a slide show creator to move between choices of content and layout for new slides. The thumbnail image to the right provides a miniature view of each possible choice as it is selected.

In the Current Page view new slides are added with the New Page button, which when clicked opens the New Page dialog window just described. Once the content and layout of a new page are selected, content is added by typing it into the appropriate section of the page's layout. Slides in the template have different sections in which content is added. These sections generally have a "Click Here" message on them. When the section is clicked, a text window opens in which text for the slide is typed, the font size can be altered, and the heading level of the section's content can be raised or lowered. This is a useful feature, because in some template slides the size of the section's text exceeds the available size of the slide. This necessitates reducing either the font size or the heading level to ensure the section is contained within the borders of the slide. Figure 8.21

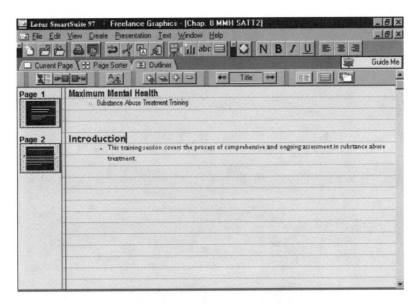

FIGURE 8.19   Lotus Freelance Graphics Outliner View

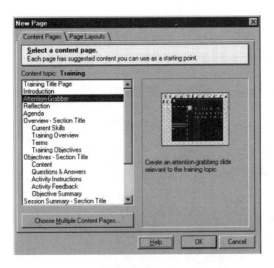

FIGURE 8.20   Lotus Freelance Graphics New Page Content Selection Window

displays the Agenda slide from the Training template. Note that both the Agenda heading and the dialog window beneath it are partially outside of the slide's borders. Each one must be clicked and dragged back inside the slide's borders in preparing the slide for viewing. The dialog box was opened after clicking the "Click here for suggested agenda" displayed on that section of the screen. The suggested agenda may either be accepted or modified for the particular needs of a presentation. Again, it will likely be necessary to reduce the font size or the heading level to ensure that this section will fix within the confines of the slide's layout. Figure 8.22 shows the Agenda page after the text and layout of the page are repositioned and resized.

Slide Transitions

Slide transitions in Freelance Graphics are added in one of two ways. One option is to add a transition to each slide individually with the Page Properties dialog box. The

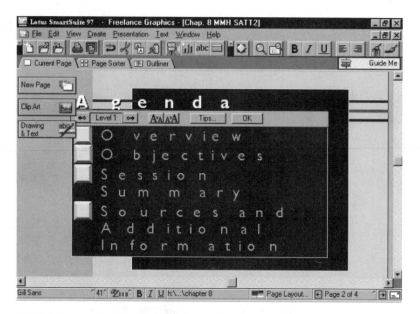

FIGURE 8.21   Lotus Freelance Graphics Agenda Slide in the Training Template

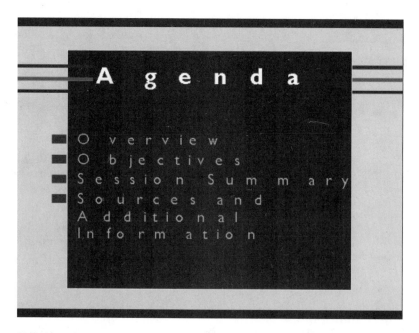

FIGURE 8.22   Lotus Freelance Graphics Presentation View of Agenda Slide

second option is to add a single type of slide transition to the entire show from the Set Up Screen Show dialog window. This option is described in the discussion of training and education slide shows.

To create individual slide transitions use the Page Properties dialog box. The Page Properties dialog box is accessed either through the menu bar with the commands Page, Page Properties or from the toolbar with the "Change properties of select object" icon. This icon is located below and slightly to the right of the Help command in the menu bar. Its name appears whenever the cursor is passed over it. The Page Properties dialog box is shown in Figure 8.23. Choices in this dialog window include type of slide transition, adding of slide transition sounds, and manual or automatic slide advancement (Eddy, 1997).

Animation of Text/Graphics

Text and Graphics animation are added in Freelance Graphics in much the same way as slide transitions. In the Current Page view, right-click on the text or graphic within a slide intended for animation. Select Text Properties from the pop-up menu that appears, then click on the movie camera icon tab at the top of the Text Properties dialog window. Figure 8.24 shows the available options for animating text and graphics. Available options include choice of the timing of the appearance of a selection of text or a graphic on screen; the effects when the text block is added, including how bullets are displayed; type of transition; and the inclusion of sound with the addition of text. Also noteworthy in the Text Properties window is the ability to generate actions when the text block is clicked. The choices here include hyperlinking to another slide in the presentation or to a URL (Web page), or running an application, sound, movie, or another Freelance Graphics show. This feature is particularly useful in developing training and education slide shows. This feature in effect makes it possible to turn text and graphics into action buttons in a slide show. If GOTO URL is selected from the drop-down menu, a dialog window appears in which to enter a Web address, thereby creating a link from the slide show to a location on the Web.

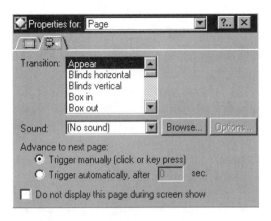

FIGURE 8.23   Lotus Freelance Graphics Page Properties Dialog Window

Training and Education Slide Shows

Staff training and client education slide shows are created in Lotus Freelance Graphics in much the same manner as described for Microsoft PowerPoint. It is possible to create linear, loop, and nonlinear presentations. Development of linear slide shows is facilitated

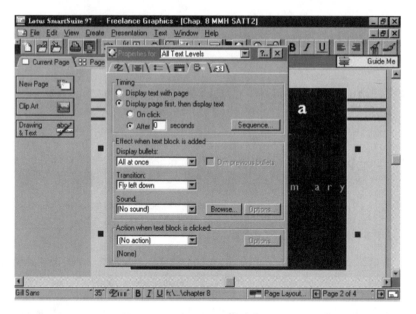

FIGURE 8.24   Lotus Freelance Graphics Text Properties Dialog Window

by the Set Up Screen Show dialog window. This dialog window, accessed from the menu bar under Presentation, Set Up Screen Show, has three tabs: Page Effects, Tools, and Options. Page Effects offers a selection of screen transitions applicable to the entire slide show and a choice of when to display the next slide. Slide transitions can be set to occur with a mouse click or the pressing of any key. Alternatively, slide transition can be automated to occur after a set number of seconds. Figure 8.25 displays the options available under the Tools tab of the Set Up Screen Show. Selecting the Display Control Panel option inserts the navigational control panel shown in the figure into each page of the presentation. The buttons in the panel allow the viewer to (a) move backwards in the slide show, (b) see a listing of all slides in the presentation and jump to a desired one, (c) move forward, and (d) exit. Adding this navigational control panel to a linear slide show makes it possible for viewers to move sequentially through a presentation. Clicking the second icon from the left in the navigational control panel opens the Screen Show Pages, which displays all the pages in the presentation. This makes it possible for viewers to move through the presentation nonsequentially.

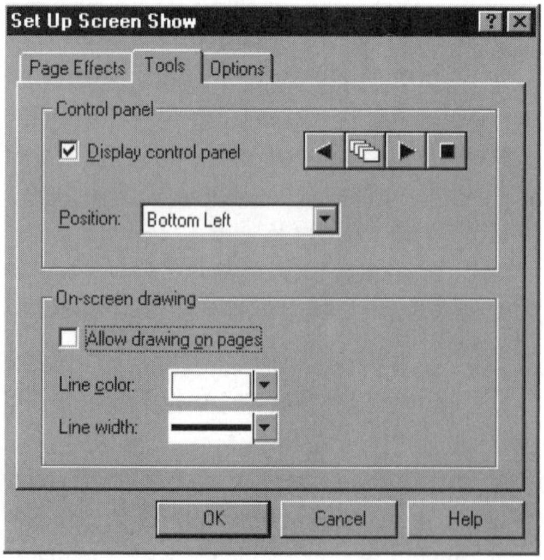

FIGURE 8.25   Lotus Freelance Graphics Set Up Screen Show Dialog Window

Looping presentations are created by selecting Options from the Set Up Screen Show dialog window. Under the Options tab, there is the Run Option of "Run screen show in a continuous loop." Selecting this option causes the slide show to loop until the Esc key is pressed. Again, this option is useful for creating standalone presentations in agency lobbies, at conventions, and as part of an information booth at conferences.

Nonlinear presentations may also be designed to employ the navigational control panel described previously. It can be used in combination with other page buttons to provide viewers the options of moving sequentially through a presentation, opening the Screen Show Pages window to move directly to a page, or clicking page buttons to follow a particular branch in the presentation. Figure 8.26 displays a slide in which the navigational control panel is included in a page in which the four arrows beside the topics have each been hyperlinked to branches in the staff training program. The hyperlinks are created by the following steps.

1. Double-click on the graphic (the arrow clip art).
2. The Properties for Group dialog box appears.
3. Select the movie camera tab.
4. Select the "Action when object is clicked" pop-up menu.
5. Select GOTO Page.
6. In the GOTO Page dialog window select the slide in the presentation corresponding with the selected topic.

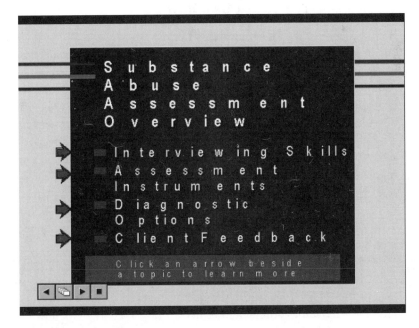

FIGURE 8.26 Lotus Freelance Graphics Slide Show with Navigational Buttons

This procedure requires the creation of all the slides for each topic before hyperlinks can be established. Once all the slides are developed, it may be necessary to use the Page Sorter view to arrange the slides in a way that creates a logical flow of information should a viewer choose to examine the presentation sequentially instead of using the nonsequential branching.

Saving and Distributing Slide Shows

Using the Save command to save a Freelance Graphics slide show saves the file with a PRZ file extension. The saved slide show is now viewable on any computer with a copy of Lotus Freelance Graphics on it. To save a copy of the slide show so viewers who do not have Freelance Graphics may still view it, use the Save As command and select "Prepare for Mobile Screen Show Player." The Mobile Screen Show Player is a standalone application available for free downloading from the Lotus Web page (http://www.lotus.com). This option allows a slide show creator to distribute a presentation via e-mail, on diskette, or as a downloadable file from a Web page. Recipients would then have to download the Mobile Screen Show Player from the Lotus Web site in order to view the presentation.

Another option for distributing a slide show is to print it. To print Freelance Graphics slide shows, select File, Print from the menu bar. Print options include printing full pages, handouts, speaker notes, and audience notes.

Creating Web Pages from a Slide Show

If an audience is likely to have access to the Web, saving a slide show as Web pages is an alternative to printing it. In Freelance Graphics, saving a slide show as Web pages is initiated with the menu bar commands File, Internet, Publish As Web Page(s). This command sequence opens the Publish As Web Page(s) Instructions window displayed in Figure 8.27. Upon clicking OK, the Publish As Web Page(s) Options dialog window shown in Figure 8.28 appears. Adding a table of contents with links to each page is a helpful option as it allows visitors to the Web site to go directly to content in the slide show of particular interest to them. Adding speaker notes is a way of providing supplemental information to the slide show. Speaker notes are created during the process of developing the slide show with the menu bar commands Create, Speaker Note. Another available option is to add an e-mail address link to the bottom of each page. This is a helpful way to receive feedback, comments, and questions for visitors to the Web pages generated from the slide show.

Click OK after making a selection of options in the Publish As Web Page(s) Options dialog window. A save file dialog window appears in which to specify where to save the HTML files of the slide show. Select a directory on the computer's hard drive or a network computer in which to save the files. Once this is complete, another dialog window appears with options to launch a Web browser in which to view

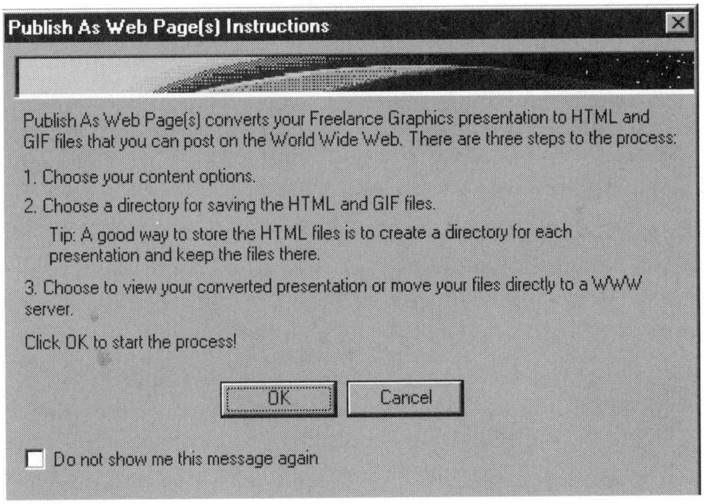

FIGURE 8.27   Lotus Freelance Graphics Publish As Web Page(s) Instructions

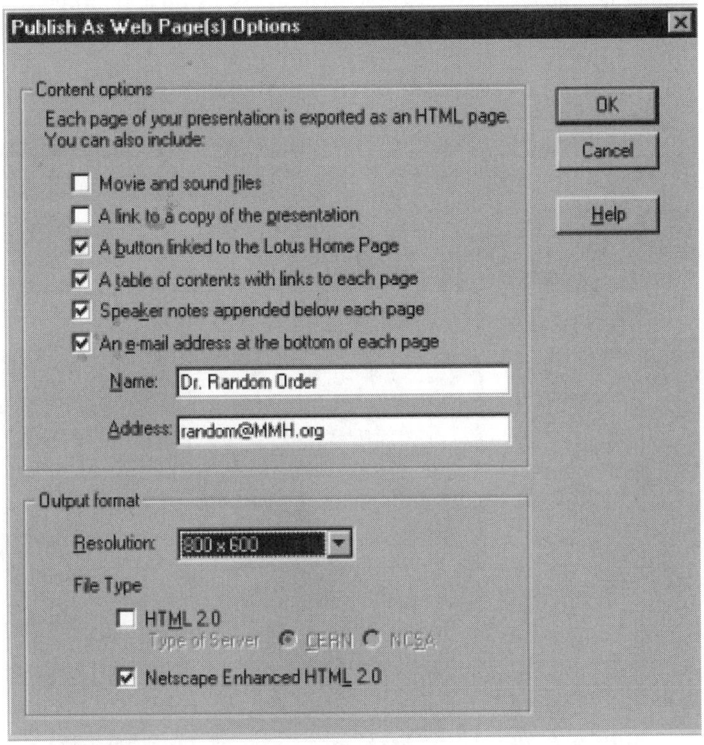

FIGURE 8.28   Lotus Freelance Graphics Publish As Web Page(s) Options Dialog Window

the saved HTML files, save the HTML files to an Internet server, or return to Free-lance Graphics. If the option to save the HTML files to an Internet server is selected, a Save to the Internet dialog window appears in which to specify the host and establish a connection to the host's Internet server. In order to save files to an Internet server, it is necessary first to have an established account with an Internet service provider. The ISP is the host. Check with the ISP for information on their Internet address and procedures for uploading files to their server. This information is inserted into the Host dialog window that is accessed from the Save to the Internet dialog window. Although this process may seem complicated, once an account is established with the ISP, placing the HTML files on the Web is a matter of completing the information in the Host dialog window and then connecting to the ISP through a modem or over a network.

Figure 8.29 displays a page from a Freelance Graphics slide show transformed into a Web page. Note both the navigational buttons at the top of the page and the table of contents on the left side of the page. The hyperlinks connecting each of the arrows on the page to different slides in the presentation are not functional on the Web page. This is because Freelance Graphics saves each slide as a GIF file and in doing so the hyperlinks are not preserved. If a slide show is intended for eventual publication on the Web, it is advisable to exclude hyperlinks, as their nonfunctionality could frustrate Web site visitors.

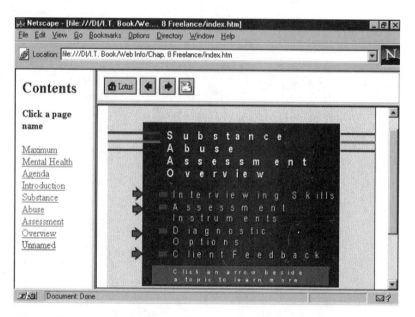

FIGURE 8.29   Lotus Freelance Graphics Slide Show as a Web Page

Using Corel Presentation

Templates

Corel Presentation takes a slightly different approach to the use of templates. Microsoft PowerPoint and Lotus Freelance Graphics offer templates with themes such as Business Overview or Marketing Plan, that offer modifiable structure to the content of the slide show. Corel Presentation takes a nonthematic approach by instead offering choices about the background appearance of the slide show. The addition of each new slide brings a new choice about the slide layout, while the background layer remains constant. This approach offers less structure to guide thinking about content for inclusion in a slide show than do the templates offered by the other two presentation applications.

When Corel Presentation starts, the user is asked to select either a new presentation or an existing one. Selecting New opens the Startup Master Gallery displayed in Figure 8.30. There are several categories of slide backgrounds to choose from. Once the selection is made, the first slide appears in the Slide Editor view. Figure 8.31

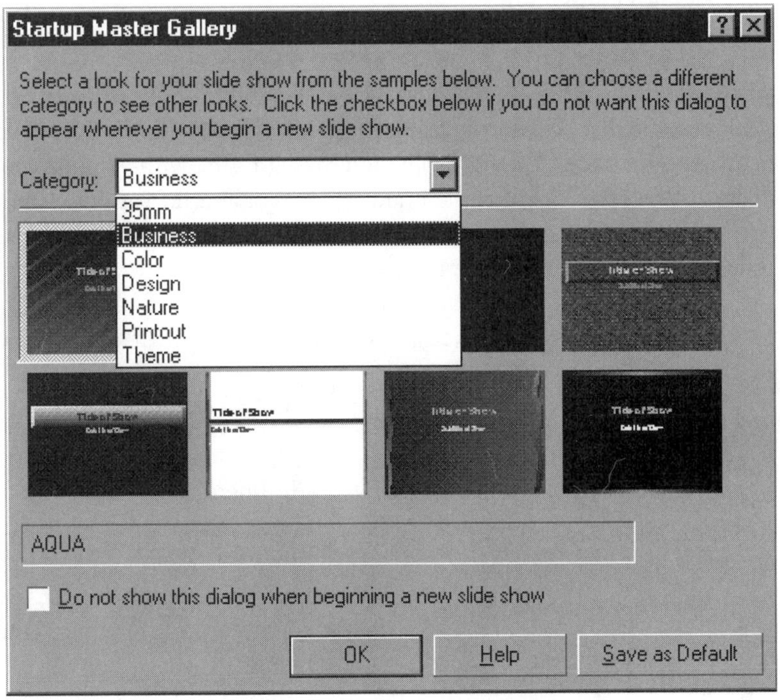

FIGURE 8.30   Corel Presentation Startup Master Gallery

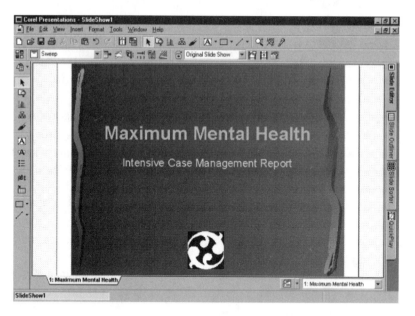

FIGURE 8.31   Slide Editor View of the First Slide in Corel Presentation Slide Show

contains the first slide in a presentation. Note the tabs on the left side of the screen for changing the slide view, the toolbar on the right side with graphics tools, and the toolbars at the top of the screen for adding content and formatting to the slide show.

After text and graphics content is added to the first slide, insert a new slide with the menu bar command Insert, New Slide. Figure 8.32 shows the New Slide selection window that offers a variety of slide layouts. Note also the "Number to add" drop-down menu with which to add more than one slide, of the same layout, at a time.

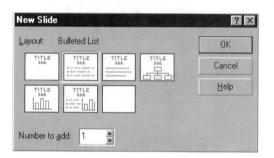

FIGURE 8.32   Corel Presentation New Slide Menu

Slide Transitions

Slide transitions are added to slide shows in one of two ways. The first option is to add a slide transition to a single slide with the Slide Transition drop-down menu in the toolbar as shown in Figure 8.31 (Sweep). The second option is to right-click on a slide, which opens a pop-up menu from which Transition is selected. This opens a Slide Properties dialog window as shown in Figure 8.33. The Transition tab of this window

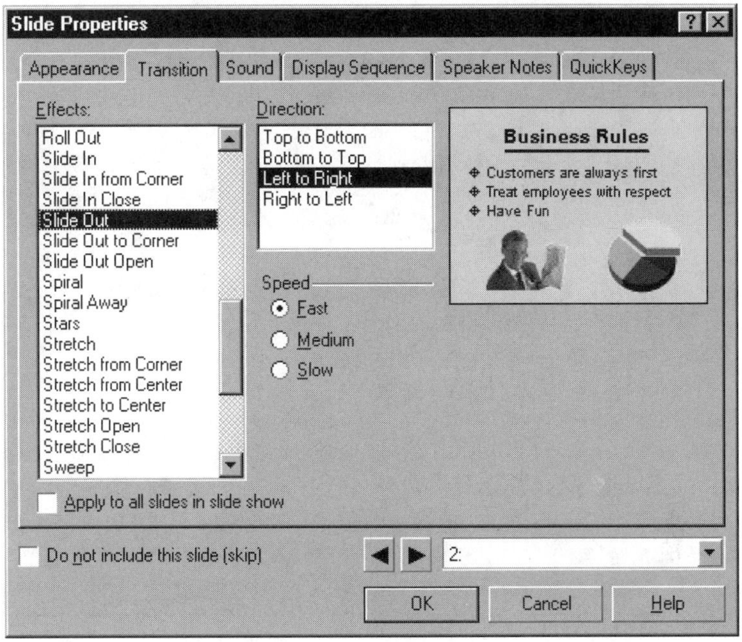

FIGURE 8.33   Corel Presentation Slide Properties Dialog Window

offers choices for transition effect, speed, direction, and for application of the same transition to all slides. It is also possible to select specific slides to exclude from the slide transition effect.

Sounds for slide transitions are added from the Sounds tab of the Slide Properties dialog window. This window offers choices of adding previously recorded WAV, MIDI, and CD sound clips. WAV and MIDI are sound file formats. The Corel WordPerfect Suite CD contains a selection of both WAV and MIDI files to choose from. Selecting CD opens a dialog window in which to record a specific track or portion of a track from a music CD. Sound transitions may be applied to the entire slide show or specific slides can be designated for exclusion from sound transitions.

Animation of Text/Graphics

Text or bulleted lists are animated in Corel Presentation by right-clicking the list and selecting Object Animation from the pop-up menu. This produces the Object Properties dialog window shown in Figure 8.34. In the case of a bulleted list, the Bulleted List Properties dialog window opens. The following instructions are applicable to either dialog window. The Object Animation tab offers choices of animating an object in place or animating it across the screen. Animating an object in place creates an animation of

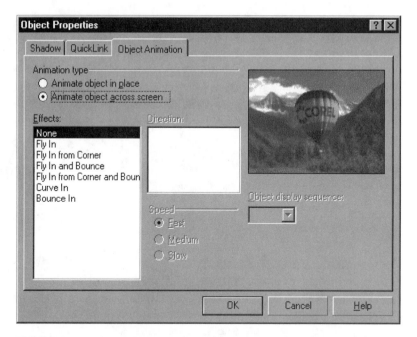

FIGURE 8.34   Corel Presentation Object Properties Dialog Window

the text box in its original location on the slide. For instance, if the animation effect "Clock" is selected, when the slide is opened, the first mouse click or keystroke causes the text box to appear in a motion resembling the sweep of a second hand around a clock face. Animating a text box across the screen causes the bulleted list to move across the slide into position. The effect, direction, and speed of animation can all be selected in this dialog window. Direction is not an option for animation in place, as the text box appears in its original position.

Graphics in a slide are animated with the same procedure. Once a graphic is inserted into a slide with the Insert, Graphics menu bar commands, right-clicking the object opens a pop-up menu from which to select Object Animation. Selecting Object Animation opens the Object Properties dialog window. Selecting the Object Animation tab makes available the animation choices described for text animation.

Movies

Video clips are inserted into a slide show with the menu bar commands Insert, Movie. The Corel WordPerfect Suite CD contains several video clips. Original video also can be digitized and added as a video clip to a slide show. The size of a video file and the intended method of distributing or showing a presentation should be taken into consideration before adding a video clip to a slide show.

Web Links

Linkages of slides in a presentation to Web sites are created by right-clicking a graphic or text box on a slide. From the pop-up menu select QuickLink, which opens the dialog window shown in Figure 8.35. Next, click the Action radio button and select Browse Internet from the drop-down menu. Either type the Web address of the page intended for linkage into the Location box, or if a Web connection is available, browse the Web for the intended page and its address. Once the Web page is found, type the address into the Location box.

Training and Education Slide Shows

Linear and nonlinear training and education slide shows are created with Corel Presentation in much the same manner as they are created in Freelance Graphics and PowerPoint. Loop slide shows are not an option in a standard Corel Presentation: however, in the Show on the Go saving option described in the next section, there is a loop option.

Movement through a linear slide show occurs with either a mouse click or with the Enter, Shift, or Directional arrow keys. Viewers can move backward in a presentation with the left directional arrow key. Another option for viewing previous slides in a presentation is to create a graphic (e.g., a left arrow) or text box (Previous Slide) with a QuickLink to

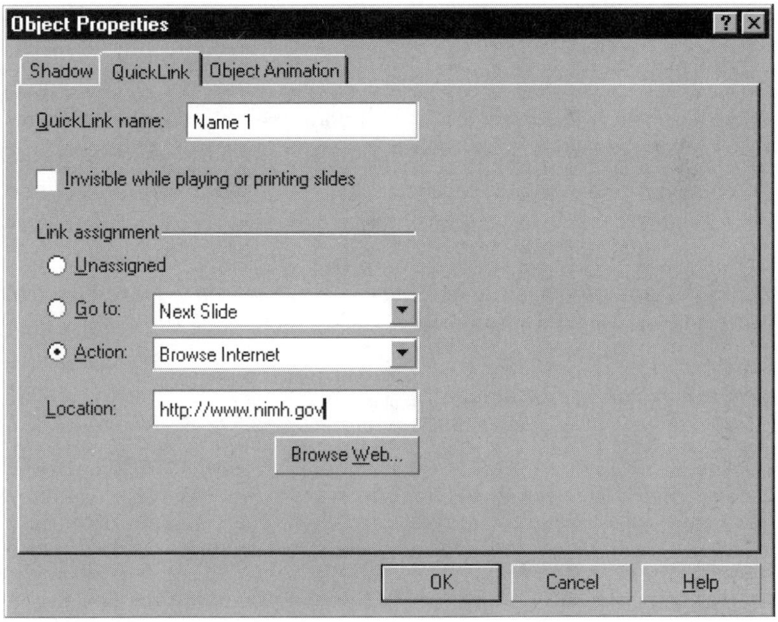

FIGURE 8.35   Corel Presentation Object Properties QuickLink Dialog Window

Previous slide. A QuickLink to a graphic or text box is created by right-clicking the object, and selecting QuickLink from the pop-up menu. Figure 8.35 shows the QuickLink dialog window. Clicking Go To and selecting Previous Slide establishes a hyperlink between the text or graphic to the previous slide. Once this Previous Slide text or graphic link is created, it can be copied and pasted in to any or all slides in the slide show. Viewers then have the option for bidirectional, linear movement through the slide show.

Nonlinear slide shows should be planned and designed as described in the discussion of nonlinear slide shows with PowerPoint and Freelance Graphics. Linkages to branches of the slide show are created using QuickLinks to specific slides. The Go To drop-down menu displays all the slides in a presentation. Once a link is established to the first slide in a branch, text or graphics with Next Slide and Previous Slide links can be used to provide bidirectional movement within the branch.

Saving and Distributing Slide Shows

The first option for saving a Corel Presentation slide show is to use the Save command, saving it as a standard Corel Presentation file. This option works well if the presentation computer has Corel Presentation on it and there is no intention to distribute the presentation. A second option is to save the slide show as a portable presentation. This option allows a presentation creator to save the slide show to a diskette or other storage medium and present it from a computer that does not have Corel Presentation installed on it. This option is accomplished with the menu bar command sequence File, Show on the Go. Figure 8.36 displays the dialog window in which the Name, Destination, System, and Display type are specified. Also note there is the option to "Repeat slide show until you press Esc." This option makes it possible to create a loop presentation. Clicking Change opens the option to change the Name, Destination, System, and Display Type. To distribute a slide show via e-mail, select e-mail under Destination.

Printing is the third option for saving and distributing a slide show. To print a presentation, use the File, Print command sequence. In the Print dialog window there are options for printing the entire document, the current view, slides, handouts, audience notes, and speaker notes. Of course, the other option is to save the slide show as Web pages.

Transforming a Slide Show to Web Pages

A Corel Presentation slide show is saved as Web pages with the menu bar command sequence File, Internet Publisher. This sequence opens a dialog window, shown in Figure 8.37, with the three options for saving a presentation. The first option saves the slide show as a standard HTML file. The second option creates a Corel Barista presentation. Corel Barista uses Java (a Web programming language) to create graphically rich slides with columns, multiple fonts, and text wrapping. Additionally, this format supports sound and slide transitions. The third option is Publish to Show It, which includes all the sounds, slide transitions, and animations in the original slide show. When viewed on the Web, slides advance by pressing the space bar or clicking the mouse. This option essentially recreates on the Web the experience of viewing the slide show.

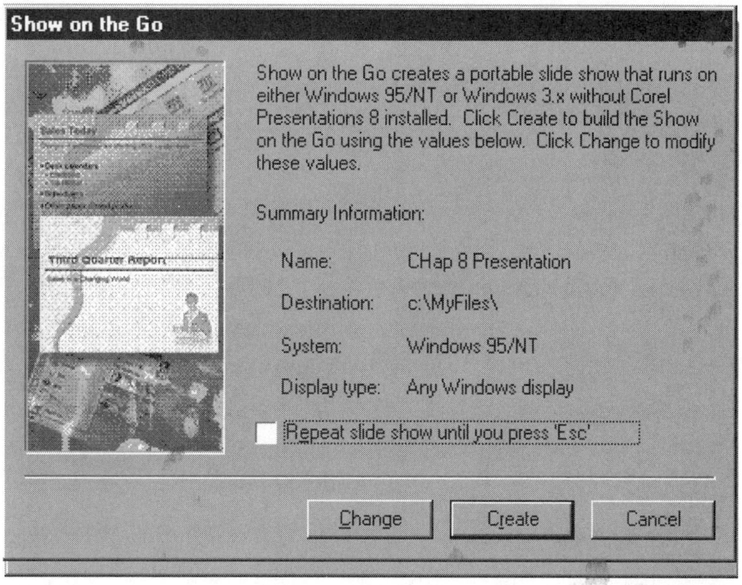

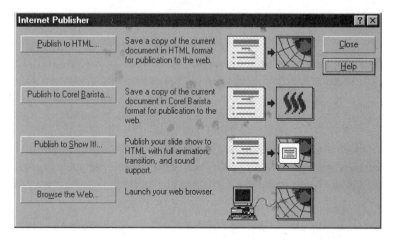

FIGURE 8.36   Corel Presentation Show on the Go Dialog Window

FIGURE 8.37   Corel Presentation Internet Publisher Window

Selecting Publish to HTML starts a wizard in which the presentation creator makes a series of decisions about the configuration of the resultant Web presentation. These choices include page layout, title of the file folder (where the pages are saved), directory to save the folder in, the use of frames, the use of navigational buttons, home page and e-mail information, display size, graphic type, and the color setting for the pages. Figure 8.38 shows one page of a Corel Presentation slide show saved as an HTML file. Note that there is a table of contents on the left of the page and navigational buttons at the top of the page. This configuration allows the viewer broad discretion in examining the content of the slide show.

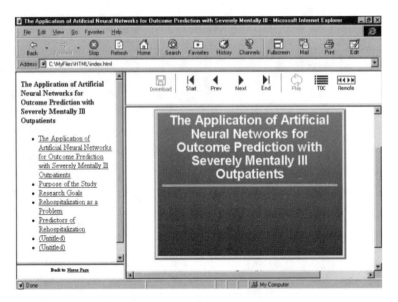

FIGURE 8.38   Corel Presentation Slide Show as a Web Page

Summary

This chapter detailed the application of presentation software in the development of slide shows. Described here were the four views of presentation software: the slide editor, slide sorter, outline view, and presentation view. The function and application of slide transitions, text/graphics animations, sounds, and video clips were explained. Described also was the use of templates to develop slide show presentations. This chapter demonstrated the process of creating slide shows in three different presentation software packages: Microsoft PowerPoint, Corel Presentation, and Lotus Freelance Graphics. The transformation of slide show presentations into Web pages was described for each of the three presentation software packages.

Exercises

1. Using presentation software, develop a presentation of at least ten slides on a topic or service related to your practice setting. Include animations and slide transitions as elements in the slide show.
2. With a group of peers, create a slide show presentation to teach, inform, or train a selected population on a specific topic. Once the training presentation is complete, transform it into Web pages. If possible, place the Web pages on a Web server and demonstrate its operation to a group of peers or colleagues.

chapter 9

The Internet as a Tool of Practice

The intention of this chapter is to articulate a range of possible applications of the Internet as a tool of social service practice. This chapter addresses the basic requirements for gaining access to the Internet, the use of e-mail software, and its application in communication via the Internet. Described here are a number of uses of the World Wide Web and procedures to find and disseminate information. Other tools of the Internet, including FTP, Usenet, and chat rooms, are discussed.

A key function in social service practice is the exchange of information. We reviewed in Chapter 7 a range of methods to provide information to clients, contributors, and other constituents in written documents including letters, flyers, brochures, and newsletters. In Chapter 8 we explored the development of slide show presentations as a tool of information sharing. Both chapters described how to create Web pages from word processing software and presentation software for the dissemination of information. Web pages are documents that reside on the World Wide Web. The World Wide Web is a network of computers on the Internet that supports documents formatted in hypertext mark-up language (Margolis, 1996). HTML enables the linkage of the vast universe of pages on the Web. The Internet is a global network of computer networks that employs a common communication protocol called TCP/IP (Transport Control Protocol/Internet Protocol). This communication protocol is the common language that allows different types of computers around the world to exchange information with one another. Increasingly, social service practitioners are employing the Internet as a means to find and exchange information with clients, supervisors, and colleagues (Giffords, 1998; Myrick & Sabella, 1995). Rivard, Madrigal, and Millan (1997) recommend the Internet as a rich source of information for developing effective practice interventions.

Marlowe-Carr (1997) surveyed 162 social workers who use online services, including dial-up networks and the Internet. (The term *dial-up networks* refers to non-Internet-based networks, such as Compuserve and America Online (AOL), which operate computer networks that have Internet access, but also maintain information resources accessible only to paying customers.) Marlowe-Carr found that 93.8% of the respondents reported the use of online services enhanced their professional capacity as social workers. She concluded that social workers have an ethical responsibility to develop the knowledge and skills necessary to use online information resources.

Shank, Roesch, Murphy-Berman, and Wright (1996) described the Nebraska Network for Children and Families (NNCF). Developed by the State of Nebraska, the NNCF is an Internet-based system designed for communication and information dissemination to at-risk families. The system is targeted at families of children with special health care needs (CSHCN). The authors report that the NNCF Web page (http://nncf.unl.edu/library.html) provides information on parent, health, government, and education resources as well as organization and new user information. This Web site is intended to facilitate parental advocacy on behalf of their children and to provide supportive interaction and empowerment.

Schopler, Abell, and Galinsky (1998) reviewed the literature on technology-based groups, including computer-based groups in which information and feedback are exchanged over online services and the Internet. Group members in computer-based groups may engage in live, online, or written dialog with other group members, or the groups may be organized so their exchanges are asynchronous. In asynchronous groups, the ongoing discussion is distributed via e-mail or posted on a secure Web page or computer bulletin board. Members are free to engage in the exchanges whenever they find it convenient. Schopler, Abell, and Galinsky (1998) cite the use of computer-based groups with a wide range of populations, including emotionally disturbed adolescents, children and adolescents with chronic illnesses, sexual abuse survivors, patients with cancer, and persons providing care to dementia and Alzheimer's patients. Cited advantages of computer-based groups include (a) flexible meeting times, (b) privacy, (c) greater accessibility, (d) minimization of racial, gender, and socioeconomic bias, and (e) improved accuracy in information exchange. The authors list several disadvantages to these types of groups, including (a) confidentiality concerns, (b) technical difficulties, (c) limited assessment, and (d) destructive interactions. Schopler, Abell, and Galinsky offer a number of recommendations for adapting group practice to computer-based interaction. Interested readers are referred to the article, as the details of the authors' recommendations are beyond the scope of this discussion.

Miller and DiGiuseppe (1998) have described an Internet-based database, the Violence Information Network (VIN), dedicated to the collection and distribution of information on violence. Accessible over the Internet, VIN publishes trends in violent activities within communities in a metropolitan area. The intended purpose of VIN is to provide a central source of information on violence in the metropolitan area and thereby heighten understanding of violence as a complex social issue facing communities.

The studies cited here are only examples of the possibilities and current applications of the Internet for the exchange of information in social service practice. This chapter describes the emerging role and the potential applications of the Internet in social service practice. The use of electronically based communication via e-mail and other methods is addressed, along with consideration of utilization of the World Wide

Web. In particular, this chapter describes how social service practitioners can employ the World Wide Web to find, collect, and use practice-relevant information. The utility of this vast information resource is illustrated with a number of social service topics. Also described are ways to retain and use information in electronic format to avoid both having to reenter information and perpetuate needless paper consumption.

A Brief History of the Internet

The Internet was developed in the late 1960s as an experimental computer network to test the feasibility of creating networks to withstand nuclear attack (Krol, 1992; Lennon, 1997). It was originally called ARPAnet as it was funded by the U.S. Defense Department's Advanced Research Projects Agency (ARPA). The ARPAnet project linked computers at the University of California Santa Barbara, University of California at Los Angeles, Stanford, and the University of Utah. The underlying idea of ARPAnet was the exchange of information over a computer network in which there was no central control and no one computer was critical to the data flow. This design meant that the loss of one or more computers in the network would not disrupt the exchange of information.

By 1971 ARPAnet had grown to a network of 23 university and government computers across the United States. In 1973 ARPAnet was expanded to include computers in England and Norway. In 1981 there were over two hundred host (file servers) computers on ARPAnet and new networks BITNET, CSNET, and Usenet were being developed. The birth of the Internet came in 1983 with the adoption of the TCP/IP communication protocol that allowed dissimilar networks and computers to talk to each other. Moreover, the adoption of TCP/IP allowed for the exchange of messages across networks and the use of information resources on geographically distant computers.

In the early days of the Internet it was a "network of networks" used primarily by researchers and scientists in academia and government. It has since become a global network used for education, entertainment, communication, and commercial purposes. It is estimated that by the year 2000 there will be 120 million host computers on the Internet and 200 million users worldwide (Green, 1997). This astonishing number of Internet users is put in some perspective by the fact that it is estimated that the world population will be almost 6 billion by the year 2000 (Hager, 1998).

Gaining Access to the Internet

Computer Requirements

If you are not one of the 200 million people who already use the Internet, then there are a few basic requirements to join the global information exchange. The first is a computer. Almost all computers produced in recent years have adequate speed, RAM, hard disk space, and graphics capabilities to interface with the Internet and, more specifically, the graphically rich World Wide Web (Vaughan-Nichols, 1996). Computers' higher processing speed, RAM, sound cards and speakers, and higher resolution monitors are able to exchange and display information from the Internet faster and with higher levels of audio and video fidelity. See Chapter 2 for more information about basic computer hardware configurations.

Modems and Digital Adapters

The second piece of equipment needed to connect to the Internet is either a modem or an ISDN adapter. Three crucial factors in determining the speed with which one connects to the Internet are the speed of the modem connected to one's computer, the speed of the modem to which one connects, and the transmission medium through which the two computers communicate. There are now three basic types of modems, analog, cable, and ADSL. An analog modem is a device that transmits data from a computer over standard phone lines to another computer (Margolis, 1996). The speed of an analog modem is measured in kilobits per second (kbps). Modern analog modem speeds range from 28.8 kbps to 55 kbps. At present, analog modems are the most commonly used device for connecting to the Internet.

The second type of modem is a cable modem. Connection to the Internet via cable (as in cable television) is becoming available in many areas of the United States. The significant advantage of a cable modem is the high-speed access to the Internet it makes available. Cable modems can download files at speeds up to 30 mbps (megabytes per second) and send (upload) files to the Internet at speeds ranging from 300 kbps to 10 mbps (Spanbauer, 1997). The speed of a cable modem is approximately 50 times the speed of a 33.6 kbps analog modem (McGrath, 1998). A cable modem connected to a cable line is presently the fastest available means to connect to the Internet short of a T1 connection. T1 lines are extremely fast and expensive direct connections to the Internet. The pricing of cable connection to the Internet is expected to be highly competitive with other Internet connection options.

A third type of modem is the ADSL (also called DSL) modem. ADSL (asymmetric digital subscriber line) is an emerging telephone line transmission technology that increases the speed at which data travels over existing telephone lines (Internet.com, 1998). The downloading speed of ADSL is 1.5 to 9 mbps, which in layman's terms is "blazingly fast." The upload speed for ADSL is estimated at 16 to 640 kbps. In other words, ADSL offers a very fast means for surfing the Web and retrieving e-mail, data files, and software. Sending or uploading e-mail and other files from a personal computer to the Internet occurs at a far slower rate than does downloading. Another drawback of ADSL is that it is not currently widely available, and the price of the service is still not fixed across regions of the country.

The fourth option for Internet connection is an ISDN (integrated services digital network) terminal adapter connected to an ISDN line. The ISDN terminal adapter is either an external or internal device (a card installed in the computer) that exchanges information digitally across an ISDN with an Internet service provider. ISDN connections currently have a maximum upload and download speed of 128 kbps, which is more than double the speed of standard phone line/analog modem transmissions. Many urban, suburban, and some rural areas now have ISDN service available. The price of an ISDN line is becoming almost comparable to standard analog Internet service access.

A fifth means to access the Internet is from a computer connected to a local area network (LAN) or wide area network (WAN). This route of access requires the LAN or WAN to have a connection to the Internet. Connecting a computer to a LAN or WAN requires both an ethernet card and network software. An ethernet card allows a computer to exchange information with a network. Some agencies and organizations have networks with established Internet connections, thereby making it possible for employees to access the Internet from their office computer. Such an arrangement opens the vast information resources of the Internet to the service of agency clients.

It should be apparent from this discussion that connecting to the Internet requires information on the types of connection technologies available—telephone line, cable, ADSL, ISDN, or network. It also requires consideration of the cost of the various services and the speed with which one wishes to interact with the Internet. In general, higher connection speed is correlated with higher cost. At present, the most popular means of connecting to the Internet is over standard phone lines with an analog modem. It is likely that as cable connection to the Internet becomes more available, many users will shift to cable because of the high-speed and potentially low-cost Internet access.

Internet Service Providers

The third major consideration in connecting to the Internet is which Internet service provider to use. For a monthly fee, an ISP makes available access to the Internet. It is the modems and computers of an ISP that one's computer connects to in order to interact with the information resources of the Internet.

Internet users may decide to use a particular ISP simply because they received a CD-ROM in the mail offering Internet access. Other users will select a service because the icon of a particular ISP appears on their new computer's desktop screen when they turn it on for the first time. All that is required is to connect a phone line to the computer's modem, click on the ISP icon, and then provide billing information, and voila!, instant Internet access. The problem with either of these "convenient" methods of choosing an ISP is that the selected service may not offer the best available match of price, service features, access speed, and access availability. For instance, an ISP provider may offer the service feature of space on their Web server for personal Web pages, but have only 28.8 kbps connections available. Another ISP provider offers faster 56 kbps connection speed, but no space for a personal Web page. When selecting an ISP, it is therefore extremely important to consider what is the best match between one's Internet access needs and the service/price offering of the available ISP.

Factors to consider in selecting an ISP include (Grimes, 1997):

1. What is the monthly fee for the service?

2. How many hours of connect time are included? Most ISPs offer unlimited connection time.

3. Is there a start-up fee?

4. Is the ISP accessible with a local phone call? Some of the large nationwide ISPs do not offer local call access to remote areas. In such situations they offer a toll-free number to call to connect to their service. This toll-free connection often comes with an additional hourly connection time fee charged in addition to the monthly fee. In such remote locations, users are advised to check their phone books and local computer shops for the names and phone numbers of local ISPs offering service to the area.

5. Does the ISP offer ISDN service and at what cost?

6. Does the ISP's service fee include space on their server for personal Web pages? If so, how much space is offered? ISPs typically offer one to five megabytes.

7. What type of technical support is available from the ISP? How many hours per day is the service available and is weekend service included?

8. Do the local cable companies have cable Internet access available? If so, ask questions 1, 2, 3, 6, and 7.

9. Does the local phone company offer ADSL service? If so, ask questions 1, 2, 3, 6, and 7.

Table 9.1 lists the names, phone numbers, and Web addresses of some of the larger national ISPs in the United States. Additional information on ISPs is available at http://thelist.com and http://www.cis.ohio-state.edu/hypertext.faq/Usenet/pdial.faq.html (Rosen & Weil, 1997).

TABLE 9.1   A Partial Listing of Internet Service Providers

Name	Web Address	Phone Number
America Online	www.aol.com	800-827-6364
AT&T Worldnet	www.att.com	800-967-5363
CompuServe	www.compuserve.com	800-848-8990
Concentric Network	www.concentric.com	800-939-4262
Earthlink Network	www.earthlink.com	800-395-8425
GTE Internet Solutions	www.gte.net	800-363-8483
IBM Internet Connection	www.ibm.net	800-821-4612
Microsoft Network	www.msn.com	800-373-3676
Mindspring	www.mindspring.com	888-677-7464
Netcom	www.netcom.com	800-638-2661
Sprynet	www.sprynet.com	800-777-9638

Once access to the Internet is established, the question that arises is how does one employ the Internet in social service practice? To answer this question it is necessary to first know what tools are available on the Internet and how they are used. E-mail and the World Wide Web are the two most commonly recognized tools of the Internet. In the following discussion we will describe their application along with the use of FTP, Usenet, and Telnet.

E-Mail as a Tool of Practice

E-mail or electronic mail is fundamentally a means to transmit a message from one computer to another. E-mail enables computer users to exchange information within a building or across the planet. The sending and receipt of an e-mail message requires that both computers are at some point connected to a computer network or the Internet. Computers on a network can receive messages sent from computers on the Internet only if the network is connected to the Internet. Messages sent on the Internet travel across town and across the globe within minutes. It is little wonder that land-based mail delivery acquired the name "snail mail" not long after e-mail became commonly available.

An important attribute of e-mail communication is its asynchronicity, that is, communication is not dependent on the sender and recipient both being available to communicate simultaneously, as is the case in a phone call. E-mail messages are not commonly read and responded to immediately after they are sent. Instead, e-mail dialog may occur over a period of minutes or months. Unlike a phone call, recipients of e-mail are free to respond, or not, at their convenience. The asynchronous nature of e-mail communication makes it possible to consider the response to an e-mail before responding. Unfortunately, contemplation and careful composition of a considered response to an e-mail are not always hallmarks of electronic communication.

E-Mail Basics

In order to begin to use e-mail as a means of communication, one first needs a computer with an Internet connection. As described previously, Internet connections are aquired from ISPs. Part of the service an ISP offers is one or more e-mail accounts for each service subscription. This makes it possible for a family that has signed up for Internet service to allow each family member to have his or her own e-mail address. Each e-mail address is unique, making it possible for messages to find their way to their intended recipients. An e-mail address is composed of (a) the recipient's name or other identifying word or number, (b) an @ symbol, and (c) a domain name. The domain name is everything to the right of the @ symbol. For instance, in the e-mail address Random @ mmh.org, the domain name is mmh.org. The org in the address is called the *top domain* (McKenzie, 1996). Commonly used top domain letters are *org,* which stands for organization, *gov* for government, *com* for commercial enterprises, and *edu* for educational institutions. These letters are found at the end of e-mail addresses originating in the United States. Other countries around the world use two letters to indicate the country of origin, such as uk for the United Kingdom.

There is a common structure to all e-mail messages. There is the message header that contains the "To:" or "Mail To:" field, the "CC" field, and the "Subject." The "To" may contain one or more e-mail addresses, which are commonly separated by a comma. The "CC" field will hold one or more addresses to which a copy of the message is sent. The "Subject" field is available for information about the subject of the e-mail. It is both helpful and courteous to include some information in the subject field in order to let the recipient(s) know what the e-mail is about. Information in the subject field helps recipients decide on the priority of opening a piece of e-mail.

Beneath the message header is the body of the message, which holds the content of the e-mail. Some e-mail software has limits on the maximum size of the message, while others place no constraints on message size or allow the user to specify the maximum length. Extremely long messages may be sent as attachments, using only a brief message in the body to alert the recipient(s) to the presence of the attachment. Creation and use of attachments are described in a later section. Figure 9.1 displays an e-mail message with a completed message header, an attachment, and the message body. Note the toolbar beneath the menu bar. Clicking the Address button opens an address book in which e-mail addresses may be stored and from which they are selected and inserted into message headers. The Attach button opens a browse window that locates files to send as attachments to the message.

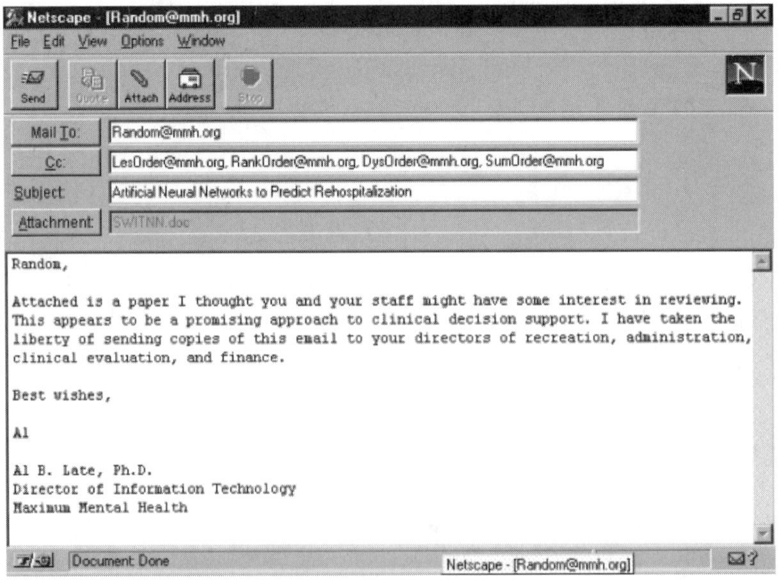

FIGURE 9.1   E-Mail Message Composed in Netscape Navigator Gold

E-Mail Software

As suggested by the preceding discussion, in addition to an e-mail account one needs e-mail software in order to interface with the ISP server. Some ISPs include e-mail software in the software they provide on subscription to their service. For instance, America Online and CompuServe, both of which provide a range of information resources along with Internet access, offer their own proprietary e-mail software (McCracken, 1997). Netscape's Navigator and Communicator Web browsers have e-mail software integrated into the browser software. Microsoft's Outlook Express is e-mail software that comes as part of Microsoft's Internet Explorer Web browser. The e-mail software in these two Web browsers is free with the browser, both of which are also currently free, and they contain a full range of features for handling e-mail. Other e-mail software packages include E-Mail Connection, Eudora Pro, Juno, and Pegasus (Levine, 1997). Reviewed next are some of the features to look for in selecting e-mail software.

FILTERS.   While composing and reading messages are the two most common functions of e-mail software, one feature included in some packages is filtering. Filters offer a variety of options for handling incoming and outgoing e-mail (Levine, 1997). Filters can be set to delete messages with certain subject headings or from specified sources, forward messages to another e-mail account, or place messages from certain individuals in a high-priority folder. In essence, filters are tools for aiding individuals to organize and control the flow of e-mail they receive. They are particularly useful if one receives a great deal of e-mail and needs to manage the flow.

ATTACHMENTS.   Another feature available in most e-mail software packages is attachment handling. An attachment is a file appended to an e-mail message. One of the great advantages of using attachments is the ability to send fully formatted documents, such as word processing documents with graphics, via e-mail. The formatting of the original document is retained when the recipient opens it—that is if the recipient has the type of software to open the document. Attaching a document to an e-mail message makes it possible to send not only word processing documents, but also graphics files, spreadsheets, databases, digital video files, and digitized audio. Just about any file that resides on a hard drive can be attached to an e-mail and a copy of it sent to one or more recipients.

This potential for the distribution of information is constrained by three factors: the size of the attached file, the recipient's e-mail software, and the recipient's application software with which to open the file. Depending on the Internet connection, extremely large files sent as attachments can take a great deal of time to send and receive. If you have to send extremely large files as attachments, it is best to compress them with compression software such as WinZip (http://www.winzip.com). The second consideration is whether the recipient's e-mail software supports the encoding standard of the received attachment. There are presently three encoding standards commonly used on the Internet, UUENCODE, MIME (or Base64), and BinHex. Encoding converts or encodes a formatted document into a text file in order for it to travel across the Internet. Upon receipt, it is decoded back to its original format. UUENCODE is the oldest encoding method of the three and is still used with some local area network e-mail systems. BinHex is commonly used with Apple Macintosh files. MIME (Multipart Internet Mail Extension) is rapidly becoming the standard for e-mail attachments. MIME attachments are recognized by most of the e-mail software packages named previously (Levine, 1997).

The third factor to consider when using an attachment is whether the recipient has the software to translate the file format of the attachment. For instance, depending on the version, someone who uses Corel WordPerfect may not be able to open a Microsoft Word file. It is often best to check with the recipient before sending an attached file to determine if they have the software that will open the file. Word processing documents can be saved as rich text format (RTF) files with the Save As command and then read by almost all widely available word processing programs. RTF can also be used to exchange word processing files between Macintosh and Windows machines.

In most e-mail software, attachments are appended to a message by clicking on an Attachment button in the software's toolbar. See Figure 9.1 for an example. Clicking the Attachment button opens a window in which to browse for files to attach to the e-mail. More than one file may be attached to an e-mail message.

STORAGE AND RETRIEVAL.   Most e-mail software makes possible the storage of messages in nested folders (Levine, 1997). The term *nested* is used here to refer to the creation of subtopic folders within a topic folder. For instance, one might have a folder for peer consultation and nested within that folder would be folders with the names of all the colleagues from whom one receives peer consultation. Each time an e-mail message is received from one of these peers, it would be saved to their folder, which is nested in the peer consultation folder. The creation of nested folders makes it possible to organize the saving of important e-mail messages and to quickly find messages when needed.

Retrieval of messages in e-mail software can be facilitated by the search or find functions it offers. There are times when it is useful to search all the e-mail one has retained to find either a particular message, a message from a specific individual, or all messages received on a given date. E-mail software packages vary in the range and type of searches they will perform. For example, Figure 9.2 displays the Find Message dialog box from Microsoft Outlook Express. Note the fact that the From, Sent to, Subject, and Message body fields make it possible to search for (a) messages from particular people, (b) messages previously sent to others, (c) messages with a particular subject heading, and (d) messages containing specified text. For instance, if one wanted to review all e-mail sent to a supervisor, entering the supervisor's name or e-mail address in the Sent to field would return a list of all messages e-mailed to the supervisor. Searches of the message body of all e-mail is a useful feature in locating all e-mail containing information about a particular topic. Note also that searches may be restricted by a range of dates defined under Received.

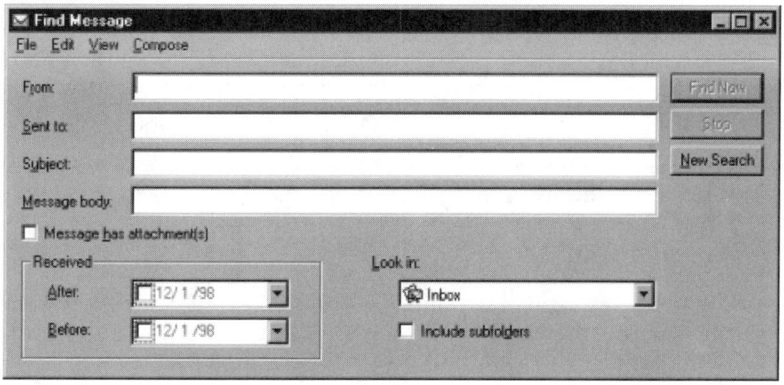

FIGURE 9.2   Find Message Dialog Window in Microsoft Outlook Express

ADDRESS BOOKS.   The address book of an e-mail software package is a small database containing e-mail addresses and other information on individuals with whom one exchanges e-mail. Figure 9.3 displays the Microsoft Outlook Express address book data entry form. Many e-mail software packages make it possible to add addresses to the address book simply by clicking or double-clicking on an address. This saves having to

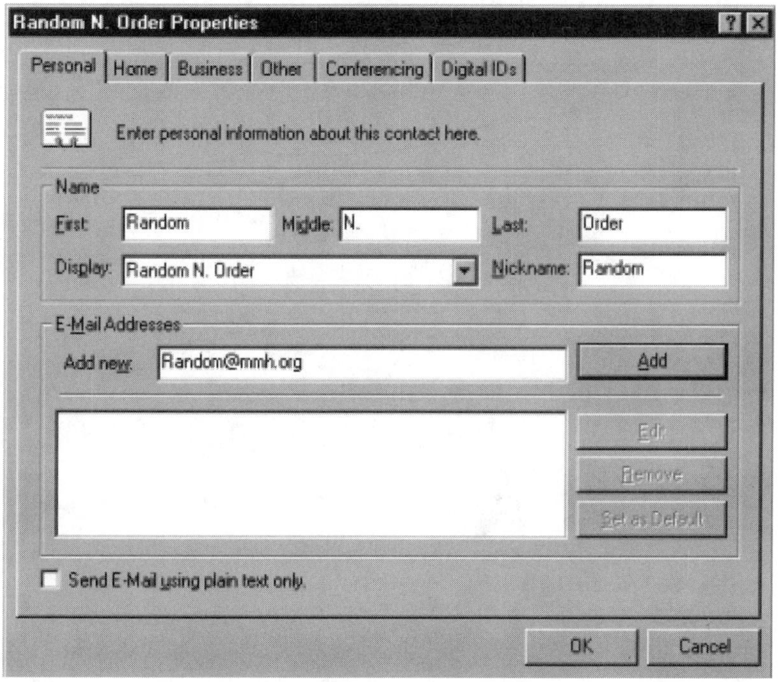

FIGURE 9.3   Microsoft Outlook Express's Address Book Data Entry Form

either type an address or copy and paste it into the address book. When composing a message, one can open the address book and select each e-mail address from one or more individuals in the address book to whom to send the e-mail. Most address books make it possible to create and save lists of addresses (distribution lists) so that a message can be sent to every address in the list by putting the distribution list's name in the To field. This saves considerable time and effort in sending messages to multiple recipients.

ACCESSING E-MAIL. To facilitate the exchange of e-mail between computers across the Internet, most e-mail software packages now use SMTP (Simple Mail Transfer Protocol) and POP3 (Point of Presence) protocols. The SMTP protocol controls the receipt by the ISP's mail server of outgoing mail and the POP3 protocol controls the handling of incoming mail. When configuring e-mail software to interact with the ISP mail server, it is often necessary to specify this information. Figure 9.4 shows a dialog window from Netscape Navigator Gold in which the names of the SMTP and POP3 servers are added. In essence, this information tells the e-mail software how to route outgoing messages to the ISP's server and where to look to find incoming e-mail.

The dialog window in Figure 9.4 also contains a field labeled POP3 User Name in which the e-mail account owner's user name is specified. In the field below that, the

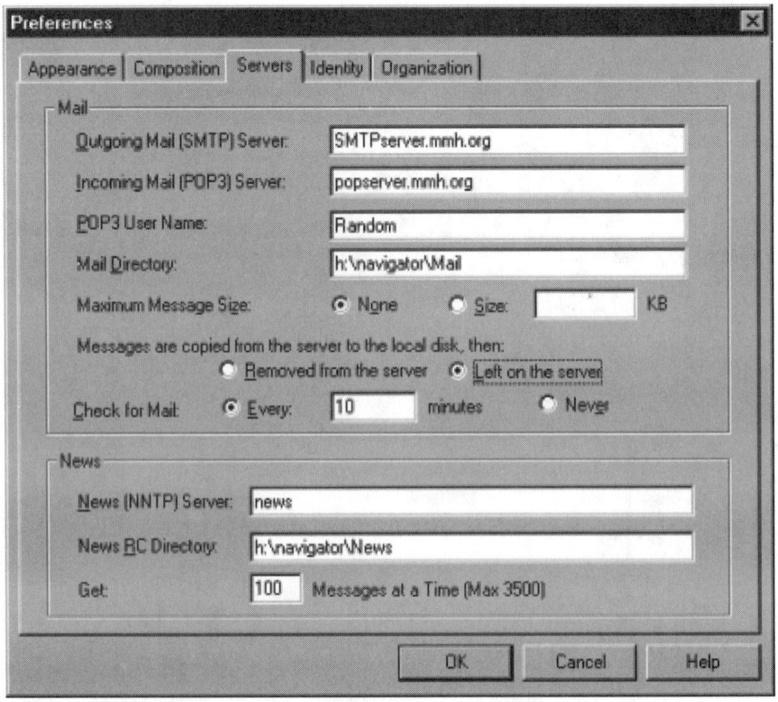

FIGURE 9.4 Netscape Navigator Gold's Server Dialog Window

location on the computer for storage of e-mail files is defined. Maximum message size is designated also in this dialog window.

The next choice, "Messages are copied from the server to the local disk, then:", is only available from some ISPs. Basically, the choice is to download a copy of all new messages from the ISP's server and leave a copy of all messages on the ISP's server each time one checks for e-mail messages or to download all new messages each time without leaving a copy on the ISP's server. As inconsequential as this decision may initially seem, it is actually rather important for a couple of reasons. Before describing these two reasons it should be pointed out that some ISPs do not allow users to keep e-mail messages on their server. In this case one must select the choice to "Remove from the server." If, however, the ISP makes available space for storage of messages on their server, then at least two advantages are gained. First, many people want to access their e-mail from more than one computer. Some people have the option to check their e-mail from both work and home. If e-mail is removed from the server whenever it is accessed, messages checked at work will be downloaded on the work machine and messages checked at home are downloaded to the home computer. This results in the messages on the work machine being unavailable from home and vice versa. This situation becomes particularly problematic if personal messages are downloaded to one's work machine or work messages are downloaded to one's home computer. This problem is a nonissue if a copy of every message stays on the ISP's server. Both the home and work computers download the same new messages, making all incoming e-mail available on both machines. Retaining copies of e-mail on the ISP's server acts as a back-up copy of e-mail correspondence should a hard drive crash and result in the loss of important messages.

Communicating with Clients

As a tool of practice, e-mail makes it possible to communicate with the full spectrum of individuals and groups one might exchange information with in most practice settings. Of course, the clients served in some practice settings may not have access to e-mail in their homes due to poverty or geographic isolation. Some clients can gain access to e-mail through community libraries with World Wide Web access. Many Web sites now offer free e-mail. A partial listing of Web sites offering free e-mail is available at http://www.csw.utk.edu/resources/misc.htm#email. In communities where libraries offer Web access, clients can sign up for free e-mail accounts and use the account to communicate with their social service worker and others.

Upon first consideration, this may seem to be a less than useful idea for many clients of social service agencies. Indeed, for some clients with significant physical and emotional impairments, travel to the community library and use of its computer system may be beyond the realm of possibility. Alternatively, in a society in which there is an increasing focus on the use of technology, individuals who do not acquire at least some minimal level of proficiency with the use of technology are likely to feel increasingly marginalized by society. This perception of technological marginalization compounds the experience of social isolation common to many individuals served by social service agencies because of economic disadvantage, physical limitation, or emotional disturbance.

Encouraging and assisting clients in getting e-mail accounts and learning to use the Web offers a number of therapeutic opportunities. First, if they cannot afford a computer and phone line, the very act of traveling to a library can offer the benefits of increased opportunities for socialization and exercise. Second, acquiring the skills necessary to log on to the Web, find their e-mail accounts, and read and respond to messages holds the potential for increasing their sense of self-efficacy and reducing the perception of technological marginalization. Third, for some clients, corresponding through e-mail may offer a greater sense of freedom to express ideas, feelings, and concerns that they might not give voice to in the confines of a social service agency office. Advocacy for a client using e-mail as a means of occasional or augmented communication with a social service worker should be considered within the context of the client's therapeutic or service provision goals. Ethical considerations regarding this practice are addressed in Chapter 10.

Communicating with Peers

E-mail makes it possible to solicit and receive the consultation, advice, and feedback of peers, or even supervision within an agency, across town, or from the far reaches of the planet. E-mail dramatically expands the potential for the exchange of information and ideas among peers. Given the nature of e-mail interaction, it is possible to pose a question or problem situation to a peer or a group of peers. Group peer consultation may be organized so each e-mail and subsequent response is delivered to all group members. This type of e-mail group peer consultation is unconstrained by geographic proximity and by the temporal imperative of synchronous communication. Answers to questions posed to a group may unfold in an iterative dialog between members. Myrick and Sabella (1995) describe a sense of comfort that arises in e-mail group consultation based on the experience of electronic proximity of assistance. Moreover, the authors report that unlike face to face communications, written thoughts and ideas shared via e-mail can be preserved for further review and consideration.

A natural extension of e-mail communication with peers is its application in the production of collaborative documents. The development of collaborative documents such as grant proposals or agency policy manuals is described in Chapter 7. For the purpose of this discussion, the term *collaborative document* refers to an electronically based document, such as a word processor file, that is shared between two or more people. While collaborative documents may be shared with the exchange of diskettes or other storage media, they are more efficiently distributed via e-mail over local networks or the Internet. Collaborative documents are commonly distributed as attachments in order to preserve the formatting of the document. Most e-mail software packages make it possible to compose a single message, address the e-mail to multiple recipients, attach a collaborative document, and then send it.

E-mail collaboration on a document may take several forms. One option is to send it to one person at a time. Each person makes a contribution to the document and then sends it back to the originator of the document. The document originator then sends it on to the next person in the work group who makes their suggested revisions and returns it to the document originator. Alternatively, the document can be e-mailed to everyone in the work group with the request that all proposed changes should be sent back to the originator, who coordinates the editing of the document and distribution of subsequent versions. Perhaps the most chaotic and ill-advised form of e-mail–based collaborative document development is for each person in the work group to mail their revisions of an originally distributed document to everyone on the mail list. This ill-fated process fosters the dissemination of multiple documents without the coordination of revisions into a single document.

Whatever procedure is followed in an e-mail–facilitated work group, it is important to make sure in advance that each member has an e-mail address and that each member has the requisite software and computer skills necessary to open the attached document. One option to consider in developing a collaborative document is to create and save it as an HTML file. Each of the three word processing programs reviewed in Chapter 7 makes it possible to create and save documents as HTML files. Netscape Communicator also has an HTML editor for the creation and saving of collaborative documents. There are three clear advantages inherent in using HTML as the file format for collaborative documents. First, HTML is a file format that can be viewed with any Web browser and readily edited with the three word processors discussed or Netscape Communicator. This common access and editing capability increases the ease of collaboration. Second, working with an HTML document increases the skill and experience of the work group members in using HTML. As a result, it advances the work group's ability to produce documents and content that can be distributed on the Web. The third advantage of using HTML format in collaborative documents is that, when appropriate, they can be posted on the Internet or on an agency's intranet. Stated differently, it is easier and faster to edit, modify, and subsequently publish on the Web a collaborative document originally developed in HTML compared to converting a word processor document into HTML, especially a graphically rich document.

Mailing Lists

A mailing list, which is often referred to as a listserv, is an e-mail distribution system that sends any message to everyone who has joined the list (McKenzie, 1996). All responses to received messages are sent to everyone subscribing to the mailing list. This distribution of messages produces an ongoing dialog among the members of the mailing list. Mailing lists are commonly organized around a particular topic or common group interest. The topics of mailing lists of professional interest to social service workers include a general social work discussion list, health care reform, psychosocial issues in HIV-AIDS patient care, child abuse, domestic violence, criminal justice, homelessness, employee assistance, computers in human services, international social work, and feminism. Web sites with information on mailing lists related to social service practice are available at http://www.sc.edu/swan/listserv.html and http://www.colostate.edu/depts/socwork/lists.html. A list of mailing lists available to the general public can be found at http://www.neosoft.com/internet.paml. To search for mailing lists related to specific topics use the search engine at http://www.liszt.com.

Subscribing to a mailing list related to a particular area of social service practice interest makes available the opinions, experience, and expertise of the entire list (Giffords, 1998). Berman (1996) studied two social work mailing lists, ABUSE-L and SOCWORK, and noted three forms of communication. He found dissemination of information, information requests, and issue discussion. Mailing lists may be particularly useful to social service practitioners in (a) agencies with limited supervision and training opportunities, (b) remote locations, or (c) for practitioners working in highly specialized fields of practice where there are limited opportunities to dialog with others facing the challenges of the specialized field.

To subscribe to a mailing list send an e-mail to the computer program that serves the mailing list. For instance, the listserv for the social work mailing lists is majordomo @uwrf.edu. The name of the social work mailing list is SOCWORK. To subscribe to this list one would send an e-mail to majordomo@uwrf.edu with the Subject heading of the message blank. When subscribing to a list, the first line of the message contains the following message: SUBSCRIBE LISTNAME *your first name your last name*. So in order to subscribe to the social work mailing list, the first line of the message would read: SUBSCRIBE SOCWORK Random Order.

Figure 9.5 shows an example of a mailing list subscription message. Future correspondence with the list should be sent to the actual mailing list address. In this case, the address for SOCWORK is currently SOCWORK@uwrf.edu.

Soon after subscribing to most mailing lists, an e-mail will arrive informing you that your subscription to the list was successful and detailing the rules and computer

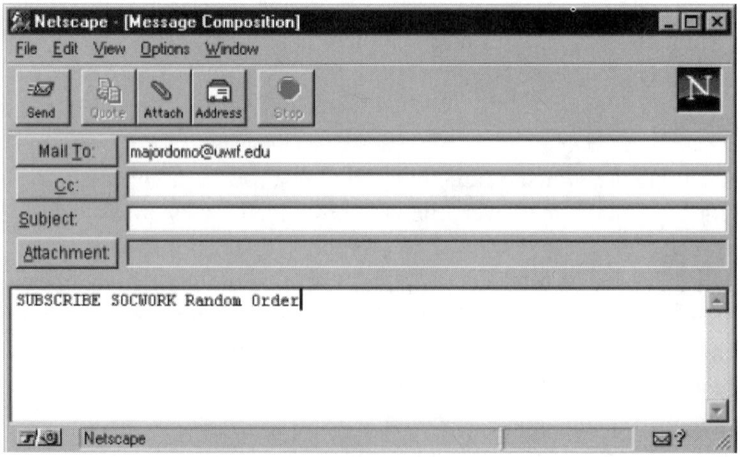

FIGURE 9.5   Mailing List Subscription Message

commands of the list. This message often contains a listing of commands for the list-serv, including how to unsubscribe to the list. It is important to save and retain this message. It is not uncommon to decide after being on a list for a while that the interest of the group is not compatible with one's own interest. Some mailing lists generate a great deal of e-mail and can rapidly overwhelm a subscriber with the sheer volume of the mail. It is therefore important to know how to unsubscribe from such a list.

After subscribing to a mailing list, there are a number of factors to consider in interacting with the list. Before sending a posting (e-mail) to the list, it is generally wise to spend some time reading the e-mail generated from the list to gain some idea of the tone and contents of the discussions (Spanbauer, 1998). This process of coming up to speed with the list may be facilitated if the list has available a frequently asked questions (FAQ) file. Check the instructions that arrive after joining the list for information on FAQs or the e-mail address of the list moderator (if there is one) who may be able to direct you to a FAQ file.

When sending questions or comments to the list, carefully consider the contents of the Subject line (maranGraphics, 1996). Many mailing list readers make decisions about what mail they will read from the list based on the information in the subject line. Subject line messages like "Read This" and "FYI" are more likely to be deleted without being read than very specific subject headings like "A Recent Substance Abuse Treatment Finding."

Each e-mail message from a mailing list will come with the address of the mailing list and the address of the individual who sent the message to the list. To send a reply to all the participants on the mailing list, use the reply command of your e-mail software. There are times when one may wish to reply privately to someone who has posted a message to a mailing list. To do this, copy and paste the individual's e-mail address into the To field of the e-mail composition tool of one's e-mail software. Make sure that the private reply is not addressed to the entire mailing list. Many a mailing list subscriber has been profoundly embarrassed by posting an intended private message to the entire mailing list.

Electronic junk mail is called *spam* and is in no way related to a canned meat product. It is not uncommon for spammers (persons who send spam) to sign on to multiple mailing lists and use e-mail address collecting programs to retrieve the e-mail addresses of individuals sending e-mail to the list (Spanbauer, 1998). These addresses are then used by the spammer to send junk e-mail or sold to other spammers who may send a stream of highly undesirable or unwanted e-mail. Fear of being spammed need not be a deterrent to joining a mailing list. E-mail filters on e-mail software, described previously, are one way to eliminate spam. Another alternative is to change the return e-mail address and signature file used by one's e-mail software to confound e-mail address collecting programs. For instance, changing the address Random@mmh.org to Random at mmh dot org would provide the spammer's e-mail address collection program with an unusable address. Most human correspondents would readily know how to translate the altered address into a usable one. Alternatively, one could use RandomDELETETHIS@mmh.com. Figure 9.6 displays the dialog window in Netscape Navigator Gold in which a faux e-mail address is inserted.

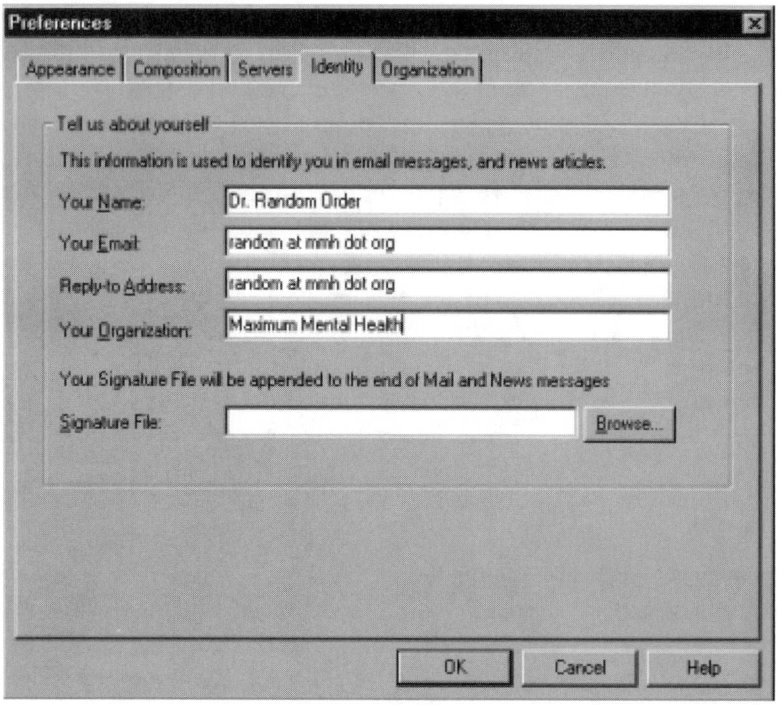

FIGURE 9.6   Dialog Window from Netscape Navigator Gold with a Faux E-Mail Address to Thwart Spammers

E-Mail Etiquette

E-mail is a social interaction and, like most forms of social interaction, it is shaped by certain implicit and explicit rules that define proper interaction. The implicit rules are difficult to articulate and are often specific to the group with which one is communicating. E-mail exchanges between colleagues in a work setting may be governed by a different set of implicit rules than communications between a group of friends or on a mailing list. The following suggestions (rules if you wish) are distilled from several sources (Krol, 1992; McKenzie, 1996; Rivard, 1997; Rodrigues, 1997). Some of them merely reflect common courtesy while others are fairly specific to e-mail communication.

1. Do not type in capital letters. It is considered yelling.

2. Be careful with both humor and sarcasm in e-mail. In face to face communications there is much more nonverbal information with which to support the good intentions of gentle humor and light sarcasm. This nonverbal information is missing in e-mail. The sender's intended humor and sarcasm often leads to misunderstandings and ill will.

3. Before sending a message, be sure to reread it to ensure that it communicates what you intend to communicate.

4. When sending messages to mailing lists, keep the message concise and to the point. Long-winded and tangential messages are likely to irritate readers and may provoke heated responses.

5. If you receive an e-mail intended for someone else, either reply to the sender that you are not the intended recipient or forward it to the intended recipient if you happened to know the address. This is not an uncommon occurrence in cyberspace. It is impolite to read any more of the message than you need to to determine it was not intended for you.

6. Remember that any e-mail you send may be fowarded to one or more people. Carefully consider this fact when composing any message.

7. A corollary of number 6 is, never say anything in an e-mail message that you would not want to become publicly known. Even deleted messages can be retrieved and disseminated.

8. Do not engage in flaming. *Flaming* is online argument that escalates to the exchange of insults. It is not uncommon to encounter flaming on mailing lists. In some cases flaming may constitute defamation of character and could result in litigation. The best thing to do is to ignore the inflammatory comments of others and focus one's comments on the central point of the ongoing discussion. If there is a moderator of the mailing list, one can send a private message of complaint about the flaming to the moderator. The moderator has the power to warn and, if necessary, remove flamers from the mailing list.

In summary, this section on e-mail as a tool of practice describes both its utility and key features. The basics of e-mail addresses and message composition are reviewed. The features of e-mail software discussed here include filters, attachments, storage and retrieval, and address books. We have examined how to access e-mail and its use in communicating with clients and peers. Also described here is how to sign on to and interact with mailing lists. Finally, some rules of e-mail etiquette are offered in the hope of forestalling preventable problems in the exchange of e-mail.

The World Wide Web as a Tool of Practice

The sixth-century BC Chinese mystical philosopher Lao-tzu said of the Tao, which is understood to be the creative energy that orders the universe, "The Tao that can be named is not the true Tao." Likewise, it is safe to say that the Web that can be named is not the true Web. Attempting to describe the World Wide Web is a bit like trying to describe global weather. Global weather displays multiple manifestations across the planet as the interconnected unfolding of the interaction between the earth's surface and its atmosphere. In other words, the Web, like the weather, is an extremely complex system that is in a continual process of becoming. Weather, like the Web, is not static. Both are dynamic systems, which may be described in increasing levels of detail, but as dynamic systems they have changed by the time an attempted description is articulated. Even in mystical states, Lao-tzu may never have envisioned the World Wide Web, but his perception of the ultimate indescribability of the Tao can inform our approach to using the Web as a tool of practice. In essence, we must concede in advance the fact that the Web offers virtually limitless potential as a tool of practice and then begin to articulate those opportunities that are most apparent at this juncture.

Moving from the metaphysical to the pragmatic, we turn our consideration to the role of the World Wide Web in social service practice. Two basic functions of the Web are evident: the acquisition of information and the dissemination of information. Acquisition of information includes finding information to inform practice, capturing it, and evaluating its validity/utility. Dissemination of information refers to the publication of information on the Web. Chapters 7 and 8 describe how to create Web pages for the purpose of presenting information on the Web. Further applications of Web publishing in social service practice are described in this chapter. But first we will turn our attention to how to find information relevant to social service practice on the Web.

Information in Support of Social Service Practice

The continuum of resources on the Web related to social service practice is vast and growing. There are resources for almost every conceivable field of social service practice. Any attempt to find and list within a book all available resources would likely soon be eclipsed by the emergence of new Web sites. There are several sites maintained on the Web that strive to provide up-to-date listings of resources for social service practice. Table 9.2 con-

TABLE 9.2   Web Social Services Resources and Information Directories

Web Page Title	Web Address
World Wide Web Resources for Social Workers	http://www.EDU/socialwork/wwwrsw
Krannert Memorial Library University of Indianapolis: Social Work Resources	http://www.uindy.edu/~kml/resources/socialwork/index.html
The University of Tennessee College of Social Work: Resource Categories	http://www.csw.utk.edu/swbookm2.htm
The George Warren Brown School of Social Work: Social Work and Social Services Web Sites	http://gwbweb.wustl.edu/websites.html
The New Social Worker: Web Sites of Interest to Social Workers	http://www.socialworker.com/websites.htm
CTI Social Work on the Web	http://www.soton.ac.uk/~chst/webconn.htm
American Public Human Services Association: Web Sites of Related Interest	http://www.aphsa.org/sites.html
American Library Association: Gateways to Social Work/Welfare on the Net	http://www.ala.org/acrl/resmar98.html
PRAXIS: Resources for Social and Economic Development	http://www.ssw.upenn.edu/~restes/praxis.html

tains a partial listing of Web sites with links to social service information and resources on the Web.

Most of the Web sites listed in Table 9.2 are directories of topic areas in social service practice. Listed under each topic area are one or more Web sites related to the topic. One advantage of using a Web directory to locate information is that one does not have to cull through numerous sites to locate information of interest. Conversely, in using a directory, one is limited to the resources listed by the Web site owner. As a result, relevant Web sites not identified or deemed irrelevant or inappropriate by the Web site owner are not listed. Therefore, relying solely on a Web directory to find resources and information leaves one vulnerable to the research diligence and editorial whims of the Web site owner. This drawback is at least partially mitigated by checking multiple directory sites. Taken together, the Web sites listed in Table 9.2 provide broad coverage of a wide range of topics germane to social service practice.

Effective Searching: Learning to Sip from a Fire Hose

There are times when it is necessary and more efficient to locate information on the Web with one or more Web-based search engines instead of using directories. *Search engines* are computer programs that have two primary components. The first is the gatherer (or robot, bot, spider, crawler), which automatically collects URLs (Uniform Resource Locator) from Web servers across the Web (Lennon, 1997). The URL is the Internet address of a Web site or other resource on the Internet. Gatherers build indexes of URLs and related information. The second component of a search engine is the inference engine. The inference engine attempts to match a user's request for information with the contents of the index created by the gatherer. Sometimes the inference engine has to match only a single search term or word to the index, while other searches require the matching of some combination of terms or a phrase.

There are numerous search engines to choose from on the Web. Some search engines like Yahoo and Infoseek arrange information in directories that are searchable. Other search engines such as AltaVista, Excite, and HotBot perform broad searches of the Internet. Some Web search sites use combined searches or metasearches in which the search terms are distributed to multiple search engines. Metacrawler and Dogpile are two metasearch engines. Table 9.3 lists a number of Web search sites along with their URLs and distinguishing features (University of Virginia, 1997, McCracken, 1998; Tweney, 1996).

The quality and usefulness of the information returned in using a Web search engine is dependent both on the search and categorization procedures of the search engine and equally on the search strategies of the user. It is often helpful to experiment with a variety of search engines until one finds one or two that seem easy to use and productive in their search results. Different search engines produce different results. After selecting one or two search engines, spend time learning to use their advanced search features. These features generally produce more refined searches and reduce the time spent looking through Web sites that are not germane to the object of one's search.

TABLE 9.3   Web Search Sites

Web Search Site	URL	Distinguishing Feature
AltaVista	http://www.alta-vista.com	Broad and fast searches. Search for audiovisual files.
Cyber 411	http://www.cyber411.com	Metasearch site
DejaNews	http://www.dejanews.com	Searches Usenet Newsgroups
Dogpile	http://www.dogpile.com	Metasearch site
Excite	http://www.excite.com	Broad and fast searches
HotBot	http://www.hotbot.com	Newsgroup and fast web searches
Inference Find	http://www.infind.com	Removes duplicates and categorized findings
Infoseek	http://www.infoseek.com	Broad searches and large directory
Lycos	http://www.lycos.com	Directory and search engine. Searches for images.
TeKCenter 35 Search Engines	http://www.tekcenter.com/search/ www/wwwsearch.htm	Metasearch site

The old saying of computing, "Garbage in, garbage out," is very applicable to conducting a search. A number of search strategies that will improve the likelihood of running a successful search of the Web are in the following list (University of Virginia, 1997; McCracken, 1998; Rodrigues, 1997; Tweney, 1996):

1. The directory Web search sites are often a good first stop when seeking information that is not highly specific. Looking in relevant categories may produce sites with the required information. Sometimes the browsing required with this strategy can be more time consuming than simply going to a search engine and entering specific terms.

2. Be as specific as possible in the selection of terms, keywords, or phrases. The terms *cannabis* or *marijuana* will produce more specific information than the phrase *substance abuse*.

3. The use of quotation marks or parentheses around a name or phrase will link the words in the search and will search sites containing that name or phrase.

4. Learn to conduct searches with Boolean operators. Named for George Boole, a nineteenth-century mathematician, Boolean operators are used to connect search terms (keywords) in order to expand or constrain the parameters of a search. The three Boolean operators are AND, OR, and NOT. Note that Boolean operators are generally capitalized. The operator AND links terms and finds sites that contain both terms. Cannabis AND "substance abuse" will limit the search to sites that use both of the terms. Some search engines allow the use of the symbols "+" or "&" in place of AND. The operator OR expands the search to find all sites with *either* term. Cannabis OR marijuana will return every site with either term. The operator NOT limits a search by linking a term to search for with a term to exclude.

"Substance abuse" NOT cannabis will find those sites with only substance abuse and filter out sites that contain both terms. Be sure to check the Help section of the search engine to determine if that particular site has a different protocol for conducting searches.

5. Prepare a list of synonyms for search terms. Using synonyms increases the likelihood of finding useful information. Most word processors now have a thesaurus for generating a list of synonyms.

6. Bookmark sites that appear promising, then move on with the search. Once the search is complete, return to the bookmarked sites for a more in-depth review of the information.

7. When reviewing a Web page for a specific term, use the <Ctrl-F> or Find command to quickly search the page for the term.

8. If one search engine is not producing results, move on to another. Although it is helpful to learn one or two search engines well, it is bad to be wed to only one or two engines.

Capturing Information and Keeping It Electronic

Once the information sought in a Web search is found, there are several options available to acquire and save the information. Printing the page is an option, but perhaps the least desirable. As discussed in previous chapters, printing ends the fluidity of electronic information. Once a Web page is printed out, use of the information or images on the page in other electronic documents is constrained by the necessity to either type the text into the new document or scan text and images to convert them back into electronic form.

Alternatively, Web pages may be saved as HTML files, viewable with a Web browser, or as text files (txt) that do not display graphics. To save a Web page in either file format option, use the File, Save As command in the browser's menu bar. Both of these options are useful ways to capture the information on a Web page for later review and citation in a document. Quotes from the saved Web page can be copied and pasted directly into word processing documents or slide show presentations. Likewise, many images and graphics on the Web can be captured and saved on a hard drive by right-clicking on the images and using the Save command in the pop-up window. With the permission of the artist, these images and graphics may be used in word processing documents or slide show presentations.

It is extremely important to recognize that the copyright to any material on the Web is retained by its author or creator unless otherwise specified. Issues of copyright are discussed in the next chapter. For present purposes, it is necessary to point out that the most prudent action to take before using any material from the Web, be it text, images, sound, databases, or video, is to e-mail or write the Web page's author and request permission to use the material (Malm, 1996a). Because of the noncommercial nature of most social service practice settings, it may be useful to explain, in requesting permission to use Web material, the nonprofit status (if this is the case) of the organization and how the material will be used, in what setting, and for how long.

Despite the constraints of copyright, the Web still represents a vast source of information to support social service practice. Information abstracted from reliable Web sites can be used to develop client information materials, guide the development of service delivery, provide content for staff training slide shows and materials, and stay abreast of governmental policies, rules, and laws. The validity of information found on the Web should always be scrutinized before using it (Rodrigues, 1997). This requires critical thinking and discernment. What is the source of the information? Is it from a university-based Web site or a known and respected news source? Are reference sources or materials listed? How old is the information or when was the Web site last modified? Is the Web site citing information from other sources or was the information generated by the site's author? If the author is citing other sources, is the information consistent or supported by other sources? If the author is responsible for generating the information on the site, what are his/her qualifications? Is the information coming from a commercial source with a vested interest in shaping the "facts" to the business's advantage? There is a great deal of information available on the Web, much of it is of questionable validity. Readers are cautioned to carefully critique any information from the Web before applying it in social service practice.

Web Publishing of Social Service Practice Information

The Web offers vast potential to both social service agencies and independent practitioners as a medium for providing information to clients, contributors, and other constituents. Some of these possibilities are discussed in Chapters 7 and 8, including home pages to provide information about an agency or practice, the use of Web pages to publish reports, the creation of pages to advertise services or special events, and the dissemination of training materials as Web pages.

Additional applications of Web pages in social service practice include:

1. Displaying street maps with directions to the agency
2. Publication of a complete listing of agency services and hours of operation
3. Showing pictures of the agency's building, location, or interior. Clients may feel more comfortable about coming to an agency if they have some advance idea of what the place looks like.
4. Providing a listing of related community resources
5. Making available client education information such as effective parenting skills
6. Publishing agency policies, rules, or procedures for staff and clients
7. Publishing brief self-assessment instruments to aid potential clients in determining if they could benefit from the agency's services. Checklists and self-assessment instruments that potential clients can take and score themselves may help clients determine if they should seek treatment.

8. Listing times and locations of support groups in the area

9. Listing links to resources on the Web related to the agency's mission

10. Providing an e-mail address to the agency for questions, comments, and suggestions

Each of these listed applications may be created with the word processing tools described in Chapter 7 or with the presentation software introduced in Chapter 8. Readers may wish to use other software with additional tools for the creation and editing of Web pages. Netscape Communicator has a composing tool for the creation of Web pages (http://www.netscape.com). Microsoft FrontPage Express is a free Web page authoring software package available at http://www.microsoft.com. Adobe Pagemill, Microsoft FrontPage, and Corel Web.SiteBuilder are standalone, full-featured software packages for the development of Web pages.

It is important to appreciate the fact that creation of basic Web pages does not necessarily require learning HTML code or Java scripting language. Java is a programming language created by Sun Microsystems. A Java applet is a small program such as a clock or calculator that operates within a Web page (Goodwin & Hammond, 1998). Java applets, animated graphics, and images may be downloaded from the Web and inserted into a page opened in a Web page editing program (Kirkly, 1996). Each Web page shown in this text was produced with software described in this book and did not require writing any raw HTML or Java code. Instead, various tools in the software's toolbar were used for formatting text, inserting objects (images/graphics and Java applets), creating tables, providing links to other documents, producing tables, and defining page colors.

Web pages created in word processing programs, with presentation software, or with Web page authoring packages can be enhanced with the addition of animated graphics and Java applets. There are numerous sites on the Web that offer free animated graphics, Web page templates, HTML tutorials, and Java applets, as well as other tools for augmenting the appearance and functionality of a Web page. Perhaps the best way to locate resources for adding animation, graphics, or functionality to a Web page is to use a search engine to locate Web sites with the required graphics or tools. For example, using the term "animated GIF" in a search engine will produce numerous sites offering animated graphics files. Before downloading any file, be sure to review the site to see if there are any stated restrictions on the use of the files available on the site.

Developing and maintaining a Web page is an iterative and ongoing process. It is important to examine a Web page with a Web browser to ensure that it looks as it should after formatting and adding text, graphics, and other objects along with creating links. Many Web editing software packages offer the option to launch the computer's designated Web browsing software in order to view the page on a browser. Doing this allows the Web page author to see how the page will appear once it is on the Web. This is useful because sometimes differences between the appearance of the page in the Web page editor and the Web browser become apparent and necessary changes to the page can then be made.

Once a Web page is complete, the page along with any associated files must be placed on a Web server. As described in Chapter 7, it is important to contact one's ISP for the details of how to transfer an electronic folder containing the Web page and associated fields to the ISP's server. Many Web page authoring/editing software packages have a Publish to the Web option that allows one to specify in a dialog window the address of the ISP's server and a requisite user name and password. Once this is done, the software uploads the folder or Web page to the ISP's server. After the file is uploaded to the ISP's server, it is important to use a Web browser to make sure the Web page is actually being published to the Web by the ISP's server.

Web pages are updated by opening the page in the Web authoring/editing software and adding or removing material. Once changes are made in the Web page, it can be reloaded to the ISP's server, replacing the prior version of the page. The frequency with which updates are made is dependent both on the content and purpose of the page as well as the time and energy one has for maintaining a page.

This section presents an overview of the creation and use of Web publishing for social service practice. What is important to appreciate is that Web pages are highly flexible and potentially very dynamic tools for the dissemination of a wide range of information in social service practice settings. The development and publication of Web pages need not be left to professional Web masters, although their services may at times be required. The potential applications of Web pages as tools of practice are evolving and should continue to do so as social service practitioners explore new ways to serve clients and constituents through the Web.

Other Internet Tools

E-mail and the World Wide Web are probably the two most commonly used tools on the Internet and as such are most germane to this discussion. There are, however, several other tools of the Internet that have varying levels of application to social service practice. These tools include FTP, Usenet, and chat rooms. Historically, these tools have required separate software that interfaced with the Internet. Increasingly, Web browsers have integrated the disparate functions of these tools into the browser's interface. Each of these Internet tools is described in the following sections.

FTP

File transfer protocol defines the rules by which files are transferred across the Internet (Hogarth & Hutchinson, 1996). It was originally developed prior to the advent of the World Wide Web and was used to transfer files between computers. FTP software is used to log on to computers on the Internet and then either upload or download files. Web browsers now make the downloading of files from a Web site transparent to the user. Once a file is located, all the user has to do is click on the desired file and then specify where on their hard drive to store the file. Uploading of files to computers on the Internet still requires FTP software. FTP software is commonly used to upload files and folders to ISPs' Web servers.

The essential functions of FTP software are to log on to a computer on the Internet and facilitate the uploading and downloading of files. To accomplish this, the Internet computer must either allow anonymous login or the user must have an account on the Internet computer. Some Internet computers (FTP servers) allow public access using "anonymous" as the login name and one's e-mail address as the password. Increasingly, FTP servers are simply making their files available on the Web and displaying their file directories as Web pages. Individuals and organizations using ISP Web servers to publish their Web pages are given accounts and passwords with which to log on to the ISP's Web server. FTP software makes it possible to log on to an ISP's Web server (assuming one has an account) and move files and folders between a personal computer and the ISP's Web server.

FTP software is commercially available and may be found on shareware sites on the Web. Figure 9.7 displays the login window of WS_FTP shareware. Note on the screen that the user must specify the address of the Internet computer (Host name) and the user's ID and password. This information is required to publish a Web page on an ISP's Web server.

After logging on to a server, FTP software typically displays a directory of the files of the local machine (one's personal computer) and a directory of files on the server (remote system). Some FTP software has "drag and drop" file copying which makes it possible to simply click on a file on one machine and drag it onto the other machine. Figure 9.8 shows WS_FTP's File Transfer Window with the directories of the local system and the remote system displayed. Files are transferred by clicking on a file in either directory and using a directional arrow to initiate the uploading or downloading of the file or folder.

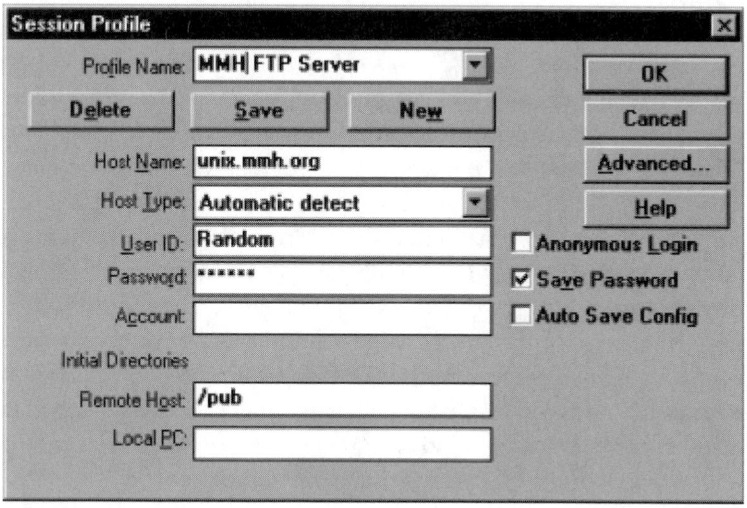

FIGURE 9.7   WS_FTP's Login Window

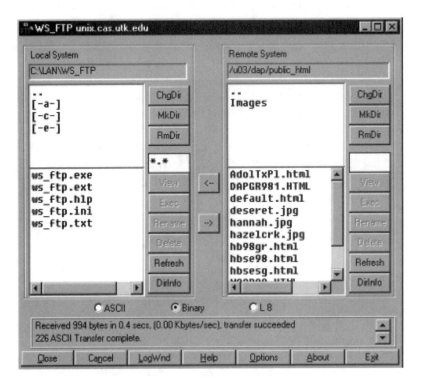

FIGURE 9.8   WS_FTP's File Transfer Window

Usenet Discussion Groups

Usenet is a large collection of discussion groups on the Internet (McKenzie, 1996; Rosen & Weil, 1997). There are tens of thousands of these groups and their topics cover an extremely broad and diverse range of subjects (Rivard, 1997). These discussion groups are commonly referred to as newsgroups. They operate like an electronic bulletin board on which members post messages and newsgroup members subsequently respond to them. The exchanges in newsgroups range from the trivial and inane to the profound. Giffords (1998) has suggested that newsgroups represent an important source of self-help support and information on the Internet. For instance, there are newsgroups devoted to supporting individuals with panic and anxiety disorders, sexual abuse recovery, depression, and a range of medical conditions. Figure 9.9 displays a selection of postings on a newsgroup devoted to supporting people with seasonal affective disorder. Moreover, there are newsgroups with discussions focused on professional issues related to practice and policy matters. These newsgroups can be an important source of information for professionals working in remote areas or in practice settings where there are limited opportunities for peer consultation and support.

There are a number of ways to find newsgroups and postings related to specific topic areas. Many search engines now will search the Usenet for postings related to a

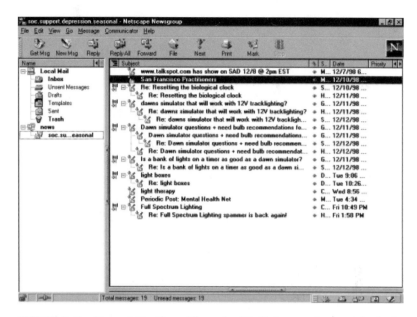

FIGURE 9.9   Usenet Postings Viewed with Netscape Communicator's Newsgroup Reader

specified topic and return messages in which the topic was discussed. Additionally, several search engines, including www.dejanews.com, www.altavista.com, and www.yahoo.com, allow users to browse newsgroups by topic. There is an annotated list of newsgroups available from Oxford University at http://www.lib.ox.ac.uk/internet/news (Hogarth & Hutchinson, 1996).

Messages on Usenet must be read with either a standalone newsreader or with the newsreader integrated into a Web browser. Both Microsoft's Internet Explorer and Netscape's Navigator and Communicator browsers have newsreaders as components. The discussion topics shown in Figure 9.9 are displayed with Netscape Communicator's Newsgroup reader. Notice the groups of messages that are linked together in descending order. These are referred to as *threads* and represent messages in response to a topic. The display of threads makes it possible for a reader to follow the flow or thread of the discussion. Standalone newsreaders that do not display topic threads show only the sequential listing of messages. This makes it difficult to track the responses to a specific topic.

As a final word of caution, it is important to recognize that the quality of information on newsgroups can vary widely. Some newsgroups are moderated. In those cases, the moderator serves as the newsgroup's editor, deciding to post messages that are appropriate and germane to the discussion, while rejecting messages deemed inappropriate or off-topic (Hogarth & Hutchinson, 1996). Most newsgroups do not have moderators. Participants are free to post their thoughts and opinions, which may be unconstrained by the facts of the matter. Any information found on newsgroups should be carefully considered for its validity and usefulness before being passed along in any type practice setting.

Chats: Real Time Interaction

Chats are live dialogs conducted over the Internet. Sometimes referred to as Internet Relay Chat (IRC), chats are a very popular feature of the Internet as they provide the opportunity to have real time dialog with one or more individuals (Malm, 1996b). These chat sessions are commonly Web based so participants can read and respond to the discussion through their Web browsers. There is a wide array of chat topics available on the Internet, including discussions on health, entertainment, politics, business, and social matters (Rivard, 1997). The numerous venues for chats cross the spectrum of Web sites, including commercial enterprises like www.cnn.com, organizations such as National Public Radio (www.npr.org), academic chats with course-specific focus, and chats conducted by health care and social service practitioners from private Web pages. As is the case with newsgroups, chats by topics are listed on several search engines, including Altavista and Yahoo.

The utility of chats as a tool of social service practice remains in question. Giffords (1998) describes the use of chats as a means of online support for people with lupus. Levenson (1997) reports that some social workers have begun to offer individual and group therapy through the use of chat technology. She goes on to raise the concern that using chat technology in counseling deprives the therapist of important visual information, including affect and body language. Levenson reports that some experts have concerns about the security of confidential information exchanged, especially in online groups. Research on the efficacy of chat group psychotherapy or the utility of chats in providing self-help support is yet to be produced. It is likely that many people derive information, support, and comfort from self-help chat groups. There may be associated risks, however, such as compulsive interaction with virtual groups to the detriment of other relationships or victimization from predatory group members. Prudence suggests that practitioners carefully review the most recent research literature on chat groups before embarking on the delivery of individual or group counseling via chat technology. Any recommendation of a specific chat support group should be accompanied with cautions about not revealing personal information or agreeing to meet any chat group member outside the virtual interaction of the chat room.

Summary

This chapter provided a brief review of some of the uses of Internet resources in social service practice as described in the professional literature. It offered a brief history of the Internet and information necessary for gaining access to the Internet was provided. This chapter discussed the basic tools of e-mail, including e-mail software, filters, attachments, address books, storage and retrieval, and remote access to e-mail. The use of e-mail as a tool to communicate with client and peers was described. A discussion of mailing lists was offered as well as guidelines for e-mail etiquette. In the discussion of the Web as a tool of practice, sites for finding social service information on the Web were listed. Strategies for conducting Web searches were offered in addition to a partial listing of Web search engines. Issues of copyright and critical assessment of the quality of information from the Web were addressed, and a listing of ideas for potential social service Web pages was provided. Finally, the chapter described several other Internet tools, including FTP, Usenet, and chats.

Exercises

1. With a group of peers, discuss how you have used e-mail in ways related to social service practice. Have you used it to communicate with clients, peers, supervisors, or other constituents of your practice setting? What problems or benefits have you experienced? What are the ethical considerations in the use of e-mail in social service practice? If you or some of your peers do not have e-mail, discuss what have been the impediments to your getting and using e-mail.

2. With a group of peers, decide on a topic of mutual interest related to the provision of social services. Independent of each other, conduct a search of the Web for information pertaining to the agreed on topic. Come back together and compare the results of your various searches. What search strategies proved most effective? Assess the quality of the information located during the searches.

3. Select an idea for a Web page from the list of applications of Web pages in social service practice. Use either word processing software or presentation software to develop a Web page that produces one of these ideas. Experiment with using graphics and Java applets from the Web to enhance the page.

4. With a group of peers, discuss your experiences in interacting with Usenet newsgroups or in chat rooms. What benefits have you found? What problems have you encountered? Were there issues or concerns about security? How useful was the information or advice you received from a newsgroup or in a chat room?

chapter 10

Ethical Applications of Information Technology in Social Service Practice

This chapter discusses the range of ethical issues posed by the use of IT in social service practice. It addresses (a) the implications of providing informed consent when providing services with IT, (b) the procedures for maintaining client confidentiality in the storage and transmission of electronic information, (c) the ethical parameters in the use of software and other IT resources, and (d) the issues involved in the use of intellectual property.

The application of personal computers to social service practice is occurring in a changing social and cultural context. Information technologies are increasingly being woven into the fabric of occupational activities and social relations. Concomitantly, some experts see a growing bifurcation of society into one group with both the resources and skills to acquire and use IT and a second group of citizens who have neither access to IT nor the training to use it (Weinbach, 1996). As described throughout this text, opportunities to improve services to clients, many of whom are among the IT alienated, are created by the growing power and capacity of personal computers in concert with networks and other information technologies. Utilization of information technologies in the service of human needs requires both an ethical framework and its conscious utilization in a range of practice circumstances in which IT is being applied.

The ethical considerations applicable to the use of information technology in social service practice settings are broad. Issues include the provision of informed consent, the necessity of protecting confidential information, the ethical use of software and other IT resources, and the appropriate use of intellectual property. Professional ethical standards provide a framework to guide professional practice in these matters. The following discussion is informed by the Code of Ethics of the National Association of Social Workers (NASW). The standards referred to are likely consistent with the ethical values of other allied social service professions. The purpose of this chapter is to:

1. Maximize practitioners' capacity to provide the informed consent of clients by detailing the risks and possible solutions associated with the provision of services via IT

2. Offer specific guidance in maximizing the protection of client confidentiality as it pertains to the storage and transmission of electronic information

3. Delineate ethical parameters in the use of software and other IT resources

4. Specify principles in the use of intellectual property.

Informed Consent

The purpose of informed consent is to ensure that clients understand the purpose of services, their rights, associated risks, costs, and alternatives. The NASW Code of Ethics (NASW, 1997) in section 1.03e makes specific reference to the responsibility service providers have to inform clients of the limitations and risks associated with services provided via computers and other electronic media, including telephone, radio, and television. The risks and limitations of the services provided by the latter three media are beyond the purview of this discussion. Regarding services provided via computers, the code is less than specific. There are a number of domains in which computers have been employed to provide services. These include but are not limited to computer-based treatment delivery (Rosen & Weil, 1997), computer-based assessment (Nurius & Hudson, 1993), and computer-mediated communication, including e-mail and chats as described in Chapter 9 of this text. Each of these domains of computer-mediated service delivery has limitations and some level of associated risk.

Computer-Based Treatment Delivery Programs

Although not previously addressed nor recommended in this text, computer-based treatment delivery refers to computer programs that provide treatment services, usually in the form of counseling. These programs commonly use a set of rules and "if, then" statements to produce responses to a client's typed remarks. Rosen & Weil's (1997) research suggests that under certain circumstances computer-based treatment delivery programs can perform adequately with some clients, but it is not sufficiently robust to remove the need for face to face treatment. These types of programs have been under development for over thirty years, but have yet to receive widespread acceptance or application in social service settings. Computer-based treatment delivery programs have been developed for specific types of therapy (Selim, Klein, Greist, Johnson, & Harris, 1982). For a more complete review of this topic, see Gould (1996). Two clear limitations of this form of counseling are (a) the program's responses are uninformed by both the visual and expressive information reflecting client mood, affect, and reaction and (b) the likelihood that the program is not sufficiently robust to respond to the range of psychosocial problems typically encountered in clinical practice settings. Given these limitations and the associated risks of inadequate and ineffective treatment, therapists have an ethical responsibility to carefully investigate the research supporting any computer-based treatment delivery program they might consider employing in a practice setting. Moreover, they have a duty to inform clients of the results of their investigations regarding the limitations and risks of the program the client might be asked to use as an adjunct or replacement for traditional face to face therapy.

Computer-Based Assessment

For the purposes of this discussion, computer-based assessment refers to computer administered and scored standardized questionnaires that do not require extensive professional training to use or interpret (Bloom, Fischer, & Orme, 1999). In other words, computer-based assessment as it is used here does not refer to computer-based psychological assessment, which lies in the professional domain of psychologists (Rosen & Weil, 1997). Hudson's (www.spspac.com/~walmyr) Computer Assisted Assessment Package (CAAP) is one example of a computer-based assessment program.

The ethical imperative of informed consent in computer-based assessment is to provide clients with information about the purpose of the assessment, its potential benefits, and costs to the client (Bloom, Fischer, & Orme, 1999). The costs may include any charges for the assessment along with the time and energy required from the client to complete the assessment. Although the energy required to complete a questionnaire is difficult to quantify, it can be a function of the ease with which a client can read and interact with the questionnaire items on the computer screen. Complex screens and instructions as well as difficult to read items and unclear response procedures may require considerable time and energy. In this sense, it is ethically incumbent on a social service practitioner to be familiar with any computer-based assessment questionnaire before asking a client to use them. Such familiarity allows the practitioner to provide clients with valid information about the limitations or risks (e.g., fatigue) associated with using the computer-based assessment.

Computer-Mediated Communications

The term computer-mediated communications as it is used here refers to e-mail, chats, and Internet video conferencing. The emerging technology of Internet video conferencing allows for two-way audio/video communications through personal computers equipped with a camera, video capture card, microphone and sound board, modem or Ethernet connection, and the necessary software (Lauriston, 1998). There are not presently documented applications of Internet video conferencing in social service practice. It is included in this discussion because with increasing access to high-speed Internet connections, it is likely that some practitioners will soon begin to experiment with this as an alternative to face to face service provision. Internet video conferencing, along with e-mail and chats, poses ethical dilemmas in both the realm of informed consent and confidentiality. Issues of confidentiality are addressed in the next section. For now we will concern ourselves with informed consent.

What are the limitations and risks of computer-mediated communications of which clients should be informed? Beyond the risk of a breach of confidentiality, there is first a question of how to provide informed consent. Levenson (1997) points out that clinicians offering online counseling face at least two problems in providing informed consent. First, the common use on a Web page of informed consent that a client clicks before starting counseling does not provide an opportunity for the client to ask questions and seek clarification about the risks and limitations of computer-mediated counseling. Second, the use of an online consent form offers no way to verify the age of the client. Proceeding with online counseling with a minor abrogates the parent's right to consent to treatment for the minor and places the practitioner at legal risk.

Aside from issues of confidentiality, perhaps the greatest limitation and potential risk of computer-mediated communication in the provision of social services is that the interaction is impoverished by a lack of visual and auditory information. Seeing a client provides information about affect, mood, body language, and reactions to the interaction. The emotion or lack thereof in what clients say can reveal a great deal about their emotional state. The pace or speed of what a client is saying as well as the presence or absence of pressure in his or her speech can convey significant clinical meaning. Often, how a client says something is almost as important as what is said. This rich body of visual and auditory information is lost in computer-mediated communications. At present, Internet video conferencing is a poor alternative to face to face communications. The quality of audio and visual information received in Internet video conferencing is insufficient for a clinician to detect much of the subtlety of verbal and nonverbal behavior commonly apparent in face to face communications. Practitioners choosing to use e-mail, chat technologies, and Internet video conferencing offer a service impaired by the medium. The risks created by computer-mediated communications include, but are not limited to, insufficient information for assessment and diagnosis, impaired ability to provide accurate feedback, an exchange constrained by the practitioner's and client's ability to express themselves in writing (except in the case of Internet video conferencing), and threats to confidentiality secondary to interception or retrieval of therapeutic exchanges. As such, practitioners bear an ethical responsibility to inform clients of the limitations of computer-mediated communications and convey to clients the possible risks.

Protecting Confidentiality

A fundamental ethical value in social service practice is the protection of client confidentiality. Several sections of the NASW Code of Ethics (NASW, 1997) make explicit reference to the protection of confidentiality related to the electronic storage and transmission of information. Other sections address the protection of confidentiality in settings and circumstances that have implications to applied information technology. These implicit and explicit responsibilities are detailed in the following sections, along with suggested IT procedures to guard confidentiality.

Electronic Storage of Information

Section 1.07l of the NASW Code of Ethics makes specific reference to the responsibility to protect confidentiality of electronic records by storing them in a secure location. Based on this ethical responsibility, two questions arise. First, in the domain of information technology, what is a secure location? Second, how is it achieved and maintained?

The answer to the first question will be addressed here from the perspective of a single personal computer user, as that is the focus of this text. There are, of course, broader data security issues in social service agencies in the domain of agency administrators and those responsible for information technology management. The ethical imperative of storing confidential electronic records in a secure location has two purposes. The first is preventing the unauthorized access to confidential information. The second, a more subtle way of understanding this section of the Code of Ethics, is recognizing that security must also protect against data loss.

PROTECTION AGAINST UNAUTHORIZED ACCESS.   The first strategy for protecting electronic records from unauthorized access is to password protect sensitive documents. One option is to password protect access to the computer on which the sensitive information is stored. One approach to doing this is to create password protection in the BIOS setup program (Lane, 1998a). The BIOS setup program is the built-in software that the computer accesses first, before starting the operating system (e.g., Windows 98). Creating a BIOS password means that the correct password must be provided before the computer will start up. This protects against anyone tampering with or copying files from the hard drive. BIOS setup programs differ from PC to PC, so check with the computer's original documentation or call the manufacturer's help desk to find out how to access the BIOS setup program.

Another alternative, somewhat less secure, is to password protect any file with confidential information on it. Each of the word processing, spreadsheet, and database programs described in this text has the capacity to password protect the contents of the document so it cannot be opened without the proper password. Password protection is generally enabled through the Save As command. Typically, the user enters the password and then reenters it in another field. This is done to ensure that the user has not made a mistake and typed the password incorrectly. When creating passwords for any purpose, there are a few rules to follow to increase the security the password provides (Lane, 1998b).

1. Avoid using real words. Programs designed to crack password protection often have dictionaries of real words that they insert one after another.

2. Avoid using names or other data from your life such as birth dates and family member names.

3. Do not use the same combination of letters and numbers for both a user login name and password.

4. Write down and store your passwords in a secret location away from your computer.

Most forms of password protection of files will not protect files from the skills of a world-class computer hacker, but most computer users seldom do anything interesting enough or potentially profitable enough to attract the attention of a world-class hacker. Security precautions need to be proportional to the threat. Littman (1998) argues that the greatest threat of data loss or breached security in organizations comes not from external hackers, but from disgruntled or troubled employees within an agency. It is therefore important to not share any passwords or file or network access with others in an agency unless they have a specific and legitimate need for access to the protected information.

PROTECTION AGAINST CONFIDENTIAL INFORMATION LOSS. Protecting confidential files from inadvertent loss or corruption requires the development of a procedure to back up files and the subsequent disciplined adherence to the procedure. Such a procedure usually means that confidential or important files are saved to another storage medium on a regular basis. Some software will automate this process and save specified files on a regularly scheduled basis. As described in Chapter 2, hard drives will and do fail. This means in order to preserve confidential information it is necessary to store the information on some other medium. Options for file back-up include storage of copies of files on a diskette, Zip drive disk or some other portable storage medium, tape drives, CD-R (compact disk recordable) or CD-RW (compact disk rewritable), or on a network file server. Each of these options offers a measure of protection against the loss of confidential files. Backing up files to a network file server can be a particularly useful strategy. Network administrators can create password protected directories for the storage of confidential files. It is important to make sure the network administrator has and follows a procedure to back up the server in case it fails. Many systems use a tape back-up system to protect against server failure. Whatever storage medium is used, the purpose of this effort is to assure that confidential information on clients is both secure and preserved. The length of time necessary to preserve such confidential information varies with both the nature of the services provided and agency policy.

Electronic Transmission of Information

Section 1.07m of the NASW Code of Ethics asserts the obligation to protect the confidentiality of information transmitted electronically. It makes specific reference to guarding the confidentiality of information through computer technology and e-mail. The code states, "Disclosure of identifying information should be avoided whenever possible" (NASW, 1997).

Compliance with this ethical obligation is most readily achieved by not communicating electronically about social service clients. This option may soon become a nonoption in many social service agencies as the use of the Internet to communicate between sites increases and the use of local area networks expands within agencies. E-mail makes it possible for supervisors and staff to communicate quickly and easily about clients. It is likely that its use to communicate about clients will expand rather than contract.

Given this possibility of increasing use of client-related e-mail, several options for maintaining confidentiality present themselves. One option is to agree upon a coding system to identify clients so that a client code is used in the e-mail instead of a name. For instance, in one university-based mental health clinic, social work interns send end of the week case summaries with coded client identifiers to their supervisors via e-mail. These summaries serve a dual purpose. They keep the supervisors up to date on client progress and provide a useful point of reference in weekly face to face supervision. The codes for identifying each client are known only by the intern and supervisor.

A second option is to use encryption software when communicating either with a client or about a client. Encryption software scrambles a message or file so that it cannot be read without a key. A key is a data file used to encrypt or decrypt a message or file. Some types of encryption software use 40-bit encryption keys while others use 128-bit keys and some encryption software packages use even larger keys. Forty-bit encryption keys may be broken by a determined hacker with significant computing resources, while 128-bit keys present a level of complexity that is not likely to be broken in this lifetime (Gibbs & Lasky, 1998). Again, the risk of a hacker devoting considerable amounts of time and energy to break the encryption key of a message sent in a social service agency seems improbable, but it is not beyond the realm of possibility.

Gibbs and Lasky (1998) suggest the safest procedure is for the sender and receiver both to have the same version of standalone encryption software such as PGP for Personal Privacy. PGP for Personal Privacy is available on the Web at www.nai.com. It uses an encryption procedure called public key/private key. Each user of the software is assigned a public key (an encrypting code) that the user may publicly distribute at the end of e-mail messages or post on a special Internet server. Each user also has a private key, known only to them, which decrypts messages encrypted by their public key. Therefore, when sending a message to someone whose public key you know, you use their public key to encrypt the message and the recipient uses their private key to decrypt the message in order to read it. This procedure provides a high level of security for protecting confidential client information or communications. With prior client authorization, this protocol may be the most secure means for sending confidential client information to third party payers such as managed care organizations.

Confidentiality Protection and Informed Consent Converge

The protection of confidentiality during the electronic transmission of information returns us to consideration of informed consent regarding the limitations and risks of providing services via electronic media. One of the risks of the use of unencrypted e-mail to communicate with clients is loss of confidentiality. This loss of confidentiality may occur at one of several points in the transmission of the e-mail. A social service worker sending e-mail from an agency to, for instance, a home-bound client, runs the risk of having the e-mail intercepted and read at several points in the transmission process. The agency's network administrator generally has access to all e-mail passing through the server. When a message moves from the agency's mail server to the ISP's mail server, the message is at risk of being read by someone in the ISP office. When the message moves from the agency's ISP to the client's ISP, it is again at risk of being read by individuals in the client's ISP office. Finally, there is a risk of the e-mail being read by someone in the client's home after the social services worker's message is downloaded to the client's computer. In all fairness it should be stated that given the shear volume of e-mail traveling through ISPs' servers, the probability of any message being intercepted and read is very low. The level of risk in an agency of an e-mail being read by a network administrator or of messages on a client's computer being read by someone other than the client is difficult to specify. Nonetheless, there is risk associated with this type of computer-mediated communication, and the NASW Code of Ethics states that the practitioner has a specific responsibility to inform clients of this risk. The level of risk connected to e-mail correspondence with clients may be dramatically reduced with the use of the encryption protocols described previously.

Chat room discussions, even if the participants are screened in advance and limited to participants in a group with a designated purpose, retain a higher level of risk due to the lack of encryption in the exchange of chat messages. Carol Lane, author of *Naked in Cyberspace,* has warned, "The cold, hard truth is that risk-proof chatting over the Net simply isn't available" (1998a, p. 132). Chat software providers warn of invasions of security and privacy, eavesdropping, harassment, fraud, and the breaking of passwords. Given these threats to confidentiality, social service providers are ill advised to use chat technologies to conduct group therapy or recommend the use of chat support groups unless there are substantial and dramatic improvements in their safety and security.

In summary, the ethical application of personal computers and information technology in the transmission and storage of client-related information requires the adoption of protocols to ensure confidentiality. The use of computer-based treatment delivery, computer-based assessment, and computer-mediated communication necessitates serious consideration of the range of limitations and risks associated with these activities. Once having investigated the limitations and risks of service provision via an electronic medium, social service practitioners have a responsibility to convey these limitations and risk to a client and obtain informed consent prior to the provision of services. In this discussion, online counseling through e-mail or chat technologies has come under particular scrutiny due to present inherent threats to confidentiality.

Ethical Use of Software and Other IT Resources

The ethical use of software and other IT resources, including computers, networks, Web pages, and the range of associated hardware, requires consideration of the potential problems and dilemmas faced in applying IT to social service practice. Social service practitioners who use illegal copies of software or who make improper use of agency IT resources are subject to legal, ethical, and organizational penalties and sanctions. Ethical and legal practice flows from a clear delineation of proper and improper behavior in the ownership and use of IT. This discussion is shaped by both the NASW Code of Ethics and relevant law. The purpose is to present the standard ethical and legal parameters for the use of software and IT resources.

Software Piracy

The unauthorized copying of software is commonly referred to as software piracy (Bowyer, 1996). The Software Publishers Association defines five categories of software piracy (SIIA, 1998).

1. Buying a single copy of a program and copying it to multiple computers or placing it on a file server

2. The copying, distribution, and/or sale of copies of a program that seem to be from legal and authorized source

3. Renting copies of software without obtaining the permission of the copyright owner. Most software is licensed for use by the purchaser, while the software creator retains the copyright.

4. The distribution and/or sale of software that has been separated or unbundled from its original bundled form

5. The downloading of copyrighted software from bulletin boards or the Internet without obtaining the permission of the copyright owner

Software piracy is an illegal act that carries fines up to $25,000 and a jail sentence of up to one year for willful copyright infringement (Bowyer, 1996). Individuals and organizations that make more than ten illegal copies of a copyrighted software title are subject to civil suit with awards up to $100,000 for each software title violation. Criminal penalties can be up to $250,000 and imprisonment up to five years for each title infringement. In addition to being an illegal act, software piracy may be construed as a violation of section 4.04 of the NASW Code of Ethics as software piracy constitutes the dishonest and fraudulent use of property one does not have license to use.

Clearly, software piracy is a nontrivial matter that deserves the careful attention of both social service practitioners and their agencies. To state the matter in the affirmative, social service practitioners are obliged to use only software they have purchased. Agencies are encouraged to take a proactive approach to assuring that they hold licenses to use all software on computers owned or operated by the agency. This upholds the rights of the software creators to profit from their efforts and that in turn encourages the creation of better software (Weckert & Adeney, 1997). It behooves any software user to carefully read the copyright and licensing information that comes with the software to understand the parameters of the licensing agreement. Moreover, ethical computing means not only understanding how one is permitted to use the software, but also what is prohibited by the licensing agreement. Application of these practices benefits not only the individual user or agency, but encourages the rule of law, upholding of professional ethics, and the protection of property rights.

Other IT Resources

Ethical computing extends beyond software to practices involved in the use of hardware and network resources. The following guidelines are drawn from the Computing Code Ethics of several universities (Boston University, 1998; Georgia State University, 1995; San Francisco State University, 1995; Western Kentucky University, 1995). They are intended to offer an ethical framework for computing in social service practice settings.

1. Users should not provide false or misleading information to gain access to computing resources.
2. Users have a responsibility to ensure that others do not use their passwords or accounts.
3. Users should not make or distribute any unauthorized copies of copyrighted software.
4. Users should not access or copy files in another's account without permission.
5. Responsible use of computing resources includes not sending or displaying offensive, harassing, threatening, libelous, or damaging information or files.
6. Users should not damage or disrupt the operation of computing or network resources.
7. Computing resources should not be used for unauthorized commercial purposes.
8. The use of agency computing resources for nonagency related activities should first be authorized by the responsible supervisor. In particular, agency e-mail systems should not be used for private correspondence unless so authorized by the agency.
9. Users should not distribute and display (on Web pages or elsewhere) the intellectual property of others without their compensation or expressed, written consent. (The concept of "fair use" may apply to the use of some copyrighted material. This concept is discussed in a later section.)
10. Responsible use of computing resources includes the reporting to responsible authorities any illegal or unethical use of computer or network resources.

Taken together, these guidelines offer both protection and a measure of security to the user, other users, and the agency or organization information infrastructure. The meaning and implications of some of these guidelines are self-evident. Some of these guidelines, however, require additional comment.

Adherence to Guideline 2 protects a user from others making inappropriate use of the user's computer identity or computer accounts. Letting someone use your computer identity is not unlike giving him or her your wallet and the key to your house. They then have access to the contents of your files and may use your identity when sending e-mail. This falls into the category of "A Remarkably Bad Idea."

Guideline 5 refers to "offensive information or files." What constitutes "offensive" is currently a matter of considerable debate in society. How then are social service practitioners to know if what they send through e-mail or display on the Web is offensive? For instance, how does one determine if sex education material intended for placement on the agency's Web page is offensive? There are no easy answers to this question. One possible solution is to ask a broad cross section of peers and supervisors if they find the material intended for distribution or display offensive. Simply asking a couple of close friends may not be sufficient to determine if the material in question meets a common understanding of "offensive," especially in an agency setting.

Guideline 8 is intended to address situations that arise when agency e-mail systems have access to the Internet. Some agencies make available only in-house e-mail systems that employees use to communicate with each other. Such systems do not have access to the Internet. However, other agencies make available to their employees access to the Internet and the Web. Problems can arise when employees use their agency e-mail address for private correspondence. The problems with this are usually related to employees spending work time sending and receiving personal correspondence. Not only is work time lost on personal correspondence, but agency servers may not be able to handle the volume of correspondence, especially if employees are signed on to numerous listservs or are receiving considerable amounts of spam. In agencies where Web access is available, one option is for employees to obtain e-mail accounts on Web sites offering free e-mail, as described in Chapter 9. Employees' private e-mail would go to the Web site and not cause congestion on the agency's mail server.

The rationale for Guideline 9 is detailed in the following section. Guideline 10 supports and upholds the responsibility that social service workers have to each other and to the community of the profession. Clearly, unethical and illegal computing harms both the agency in which it occurs and the professional community. If the application of information technology in the service of clients is to continue, the self-governance implicit in Guideline 10 is essential.

Use of Intellectual Property

The World Wide Web is filled with the intellectual property of people around the globe. Intellectual property is generally understood to mean products of the mind, including but not limited to text, images, graphics, music, video, and software (Gorman, 1988). Almost all of this material is protected by copyright law (Malm, 1996). Copyright protects a work from unauthorized use or reproduction. The extension of copyright protection both preserves the rights of the work's creator and encourages the creation of new works. Copyright is extended to a person who creates a work, unless the work was either commissioned by someone else or the work was produced as part of the individual's duties as an employee of a company. Intellectual property is considered to be covered by copyright law when it becomes "fixed in a tangible form of expression" (Malm, 1996, p. 688). In other words, the copyright starts when a work is recorded or produced in some fashion. Conversation, unless recorded or videotaped, is not copyrighted. A work need not be registered with the United States Copyright Office for it to be copyrighted. For more specific information on copyright law, visit the Copyright Office's Web page at http://lcweb.loc.gov/copyright/copy1.html.

As has been described throughout this text, the advent of digital technology has made it possible to both create and transform intellectual property into digital form. In digital form, intellectual property is readily transportable. It moves between computers on diskettes and other storage media. Intellectual property moves across the Internet in the form of software, data files, images, sounds, and videos. Each time we click on a Web page, we download someone's intellectual property.

The increased ease of flow of digital information comes with a heightened risk of copyright violation. Despite the ease with which intellectual property may be digitized (for example, running this page through a page scanner) or may be obtained in digital form, as in downloading it from the Web, the copyright ownership of the material does not change. The creator of any piece of intellectual property retains the rights to the use and distribution of the work. The creator may sell or give away the copyright to the work or may give permission for the work to be used by another in some specified manner. In this legal framework, the use of intellectual property without either the compensation or the permission of the owner is a violation of copyright law.

It is, of course, permissible and legal to visit Web sites and view their contents. That is why most of them exist. It is, however, a violation of copyright law to copy any part of the site and use, distribute, or sell its contents or underlying HTML code without either compensation or permission of the Web site owner. There are Web sites that make images, graphics, and other forms of intellectual property freely available for downloading. These sites can be a rich resource for creating Web pages, word processing documents, and slide show presentations applicable to a wide range of social service activities. The question that arises is whether the contents of these Web pages are owned by the Web site author who is publishing them. Carefully examine the documentation on any Web page to determine the ownership and any limitations placed on the use of the material being offered before downloading content from a Web site.

Public Domain Material

To complicate the problem even further, there is a considerable amount of content on the Web that exists in the public domain. The term *public domain* refers to work that is available to the public and not subject to copyright protection (Margolis, 1996). As such, digital material that is placed in the public domain may be freely used.

A search of the Web using the term "public domain" returns numerous Web sites with public domain content available. Again, it is prudent to read all available documentation to be sure the material offered as being in the public domain is in fact in the public domain. Additionally, some Web sites use the term "public domain" to draw visitors to the site in order to sell digital material or services. A quick review of such a site usually makes clear the Web author's intention and one may wish to simply move on to another site to find material truly in the public domain.

Fair Use

The prohibition against using copyrighted material without permission is not absolute. The rights of a copyright owner are limited by the "fair use" doctrine. Under the doctrine of fair use an author may be permitted to make limited use of portions of a pre-existing copyrighted work without the permission of that work's author. The fair use doctrine is designed to allow for the advancement of knowledge and was intended to support teaching, scholarship, criticism, commentary, research, and news reporting (Bowyer, 1996). It is difficult to specify exactly what qualifies as fair use as there are no fixed rules for its application (Malm, 1996a). The United States Copyright Office offers the following guidelines:

Four factors to be considered in determining whether or not a particular use is fair:

(1) the purpose and character of the use, including whether such use is of commercial nature or is for nonprofit educational purposes;

(2) the nature of the copyrighted work;

(3) the amount and substantiality of the portion used in relation to the copyrighted work as a whole; and

(4) the effect of the use upon the potential market for or value of the copyrighted work.

The distinction between fair use and infringement may be unclear and not easily defined. There is no specific number of words, lines, or notes that may safely be taken without permission. Acknowledging the source of the copyrighted material does not substitute for obtaining permission.

Copyright protects the particular way an author has expressed something; it does not extend to any ideas, systems, or factual information conveyed in the work. The safest course is always to get permission from the copyright owner before using copyrighted material. The Copyright Office cannot give this permission. When it is impracticable to obtain permission, use of copyrighted material should be avoided unless the doctrine of fair use would clearly apply to the situation. The Copyright Office can neither determine if a certain use may be considered fair nor advise on possible copyright violations. If there is any doubt, it is advisable to consult an attorney (Copyright Office, 1993).

The degree to which social service agencies and practitioners are covered by the "nonprofit educational purposes" guideline is dependent upon both the legal organizational status of the agency or practitioner and the purpose for which the copyrighted material is used. It is clear from the Copyright Office's guidelines that the most prudent course is to seek permission from a work's author and/or consult an attorney before using any copyrighted material without permission.

Summary

This chapter addressed the ethical issues of applying personal computers and information technology to social service practice. It discussed the responsibility to provide informed consent to clients about the limitations and risks associated with the use of computer-based treatment delivery programs, computer-based assessment, and computer-mediated communications. This chapter detailed the ethical implications of protecting confidentiality as it relates to the electronic storage and transmission of client information. Guidance was offered in relation to the ethical use of software and other IT resources with particular attention to software piracy and ethical computing within social service agencies. Finally, the chapter addressed the ethical and legal use of intellectual property and copyrighted material.

Exercises

1. With a group of peers, discuss your thoughts and beliefs about the necessity of providing informed consent when using computer-based treatment delivery, computer-based assessment, and computer-mediated communications. In your practice experience, have you seen any of these methods of service delivery used? Was informed consent sought and obtained?
2. With a group of peers, discuss your practice experience with the protection of confidentiality on electronically stored and transmitted information. How are client data protected in your practice setting? What precautions are taken to prevent data loss? What measures exist to protect confidentiality of electronically transmitted client information?
3. Conduct a search of the Web for available encryption software. What types are available? What do they cost and how do they work? Do they have potential for use in your practice setting?

4. With a group of peers, discuss the problems associated with software piracy and copyright infringement. Has any one in the group ever used pirated software? How, if at all, have their views on software piracy changed? How should practice settings protect themselves against software piracy and copyright infringement?

5. Review the ethical computing guidelines in this chapter. What would you add or take away from these guidelines? How comfortable are you with adhering to these guidelines?

References

Alter, C., & Evens, W. (1990). *Evaluating your practice: A guide to self-assessment.* New York: Springer.

American Psychological Association. (1994). *Publication manual of the American Psychological Association* (4th ed.). Washington, DC: author.

Andrews, D. (1998, January). DVD finally. *PC World,* 195–208.

Benbenishty, R. (1991). Monitoring practice on the agency level: An application in a residential care facility. *Research on Social Work Practice, 1*(4), 371–86.

Berman, Y. (1996). Discussion groups on the Internet as sources of information: The case of social work. *ASLIB Proceedings, 48*(2), 31–36.

Bloom, M., Fischer, J., & Orme, J. G. (1999). *Evaluating practice: Guidelines of the accountable professional* (2nd ed.). Boston: Allyn and Bacon.

Boston University. (1998). *Conditions of use and policy on computing ethics.* Retrieved from the World Wide Web: polymer.bu.edu/cpshelp/ethics.html.

Boyce, J. (1997). Simplifying and automating tasks. In T. F. Hayes (Ed.), *Special edition using Microsoft Office 97 Professional, Best Sellers Edition* (pp. 57–83). Indianapolis, IN: Que Corporation.

Boyce, J. (1997). Using outlines, templates, and styles. In T. F Hayes (Ed.), *Special edition using Microsoft Office 97 Professional, Best Sellers Edition* (pp. 85–107). Indianapolis, IN: Que Corporation.

Bowyer, K. W. (1996). *Ethics and computing: Living responsibly in a computerized world.* Los Alamitos, CA: IEEE Computer Society Press.

Caputo, R. K. (1988). *Management and information systems in human services: Implications for the distribution of authority and decision making.* New York: Haworth Press.

Cleveland, W. S., & McGill, R. (1984). Graphical perception: Theory, experimentation, and application to the development of graphical methods. *Journal of the American Statistical Association, 79,* 531–554.

Cohen, C. S., & Phillips, M. H. (1997). Building community: Principles for social work practice in housing settings. *Social Work, 42*(5), 471–480.

Cohen, J. (1977). *Statistical power analysis for the behavioral sciences.* New York: Academic Press.

Concise Columbia Encyclopedia. (1991). New York: Columbia University Press.

Copyright Office. (1993). Library of Congress. Washington, DC. Retrieved from the World Wide Web: http://lcweb.loc.gov/copyright/fls/fl102.htm.

Drew, C. J., & Hardman, M. L. (1985). *Designing and conducting behavioral research.* New York: Pergamon Press.

Eddy, S. (1997). *Mastering Lotus SmartSuite 97 for Windows 95.* San Francisco: Sybex.

FamilyPC. (1998, January). *Backing up your computer.* Ziff-Davis. Retrieved from the World Wide Web: www.zdnet.com/familypc/content/9712/survival/backup_index.html.

Finn, J. (1996). Computer-based self-help groups: On-line recovery for addicts. *Computers in Human Services, 13*(1), 21–41.

Fuller, S. (1997). Generating reports. In T. F. Hayes (Ed.), *Special edition using Microsoft Office 97 Professional, Best Sellers Edition* (pp. 657–688). Indianapolis, IN: Que Corporation.

Fuller, S., & Pagan, K. (1997). Access quick start guide. In T. F. Hayes (Ed.), *Special edition using Microsoft Office 97 Professional, Best Sellers Edition* (pp. 583–590). Indianapolis, IN: Que Corporation.

Furger, R. (1997, September). What a pain! The first six months of owning a PC. *PC World,* 189–198.

Georgia State University. (1995). *Computer ethics policy.* Retrieved from the World Wide Web: www.gsu.edu/welcome/policy.html.

Gerstman, K. L. (1996). Influence of director's attitude and involvement with agency computer use. *Computers in Human Services, 13*(3), 37–55.

Gibbs, M., & Lasky, M. S. (1998, September). The defenders: The best cookie killers, spam stoppers, email encryptors, and a full lockbox of other security essentials. *PC World,* 140–158.

Giffords, E. D. (1998). Social work on the Internet: An introduction. *Social Work, 43*(3), 243–251.

Gilgen, R. (1997). PowerPoint quick start guide. In T. F. Hayes (Ed.), *Special edition using Microsoft Office 97 Professional, Best Sellers Edition* (pp. 475–488). Indianapolis, IN: Que Corporation.

Glastonbury, B. (1997). *Dreams and realities: Information technology in the human services.* Helsinki, Finland: Stakes.

Goldman, H. H., Skodol, A. E., & Lave, T. R. (1992). Revising axis V for DSM-IV: A review of measures of social functioning. *American Journal of Psychiatry, 149,* 1148–1156.

Goodwin, M., & Hammond, S. (1998, April). Painless web pages. *PC World,* 139–154.

Gorman, R. A. (1998, May–June). Intellectual property: The rights of faculty as creators and users. *Academe,* 14–18.

Gould, R. L. (1996). The use of computers in therapy. In T. Trabin (Ed.), *The computerization of behavioral healthcare: How to enhance clinical practice, management, and communications.* San Francisco: Jossey-Bass.

Green, J. (1997). *The new age of communications.* New York: Henry Holt.

Grimes, B. (1997, February). Best routes to the net: Top internet service providers. *PC World,* 125–140.

Hager, M. (1998, November 2). How "demographic fatigue" will defuse the population bomb. *Newsweek,* 12.

Halfhill, T. R. (1998, February). Disposable PCs. *Byte* 62–74.

Hartman, A. (1978). Diagrammatic assessment of family relationships. *Social Casework, 59,* 465–476.

Henry, G. T. (1998). Graphing data. In L. Bickman & D. J. Rog (Eds.). *Handbook of applied social research methods.* Thousand Oaks, CA: Sage.

Hogarth, M., & Hutchinson, D. (1996). *An Internet guide for the health professional.* Davis, CA: New Wind Publications.

Holmes, N. (1984). *Designer's guide to creating charts and diagrams.* New York: Watson-Guptill.

Holsinger, E. (1997, July). CD-Rewritable drives record and erase. *PC World,* 152.

Howard, M. D. (1995). From oral tradition to computerization: A case study of a social work department. In J. Rafferty, J. Steyaert, & D. Colombi (Eds.), *Human services in the information age* (pp. 203–219). London: The Haworth Press.

Howe, D. (1999). *Free on-line dictionary of computing.* Retrieved from the World Wide Web: http://wombat.doc.ic.ac.uk/foldoc/index.html.

Hudson, W. W. (1996). *Computer assisted social services.* Tempe, AZ: WALMYR Publishing Co.

Hudson, W. W., & McMurtry, S. L. (1997). Comprehensive assessment in social work practice. *Research on Social Work Practice, 7*(1), 79–98.

IBM. (1995). *ThinkPad 701C/701CS user's guide.* Portsmouth, England: International Business Machine Corporation.

Intel Corporation. (1999). *Press kits: Desktops.* Retrieved from the World Wide Web: http://www.intel.com/pressroom/kits/processors/desktop.htm.

Internet.com. (1997). *PC webopaedia.* Retrieved from the World Wide Web: http://www.pcwebopedia.com.

Internet.com. (1998). *PC webopaedia.* Retrieved from the World Wide Web: http://www.pcwebopedia.com.

James, V., & Jansen, E. (1998). *Netlingo: The Internet language dictionary.* Retrieved from the World Wide Web: http://www.netlingo.com.

Janzen, F. V., & Lewis, R. E. (1990). Spreadsheet analysis in human services. *Computer literacy in human services, 6*(1–3), 51–67.

Jarvenpaa, S. L., & Dickson, G. W. (1988). Graphics and managerial decision making: Research based guidelines. *Communications of the ACM, 31,* 764–774.

Johnson, D. I. (1994). Take word processing one step further. *Computers in Nursing, 12*(3), 128–131.

Kachigan, S. K. (1986). *Statistical analysis: An interdisciplinary introduction to univariate and multivariate methods.* New York: Radius Press.

Kimbler, D. L. (1998). *Continuous quality improvement server.* Department of Industrial Engineering, Clemson University. Retrieved from the World Wide Web: http://deming.eng.clemson.edu/pub/tutorials/qctools/flowm.htm.

Kirkly, J. (1996). Java/Java script and the Web. In S. Kearns (Ed.), *Inside the World Wide Web* (2nd ed., pp. 478–516). Indianapolis, IN: New Riders Publishing.

Kozierok, C. (1997). *The PC guide.* Retrieved from the World Wide Web: http://www.PCGuide.com.

Kraynak, J. (1997). Creating and publishing web documents. In T. F. Hayes (Ed.) *Special edition using Microsoft Office 97 Professional, Best Sellers Edition* (pp. 909–934). Indianapolis, IN: Que Corporation.

Krol, E. (1992). *The whole Internet: User's guide and catalog.* Sebastopol, CA: O'Reilly & Associates, Inc.

Lachiusa, T. A. (1996). Development of the graphic social network measure. *Journal of Social Service-Research, 21*(4), 1–35.

Lamb, J. A. (1990). Teaching computer literacy to human service students. *Computers in Human Services. 7*(1–2), 31–45.

Lane, C. (1998a, September). Going private: How to protect yourself from hackers, snoops, and spammers. *PC World,* 115–132.

Lane, C. (1998b, September). And the password is . . . *PC World,* 123.

Lasky, M. S., & McCracken, H. (1997, May). Put a PC in your pocket. *PC World,* 153–168.

Lauriston, R. (1998, August). What's wrong with this picture? *PC World,* 171–182.

Lefferts, R. (1981). *Elements of graphics: How to prepare charts and graphs for effective reports.* New York: Harper & Row.

Lennon, J. A. (1997). *Hypermedia systems and applications: World Wide Web and beyond.* New York: Springer.

Levenson, D. (1997, September). Online counseling: Opportunity and risk. *NASW News,* 3.

Levine, D. B. (1997, August). First class e-mail: Six tools that get your Internet messages across. *PC World,* 169–184.

Littman, J. (1998, September). Inside job. *PC World,* 163–170.

Mahler, C. R., & Meier, S. T. (1993). The microcomputer as a psychotherapeutic aid. *Computers in Human Services, 10*(1), 35–40.

Malm, L. (1996a). Legal issues. In S. Kearns (Ed.), *Inside the World Wide Web* (2nd ed., pp. 672–710). Indianapolis, IN: New Riders Publishing.

Malm, L. (1996b). Internet connection alternatives. In S. Kearns (Ed.), *Inside the World Wide Web,* (2nd ed. pp. 172–194). Indianapolis, IN: New Riders Publishing.

maranGraphics. (1996). *Teach yourself computers and the Internet visually.* Foster City, CA: IDG.

Margolis, P. E. (1996). *Random House personal computer dictionary* (2nd ed.). New York: Random House.

Marlowe-Carr, L. C. (1997). Social workers on-line: A profile. *Computers in Human Services, 41*(1), 59–70.

Mattaini, M. A. (1993). *More than a thousand words: Graphics for clinical practice.* Washington, DC: NASW Press.

McCracken, H. (1996, December). Personal printers: Great values for every budget. *PC World,* 161–175.

McCracken, H. (1997, February). Microsoft Office: What's new for 97. *PC World,* 106–118.

McCracken, H. (1997, August). Better email for America Online and CompuServe. *PC World,* 174.

McCracken, H. (1998, March). Start your engines: The best search sites. *PC World,* 158–164.

McEvoy, A., Freeman, A., McCraken, H. Scisco, P., & Spanbauer, S. (1998). Store wars: The best and worst places to buy a PC. *PC World, 16*(2), 122–135.

McGoldrick, M., & Gerson, R. (1985). *Genograms in family assessment.* New York: W. W. Norton.

McGrath, P. (1998, November 23). Fast lane on the infobahn. *Newsweek,* 90–93.

McKenzie, B. C. (1996). *Medicine and the Internet: Introducing online resources and terminology.* New York: Oxford University Press.

Meyer, C. H. (1993). The impact of visualization on practice. In M. A. Mattaini (Ed.), *More than a thousand words: Graphics for clinical practice* (pp. 261–270). Washington, DC: NASW Press.

Miastkowski, S. (1997, March). Virus killers. *PC World,* 189–204.

Miller, D. B., & DiGiuseppe, D. (1998). Fighting social problems with information: The development of a community database—the Violence Information Network. *Computers in Human Services, 15*(1), 21–34.

Miller, H. (1970). *The world of sex.* London: Calder and Boyars, p. 101.

Morrison, J. D., Howard, J., Johnson, C., Navarro, F. J., Plachetka, B., & Bell, T. (1997). Strengthening neighborhoods by developing community networks. *Social Work, 42*(5), 527–534.

Murphy, J., & Pardeck, J. (1988). Technology in clinical practice and the technological ethic. *Journal of Sociology and Social Welfare, 15*(1), 119–128.

Murphy, J., & Pardeck, J. (1986). Technologically mediated therapy: A critique. *Social Casework: The Journal of Contemporary Social Work, 67*(10), 605–612.

Murphy, J., & Pardeck, J. (1992). Computerization and the dehumanization of social services. *Administration in Social Work, 16*(2), 61–72.

Mutschler, E., & Hoefer, R. (1990). Factors affecting the use of computer technology in human service organizations. *Administration in Social Work, 14*(1), 87–101.

Myrick. R., & Sabella, R. (1995). Cyberspace: New place for counselor supervision. *Elementary School Guidance & Supervision, 30,* 35–44.

NASW. (1997). *NASW code of ethics. NASW On-line.* Retrieved from the World Wide Web: www.naswdc.org/CODE.HTM.

Negroponte, N. (1995). *Being digital.* New York: Alfred A. Knopf.

Nelson, T. H. (1974). *Dream machines: New freedom through computer screens—A minority report.* Chicago: Hugo's Book Service.

Nurius, P. S., & Hudson, W. W. (1993). *Human services practice, evaluation, and computers: A practical guide for today and beyond.* Grove Park, CA: Brooks/Cole.

Ogilvie, D. M. (1996). Use of graphic representation of self-dynamisms in clinical treatment. *Crisis-Intervention, 1*(2), 125–40.

Pardeck, J. T., Collier Umfress, K., & Murphy, J. W. (1990). The utilization of computers on social service agencies. In J. T. Pardeck & J. Murphy (Eds.), *Computers in human services: An overview for clinical and welfare services* (pp. 121–128). Chur, NY: Harwood Academic Publishers.

Parsons, J. J., Oja, D., & Auer, D. (1995). *Comprehensive Microsoft Excel 5.0 for Windows.* Cambridge, MA: Course Technology.

Patterson, D. A., & Cloud, R. N. (in press). The application of artificial neural networks for outcome prediction in a cohort of severely mentally ill outpatients. *Journal of Technology in Human Services.*

Patterson, D. A., & Lee, M. S. (1995). Field trial of the global assessment of functioning scale—modified. *American Journal of Psychiatry, 152*(9), 1386–1388.

Patterson, D. A., & Lee, M. S. (1998). Intensive case management and rehospitalization: A survival analysis. *Research on Social Work Practice, 8*(2), 152–171.

Patterson, D. A., Pullen, L., Evers, E., Champlin, D. L., & Ralson, R. (1997). An experimental evaluation of HyperCDTX: Multimedia substance abuse treatment education software. *Computers in Human Services, 14*(1), 21–38.

Patterson, D. A., & Yaffe, J. (1993). An evaluation of computer-assisted instruction in teaching axis II of DSM-III-R to social work students. *Research on Social Work Practice, 3*(3), 343–357.

Patterson, D. A., & Yaffe, J. (1994). Hypermedia computer-based education in social work education. *Journal of Social Work Education, 30*(2), 267–277.

Phillips, D., & Berman, Y. (1995). *Human services in the age of new technology: Harmonising social work and computerisation.* Aldershot, England: Avebury.

Pirsig, R. M. (1974). *Zen and the art of motorcycle maintenance: An inquiry into values.* New York: Morrow.

Plant, P. (1991). Vikings on the Seine: Policy challenges confronting career guidance counsellors in Denmark. *British Journal of Guidance and Counseling, 19,* 258–266.

Rafferty, J., Steyaert, J., & Colombi, D. (Eds.). (1995). *Human services in the information age.* London: Haworth Press.

Rivard, J. D., Madrigal, C., & Millan, A. (1997). *Quick guide to the Internet for social workers.* Boston: Allyn and Bacon.

Robb, J. (1997, March). Lotus SmartSuite 97: Now smart enough? *PC World,* 163–174.

Rodrigues, D. (1997). *The research paper and the World Wide Web.* Upper Saddle River, NJ: Prentice Hall.

Rondero, V. (1998). Computer technology in social work practice settings: Issues, considerations, and implications for the profession. In *The proceedings of the 2nd annual Information Technology for Social Work Education and Practice Conference* (pp. 40–50). Columbia: College of Social Work, University of South Carolina.

Rose, S. D. (1989). *Working with adults in groups: Integrating cognitive and behavioral and small group strategies.* San Francisco: Jossey-Bass.

Rosen, L. D., & Weil, M. M. (1997). *Mental health technology bible.* New York: John Wiley & Sons.

Royse, D. (1992). *Program evaluation.* Chicago: Nelson-Hall.

Royse, D. (1995). *Research methods in social work* (2nd ed.). Chicago: Nelson-Hall.

Rubin, A., & Babbie, E. (1997). *Research methods for social work* (3rd ed.). Pacific Grove, CA: Brooks/Cole.

Rutledge, P. A. (1997). Using lists and databases. In J. Boyce (Ed.), *Using Microsoft Office 97 Professional* (347–364). Indianapolis, IN: Que.

San Francisco State University. (1995). *Computing ethics and security.* SFSU Computing Services. Retrieved from the World Wide Web: www.sfsu.edu/~helpdesk/docs/rules/ethics.htm.

Schoech, D. (1990). *Human service computing: Concepts and applications.* New York: Haworth Press.

Schopler, J. H., Abell, M. D., & Galinsky, M. J. (1998). Technology-based groups: A review and conceptual framework for practice. *Social Work, 43*(3), 254–267.

Schorr, J. (1997, November). Print it. *Macworld,* 115–118.

Selim, P. M., Klein, M. H., Greist, J. H., Johnson, J. H., & Harris, W. (1982). An investigation of computer-assisted cognitive-behavior therapy in the treatment of depression. *Behavior Research Methods and Instrumentation, 14,* 181–185.

Sengstack, J. (1998, February). 32X CD-ROMs up ante—But add little value. *PC World,* 78.

Shank, N. C., Roesch, S. C., Murphy-Berman, V. A., & Wright, G. F. (1996). The use of the Internet for at-risk families receiving services co-ordination. In B. Glastonbury (Ed.), *Dreams and realities: Information technology in the human services.* Helsinki, Finland: Stakes National Research and Development Centre for Welfare and Health.

SIIA. (1998). *SPA Anti-piracy division's copyright protection campaign.* Software & Information Industry Association. Retrieved from the World Wide Web: http://www. siia.net.

Simkin, D., & Hastie, R. (1987). An information-processing analysis of graph perception. *Journal of the American Statistical Association, 82,* 454–465.

Spanbauer, S. (1997, August). Bandwidth on demand. *PC World,* 159–168.

Spanbauer, S. (1998, June). Get on the list. *PC World,* 136–137.

Steward, W., & Perry, G. (1997). *WordPerfect Suite 8: The comprehensive guide.* Research Triangle Park, NC: Ventana Communications Group.

Steyaert, J., Colombi, D., & Rafferty, J. (1996). *Human services and information technology: An international perspective.* Aldershot, England: Ashgate Publishing Limited.

Trivette, D. (1997). How to buy laptops. *ComputerLife Online Reviews.* Ziff-Davis. http://www.zdnet.com/complife/rev/9702/buynote1.html.

Tsai, C. J. (1988). Hypertext: Technology, applications, and research issues. *Journal of Educational Technology Systems, 17*(1), 3–14.

Tweney, D. (1996, December). Searching is my business: A gumshoe's guide to the web. *PC World,* 182–196.

University of Virginia. (1997). *Drinking from a fire hose? Tips for managing web overload.* Inside Information. Information Management and Computing at the University of Virginia Health Sciences Center. Retrieved from the World Wide Web: http://www.med.virginia.edu/hs-library/newsletter/1997/january/toc.html.

Vaughan-Nichols, S. (1996). What you need to link to the web. In S. Kearns (Ed.), *Inside the World Wide Web* (2nd ed., pp. 143–170). Indianapolis, IN: New Riders Publishing.

Warner, N. (1997). Document collaboration. In T. F. Hayes (Ed.), *Special edition using Microsoft Office 97 Professional, Best Sellers Edition* (pp. 1099–1115). Indianapolis, IN: Que Corporation.

Weckert, J., & Adeney, D. (1997). *Computer and information ethics.* Westport, CT: Greenwood Press.

Weinbach, R. (1996). A glimpse into the future: Anticipating the computer-mediated communication underclass. In B. Glastonbury (Ed.), *Dreams and realities: Information technology in human services* (pp. 103–112). Helsinki, Finland: Stakes National Research and Development Centre for Welfare and Health.

Weinbach, R. W., & Grinnell, R. M. (1991). *Statistics for social workers* (2nd ed.). New York: Longman.

Western Kentucky University. (1995). *Ethics policy.* Academic Computing & Research Services. Retrieved from the World Wide Web: www2.wku.edu/www/acrs/policy.html.

White, J. V. (1984). *Using charts and graphs: 1000 ideas for visual persuasion.* New York: R. R. Bowker.

Williams, M., Unrau, Y. A., & Grinnell, R. M. (1998). *Introduction to social work research.* Itasca, IL: F. E. Peacock Publishers.

Williams, S., & Foster, J. (1988). Technology on trial. In B. Glastonbury, W. LaMendola, & S. Toole (Eds.). *Information technology and the human services* (pp. 214–222). Chichester, England: Wiley.

Williamson, D. J. (1992). Computers in psychiatry: An introductory course—2. Word processing. *Psychiatric Bulletin, 16,* 435–436.

Yalom, I. D. (1995). *The theory and practice of group psychotherapy* (4th ed.). New York: BasicBooks.

Glossary

ADSL (asymmetric digital subscriber line) An emerging telephone line transmission technology that increases the speed at which data travels over existing telephone lines.

Applet A small program (application), often created with the Java programming language.

Application A program designed to carry out a function or set of functions for the user.

Archive To store a file or set of files on a storage medium.

Asynchronous Not occurring at the same time. For instance, e-mail exchanges are asynchronous.

Attachment Compressed or uncompressed file(s) appended to an e-mail message.

Back-up To copy a file to another storage medium.

Bandwidth A measurement of the quantity of information that can be transmitted over a fixed period of time, usually measured in bits or bytes.

BinHex A data encoding standard commonly used with Apple Macintosh files.

BIOS Setup program is the built-in software that the computer accesses first, before starting the operating system.

Bit The smallest unit of information in computing. The presence or absence of an electronic pulse or magnetized spot on a disk.

Bitnet (Because it's time network) An early, largely university-based wide area network.

Bookmark A link to a Web page or file on a server.

Browser An application for interacting with Web pages and other HTML documents.

Button A graphic that is clicked to activate a command or select an option.

Byte Eight bits equal a byte. A byte can be thought of as a word in computer language, as computers are designed to process a byte as a single unit.

CD-R (compact disk—recordable) A compact disk on which information can be recorded by someone other than a CD-ROM vendor. CD-R drives allow personal computer users to save information on CDs.

CD-RW (compact disk—rewritable) A compact disk that can be erased and used again.

CD-ROM Compact disk—read only memory.

Cell A single box in a spreadsheet, which is the intersection of a row and a column.

Chat (aka chat room)   Live, text-based dialogs conducted over the Internet.

Chip   An electronic device with embedded circuitry. The two most common types of chips are microprocessors (CPUs) and memory chips.

Clip art   Electronic illustrations which may be inserted into documents.

CPU   Central processing unit. The brain of the computer.

Cursor   An on-screen symbol, such as an arrow, blinking line, or rectangle, that indicates where text may be inserted. In a graphic user interface environment it is the primary means to select objects and activate commands in the menu bar.

Cyberspace   A metaphor for the nonphysical territory of the Internet, including the World Wide Web.

Data   Factual information encoded into a form allowing for transmission and processing.

Database   Data organized in a form that allows for updating, searching, and retrieval.

Decrypt   To remove encryption.

Desktop   A metaphorical representation on a computer screen of a personal work environment with icons representing available tools, folders, and files.

Dial-up   A computer connection to another computer via a modem and standard phone lines.

Digital   Electronic technology that represents information as either 1's or 0's. Digitized information is converted into strings of 1's and 0's.

Directory   A file holding other hierarchically organized files, commonly represented as a folder in graphical user interfaces.

Diskette   A portable, magnetic disk used for storage and transportation of information.

Domain   A sphere of knowledge, influence, or activity. On the Internet, this term refers to a group of associated network addresses.

Download   Receipt of information or software from another computer.

DPI (dots per inch)   A measurement of the clarity or sharpness of a display screen or printer output.

DSL (digital subscriber line)   See ADSL.

Dual-scan   A passive matrix liquid crystal display (LCD) that is faster than standard passive matrix screens, but slower and not as bright as active matrix screens.

DVD (digital versatile disk)   An optical data storage disk that holds up to 4.7 gigabytes on one side. Using two layers on two sides of the disk, there is the potential to store 17 gigabytes of information on a single disk.

DVD-ROM   Digital versatile disk—read only memory.

DVD-RW   Digital versatile disk—rewritable.

E-mail (electronic mail)   A message exchanged between computers over a network or the Internet.

Encryption   An approach to data security that transforms or translates data to a form that cannot be read by someone intercepting the data.

Ethernet   A widely used technology for local area networks.

FAQ   Frequently asked questions.

Filter   Software that applies certain criteria to the input, sorting, or output of data. For instance, an e-mail filter might be set to exclude all e-mail from a certain address.

Flaming   An online argument that escalates to the exchange of insults.

Floppy disk   A magnetic data storage medium used to store and transfer files.

Font   Text characters of a specific style and size. The height of a font is measured in points, for example, a 12-point font. A point is about 1/72 of an inch.

Footprint   The space on a desk or floor required for a device such as a computer or printer.

Frame   A rectangular space in which graphics or text can appear.

FTP (file transfer protocol)   A protocol for exchanging files between computers.

GIF (graphics interchange format)   A file format for graphical images commonly used on the Web and in graphics software.

Gigabyte   A unit of measurement in computer storage space equal to 1,024 megabytes or approximately one billion bytes.

GUI (graphical user interface)   The visual representation of the options or features available in an operating system or a software application. A mouse is used to point, click, and select icons or menu options in the operating system or software.

Hacker   Generally used to refer to a person who is a clever programmer. It may be used to refer to someone who lacks formal training in programming. The term also is used to describe an individual who breaks into computers without permission.

Hard copy   A printed version of a document or data file.

Hard disk   A magnetic disk that generally is not portable used to store data, software, and documents.

Hardware   Refers to the physical objects of information technology such as computers, monitors, printers, chips, drives.

Home page   The first Web page a user sees when visiting a Web site. It usually has an index or directory to other documents or Web pages at the site.

HTML (hypertext markup language)   The language used to author documents for the World Wide Web. It essentially tells the Web browser how to display the information contained on the Web page.

Hyperlink   Electronic addresses within a document or a Web page that connect to files, other Web pages, e-mail addresses, or FTP servers.

Hypermedia   Derived from the term *hyperlink,* referring to software that contains links to multimedia such as text, images, animations, video, and sound.

Hypertext   The nonlinear linkage of information that allows users to decide what information they wish to view. This is a central feature of the World Wide Web.

Icon   A small graphic or picture that represents a function, file, window, or software application.

Information technology   Computer hardware and software, the networks that link computers, and the mechanisms that change information and images into digital formats, such as digital cameras and scanners.

Input   Data entered into a computer.

Internet   A global network of computer networks linking millions of computers around the world which allows for the exchange of messages and data.

Intranet   A network that links networks (LANs and WANs) across the Internet for the purpose of sharing information within an organization. Access to an intranet is limited to individuals within the organization or others outside of the organization who are given access. Intranets use standard TCP/IP protocols and format documents in HTML.

ISDN (integrated services digital network)   A communications standard for the transmission of digital information on copper phone lines and other media.

ISP (internet service provider)   A company or organization that makes available access to the Internet and Web page hosting services.

Java   A programming language created by Sun Microsystems for the computing environment of the Internet. Applications created with Java may run on a single computer or between two or more computers (distributed computing).

JPEG (Joint Photographic Experts Group)   A graphic image compression format that allows for specification of image quality. It is commonly used for images on the Web.

Kbps (kilobits per second)   A measure indicating the speed of data transfer.

Kilobit   A thousand bits.

Kilobyte   A thousand bytes (technically, 1,024 bytes).

Kiosk   An information booth containing a computer and a screen or monitor.

LAN (local area network)   A computer network established within a building or between buildings in close proximity to each other.

LCD (liquid crystal display)   A technology used for display screens in laptops and for some monitors.

Link   A connection from a word, image, or icon that can be selected in order to connect to other information resources such as a Web page.

Listserv   An e-mail distribution system that sends any message sent to it to every name on the mailing list.

Login   To gain access to a computer or network. The same as log on.

Mainframe   A large and commonly expensive computer serving hundreds or thousands of users.

Mbps   Millions of bits per second. Used as a measure of data transmission speed.

Megabyte   Approximately one million bytes of information. Commonly referred to as a Meg. Used as a measurement of RAM in a computer.

Megahertz   Abbreviated as MHz. A measure of computing speed. One MHz is one million cycles per second.

Modem   A device that transmits data from a computer over standard phone lines to another computer.

Motherboard   A piece of hardware inside the computer that links the various components together and allows them to communicate with each other via the CPU.

Mouse A hand-held device with one or more buttons used to point at and select objects on a computer screen.

Multimedia One or more media presented simultaneously on a computer, for example, text and video, sound and images.

Nanosecond One billionth of a second. A measurement of the speed at which information is exchanged in RAM chips.

Net A term generally used to refer to the Internet.

Network Two or more computers connected to each other. A network may be linked to other networks.

Newsgroup Discussion about a particular topic written to a central location and then distributed across the Internet through Usenet; much like an electronic bulletin board.

Newsreader Software for reading messages on Usenet. Newsreaders are now commonly integrated into Web browsers.

OCR (optical character recognition) Technology for translating images of characters on a page into information a computer can process. It transforms the information on a printed page into an electronic file that can be opened and altered by word processing software.

Online To be connected to another computer or network. To be turned on, as in "the printer is online."

Password A secret set of characters used to access a computer, network, program, or file.

PC (personal computer) A computer used by a single individual. The term is also used to distinguish Intel/Windows–based personal computers from Apple Macintosh computers.

Pixel A word abbreviated from *picture element*. The basic unit of or single point in a graphic image.

POP3 (point of presence or post office protocol) The Internet protocol for handling incoming e-mail.

Private key A value or decryption cipher used by an individual to open encrypted messages sent from someone else using the intended recipient's public key. When sending a message to someone whose public key you know, you use their public key to encrypt the message and the recipient uses his or her private key to decrypt the message in order to read it.

Program A set of ordered instructions for a computer to execute in order to accomplish one or many tasks.

Public key A value or cipher used to encrypt a message for a specific individual who will subsequently open or decrypt the message with his or her private key.

RAM Random access memory.

Resolution Designates the clarity and sharpness of an image. May reference the ability of a monitor or printer to display an image: a printer produces 600 dpi output. The resolution of monitors is measured in pixels.

RTF (rich text format) A file format used to exchange documents between different word processing applications.

Scanner   An optical device for capturing images of text, graphics, or photographs from hardcopy. The image is digitized by the scanner and turned into an electronic file.

Scroll   The capacity to view portions of a document that do not appear on the screen. As one scrolls down through a document, successive lines of the document appear at the bottom of the page and lines at the top disappear. Many applications allow for vertical and horizontal scrolling.

Server   A computer or program on a computer that provides files, software, or other resources to other computers on a network.

SIMM (single in-line memory module)   A device holding one or more RAM chips that resides on the motherboard of a computer.

Slot   Sometimes referred to as an expansion slot. A location in a computer into which a card that expands the functionality of a computer may be inserted, for example, a modem card, ethernet card, or video capture card.

SMTP (simple mail transfer protocol)   A protocol for handling the transmission of e-mail across the Internet.

Software   Electronically stored instructions for the operation of a computer. Two general categories of software are applications and operating systems.

Spam   Junk e-mail. Unsolicited e-mail received from sources on the Internet.

Spammer   One who sends spam.

Spreadsheet   A scrollable table of rows and columns into which labels, values, and formulas may be inserted. Commonly used for data collection, organization, graphing, and analysis.

TCP (transmission control protocol)   A protocol for tracking elements of messages sent over the Internet.

Telnet   An Internet tool that allows one to log on to and interact with other computers on the Internet (assuming one has permission to do so).

Text box   A rectangular space in an application into which text may be inserted or typed.

TFT (thin film transistor)   Another name for the liquid crystal display screen also known as an active matrix screen.

Thread   A succession of responses to a posting on a specific topic or subject on a bulletin board or in a Usenet newsgroup.

Toolbar   The graphical representation with icons of a collection of functions or commands in a software application.

txt   The file extension of a text file. Also known as an ASCII file.

URL (universal resource locator)   The address of a file, Web page, or some other resource on the Internet.

Usenet   A large collection of discussion groups (newsgroups) on the Internet.

Utility   A small program that performs a specific task.

WAN (wide area network)   A computer or telecommunications network that covers a geographically large area.

Web   Short for the World Wide Web.

World Wide Web   An Internet-based collection of computer and information resources that use HTML formatted documents.

Index